Data-Driven Services with Silverlight 2

John Papa

Beijing · Cambridge · Farnham · Köln · Sebastopol · Taipei · Tokyo

Data-Driven Services with Silverlight 2
by John Papa

Copyright © 2009 John Papa. All rights reserved.
Printed in the United States of America.

Published by O'Reilly Media, Inc., 1005 Gravenstein Highway North, Sebastopol, CA 95472.

O'Reilly books may be purchased for educational, business, or sales promotional use. Online editions are also available for most titles (*http://safari.oreilly.com*). For more information, contact our corporate/institutional sales department: (800) 998-9938 or *corporate@oreilly.com*.

Editor: John Osborn	**Indexer:** Ellen Troutman
Production Editor: Sumita Mukherji	**Cover Designer:** Karen Montgomery
Copyeditor: Audrey Doyle	**Interior Designer:** David Futato
Proofreader: Nancy Kotary	**Illustrators:** Robert Romano and Maria Amodio

Printing History:

    December 2008:   First Edition.

RepKover™

This book uses RepKover, a durable and flexible lay-flat binding.

ISBN: 978-0-596-52309-1

[M]

1229008878

Dedicated to my family: Colleen, Haley, Madelyn, Ella, and soon, Landon. Through you, God has truly blessed me.

Table of Contents

Foreword

I recall a time in March 2006 when I was in Las Vegas, sitting in the back of a packed room waiting to hear someone from Microsoft start his session titled "WPF/E," and wondering what it would be about. In the hour that followed, attendees got their first glimpse of gradients and animations (as they were to become known) as they ran within a browser and on multiple operating system platforms. We all left curious and inspired and wondering what would come next for this little side project code-named "WPF/E."

We now know, of course, that WPF/E became Microsoft Silverlight. What we didn't know then was how much energy and excitement this new platform would generate. Perhaps not since the unveiling of the .NET Framework itself has a platform generated so much interest within a developer ecosystem.

Silverlight is a rich Internet application platform that extends the reach of the .NET developer, and the capabilities already enjoyed in Windows Presentation Foundation (WPF) applications, to the browser. As a technology, it immediately opened new opportunities for organizations to extend the reach of their applications while leveraging their existing knowledge of .NET development to create web applications more quickly and more reliably than before. Silverlight has also caused new competition among other interactive platforms, challenging dominant market leaders and forcing everyone to innovate in a market that had grown complacent. Silverlight made its first public appearance in a small room around the corner from the normal bustle of a Microsoft conference and has quickly become the platform of choice for Microsoft developers wishing to extend their reach onto the Internet.

Of course, we know that applications aren't just made up of gradient color schemes or animations. Most who look at "traditional" line-of-business applications know that there are very few spinning rectangles in the UI they use to perform their daily operations on their customer service, human resources, or order management systems. Any platform wishing to survive in any organization must be able to handle the basics of acting upon information provided by the end user. *Central to any application is data.* Breaking outside the realm of "traditional" applications, even online games rely on data in some form or other. Our world of technology is surrounded by data coming to and from our applications, whether in the form of syndication, user input, automated services, or something else—data is king.

Beyond whatever excites you about Silverlight as a platform, data will still be king in all of your applications as well. Whether you are developing the next greatest game, an enhanced user experience for your human resources application, or a kiosk at an airport, your application will be interacting with data. Understanding the different ways to receive and provide that data within Silverlight is what will ultimately result in a successful implementation for you as a developer. What is great about Silverlight is that at its core, it is .NET! Most of what you already know about accessing data applies in your implementation of another platform.

Silverlight does, however, provide some unique opportunities for the developer, and perhaps some challenges. With past experience in working with data on Microsoft platforms, author John Papa is able to bring his unique perspective to understanding data in the Silverlight platform. Whether it is traditional ASP.NET web services, Windows Communication Foundation, RSS syndicated content, or RESTful data sources, John's expertise will help you, the developer, understand how these different sources interoperate with Silverlight and the best practices with which to implement them. John will walk you through each concept and point out the tools and techniques that will no doubt help you to be successful in your Silverlight application.

Data-Driven Services with Silverlight 2 should be a staple title on any Silverlight developer's shelf. John's in-depth coverage of accessing data with Silverlight 2 is an indispensible guide for anyone working with data. John covers more than what you need to know, but explains why you should do things in a certain manner to help you gain a better understanding of what happens behind the curtain with regard to Silverlight and data access.

No matter how you use *Data-Driven Services with Silverlight 2*—either as a guide or as a reference—it will prove to be invaluable to you in your learning, and even later down the road. Having read this has already made me a better data developer with regard to Silverlight, and I know it will make you one as well.

—Tim Heuer
Program Manager, Microsoft

Preface

Ideally, every application should have a robust user interface, be available over the Web in any browser, and be rich in functionality. Attempts at achieving that ideal, however, have been fraught with challenges. Throughout the years, developers have had to battle cross-browser issues regarding DOMs as well as HTML, JavaScript, and DHTML implementations. It has always taken longer than it should to implement a cross-browser web application. And even after all of the effort was expended, sometimes the result was a poor excuse for a user interface due to the lowest-common-denominator principle of building web applications that work in various web browsers. There always seemed to be a sacrifice to the user experience when building an application for the Web. That's why when whispers of what we now know as Silverlight were coming out of the dark recesses of Redmond, I watched intently for its arrival.

The first version of Silverlight was certainly impressive: a plug-in to the browser that made richer UIs than were possible with standard web technologies using HTML. Like any first-generation product, aspects were missing in Silverlight 1. In version 2 of Silverlight, significant advances were made by adding the new Silverlight control library and support for .NET code in the browser. In one fell swoop, developers can leverage their .NET skills to develop Silverlight 2 applications that run in Firefox, Safari, Google Chrome, and Internet Explorer.

The creativity and passion of many developers bore new examples of graphical wonders popping up like flowers in the spring. A new era of rich interfaces with XAML and Silverlight was dawning. Amid this UI splendor is another facet of Silverlight that is just as important: the ability to link these robust Silverlight user interfaces to fully functional line-of-business solutions. Silverlight 2 enables developers to create rich cross-browser web UIs that can communicate over HTTP with REST services and with web services.

Instantly, the development playing field was altered. Silverlight 2 applications can leverage existing business object and data access layers that companies may already have in place. Developers can also take advantage of new technology frameworks such as the ADO.NET Entity Framework, LLBLGen Pro, LINQ to SQL, NHibernate, and other middle-tier frameworks to build a domain entity model, query the model with LINQ, serialize the entities, and pass them through Windows Communication Foundation (WCF) services to a Silverlight 2 application. Developers can use entities in the client application in the browser and apply them to the new Silverlight 2 controls using rich data-binding techniques. Silverlight 2 applications can easily access existing or new models through a variety of web services, including RESTful-style web services, syndicated feeds with RSS and Atom, services that return XML or JSON, and SOAP-based services.

Silverlight Backdrop

Since Microsoft announced Silverlight, there has been tremendous interest in building applications with it. Silverlight provides the means to design robust user interfaces that work in a variety of browsers and communicate with highly scalable web server applications. Historically, desktop applications have cornered the market on rich user interfaces, whereas web applications have been more limited. This was largely due to the vast resources available to desktop applications, while Internet applications have had to contend with working on many browsers and operating systems. Silverlight changes this balance and opens the doors for web applications to provide rich and interactive user experiences.

Silverlight 2 helps developers to build rich Internet applications (RIAs) that work in several browsers and operating systems. It provides an extremely rich user experience and leverages developer experience with .NET technologies. Microsoft is vested heavily in this product, which is gaining a lot of momentum. Thanks to Silverlight 2, developers can use their .NET and XAML skills to develop RIAs. Silverlight 2 introduced an extensive set of controls and has promised to increase the control suite through a Silverlight Toolkit.

Who Should Read This Book

Developers who are interested in developing data-driven applications or who communicate with web services with Silverlight 2 will benefit from reading this book. This book focuses on planning and developing applications that present data, save data, and manipulate data with Silverlight 2. Whereas other books may focus on advanced animations and graphical spectaculars that can truly inspire artistic creativity, this book targets users who want to use Silverlight 2 to build applications that perform data-centric and business logic functions with robust user interfaces. You can use Silverlight 2 to build any business application that will operate over the Internet. Although Silverlight is great for web-based applications, using Windows Presentation Foundation (WPF) and XBAP applications is a solid and arguably better alternative for intranet-based applications.

The controls from the examples in this book use templates and styles that are elegant, are robust, are changeable, and most importantly, support business functionality. This book can serve as a reference for you to fall back on for certain scenarios; however, its true value is in demonstrating how to solve real problems that involve writing data-driven solutions with Silverlight 2.

Why You Should Read This Book

Silverlight 2 is cool. The graphical expressions and the user experience that it provides far exceed what traditional web technologies such as ASP.NET can do on their own. Silverlight 2 adds to the expanding group of technologies from which developers can choose to create applications. This includes WINForms, Web Forms with ASP.NET, and technologies such as Ajax, WPF, and even Flex. Silverlight works well as an Internet-based application when there are services to consume and a rich user interface is required. WPF and WINForms are great for internal applications (behind a firewall). WPF with XBAP is a solid choice for web-based solutions for internal applications as well. Silverlight 2 fills the niche of a rich user interface on a web browser without losing the powerful array of interactivity you can get by consuming and interacting with remote services.

Styles, templates, animations, storyboards, transitions, and many other features of Silverlight 2 make it a great tool for creating rich interfaces. But developers build applications, usually for businesses, and most often these applications are data-driven and interact with web services. This capability, combined with the glitz of its rich interactive nature, is where Silverlight 2 really shines.

Silverlight 2 is a fantastic tool for designing rich interfaces that work in various browsers. It has extensive support for consuming and pushing data across web services. It also supports a variety of LINQ features, including LINQ to XML, LINQ to Objects, and LINQ to JSON, which makes consuming data from services and manipulating it an easy task. All of these features make Silverlight a viable solution for business applications. This book arms the reader with the knowledge to build visually and functionally robust applications with Silverlight 2.

What This Book Will Cover

In a nutshell, this book explores how to build data- and web-service-driven applications with Silverlight 2. It explains XAML-based data-binding techniques, binding to lists, notifications and modes for bindings, and handling data binding and converters through both Expression Blend and Visual Studio. Web service communication is a critical aspect in building Silverlight 2 applications. This book covers many ways in which Silverlight can consume and work with web services and the requests/responses from them, including communication with WCF, consuming SOAP-based and RESTful services, working with RSS services, and retrieving Plain Old XML (POX) and JSON. Sometimes it is necessary to design and build web services for Silverlight 2 applications. This book covers creating SOAP-based and RESTful services that Silverlight 2 can communicate with using ASMX and WCF.

Communications with web services from Silverlight 2 often travel across different domains. The server hosting the remote web service must allow its web services to be accessed using cross-domain policies. This book discusses how the policies work, when they are enforced, how to work with them, and how to debug common issues stemming from cross-domain policies. It also discusses consuming and manipulating serialized entities from domain models, incorporating binding techniques and notifications into a Silverlight application, and using ADO.NET Data Services to interact with middle-tier domain entity models via REST-style URI templates to access resources.

This book also covers many varieties of LINQ queries that help to define complex queries that consume and manipulate data in Silverlight 2 applications. LINQ is an essential tool in the modern .NET developer's arsenal. LINQ to Entities is a critical tool for querying objects when using the ADO.NET Entity Framework to implement a domain model. After the entities are retrieved using LINQ to Entities, they can be passed to and from the client layer of a Silverlight application architecture through WCF services. Likewise, custom domain models, NHibernate, LINQ to SQL, and other modeling frameworks can all be used as the underlying model and data persistence layer for a Silverlight 2 application, as long as services are written to transport the communications between the middle tier on a server and the client-based Silverlight application. Each of these business models and data access tools lives on the server and can communicate in varying degrees with Silverlight 2 applications through SOAP, REST, and web service protocols.

LINQ to Objects is the generic screwdriver of this toolset. You can use it to query lists of objects on the client in the Silverlight application code. These lists may be returned serialized from any source. LINQ to Objects is great for creating queries to manage lists of entities and objects in Silverlight that may be passed to and from a web service.

LINQ to XML is also very valuable in a Silverlight 2 application for querying and managing XML data. Often, web applications must communicate with applications directly over HTTP and without the benefit of a contract via a WCF service. For example, a Silverlight application can contact a REST service and consume its XML data stream. This stream could be read through one of the various .NET libraries of XML readers, or it could be read using LINQ to XML. LINQ to XML makes it easy to process XML data returned from web service responses and RSS feeds. Web services can also return JSON in their message responses. LINQ to JSON is a valuable tool for parsing JSON data and translating it into entities or other data structures to be bound or passed to other applications from Silverlight 2.

Problems This Book Solves for Readers

This book aims to solve a variety of problems that developers frequently encounter, including how to do the following:

- Develop data-centric Silverlight 2 applications with Blend and Visual Studio

- Implement commonly required Silverlight data-binding techniques
- Develop communicative data-binding operations that include notifications
- Retrieve cross-domain data and work with cross-domain policies
- Debug web services and communications from Silverlight 2 applications
- Request and send data to and from SOAP-based web services from Silverlight 2
- Communicate with RESTful web services from Silverlight 2
- Manage XML from noncontractual services such as REST and RSS using LINQ
- Design and build SOAP and RESTful web services for Silverlight applications
- Build Silverlight 2 applications on top of multitier application architectures with customer domain entity models
- Build Silverlight 2 applications that interact with entity domain models built with custom classes, the ADO.NET Entity Framework, and LINQ to SQL
- Use ADO.NET Data Services to retrieve/send data with Silverlight 2

How This Book Is Organized

Chapter 1 provides some background on some skills needed to read this book. Chapters 2–4 discuss in detail the process of building Silverlight 2 applications as they pertain to data binding. Chapters 5 and 6 demonstrate how to design SOAP applications with ASMX and WCF to communicate with third-party SOAP web services. Chapters 7–9 delve into how to get and manipulate complex data in Silverlight applications using REST and how to build RESTful services. Chapter 10 shows how to communicate with and consume RSS services. Finally, Chapter 11 discusses how to design a Silverlight 2 application that communicates with ADO.NET Data Services. Where relevant, code examples in this book are shown in C# and VB.

Here is a short summary of the chapters in this book and what you'll find inside (many of the code samples in this book use style resources found in the respective project's *app.xaml* file):

Chapter 1, *Getting Started with Silverlight 2*
> This chapter covers the steps to develop applications with Silverlight 2 and explains the various tools and their purposes. It also examines the fundamentals of Silverlight 2, its control set, and the importance of XAML and its data-binding features, and includes a primer on XAML as it pertains to data and Silverlight.

Chapter 2, *Silverlight Data-Binding Foundations*
> This chapter discusses different ways to use data binding with XAML and with .NET code in Silverlight 2. It examines the controls and provides examples on how to bind custom objects to them. It also examines the `DataContext` property in depth, as well as situations in which you can apply binding through XAML or .NET code.

Chapter 3, *Modes and Notifications*

This chapter demonstrates situations in which different binding modes can be most beneficial when used with objects and controls. It also explores how to make the Silverlight 2 controls listen for and respond to notifications through `INotifyPropertyChanged` that can be implemented on objects.

Chapter 4, *Managing Lists, Templates, and Converters*

This chapter explores various techniques for binding and presenting lists of data in list-based controls. It also discusses how to use templates to stylize and present data more efficiently in controls. Examples use LINQ to Objects to query lists of custom entities, converting bound data between the data source and the target controls, and to implement notifications for list-based collections using `INotifyCollectionChanged` and `ObservableCollection<T>`.

Chapter 5, *WCF, Web Services, and Cross-Domain Policies*

This chapter demonstrates how to communicate between Silverlight 2 applications and WCF services—both custom and from third parties. It demonstrates how to build an application in Silverlight 2 that communicates with web services on different domains using SOAP either through WCF or ASMX web services. Also, it discusses what cross-domain policies are, how to account for them, and how to debug applications using network-sniffing tools.

Chapter 6, *Passing Entities via WCF*

This chapter shows how to send and retrieve custom domain entities filled from ADO.NET-driven data mappers in the middle tier, and expose them through WCF contracts and serialization techniques. It also shows how to pass entities from tools such as LINQ to SQL and from the ADO.NET Entity Framework to and from Silverlight 2 applications.

Chapter 7, *Consuming RESTful Services with WebClient and HttpWebRequest*

This chapter discusses how to consume and present data retrieved from REST services and manipulate it using LINQ to XML. It demonstrates how to use `WebClient` and `HttpWebRequest` from Silverlight 2 to invoke RESTful communications with web services, and also includes a primer on RESTful services and how Silverlight 2 can communicate with them.

Chapter 8, *Consuming Amazon's RESTful Services with Silverlight 2*

This chapter demonstrates how to send and receive data using the RESTful API exposed by the Amazon E-Commerce Service (also known as Amazon Associates Web Service). This case study shows how to build a Silverlight 2 application that allows users to search for and add items to a shopping cart stored at Amazon.

Chapter 9, *Creating RESTful Services and Introducing SilverTwit*

This chapter discusses how to build a RESTful service with which Silverlight 2 applications can communicate. The services allow `GET`s and `POST`s to be sent from Silverlight 2 applications passing XML and JSON. The chapter also demonstrates LINQ to XML and LINQ to JSON, and includes a case study of the SilverTwit

Twitter client to demonstrate how building a RESTful WCF application can be an important component of a Silverlight 2 application.

Chapter 10, *Syndication Feeds and Silverlight 2*

This chapter explains issues with consuming syndicated feeds from Silverlight 2 applications and how to overcome them. It also demonstrates the `Syndication Feed` class and how to use it to build a robust Silverlight 2 application that uses web services to aggregate Atom and RSS feeds.

Chapter 11, *Silverlight 2 and ADO.NET Data Services*

This chapter demonstrates how ADO.NET Data Services is uniquely qualified to pass data to and from Silverlight 2 applications using REST-style web services. It also shows how ADO.NET Data Services can communicate with and issue LINQ queries against entity data models in a middle tier to save and retrieve data.

Appendix A, *ADO.NET Data Services Quick Reference*

This appendix includes enumerations and values specific to ADO.NET Data Services that are helpful when coding with ADO.NET Data Services.

Appendix B, *Silverlight 2 Debugging with HTTP Sniffing Tools*

This appendix demonstrates how to use Fiddler2, Firebug, and the Web Development Helper tools to troubleshoot communication problems between Silverlight and web services.

What You Need to Use This Book

Developing the Silverlight 2 applications in this book requires .NET 3.5 Service Pack 1, the Silverlight runtime, the Silverlight SDK, and the Silverlight Tools add-on. This book demonstrates how to design and develop aspects of Silverlight applications using Expression Blend and Visual Studio 2008. Therefore, I recommend that you have these tools installed.

Conventions Used in This Book

The following typographical conventions are used in this book:

Italic

Indicates new terms, URLs, email addresses, filenames, file extensions, pathnames, directories, and Unix utilities

`Constant width`

Indicates commands, options, switches, variables, attributes, keys, functions, types, classes, namespaces, methods, modules, properties, parameters, values, objects, events, event handlers, XML tags, HTML tags, macros, the contents of files, or the output from commands

`Constant width bold`

Shows commands or other text that should be typed literally by the user

Constant width italic

Shows text that should be replaced with user-supplied values

C#

This icon (placed at the start of the code block) signifies C# code

VB

This icon (placed at the start of the code block) signifies VB code

This icon signifies a tip, suggestion, or general note

This icon indicates a warning or caution

Using Code Examples

This book is here to help you get your job done. In general, you may use the code in this book in your programs and documentation. You do not need to contact us for permission unless you're reproducing a significant portion of the code. For example, writing a program that uses several chunks of code from this book does not require permission. Selling or distributing a CD-ROM of examples from O'Reilly books *does* require permission. Answering a question by citing this book and quoting example code does not require permission. Incorporating a significant amount of example code from this book into your product's documentation *does* require permission.

We appreciate, but do not require, attribution. An attribution usually includes the title, author, publisher, and ISBN. For example: "*Data-Driven Services with Silverlight 2*, by John Papa. Copyright 2009 John Papa, 978-0-596-52309-1."

If you feel your use of code examples falls outside fair use or the permission given here, feel free to contact us at *permissions@oreilly.com*.

Accompanying Website

You can download many of the examples in this book from *http://www.Silverlight-Data .com*. Also available on this website are updates and comments from the author.

Templates

This book uses a series of styles and templates that provide a consistent and elegant appearance to the controls. The templates provided are free for you to use or modify at your own discretion. You can find the template source code on the book's website, at *http://www.Silverlight-Data.com*. Special thanks to Corrina Barber for supplying the templates and granting permission to use them in this book.

Safari® Books Online

When you see a Safari® Books Online icon on the cover of your favorite technology book, that means the book is available online through the O'Reilly Network Safari Bookshelf.

Safari offers a solution that's better than e-books. It's a virtual library that lets you easily search thousands of top tech books, cut and paste code samples, download chapters, and find quick answers when you need the most accurate, current information. Try it for free at *http://safari.oreilly.com*.

Comments and Questions

Please address comments and questions concerning this book to the publisher:

> O'Reilly Media, Inc.
> 1005 Gravenstein Highway North
> Sebastopol, CA 95472
> 800-998-9938 (in the United States or Canada)
> 707-829-0515 (international or local)
> 707-829-0104 (fax)

We have a web page for this book, where we list errata, examples, and any additional information. You can access this page at:

> *http://www.oreilly.com/catalog/9780596523091*

To comment or ask technical questions about this book, send email to:

> *bookquestions@oreilly.com*

For more information about our books, conferences, Resource Centers, and the O'Reilly Network, see our website at:

> *http://www.oreilly.com*

Acknowledgments

A special thank you to everyone on the technical review team for my book, including Rob Bagby, Andrew Conrad, Elisa Flasko, Tim Heuer, Jay Kimble, Sebastien Lambla, Gio Montrone, Jason Peron, Beatriz Stollnitz, Derik Whittaker, and Shawn Wildermuth. Each of you played an important role in fine-tuning the content in this book. An extra special thank you goes to these Silverlight warriors for their fellowship on our trek through the beta days of Silverlight 2: Adam Kinney, Tim Heuer, Shawn Wildermuth, and Jesse Liberty. Your collaboration was invaluable.

Thank you to those who read and comment on my blog, attend my conference sessions, and read my magazine articles. I considered much of your input while writing this book and added many subtopics based on your feedback.

Thanks to Jonathon Goodyear and my colleagues at ASPSOFT for encouraging me and this book. As the hours mounted, so did their support.

Thanks to Dave Doknjas and Tangible Software Solutions for providing me with their Instant VB and Instant C# software programs, which were invaluable in helping me convert small samples and full solutions for the book between C# and VB. I can't tell you all how many hours this saved me.

Thanks to Corrina Barber of Microsoft for providing the styles used in many of the solutions. Corrina was kind enough to provide the styles and work with me on getting them converted for the book for each iteration in the beta process through the release version of Silverlight 2. Corrina is a designer with a strong desire to create compelling applications that offer significant utility, usability, and beauty. Her current passion is Silverlight and it certainly shows in the work she has done.

Thanks to the great people at O'Reilly Media—including Laurel Ruma, Laurel Ackerman, Rachel Monaghan, Marsee Henon, Anna Freeman, Audrey Doyle, Sumita Mukherji, Nancy Kotary, Ellen Troutman, Karen Montgomery, David Futato, Rob Romano, Maria Amodio, and Marcia Friedman—for helping to get this book out of the nooks of my mind, into the bookstores, and ultimately into the hands of the readers. Thanks especially to John Osborn, my editor, for guiding me through the process, and most importantly, for believing that this book had an important story to tell.

Thanks to all the members of my family for supporting me the way families do. I am blessed to count you all as part of my family: Dad, Mom, Julie, Sandy, Laurie, Debbie, Scott, Jeff, Jack, Terry, John, James, Aly, Zach, Alyssa, Julia, Sean, Kyle, Jenna, Jessica, Danielle, Donna, Jim, Matt, Suzanne, Jeff, Nancy, Kevin, Denise, Anna, Ben, Alicia, Brittini, and of course, Kadi.

Most importantly, an enormous thank you to my family. Colleen—thank you for sharing your heart with me. You are my soul mate, my best friend, my love. Landon—I can't wait to walk, run, and fall through this world with you. Tackle life head on. Ella—you have a never-ending supply of hugs, high fives, and kisses for everyone. Daddy's littlest princess has a huge heart. Madelyn—you share so much love and caring from your heart—I am so proud of you, my rock star. Haley—your kindness is legendary—you are truly an angel amongst us. This book is dedicated to you all. Watching movies, special one-on-one days out, game nights, cuddling on the couch, holding hands, and hop on pop were never so good!

CHAPTER 1

Getting Started with Silverlight 2

You've learned how Silverlight can produce stylish interfaces and highly interactive applications in a variety of browsers, and now you want to build a Silverlight application. Not just a bouncing ball, an embedded video, or a spiffy-looking series of buttons, but a walking, talking, fully functional line-of-business application. Of course, you still want the snazzy interface, too. The good news is that you can have it all with Silverlight 2.

In this chapter, I will review some of the critical areas that you need to be familiar with to develop data-driven Silverlight applications, including required software installations and tools. Before developing with Silverlight 2, it is important to understand the major differences between versions 1 and 2 of Silverlight. This chapter will review those differences and point out why each advancement in Silverlight 2 is important to developing data-driven applications.

One important advancement that Silverlight 2 introduces is the ability to write .NET code. This allows developers to leverage their existing skills to create robust Silverlight 2 applications. The .NET 3.5 language features in Silverlight 2, such as LINQ and implicitly typed variables, can also significantly aid in the development of these applications. This chapter will discuss some of these .NET 3.5 language enhancements as they are used throughout this book. I will also walk through the steps of creating a simple data-driven Silverlight 2 application to help get you started.

The Importance of Data Access

Beyond the rich user interfaces, video streaming, and stylish templates in Silverlight 2 lies a robust framework that works very well with various types of data sources. Silverlight applications run in the client machine's browser, where they have the Internet between them and any server applications. Silverlight applications are disconnected from remote data sources, so they must communicate with remote servers through various types of web services to send and receive data.

Silverlight 2 provides several ways to get data from remote servers using HTTP and sockets. Some of the most popular and useful techniques are to communicate with a

SOAP-based web service on a remote server (as we'll explore in Chapters 5 and 6), and to receive data from a REST service (which we'll discuss in Chapters 7–9). Several tools and techniques are available for receiving the data, manipulating it, binding it, presenting it to the user, and handling all of the data-driven aspects of the application, all inside Silverlight 2.

Most applications require some sort of data interaction. The data might be from a database, an RSS feed, a web service, or a REST service that returns Plain Old XML (POX). Silverlight applications can communicate with services and return data in a variety of ways. Although Silverlight can be a very rich and compelling tool for end users, the data for the application is just as important as its delivery.

Data access has taken on several meanings in recent years. *Data access* really is a term that describes the act of accessing data from any number of sources. This can mean accessing data from a database directly through ADO.NET, the ADO.NET Entity Framework, NHibernate, LLBLGen Pro, Enterprise Library, or some custom business object and data access layer. It can also mean accessing data through web services, ASMX, Windows Communication Foundation (WCF), RSS feeds, REST-style web services, and HTTP requests. Obviously, you can access data in several ways, and once you've retrieved it, you often need to manipulate it in some way. Developers often use LINQ to organize data that has been retrieved so that it can be in a more usable shape for the task at hand. All of these aspects define *data access*, and you can use all of these directly or indirectly through Silverlight 2.

Jumping In

Silverlight is a fantastic tool for designing rich interfaces that work in various browsers. However, its extensive support for data programmability is what makes Silverlight a viable solution for business applications. This book arms the reader with the knowledge to build visually and functionally robust applications with Silverlight 2.

Before diving into any examples in this book, make sure that you have the prerequisites for Silverlight 2 installed and set up. You must install the Silverlight 2 runtime to view and run Silverlight applications in the browser. This runtime works in (and is officially supported in) Internet Explorer, Google Chrome, Firefox, and Safari. Runtimes are available for Windows and Mac OS X. The following browsers support Silverlight 2:

- Microsoft Internet Explorer versions 6.0, 7.0, and 8.0 beta
- Mozilla Firefox versions 1.5, 2.0, and 3.0
- Apple Safari versions 2.0 and 3.0 beta
- Google Chrome

Silverlight 2 Tools is an add-on to Visual Studio 2008 that allows you to create Silverlight 2 applications using .NET and Silverlight 2. The Silverlight Tools installation program also installs the Silverlight 2 runtime and the Silverlight 2 SDK. The Silverlight

2 SDK contains examples, documentation, and tools to assist in the development of Silverlight applications.

The following components are required for developing and experiencing Silverlight 2. All of these are contained within a *single* installation file:

- Silverlight 2 Runtime
- Silverlight 2 SDK
- Silverlight 2 Tools for Visual Studio

The following debugging tools can greatly assist in identifying communication problems with Silverlight 2 applications and services. All are free and can clarify problem points as well as help you to identify solutions. Appendix B discusses tips and tricks when using these tools to debug communications between Silverlight 2 and services.

- Firebug (for Firefox)
- Web Development Helper (for Internet Explorer)
- Fiddler2 (for all network traffic sniffing)

It is also recommended that you install Visual Studio 2008 and Expression Blend with SP 1. Visual Studio 2008 is great for editing XAML, using IntelliSense, and of course, writing .NET code for Silverlight 2 applications. Expression Blend is fantastic for arranging complex designs and layouts within Silverlight 2. Both are valuable tools that you should use side by side when developing with Silverlight 2.

Silverlight 2 Features

Silverlight 2 introduced support for .NET code in Silverlight applications, but that is not the only major improvement it offered. Table 1-1 lists many of the major improvements to Silverlight 2, including several that are integral to developing data-driven applications with Silverlight. Table 1-1 singles out these specific features, as it is important to be aware of how they can help developers build solid, data-driven applications with Silverlight 2.

Table 1-1. Key Silverlight 2 features

New features in Silverlight 2	Notes
Framework languages and .NET support	Silverlight 2 includes a portion of the .NET Framework, and supports Visual Basic, Visual C#, IronRuby, and IronPython.
Data binding and notifications	XAML-based data binding and notifications through the INotifyCollection Changed and INotifyPropertyChanged interfaces are now available in Silverlight 2.
Isolated storage	Silverlight 2 can store information in a protected area on a client computer.

New features in Silverlight 2	Notes
Contractual and noncontractual data services: JSON, REST, SOAP, POX, and Atom-based RSS web services	Various data services are accessible via Silverlight 2. This makes reading data from web services simple.
Cross-domain network access	Silverlight 2 can access services that do not originate from the server hosting the Silverlight 2 application.
LINQ, lambdas, extension methods, and object initializers	LINQ to Objects, LINQ to XML, and LINQ to JSON are included in Silverlight 2 to define queries against complex data structures.
StackPanel, Grid, and Canvas layout support	Silverlight 2 introduces support for the three major layout panels native to WPF and XAML.
Suite of bindable controls and panels	Silverlight 2 introduces a wide array of controls that you can integrate into Silverlight 2 applications and bind to data sources.

 Originally, Microsoft was going to release Silverlight 2 as Silverlight 1.1, but with all of the improvements it made to the application, the company deemed the new version to be different enough to warrant its own major release number.

Looking at the new features in Table 1-1, it is obvious that Silverlight 2 boasts a lot of major new capabilities. It is important to touch on each enhancement that directly affects data-driven application development. We will explore many of these thoroughly in upcoming chapters, so for now I'll cover them only briefly to introduce you to them.

Framework Languages and .NET Support

I cannot overstate the fact that developing a Silverlight application is much easier when you can leverage your existing .NET development experience. This starts with being able to write .NET code in the Silverlight client application to handle various aspects of that application, including event handlers, referencing the extensive .NET Framework, and creating complex user controls. The Silverlight 2 runtime contains a small but powerful subset of the .NET Framework library so that developers can take advantage of their .NET skills and transition to Silverlight 2 with minimal effort.

Self-Describing Data Services

Silverlight 2 can communicate with SOAP-based web services (e.g., using WCF or ASMX) to pass defined data structures between a Silverlight client and a remote server. These services expose a contract through WSDL with which the client can communicate by generating proxy classes. This contract defines the services that you can call and how to call them, and it exposes the data structures that you can pass into and out of the services. This is key to exposing web services that return or accept serializable entities as parameters. With contractual data services, Silverlight 2 can communicate with remote services that return entities from LINQ to SQL, NHibernate, the ADO.NET Entity Framework, or even custom domain entity models. It also opens the door to being able to communicate with third-party SOAP-based services that expose WSDL, such as Live Search.

Loose Coupling with Data Services

Silverlight 2 can also consume data services without generating proxy classes using SOAP, RSS, Atom, JSON, POX, or REST. Many sources of information are available that return data using a noncontractual service. For example, Digg.com (*http://www .digg.com*), Amazon.com (*http://www.amazon.com*), Twitter.com (*http://www.twitter .com*), and Flickr.com (*http://www.flickr.com*) all expose REST services that return XML. Silverlight 2 applications can request information from all of these services and integrate the results into an application. In Chapters 7–9, we will delve deeply into these areas, as well as discuss how to communicate with them across domains and how to manage the XML and JSON they may return via LINQ to XML and LINQ to JSON, respectively.

Control Model

The new control model that Silverlight 2 provides makes it much easier to write Silverlight 2 applications. You can organize the new controls within the XAML layout panels, such as `Grid`, `Canvas`, and `StackPanel`, to create rich interfaces. The controls support XAML-based data binding and dependency properties, which we will discuss in detail in Chapters 2–4.

Silverlight 2 introduced more than two dozen controls that you can use to build Silverlight 2 client applications. It offers layout panels such as `Grid`, `StackPanel`, and `Canvas`, as well as several input controls that you can customize using templates and styles. You can completely replace the content of some of the controls to achieve a more complex solution. For example, you can replace the header of a `DataGrid` control with a series of controls that allow you to sort the `DataGrid`. Or you can replace a button's default look with another element such as an `Ellipse` and fill it with another `FrameworkElement` such as an image. Chapters 2–4 will dive deeply into the controls and explain how data binding works with them, as well as offer best practices for binding and presenting data. Figure 1-1 shows the controls available in Expression Blend 2 with SP 1 and Figure 1-2 shows the controls available in Visual Studio 2008.

LINQ to Objects and LINQ to XML

Silverlight 2 supports the use of LINQ to Objects, which can simplify the querying of data in arrays and collections in a Silverlight application. LINQ to XML (also supported in Silverlight 2 applications) is very useful when consuming noncontractual data services that return XML. The XML can be read into a variety of XML-consuming libraries,

Figure 1-1. Silverlight 2 controls shown in Expression Blend

but consuming it with LINQ to XML's objects allows you to query the XML using the familiar and powerful LINQ syntax. Also, with LINQ at your disposal you can combine XML and object data structures in the same LINQ query. Many of the examples in this book will use LINQ in some fashion to query data from XML or objects.

LINQ

Data-driven applications written with Silverlight 2 make extensive use of LINQ and the .NET 3.5 language enhancements in one way or another, as many of the examples in this book will demonstrate. Because of the importance of these features, it is worth taking a look at how they work. C# 3 and Visual Basic (VB) 9 introduced several language enhancements, some of which are integral to writing queries with LINQ. Silverlight 2 applications can consume XML, JSON, objects, entities from LINQ to SQL, and entities from the ADO.NET Entity Framework, to name a few sources.

Silverlight 2 applications often need to gather values from arrays and/or lists of custom entities (e.g., a List<T>). In these cases, LINQ to Objects comes in handy, as it allows you to query any IEnumerable list. Although you can consume and manage XML

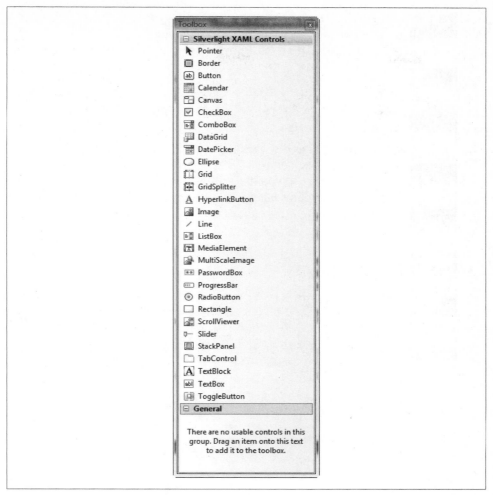

Figure 1-2. Silverlight controls shown in Visual Studio 2008

through a variety of .NET libraries, such as XmlReader, LINQ to XML provides a simpler and often more powerful way to consume XML. This makes it easy for Silverlight applications to consume XML from RSS feeds or REST services and massage the data without resorting to verbose loops. LINQ queries can also join a list of objects and XML, which is very useful when an application is pulling data from multiple sources. This book makes extensive use of LINQ to Objects and LINQ to XML in several chapters in appropriate places where Silverlight applications can take advantage of them.

LINQ to Entities is used heavily in querying the Entity Data Model that the ADO.NET Entity Framework produces. The ADO.NET Entity Framework builds an Entity Data Model that maps an object-oriented conceptual model of entities to a relational store, such as SQL Server (although the ADO.NET Entity Framework supports a provider model, so other database servers such as Oracle are also supported). Queries are written with LINQ to Entities against the conceptual model and the queries are translated through the mapping layer to SQL statements that execute against the relational store. Once the entities have been returned from the LINQ to Entities query, the entities can be serialized and passed to other application tiers. For example, a Silverlight client application could request an entity from a WCF service on a remote server that exposes entities from the Entity Data Model. The Silverlight application could then use LINQ to Objects on those entities as well.

The fourth flavor of LINQ that this book will discuss is LINQ to SQL. LINQ to SQL allows a one-to-one mapping from entities to SQL Server objects. It does not support the rich mapping schema that the ADO.NET Entity Framework supports; neither does it have a provider model, so it works only with SQL Server. For example, you can write queries with LINQ to SQL that return entities that can then be serialized and passed to a Silverlight application.

Language Enhancements

Several .NET language enhancements were introduced with .NET 3.5. These language enhancements, along with features such as generics, are important pieces to building queries with LINQ.

This section will demonstrate and discuss several key language features, including:

- Automatic property setters/getters
- Object initializers
- Collection initializers
- Extension methods
- Implicitly typed variables
- Anonymous types

Figure 1-3 shows the .NET 3.5 language enhancements.

Automatic Properties in C#

Creating properties can be a very redundant process, especially when the getters and setters contain no logic other than getting and setting the value of the private field. Using public fields would reduce the amount of code; however, public fields do have some drawbacks. Most importantly, public fields are not fully supported by data binding.

One way to avoid having to type the code for a private field and its public property getter and setter is to use a refactoring tool. However, automatic properties allow you

```
List<Customer> customerList = new List<Customer>
    {  ◄─────────────────────────────────── Collection Initializer
        new Customer {ID = 101, CompanyName = "Foo Company",
                BusinessAddress = new Address {State="FL"}},
        new Customer {ID = 102. CompanyName = "Goo Company".
                BusinessAddress = new Address {State="NY"}}, ◄── Object Initializer
        new Customer {ID = 103, CompanyName = "Hoo Company",
                BusinessAddress = new Address {State="NY"}},
        new Customer {ID = 104. CompanyName = "Koo Company".
                BusinessAddress = new Address {State="NY"}}◄─── Embedded
    };                                                         Object
                                                               Initializer

    var query = from c in customerList
                where c.BusinessAddress.State.Equals("FL")
                select new { Name = c.CompanyName,
                        c.BusinessAddress.State };◄──────── Anonymous Type
       ▲
Implicitly Typed Variable
```

Figure 1-3. .NET 3.5 language enhancements at a glance

to type less code and still get a private field and its public getter and setter. You create an automatic property using shortened syntax. The compiler will generate the private field and the public setter and getter for you. In Example 1-1, a `Customer2` class and an `Address2` class have several private fields that are exposed through a series of corresponding public property getters and setters.

 C# supports automatic properties, but VB does not.

Example 1-1. Explicit getters and setters in C#

```
public class Customer2
{
    private int id;
    private string companyName;
    private Address2 companyAddress;

    public int ID
    {
        get { return id; }
        set { id = value; }
    }

    public string CompanyName
    {
        get { return companyName; }
        set { companyName = value; }
```

```
        }

        public Address2 CompanyAddress
        {
            get { return companyAddress; }
            set { companyAddress = value; }
        }
    }

public class Address2
{
    private int id;
    private string city;
    private string state;

    public int ID
    {
        get { return id; }
        set { id = value; }
    }

    public string City
    {
        get { return city; }
        set { city = value; }
    }

    public string State
    {
        get { return state; }
        set { state = value; }
    }
}
```

Example 1-2 shows how you can achieve the same result through automatic properties with less code than Example 1-1. The Customer and Address classes use automatic properties to create the class properties without requiring all of the code to declare a field and its property getter and setter.

Example 1-2. Automatic properties

```
public class Customer
{
    public int ID { get; set; }
    public string CompanyName { get; set; }
    public Address CompanyAddress { get; set; }
}

public class Address
{
    public int ID { get; set; }
    public string City { get; set; }
    public string State { get; set; }
}
```

Object Initializers

Object initializers allow you to pass in named values for each public property that will then be used to initialize the object. For example, you could initialize an instance of the Customer class using the code shown in Example 1-3.

Example 1-3. Creating and initializing a class

C#
```csharp
Customer customer = new Customer();
customer.ID = 1001;
customer.CompanyName = "Foo";
customer.CompanyAddress = new Address();
```

VB
```vb
Dim customer As New Customer()
customer.ID = 1001
customer.CompanyName = "Foo"
customer.CompanyAddress = New Address()
```

However, by taking advantage of object initializers, you can create an instance of the Customer class using the syntax in Example 1-4.

Example 1-4. Using object initializers

C#
```csharp
Customer customer = new Customer
{
    ID = 1001,
    CompanyName = "Foo",
    CompanyAddress = new Address()
};
```

VB
```vb
Dim customer = New Customer() With _
    {.Id = 1001, .CompanyName = "Foo", _
    .CompanyAddress = New Address()}
```

Object initializers allow you to pass any named public property to the constructor of the class. This feature removes the need to create multiple overloaded constructors using different parameter lists to achieve the same goal. The IntelliSense feature of the IDE will help you by displaying a list of the named parameters as you type. You do not have to pass in all of the parameters, and you can use a nested object initializer, as shown in Example 1-4.

Collection Initializers

Initializing collections generally takes up several lines of code as you create the collection, create each object instance, and then add each item one by one to the collection in separate statements. The following statement demonstrates how to initialize a List<Customer> by passing in three instances of a Customer class.

C# supports collection initializers, but VB does not.

```
List<Customer> custList =
    new List<Customer> { customer1, customer2,  customer3 };
```

Using the combination of object initializers and collection initializers, you can create a collection and initialize it with a series of objects in a single statement. Using collection initializers, you can create a `List<Customer>` and add three `Customer` instances to the `List<Customer>`, as shown in Example 1-5.

Example 1-5. Collection initializers

```
List<Customer> custList = new List<Customer>
    {
        new Customer {ID = 1001, CompanyName = "Foo"},
        new Customer {ID = 1002, CompanyName = "Goo"},
        new Customer {ID = 1003, CompanyName = "Hoo"}
    };
```

Without these features, the syntax to create a `List<Customer>` and add three new instances of `Customer` to it is a bit more methodical, as shown in Example 1-6.

Example 1-6. Creating and initializing a collection

```
Customer customerFoo = new Customer();
customerFoo.ID = 1001;
customerFoo.CompanyName = "Foo";
Customer customerGoo = new Customer();
customerGoo.ID = 1002;
customerGoo.CompanyName = "Goo";
Customer customerHoo = new Customer();
customerHoo.ID = 1003;
customerHoo.CompanyName = "Hoo";
List<Customer> customerList3 = new List<Customer>();
customerList3.Add(customerFoo);
customerList3.Add(customerGoo);
customerList3.Add(customerHoo);
```

Extension Methods

Extension methods allow you to enhance an existing class by adding a new method to it, without modifying the actual code for the class. For example, a requirement may exist to provide the area of a square surface given the length of one side. You could easily write an extension method to accomplish this. Because all the sides are the same length, you could create an extension method that calculates the square of an integer. An extension method would allow you to expose a method named `SquareIt` on the `int` datatype in this case.

You must create extension methods in a static class and define the extension methods as static. The first parameter of the extension method must use the keyword this to signify that the first parameter is the type that the extension method will extend. The code in Example 1-7 uses a static method named SquareIt that accepts a single parameter.

Example 1-7. Extension method

C#
```csharp
public static class MyExtensions
{
    public static int SquareIt(this int num)
    {
        return num*2;
    }
}
```

VB
```vb
Public Module MyExtensions
    <System.Runtime.CompilerServices.Extension> _
    Public Function SquareIt(ByVal num As Integer) As Integer
        Return num * 2
    End Function
End Module
```

When you create an extension method, the method appears in IntelliSense in the IDE. Once you have defined the extension method, you can use it to calculate the square of an integer using the code sample in Example 1-8.

Example 1-8. Implementing the extension method

C#
```csharp
int x = 7;
int squaredX = x.SquareIt();
```

VB
```vb
Dim x As Integer = 7
Dim squaredX As Integer = x.SquareIt()
```

Extension methods can be a great help; however, I recommend that you use them in situations where they truly do extend a class. For example, I would not create a TrimIt extension method for a string class, because there is already one called Trim. If you wanted to create a method to operate on a Customer class to calculate a customer's credit limit, a best practice would be to add this method to the Customer class itself. Creating an extension method in this case would violate the encapsulation principle by placing the code for the customer's credit limit calculation outside the Customer class. However, extension methods are very useful when you do not have the ability to add a method to the class itself, as in the case of creating a SquareIt method on the int class.

You also should use extension methods when doing so assists a class that you cannot extend because it is part of the .NET Framework. For example, the ADO.NET Entity Framework has a lot of operations that you can perform on its objects. But sometimes you can find yourself performing the same operations repeatedly. I find that it is sometimes convenient to set all of the properties of a class in an entity data model to the modified state. Example 1-9 shows how you can do this using an extension method. A good practice is to organize your extension methods in static classes with other like extension methods.

Example 1-9. Using an extension method to set all of the properties of a class in an entity data model to a modified state

C#
```
public static class EFExtension
{
    public static void SetAllModified<T>(this T entity, ObjectContext context)
    where T : IEntityWithKey
    {
        var stateEntry =
            context.ObjectStateManager.GetObjectStateEntry(entity.EntityKey);
        var propertyNameList =
            stateEntry.CurrentValues.DataRecordInfo.FieldMetadata.Select
            (pn => pn.FieldType.Name);
        foreach (var propName in propertyNameList)
        {
            stateEntry.SetModifiedProperty(propName);
        }
    }
}
```

VB
```
Public Module EFExtension
    <System.Runtime.CompilerServices.Extension> _
    Public Sub SetAllModified(Of T As IEntityWithKey) _
        (ByVal entity As T, ByVal context As ObjectContext)
        Dim stateEntry = _
            context.ObjectStateManager.GetObjectStateEntry(entity.EntityKey)
        Dim propertyNameList = _
            stateEntry.CurrentValues.DataRecordInfo.FieldMetadata. _
                Select(Function(pn) pn.FieldType.Name)
        For Each propName In propertyNameList
            stateEntry.SetModifiedProperty(propName)
        Next propName
    End Sub
End Module
```

Implicitly Typed Variables

Implicitly typed variables declare the type on which they operate as a specific type based on what they are being set to. You can declare implicitly typed variables using the **var** keyword (or Dim in VB). The following example shows an implicitly typed variable that represents a string:

C#
```
var x = "Foo";
```

VB
```
Dim x = "Foo"
```

The variable x becomes a string, because that is the type of the value that it is being set to. As long as the righthand side's type can be determined, the lefthand side will take on the same type. This syntax can shorten some code samples, too, as shown here with a declaration of a `List<T>`. There is no need for the redundant `List<string>`, because the righthand side already shows you the type:

C#
```csharp
var stringList = new List<string>();
```

VB
```vb
Dim stringList = New List(Of String)()
```

Anonymous Types/Implicit Types

You can use implicitly typed variables to help create anonymous types, too. Anonymous types allow you to create an object instance that is not of a predefined class type that you have already created. Rather, it is a new and custom class type that you can use within the local scope. When you create an anonymous type, you need to declare a variable to refer to the object. Because you do not know what type you will be getting (because it is a new and anonymous type), you can declare the variable with the `var` keyword.

For example, you could create an anonymous type that describes a car. The `car` variable will represent the instance of the class and it will expose the `Make`, `Model`, and `Coolness Factor` properties. You can use the following code to create this new object without having to create a `Car` class explicitly. This feature comes in handy when you're using LINQ to project the results of queries. Example 1-10 demonstrates how to create an instance of a class with `Make` and `Model` properties.

Example 1-10. Anonymous type creation

C#
```csharp
var car = new { Make = "Chevrolet",
    Model = "Camaro", CoolnessFactor = 1 };
```

VB
```vb
Dim car = New With {Key .Make = "Chevrolet", _
    Key .Model = "Camaro", Key .CoolnessFactor = 1}
```

Anonymous Types and LINQ

When writing a LINQ query expression you may return various pieces of information. Anonymous types are a great way to collect this information within a single object instance. For example, an enumerable list could be queried using LINQ that returns an anonymous type containing the `CompanyName` from a `Customer` class and each customer's city. The `City` may be from an associated `Address` class that is a property of the `Customer` class. Example 1-11 shows one way to accomplish this using an anonymous type.

Example 1-11. Anonymous types with LINQ

C#
```csharp
var query = from c in customerList
            where c.CompanyAddress.State == "FL"
            select new { Name = c.CompanyName, c.CompanyAddress.City };

foreach (var info in query)
```

```
        Console.WriteLine(string.Format("{0} is in {1}, Florida",
            info.Name, info.City));
```

```
Dim query = From c In customerList _
    Where c.CompanyAddress.State = "FL" _
    Select New With {Key .Name = c.CompanyName, Key c.CompanyAddress.City}

For Each info In query
    Console.WriteLine(String.Format("{0} is in {1}, Florida", _
        info.Name, info.City))
Next info
```

The select clause in the LINQ query expression creates an instance of an anonymous type that will have Name and City properties. These values come from the Customer and Address objects. The properties can be renamed (CompanyName is renamed to Name) or they can implicitly take on the name. The resultant anonymous type is available as a local variable in scope.

Summary

Silverlight 2 supports code to be written using .NET that includes many features, such as generics, collections, LINQ to Objects, and LINQ to XML. This support, along with the new language enhancements in Silverlight 2, allows developers to create rich, data-driven applications using Silverlight 2 and their existing .NET skill sets. The new control suite, XAML binding techniques, LINQ support, and rich communications features in Silverlight 2 greatly simplify the process of developing data-centric, line-of-business applications.

CHAPTER 2

Silverlight Data-Binding Foundations

Data binding provides a simple way to present and manage data in a Silverlight 2 client application. Data binding handles the process of pushing data from a data source into the target (the Silverlight 2 application's controls), and in some cases pulling the data from the target back to the source. You can perform this process manually without the data-binding techniques by writing a series of event handlers and manually pushing and pulling data. However, the data-binding techniques are built specifically to help alleviate the redundant code required to handle data binding that goes into each client application. XAML provides a rich set of features for data binding from which Silverlight 2 applications also benefit.

ASP.NET and Windows Forms applications have their own flavor of data-binding controls. For example, ASP.NET has an `ObjectDataSource` control and Windows Forms has the `BindingSource` control. The role of these controls is to tie a data source to a series of controls. The data source object feeds the data source, and its property values are presented in controls that tie to the data-binding control. When the values are changed, the binding control sends the values back to the object that is the data source. This model has worked in the sometimes awkward evolution of data binding.

There is no specific data-binding control with Silverlight. Instead, you bake the data-binding functionality right into Silverlight 2 and XAML using tools such as `DataContext` and binding markup extensions. Silverlight 1 did not support data binding to controls because, well, Silverlight 1 did not have controls. XAML-based data binding is very powerful, and Silverlight 2 applications now support it. This chapter demonstrates how to push values from a source entity into a set of controls and then pull them back out using manual binding. It also examines the foundations of data binding with Silverlight 2 and its controls, the importance of the dependency property in data binding, and the basic rules of data binding. We will also discuss how to bind a data source (such as a business object entity), how to bind a data source to a set of Silverlight 2 controls, the effect of an inherited `DataContext`, and the role of data-bound targets and sources.

Life Without Binding

Fully understanding how XAML-based data binding works—and its advantages over pushing and pulling data through explicit code without binding—becomes much clearer after seeing life without data binding. Data can flow from an entity to a control and back without using data binding. Data binding is an automated vehicle that facilitates the connection between an entity and a set of controls. Without binding, you can use a technique to push data into a set of controls to be presented, and then pull it back out of the controls and into an entity data source.

The XAML shown in Example 2-1 will display three TextBox controls and a button, laid out in a grid. The controls are not bound declaratively and will not display any values until an event handler pushes values into them.

Example 2-1. Manual binding of a XAML layout

```xml
<Grid x:Name="LayoutRoot">
    <Grid.RowDefinitions>
        <RowDefinition/>
    </Grid.RowDefinitions>
    <Grid.ColumnDefinitions>
        <ColumnDefinition/>
    </Grid.ColumnDefinitions>
    <Rectangle Fill="#FFDEE6FB" Grid.Column="0" Grid.Row="0"
     RadiusX="20" RadiusY="20" Opacity="0.8" StrokeThickness="0" />
    <Grid Grid.Column="0" Grid.Row="0" Margin="10,10,10,10">
        <Grid.ColumnDefinitions>
            <ColumnDefinition Width="80"/>
            <ColumnDefinition Width="260"/>
        </Grid.ColumnDefinitions>
        <Grid.RowDefinitions>
            <RowDefinition Height="40"></RowDefinition>
            <RowDefinition Height="40"></RowDefinition>
            <RowDefinition Height="40"></RowDefinition>
            <RowDefinition Height="40"></RowDefinition>
        </Grid.RowDefinitions>
        <TextBlock Text="First Name" Grid.Row="0" Grid.Column="0"
        Margin="10,5,10,5" Style="{StaticResource TextBlockCaptionStyle}"/>
    <TextBlock Text="Last Name" Grid.Row="1" Grid.Column="0" Margin="10,5,10,5"
        Style="{StaticResource TextBlockCaptionStyle}"/>
    <TextBlock Text="Company" Grid.Row="2" Grid.Column="0" Margin="10,5,10,5"
        Style="{StaticResource TextBlockCaptionStyle}"/>
    <TextBox x:Name="tbFirstName" Grid.Column="1" Grid.Row="0"
        Margin="10,5,10,5" HorizontalAlignment="Left" Height="30"
        Width="240" Style="{StaticResource TextBoxStyle}"/>
    <TextBox x:Name="tbLastName" Grid.Column="1" Grid.Row="1"
        Margin="10,5,10,5" HorizontalAlignment="Left" Height="30" Width="240"
        Style="{StaticResource TextBoxStyle}"/>
    <TextBox x:Name="tbCompany" Grid.Column="1" Grid.Row="2" Margin="10,5,10,5"
        HorizontalAlignment="Left" Height="30" Width="240"
        Style="{StaticResource TextBoxStyle}"/>
    <Button x:Name="btnSave" Content="Save" Grid.Column="2" Grid.Row="3"
        Margin="10,5,10,5" HorizontalAlignment="Right" Height="30"
```

```
            Width="100" Style="{StaticResource ButtonStyle}"/>
    </Grid>
</Grid>
```

Reusable Styles

The XAML in Example 2-1 sets the `Style` property of several elements to a
`StaticResource`. For example, the `Style` property of the `TextBox` controls is set to the
`TextBoxStyle` style. This style refers to a resource that can be defined in this page or in
the *app.xaml* file. If the style is defined in the local page, any control on the page can
use it as a `StaticResource`. However, if the style is defined in the *app.xaml* file, any page
or control in the application can use it. As the code in this book uses these styles in
several examples, these styles are defined in *app.xaml*.

The `TextBoxStyle` style shown in the following code is assigned an `x:Key` value that any
`TextBox` control that should use this style can reference. The `TargetType` indicates that
this style can be applied to any `TextBox` control. Each `Setter` element accepts a
`Property` and `Value` attribute. Each of these represents the name of the property of the
`TextBox` and a value to set the property to, respectively.

```
<!--TextBox-->
<Style x:Key="TextBoxStyle" TargetType="TextBox">
    <Setter Property="FontSize" Value="11"/>
    <Setter Property="Foreground" Value="#FF313131"/>
    <Setter Property="FontFamily" Value="Trebuchet MS"/>
    <Setter Property="Template">
        <Setter.Value>
            <ControlTemplate TargetType="TextBox">
                <Border x:Name="BackgroundBorder"
                        VerticalAlignment="Bottom"
                        BorderBrush="#FF888888"
                        CornerRadius="2.5"
                        BorderThickness="2.5"
                        Background="#FFFFFFFF">
                    <Border x:Name="InnerBorder" Margin="0"
                            CornerRadius="2"
                            BorderBrush="#FF5B0000"
                            BorderThickness="1.5"
                            Background="#FFFFFFFF">
                        <Border x:Name="HoverBorder"
                                Background="#FFFFFFFF"
                                BorderBrush="#66D6A5A5"
                                BorderThickness="3">
                            <Border
                                x:Name="ELEMENT_Content"
                                Margin="1"/>
                        </Border>
                    </Border>
                </Border>
            </ControlTemplate>
        </Setter.Value>
    </Setter>
</Style>
```

The `Template` property of a control is used to define a template to replace the default template for a control. In other words, instead of using the default visual representation of a `TextBox`, the `Template` property provides a way to define a custom visual representation. In this style, the `ControlTemplate` defines a series of `Border` controls that will give the `TextBox` control to which they are applied a fancier appearance (see Figure 2-1, shown later in this chapter).

This book uses a series of styles and templates that are defined in the code examples available for download from the book's website, at *http://www.Silverlight-Data.com*.

The controls that are rendered using the code in Example 2-1 are loaded manually by pushing property values from an entity instance into its corresponding controls. Example 2-2 shows the `BoundManually_Load` event handler that pushes data values into the controls from an entity. This code shows a `Person` class that is created and initialized, using its object initializer, to hold a person's information. This information is then accessed through the entity's properties and pushed into the UI's controls.

You can set event handlers in Silverlight 2 either through XAML or in the code-behind. Event handlers are not part of the visual presentation of the user interface, and in general it is a good practice to separate the visual presentation from any presentation logic. Therefore, the examples in this book create event handlers in .NET code in the code-behinds instead of declaratively through XAML. Example 2-2 demonstrates this through the `BoundManually()` constructor.

Example 2-2. Manually pushing into controls

```
public partial class BoundManually : UserControl
{
    public BoundManually()
    {
        InitializeComponent();
        this.Loaded += new RoutedEventHandler(BoundManually_Loaded);
        //...
    }

    private void BoundManually_Loaded(object sender, RoutedEventArgs e)
    {
        var person = new Person { FirstName = "John",
         LastName = "Smith", Company = "Foo Company" };
        tbFirstName.Text = person.FirstName;
        tbLastName.Text = person.LastName;
        tbCompany.Text = person.Company;
    }
}

public class Person
{
    public string FirstName { get; set; }
    public string LastName { get; set; }
```

```vb
    public string Company { get; set; }
}

Partial Public Class BoundManually
    Inherits UserControl
    Public Sub New()
        InitializeComponent()
        AddHandler Loaded, AddressOf BoundManually_Loaded
        ' ...
    End Sub

    Private Sub BoundManually_Loaded(ByVal sender As Object, _
            ByVal e As RoutedEventArgs)
        Dim person = New Person With {.FirstName = "John", _
            .LastName = "Smith", .Company = "Foo Company"}
        tbFirstName.Text = person.FirstName
        tbLastName.Text = person.LastName
        tbCompany.Text = person.Company
    End Sub
End Class

Public Class Person
    Private privateFirstName As String
    Public Property FirstName() As String
        Get
            Return privateFirstName
        End Get
        Set(ByVal value As String)
            privateFirstName = value
        End Set
    End Property
    Private privateLastName As String
    Public Property LastName() As String
        Get
            Return privateLastName
        End Get
        Set(ByVal value As String)
            privateLastName = value
        End Set
    End Property
    Private privateCompany As String
    Public Property Company() As String
        Get
            Return privateCompany
        End Get
        Set(ByVal value As String)
            privateCompany = value
        End Set
    End Property
End Class
```

The values are pushed into the controls on BoundManually_Load and are presented in the user interface. Figure 2-1 shows the page that is displayed after the data has been pushed into the controls through manual binding.

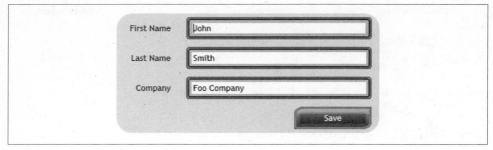

Figure 2-1. Manually bound controls

You can pull the data out of the controls and back into the entity's properties through a number of events, the most common of which is an event that may fire when a user clicks a Save button. Example 2-3 shows the `btnSave_Click` event handler, which creates an instance of a `Person` class and initializes its values by pulling the values from the `TextBox` controls.

Example 2-3. Pulling control values into an entity

C#
```csharp
private Person  person;

public BoundManually()
{
    //...
    btnSave.Click += new RoutedEventHandler(btnSave_Click);
}


private void btnSave_Click(object sender, RoutedEventArgs e)
{
    person = new Person
                {
                    FirstName = tbFirstName.Text,
                    LastName = tbLastName.Text,
                    Company = tbCompany.Text
                };
}
```

VB
```vb
Private person As Person

Public Sub New()
    ' ...
    AddHandler btnSave.Click, AddressOf btnSave_Click
End Sub


Private Sub btnSave_Click(ByVal sender As Object, ByVal e As RoutedEventArgs)
    person = New Person With {.FirstName = tbFirstName.Text, _
        .LastName = tbLastName.Text, .Company = tbCompany.Text}
End Sub
```

This technique is quite simple, but the code gets very redundant, especially when a lot of controls and properties need to be bound in a Silverlight user control. Each property requires a push and a pull, as well as a firing mechanism (an event handler) to perform the push and pull binding. This technique is known as *manual binding* because of its reliance on the firing mechanisms and the code that is required to perform the pushing and pulling.

Data Binding in Silverlight

Although binding can be established using a manual push-and-pull process, the data-binding capabilities of XAML and Silverlight 2 offer more power and flexibility with less runtime code. The result as a more robust data-bound user interface with fewer failure points than what you would get with manual binding.

Automated data binding in Silverlight 2 is the process that links a UI FrameworkElement to a data source entity and back. The entity contains the data that will flow to the FrameworkElement control for presentation. The data can also flow from the control in Silverlight 2 back to the entity. For example, an entity may be bound to a series of controls, each linked to a specific property on the entity, as shown in Figure 2-2.

The entity class instance is set to the DataContext for a control that then allows that control or any child control of that control to be bound directly to the entity. This process involves many important players that we'll explore in this chapter, including the DataContext, binding modes, and dependency properties on FrameworkElement controls. Each plays a critical role in customizing how the data-binding process operates in a Silverlight application.

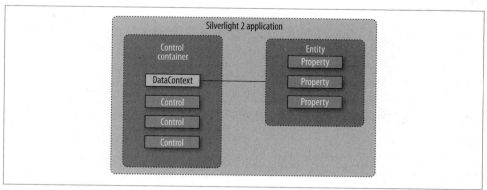

Figure 2-2. Data binding in Silverlight 2

There are some basic rules to follow when setting up data binding in Silverlight. Rule 1 states that the target element of a data-binding operation must be a FrameworkElement. Rule 2 says that the target property must be a dependency property.

Rule 1: FrameworkElement

The target of the data binding must be a `FrameworkElement`. This may sound limiting, but it is quite the opposite. Many subclasses inherit from `FrameworkElement`. Figure 2-3 shows several controls that inherit from `FrameworkElement`. `FrameworkElement` extends the `UIElement` class and adds capabilities that allow it to control layout and support data binding.

```
System.Object
  System.Windows.DependencyObject
    System.Windows.UIElement
      System.Windows.FrameworkElement
        System.Windows.Controls.Border
        System.Windows.Controls.Control
        System.Windows.Controls.Image
        System.Windows.Controls.ItemsPresenter
        System.Windows.Controls.MediaElement
        System.Windows.Controls.MultiScaleImage
        System.Windows.Controls.Panel
        System.Windows.Controls.Primitives.Popup
        System.Windows.Controls.TextBlock
        System.Windows.Documents.Glyphs
        System.Windows.Shapes.Shape
```

Figure 2-3. FrameworkElement class hierarchy

Any XAML element that derives from `FrameworkElement` can be used for layout on a page or user control, and can be involved in data binding as a target. Figure 2-3 shows many of the controls that derive from `FrameworkElement`. There are also controls that derive from the `System.Windows.Controls.Control` class, such as `TextBox`, `Calendar`, and `DataGrid`. In data binding, both a data source and at least one target are required. The target can be a control or set of controls on a page (or within a user control). Basically, the data can travel between the source and the target in both directions. Sources of data are generally instances of objects, such as a domain entity. The properties of the data source are referred to in the targets so that each target control knows to which property of the entity it should be bound.

Rule 2: Dependency Properties

As mentioned previously, the second rule of data binding in Silverlight 2 is that the target must be a dependency property. At first thought, this may sound limiting, especially as one of the first controls people think about when they think of data binding is the `TextBox`'s `Text` property. However, if you look in the Silverlight 2 documentation or at the source code (using a tool such as Lutz Roeder's .NET Reflector) for the `Text` property of a `TextBox` you will see that it too is a dependency property. Example 2-4 shows the source code for the `TextBox`'s `Text` property. In fact, most properties that you can think of are dependency properties, which is great because that means that you can use data binding with so many properties.

Example 2-4. Source code for TextProperty and Text

```csharp
public static readonly DependencyProperty TextProperty;

public string Text
{
    get
    {
        string str = (string) this.GetValue(TextProperty);
        if (str != null)
        {
            return str;
        }
        return string.Empty;
    }
    set
    {
        if (value == null)
        {
            throw new ArgumentNullException("Text");
        }
        base.SetValue(TextProperty, value);
    }
}
```

```vb
Public Shared ReadOnly TextProperty As DependencyProperty

Public Property Text() As String
    Get
        Dim str As String = CStr(Me.GetValue(TextProperty))
        If str IsNot Nothing Then
            Return str
        End If
        Return String.Empty
    End Get
    Set(ByVal value As String)
        If value Is Nothing Then
            Throw New ArgumentNullException("Text")
        End If
        MyBase.SetValue(TextProperty, value)
    End Set
End Property
```

Dependency properties are just like CLR properties, but with the added capability of supporting data binding and styling. The purpose of dependency properties is to provide a way to determine the value of a property based on inputs, including but not limited to user preferences, resources, styles, and data binding. The Fill property in the following code shows an example of a dependency property:

```xml
<Rectangle Fill="#FFDEE6FB" Grid.Column="0" Grid.Row="0"
    RadiusX="20" RadiusY="20" Opacity="0.8" StrokeThickness="0" />
```

The Rectangle control's Fill property is a dependency property that can be set to a color. You can determine the Fill property's value using a resource or by data-binding to an object. This would allow the color of the rectangle to be determined at runtime.

You do not declare dependency properties as a standard .NET CLR type, but rather with a backing property of type `DependencyProperty`. The code in Example 2-5 shows the public facing property, `Fill`, and its type, `Brush`. However, notice that the backing property for it is not `Brush`, but rather the `DependencyProperty` type. You can always identify a dependency property by looking at its backing property's name. If the backing property name has the *Property* suffix, it is generally the backing property for a dependency property.

Example 2-5. DependencyProperty

C#
```
public static readonly DependencyProperty FillProperty;

public Brush Fill
{
    get { return (Brush) this.GetValue(FillProperty); }
    set { base.SetValue(FillProperty, (DependencyObject) value); }
}
```

VB
```
Public Shared ReadOnly FillProperty As DependencyProperty

Public Property Fill() As Brush
    Get
        Return CType(Me.GetValue(FillProperty), Brush)
    End Get
    Set(ByVal value As Brush)
        MyBase.SetValue(FillProperty, CType(value, DependencyObject))
    End Set
End Property
```

There are a few key points to remember when thinking about dependency properties. First, Table 2-1 is a quick reference of some key terms applied to the code in Example 2-5.

Table 2-1. Fill dependency property

Term	Description
Dependency property	The property named `Fill`.
DependencyProperty	The type of `FillProperty`.
Dependency property identifier	The instance of the backing property, `FillProperty`. You refer to this in the CLR wrapper code with the `GetValue` and `SetValue` methods.
CLR wrapper	The setter and getter accessor code for the `Fill` property.

Second, a dependency property can also get its value through a data-binding operation. Instead of setting the value to a specific color or a `Brush`, you can set the value through data binding. When using data binding, the property's value is determined at runtime from the binding to the data source.

The following XAML example sets the `Fill` for a `Rectangle` using data binding. The binding uses an inherited data context and an instance of an object data source (referred to as `MyShape`). We will explore the binding syntax and the `DataContext` later in this chapter.

```
<Rectangle Fill="{Binding MyShape.FillColor}"
    Grid.Column="0" Grid.Row="0"
    RadiusX="20" RadiusY="20" Opacity="0.8" StrokeThickness="0" />
```

 Besides basic data binding, styles, animations, and templates are huge beneficiaries of using dependency properties. Most of the examples in this book show controls that use styles indicated through a `StaticResource` (mostly defined in *app.xaml*). The style resources are often set to a `Style` dependency property to achieve a more elegant appearance.

A third point to remember is that dependency property values are determined using an order of precedence. For example, a style resource may set the `Background` dependency property to `White` for a canvas control. However, you can override the `Background` color in the control itself by setting the `Background` property to `Blue`. The order of precedence exists to ensure that the values are set in a consistent and predictable manner. The previous example of the `Rectangle` control shows that the locally set property value has a higher precedence than a resource.

When creating a binding, you must assign a dependency property of a `FrameworkElement` to the binding. This is the target of the binding operation. You can assign the source of the binding through the `DataContext` property of the UI element, or any UI element that is a container for the bound UI element.

XAML's Binding Markup Extensions

One of the main pieces of functionality that dependency properties offer is their ability to be data-bound. In XAML, the data binding works through a specific markup extension syntax. Alternatively, you can establish the binding through .NET code. Both ways are effective and will be demonstrated in this chapter.

A set of XAML attributes exists to support the data-binding features. The following pseudocode examples represent basic usage of these extensions:

```
<someFrameworkElement property="{Binding}" .../>

<someFrameworkElement property="{Binding pathvalue}" .../>

<someFrameworkElement property="{Binding Path=pathvalue}" .../>

<someFrameworkElement
    property="{Binding oneOrMoreBindingProperties}" .../>

<someFrameworkElement property
    ="{Binding pathvalue, oneOrMoreBindingProperties}" .../>
```

In the preceding code, the element must be a `FrameworkElement` (thus, the name *someFrameworkElement*). You would replace *property* with the name of the property that will be the target of the binding. For example, the element might be a `TextBox` and the property might be `Text`. To bind the value of the property to a source, you can use the binding markup extensions.

The `Binding` attribute indicates that the value for the dependency property will come from a data-binding operation. The binding gets its source from the `DataContext` for the element. If the element does not have a `DataContext`, the XAML hierarchy is examined to see whether any parent XAML container element has a `DataContext`. All that is needed to bind an element to an object that is the `DataContext` (and not to a property of the object) is the `Binding` attribute (see the first line of XAML from the previous example). For instance, this is commonplace when binding a `ListBox` to an object that is a list.

The second usage of the binding markup syntax is to specify a `pathvalue`. This can be the name of a property that exists on the bound object. For example, to bind a `TextBox`'s `Text` property to the `CompanyName` property of an object in the inherited `DataContext`, you could use the following XAML:

```
<TextBox x:Name="tbCompany" Text="{Binding CompanyName}"/>
```

Optionally, you can use the `Path` keyword to set the `pathvalue`. The following code also binds the `CompanyName` property of the `DataContext`, but uses the optional `Path` keyword:

```
<TextBox x:Name="tbCompany" Text="{Binding Path=CompanyName}"/>
```

Binding Extension Properties

Additionally, you can set a handful of other binding properties (referred to in the previous example as `oneOrMoreBindingProperties`) with the XAML binding extensions in Silverlight. These properties are:

- `Converter`
- `ConverterCulture`
- `ConverterParameter`
- `Mode`
- `NotifyOnValidationError`
- `Path`
- `Source`
- `ValidatesOnExceptions`

All of the properties are optional, including `Path`. You can set `Path` to a `pathvalue`. When the binding source object is a business entity the `pathvalue` would be a property on the object. If the `Path` property and its value are omitted, the binding is bound to the instance of the binding source object. The following two code examples produce the same result. They both bind to an inherited `DataContext` and use the `Company` property. The `Path` binding markup property is optional:

```
<TextBox x:Name="tbCompany" Grid.Column="1" Grid.Row="2"
    Margin="10,5,10,5" HorizontalAlignment="Left" Height="30" Width="240"
    Text="{Binding Path=Company}"/>
<TextBox x:Name="tbCompany" Grid.Column="1" Grid.Row="2"
    Margin="10,5,10,5" HorizontalAlignment="Left" Height="30" Width="240"
    Text="{Binding Company}"/>
```

The `Mode` property indicates the binding mode that specifies the direction(s) in which the binding will operate and whether the binding will listen for change notifications. Valid values for the `Mode` property are `OneTime`, `OneWay`, and `TwoWay`. An object reference can be set to the `Source` property. If the `Source` property is set, the object reference will override the `DataContext` as the data source for this binding. All of these properties are optional. The default value for the `Mode` is `OneWay` for most dependency properties (it depends on the dependency property), and if the `Source` property is omitted, the data source will defer to the `DataContext`.

 It is a good practice to explicitly set the `Mode` to the desired value instead of relying on the default value. This improves code readability and reduces the chance that the `Mode` will be set to an unintended value.

Use the `Converter` property to indicate the converter class (which implements the `IValueConverter` interface) that will convert the value for the data-binding operation. `ConverterCulture` and `ConverterParameter` are supporting properties for the converter class. Chapter 4 discusses converters in detail.

The `NotifyOnValidationError` property accepts a `boolean` value that indicates whether the `BindingValidationError` event is raised when a validation error occurs. The `ValidatesOnExceptions` property accepts a `boolean` value that indicates whether validation exceptions will be reported when an exception occurs. In Silverlight, the only type of validation that exists is validation on exceptions. You must set both of these properties for the `BindingValidationError` event to be raised.

Keep in mind that a dependency property follows an order of precedence based on the timing of the binding to determine its value. If a dependency property is bound and in code the property is set to a value explicitly, the binding is removed. For example, the `tbCompany` `TextBox` in the previous example is bound to the `CompanyName` property of the `DataContext`. If in code the `Text` property of `tbCompany` is set to `Foo`, the binding is removed.

Simplified Binding

Using the Silverlight XAML binding syntax, you can greatly simplify the user control in Examples 2-1 and 2-2. If you add the binding syntax to each `TextBox` control in the XAML in Example 2-2, you will bind the `Text` property of each `TextBox` to the specified property of the data source. For example, adding the following code to the `TextBox` named `tbFirstName` from Example 2-1 will establish the binding for this control:

```
Text="{Binding FirstName}"
```

This code indicates that the value for the `Text` property (a dependency property) will be determined by evaluating the inherited `DataContext` and accessing that object's `FirstName` property.

Now you can replace the event handlers from Example 2-2 that pushed the values from the `Person` instance into the `TextBox` controls with the code in Example 2-7 (shown later in this chapter). The instance of the `Person` is created and initialized, and then the object is set to the `DataContext` of the user control. The `DataContext` is inherited by any children controls of the user control, so the `TextBox` automatically is aware and able to be bound to this `DataContext`. (The full code for this example and the manual binding example are available on the book's website, *http://www.Silverlight-Data.com*.)

Alternatively, you can set the binding through XAML by setting the `DataContext` to a `StaticResource`. The following XAML shows a `TextBox` whose `Text` property is bound to the `Company` property of the object instance represented by the `DataContext`:

```
<TextBox Text="{Binding Company}" DataContext="{StaticResource myPerson}"/>
```

In Example 2-7, the `DataContext` for the `TextBox` is set to a `StaticResource` named `myPerson`, which is defined as a resource on the page (as shown in the XAML in Example 2-6).

Example 2-6. Instance of the Person class as a resource

```
<UserControl x:Class="Bindings.BindingSimple"
    xmlns="http://schemas.microsoft.com/client/2007"
    xmlns:x="http://schemas.microsoft.com/winfx/2006/xaml"
    xmlns:Bindings="clr-namespace:Bindings"
    Width="380" Height="200">
    <UserControl.Resources>
        <Bindings:Person x:Key="myPerson"
            Company="Some Company"
            FirstName="Joe"
            LastName="Someone"/>
    </UserControl.Resources>
...
...
```

Example 2-7. Simple binding

```csharp
private void BindingTags_Loaded(object sender, RoutedEventArgs e)
{
    var person = new Person { FirstName = "John",
        LastName = "Smith", Company = "Foo Company" };
    this.DataContext = person;
}
```

```vb
Private Sub BindingTags_Loaded(ByVal sender As Object, ByVal e As RoutedEventArgs)
    Dim person = New Person With {.FirstName = "John", _
        .LastName = "Smith", .Company = "Foo Company"}
    Me.DataContext = person
End Sub
```

Runtime Binding

Although you can bind Silverlight 2 applications using the XAML syntax shown in the previous examples, you also can set up binding entirely through .NET code. This technique allows a developer to change the bindings at runtime, which is good in situations when the source or property may not be known at design time. For example, a TextBox might need to be bound to a different property based on business logic that is executed at runtime. In this case, the bindings could be created conditionally based on the logic.

You can create the bindings using the System.Windows.Data namespace and an instance of the Binding class. The Binding class is the same class that you can create through the markup extensions shown in Example 2-6. Therefore, it has the same five properties, as shown in the IntelliSense menu in Figure 2-4.

Creating Runtime Bindings

A runtime binding first requires that a binding be created and a target property specified. Then the binding must either use the inherited DataContext or indicate a specific source object. Once the binding is created, it is bound to the target using the SetBinding method of the target object.

> It is always easy to tell what objects support binding, because the object will have the SetBinding method. SetBinding is a method of the FrameworkElement base class.

First, an examination of the example application that demonstrates runtime binding is in order. The user control in Figure 2-5 shows the state of the controls when they are first loaded. The controls display the default values that were set up in XAML using each TextBox's Text property. The default values are there simply as placeholders. This is the initial state, which you can change by clicking one of the buttons.

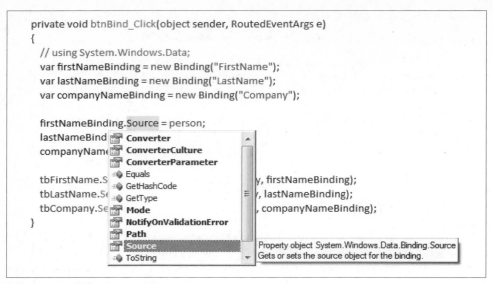

```
private void btnBind_Click(object sender, RoutedEventArgs e)
{
  // using System.Windows.Data;
  var firstNameBinding = new Binding("FirstName");
  var lastNameBinding = new Binding("LastName");
  var companyNameBinding = new Binding("Company");

  firstNameBinding.Source = person;
  lastNameBind                Converter
  companyName                 ConverterCulture
                              ConverterParameter
                              Equals
  tbFirstName.S               GetHashCode        y, firstNameBinding);
  tbLastName.Se               GetType            , lastNameBinding);
  tbCompany.Se                Mode               , companyNameBinding);
}                             NotifyOnValidationError
                              Path
                              Source
                              ToString
```

Property object System.Windows.Data.Binding.Source
Gets or sets the source object for the binding.

Figure 2-4. Binding class members

First Name	First Name Goes Here
Last Name	Last Name Goes Here
Company	Company Goes Here

Bind   Override

Figure 2-5. Runtime binding, after load

When the Bind button is clicked, the btnBind_Click event handler (shown in Figure 2-6) executes. First the code creates a new instance of a Binding object for each target and source pair. The Binding class's constructor accepts the path, which points to the Source object's property.

Once the Binding has been created, the Source property is set to the instance of the Person class. The Source points to the source object and the path points to the Source object's property. At this point, half of the binding is completed, with only the Target control and Target property left to handle.

The next step in binding is to link the Binding instances with their corresponding Targets. You do this by invoking the SetBinding method of each FrameworkElement (in this case, each TextBox). Example 2-8 shows that each TextBox's SetBinding method is

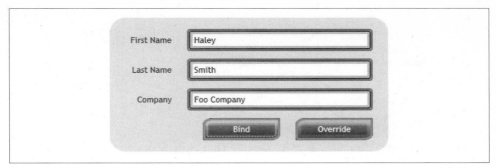

Figure 2-6. Runtime binding, after binding

invoked and is passed the name of the dependency property of the `Target` as well as the instance of the `Binding` object. These few steps establish the binding and effectively push the values from the `Person` entity into the `TextBox` controls, as shown in Figure 2-6.

Three `Binding` class instances are created: one for each property of the `person` object to point to three different `TextBox` controls. It is important to note that runtime binding certainly requires more code than binding via XAML. Of course, you could reduce the code if you refactored it into a helper method. However, if the binding is known at design time, it is often better to use XAML binding than runtime binding and to reserve runtime binding for cases when the binding must be determined on the fly.

Example 2-8. Runtime binding

```
private void RuntimeBinding_Loaded(object sender, RoutedEventArgs e)
{
    person = new Person { FirstName = "Haley",
        LastName = "Smith", Company = "Foo Company" };
}

private void btnBind_Click(object sender, RoutedEventArgs e)
{
    var firstNameBinding = new Binding("FirstName");
    var lastNameBinding = new Binding("LastName");
    var companyNameBinding = new Binding("Company");

    firstNameBinding.Source = person;
    lastNameBinding.Source = person;
    companyNameBinding.Source = person;

    tbFirstName.SetBinding(TextBox.TextProperty, firstNameBinding);
    tbLastName.SetBinding(TextBox.TextProperty, lastNameBinding);
    tbCompany.SetBinding(TextBox.TextProperty, companyNameBinding);
}
```

```
Private Sub RuntimeBinding_Loaded(ByVal sender As Object, _
        ByVal e As RoutedEventArgs)
    person = New Person With {.FirstName = "Haley", _
        .LastName = "Smith", .Company = "Foo Company"}
```

```
End Sub

Private Sub btnBind_Click(ByVal sender As Object, _
      ByVal e As RoutedEventArgs)
   Dim firstNameBinding = New Binding("FirstName")
   Dim lastNameBinding = New Binding("LastName")
   Dim companyNameBinding = New Binding("Company")

   firstNameBinding.Source = person
   lastNameBinding.Source = person
   companyNameBinding.Source = person

   tbFirstName.SetBinding(TextBox.TextProperty, firstNameBinding)
   tbLastName.SetBinding(TextBox.TextProperty, lastNameBinding)
   tbCompany.SetBinding(TextBox.TextProperty, companyNameBinding)
End Sub
```

When setting up a binding, there must be both a target and a source. The target is usually the control that you will present to the user and the source is usually an object that contains the data you want to present. Table 2-2 shows an example of the target and source from the code from Example 2-8. The `Target` is the `TextBox` control named `tbFirstName`, and the property of the `Target` that is being bound to the object's property is the `TextBox`'s `Text` property (a dependency property). The `Target` object is tied to the `Source` object and the `Target` property is tied to a property of the `Source` object.

Table 2-2. Target and source

Binding targets and sources	Value
Target object	tbFirstName
Target property	Text
Source object	Person
Source property	FirstName

SILVERLIGHT 2 AND WPF DATA BINDING

Key Differences

XAML supports data binding using various constructs. Just as the .NET libraries that Silverlight supports are a subset of the complete .NET library, the data-binding-oriented XAML that Silverlight 2 supports is a subset of the XAML data-binding features supported in WPF. For example, the `Binding` object exists in both Silverlight 2 and WPF; however, it is greatly scaled down in Silverlight 2, as it supports only eight properties: `Converter`, `ConverterCulture`, `ConverterParameter`, `Mode`, `Source`, `Path`, `NotifyOnValidationError`, and `ValidatesOnExceptions`.

WPF's `Binding` object supports these eight properties as well as several others, including `ElementName` (which allows binding to a `FrameworkElement`) and `XPath` (the XPath name to bind to when binding to XML). Another difference between the data-binding features supported in Silverlight 2 and WPF is that in Silverlight 2 a `FrameworkElement` cannot

---

be bound to another `FrameworkElement` directly. For example, in WPF you could set a `Brush`'s `Fill` color to the value from another XAML element (perhaps a selected value from a `ListBox`). Silverlight 2's XAML-based data binding does not support binding to elements directly. However, a workaround is to create a custom class that stores the color, and bind to it both the `ListBox` that lists the color names and the `Brush`'s `Fill` property, using a converter to translate the value to a `Brush`. This workaround is effective, but it is not as simple as binding directly to an element.

Removing a Binding

When the Override button from Figure 2-7 is clicked, the bindings are removed and replaced with local values. The event handler, shown in Example 2-9, simply sets each `TextBox`'s `Text` property with a string value. This step effectively removes the `Binding` object, if one existed, and replaces it with the local value. A `Binding` cannot be placed on a target property and coexist with a locally set property value at the same time.

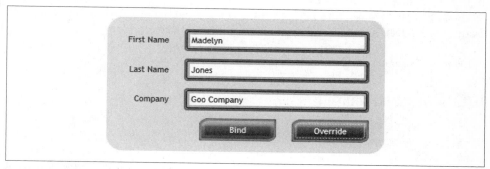

Figure 2-7. Runtime binding, after replacing the bindings

Example 2-9. Removing bindings

C#
```csharp
private void btnOverride_Click(object sender, RoutedEventArgs e)
{
    //Set the values manually, removing the bindings
    tbFirstName.Text = "Madelyn";
    tbLastName.Text = "Jones";
    tbCompany.Text = "Goo Company";
}
```

VB
```vb
Private Sub btnOverride_Click(ByVal sender As Object, ByVal e As RoutedEventArgs)
    'Set the values manually, removing the bindings
    tbFirstName.Text = "Madelyn"
    tbLastName.Text = "Jones"
    tbCompany.Text = "Goo Company"
End Sub
```

DataContext

Up to this point, I have alluded to the `DataContext` property but haven't discussed it in depth. It is time to give it some attention by examining where it is used, what it does, and how it can benefit a Silverlight application.

The `DataContext` property refers to a source of data that you can bind to a target. The `DataContext` often is set to an instance of an entity, such as a `Person` in the previous examples. Once you set the `DataContext`, you can bind it to any controls that have access to it. For instance, you can use it to bind all controls within a container control to a single data source. This approach is useful when several controls use the same binding source. It could become repetitive to indicate the binding source for every control. Instead, you can set the `DataContext` for the container of the controls.

Each `FrameworkElement` has a `DataContext`. This includes the instances of the `UserControl` class that the examples in this chapter have demonstrated, as the `UserControl` class inherits from the `Control` class, which in turn inherits from the `FrameworkElement` class. This means that on a single `UserControl`, objects could be assigned to dozens of `DataContext` properties of various `FrameworkElement` controls. For example, the `UserControl`, a layout control such as a `Grid`, and a series of interactive controls such as `TextBoxes`, `CheckBoxes`, and `ListBoxes` might all have their `DataContext` property set.

DataContext and Source

You can assign the binding source via the `Source` property of a `Binding`, or via the `DataContext`. Setting the data source through a `Binding` instance's `Source` property allows a specific object to be set. You could set the same data source using the `DataContext` to achieve the same results, and often with more flexibility than if you set it through the `Source`.

A good rule of thumb is to set the data source using the `Source` property if you do not want other target controls to inherit the data source. If you must bind a set of controls to a data source, the `DataContext` is an optimal choice. If you must bind multiple `Target` properties to the same data source, you can do this most easily by setting the `DataContext` of the `FrameworkElement` control that contains all of the controls that must be bound.

For instance, the code in Example 2-8 sets the `Source` property of each `Binding` directly to the `person` instance. Instead of setting the `Source` property for each control, you could set the `DataContext` property for each control. To use the `DataContext`, you must also modify the XAML using the binding markup extension syntax. The code in Example 2-10 shows the newly modified XAML for the `UserControl` named `DataContextBinding`. The code in this example is only a piece of the entire XAML file and shows only the elements that differ from the previous XAML examples.

Example 2-10. Binding through XAML

```
<TextBox x:Name="tbFirstName" Grid.Column="1" Grid.Row="0"
    Margin="10,5,10,5" HorizontalAlignment="Left" Height="30"
    Width="240" Style="{StaticResource TextBoxStyle}"
    Text="{Binding FirstName}"/>
<TextBox x:Name="tbLastName" Grid.Column="1" Grid.Row="1"
    Margin="10,5,10,5" HorizontalAlignment="Left" Height="30"
    Width="240" Style="{StaticResource TextBoxStyle}"
    Text="{Binding LastName}"/>
<TextBox x:Name="tbCompany" Grid.Column="1" Grid.Row="2"
    Margin="10,5,10,5" HorizontalAlignment="Left" Height="30"
    Width="240" Style="{StaticResource TextBoxStyle}"
    Text="{Binding Company}"/>
```

This XAML shows that the Text property of each TextBox is bound to a property of the data source. The data source is not listed anywhere in this XAML code. Therefore, it is inferred that the Binding will use the DataContext that is closest in the inheritance hierarchy to the Target. If the TextBox itself has its DataContext property set, it will use the object from its own DataContext.

The code in Example 2-11 shows the event handler that will execute when the UserControl is loaded. First, an instance of the Person class is created and initialized. Then the DataContext property (also a dependency property) of each TextBox is set to the person instance. This gives each TextBox's Binding a valid DataContext to use as the data source. Figure 2-8 shows the result of the binding. The code using the DataContext is much shorter than it would be if you used the Source through runtime binding.

Example 2-11. DataContext binding

C#
```csharp
private void DataContextBinding_Loaded(object sender, RoutedEventArgs e)
{
    person = new Person { FirstName = "Ella",
        LastName = "Johnson", Company = "Hoo Company" };
    tbFirstName.DataContext = person;
    tbLastName.DataContext = person;
    tbCompany.DataContext = person;
}
```

VB
```vbnet
Private Sub DataContextBinding_Loaded(ByVal sender As Object, _
        ByVal e As RoutedEventArgs)
    person = New Person With {.FirstName = "Ella", _
        .LastName = "Johnson", .Company = "Hoo Company"}
    tbFirstName.DataContext = person
    tbLastName.DataContext = person
    tbCompany.DataContext = person
End Sub
```

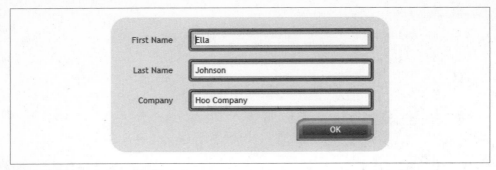

Figure 2-8. DataContext binding

DataContext Propagation

Notice that in Example 2-11 the `DataContext` property is set on each `TextBox` control. Although this achieves the desired result, there is a more efficient way to set the data source for each binding. The `DataContext` is a special object that allows itself to be accessed from a container `FrameworkElement`. For example, consider the XAML in Example 2-12 that shows a `Canvas` control containing a `StackPanel` that contains a `TextBlock` and a `TextBox`.

Example 2-12. Two TextBox controls within container panels

```
<Canvas x:Name="myCanvas">
    <StackPanel x:Name="myStackPanel">
        <TextBox x:Name="tbName" Height="30" Width="80" Text="{Binding Name}"/>
        <TextBox x:Name="tbAge" Height="30" Width="80" Text="{Binding Age}"/>
    </StackPanel>
</Canvas>
```

The `TextBox` controls are bound to a data source that is as yet undefined. However, each control indicates the source property to which the control will be bound. The `DataContext` could be set on each `TextBox`, or on the `StackPanel`, or on the `Canvas`, or ultimately on the `UserControl`. The `TextBox` will first examine its own `DataContext` property to see whether a data source exists. If so, the `TextBox` will use it. If not, the `TextBox` will go up to the container control (the `myStackPanel StackPanel`) and see whether a `DataContext` is set on the container control. This process is repeated until a `DataContext` is found in the inheritance hierarchy that can be used.

You can apply this concept to the code in Example 2-11 so that you do not have to set the `DataContext` for each control individually. Instead, you can set the `DataContext` for a container control such as the `Grid` named `LayoutRoot`. The code in Example 2-13 shows the revised code from Example 2-10, now using the inherited `DataContext`. The result of running this shortened code is the same as that shown in Figure 2-8.

Example 2-13. Inherited DataContext

```csharp
private void DataContextBinding_Loaded(object sender, RoutedEventArgs e)
{
    person = new Person { FirstName = "Ella",
        LastName = "Johnson", Company = "Hoo Company" };
    LayoutRoot.DataContext = person;
}
```

```vb
Private Sub DataContextBinding_Loaded(ByVal sender As Object, _
        ByVal e As RoutedEventArgs)
    person = New Person With {.FirstName = "Ella", _
        .LastName = "Johnson", .Company = "Hoo Company"}
    LayoutRoot.DataContext = person
End Sub
```

Binding in Blend

So far, this chapter has focused on handling binding via XAML using Visual Studio 2008. Visual Studio 2008 makes writing XAML easy through its IntelliSense and other text-editing features. However, Expression Blend is also a very viable tool for creating Silverlight 2 applications. Expression Blend shows both the XAML and a visual designer in a split screen. Though Expression Blend currently lacks some of the IntelliSense and other text-editing features that are inherent in Visual Studio 2008, it has a much richer designer. This makes Blend a great choice for designing Silverlight applications. An ideal choice is to use both Blend and Visual Studio 2008 to edit a Silverlight project at the same time.

Besides basic designer features, Blend also provides ways to create event handlers and establish data binding. This makes it easy to use Blend to design a user control and bind its child controls to a binding source. First, to demonstrate this example, Figure 2-9 shows a user control that is created through Blend.

Next, you can add the code to the code-behind for the *BlendBinding.xaml* user control. You can do this by right-clicking the *BlendBinding.xaml.cs* file in the project window in Blend and selecting the Edit in Visual Studio menu option, as shown in Figure 2-10.

The event handler for the user control's Loaded event and an instance of the Person class are created. The instance of the Person class is then used as the binding source object for the LayoutRoot control which is the grid layout control. The DataContext of the LayoutRoot control is set to the instance, and because the DataContext is inherited by child controls contained within the grid, any child controls will have access to the Person instance. Example 2-14 shows the code for the BlendBinding user control.

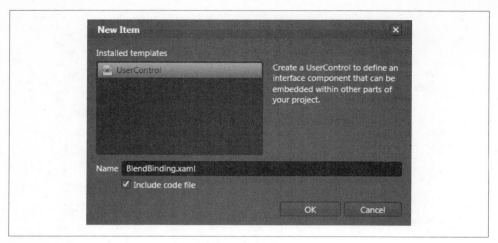

Figure 2-9. Creating a user control in Expression Blend

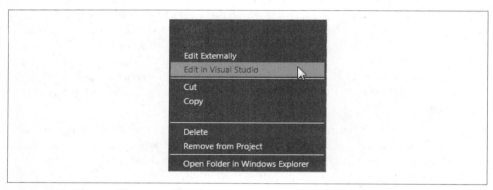

Figure 2-10. Editing a file in Visual Studio

Example 2-14. Code-behind for BlendBinding.xaml

```csharp
public partial class BlendBinding : UserControl
{
    private Person person;

    public BlendBinding()
    {
        // Required to initialize variables
        InitializeComponent();
        this.Loaded += new RoutedEventHandler(BlendBinding_Loaded);
    }

    private void BlendBinding_Loaded(object sender, RoutedEventArgs e)
    {
        person = new Person { FirstName = "Ella",
                LastName = "Johnson", Company = "Hoo Company" };
        LayoutRoot.DataContext = person;
```

```
        }
}
```

```
Partial Public Class BlendBinding
    Inherits UserControl
    Private person As Person

    Public Sub New()
        'Required to initialize variables
        InitializeComponent()
        AddHandler Loaded, AddressOf BlendBinding_Loaded
    End Sub

    Private Sub BlendBinding_Loaded(ByVal sender As Object, _
            ByVal e As RoutedEventArgs)
        person = New Person With {.FirstName = "Ella", _
        .LastName = "Johnson", .Company = "Hoo Company"}
        LayoutRoot.DataContext = person
    End Sub
End Class
```

Once you've written the code in Example 2-14, you can lay out the design for the user control. Figure 2-11 shows one way to lay out the user control with three `TextBox` controls to represent the `Person` class's information.

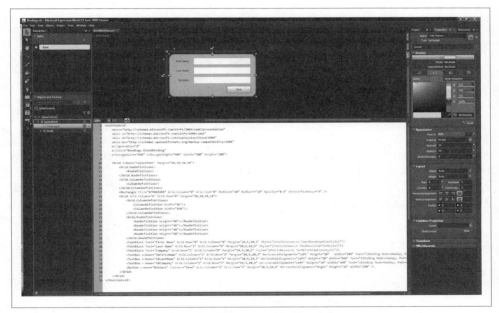

Figure 2-11. Designing the user control in Expression Blend

At this point, the user control has been designed and the code has been written to bind the `Person` instance to the `DataContext` of the `LayoutRoot` `Grid` control. The next step is to set up the data binding for the `TextBox` controls. You can do this by selecting a `TextBox` control, going to its properties, finding the `Text` property, clicking the small square to its right, and then clicking on the DataBind menu option. This opens the Create Data Binding dialog window where you can configure the binding.

The `tbFirstName` `TextBox` should be bound to the `Person` class instance's `FirstName` property. You can do this by going to the Explicit Data Context tab of the dialog, checking the "Use a custom path expression" checkbox, and typing **FirstName** into the text box next to it, as shown in Figure 2-12. You can also set the other binding markup extensions through this dialog. These are available by clicking the down arrow at the bottom of the dialog which shows the additional configuration options.

Notice that you need not set the `DataContext` for the specific control. This is because the control will inherit the `DataContext` from the `LayoutRoot` control's `DataContext`. You can repeat this process for each control that must be bound to the inherited `DataContext`. The result will show the code for the three `TextBox` controls, as shown in Example 2-15.

Example 2-15. XAML written by Blend

```
<TextBox x:Name="tbFirstName" Grid.Column="1" Grid.Row="0"
    Margin="10,5,10,5" HorizontalAlignment="Left" Height="30"
    Width="240" Text="{Binding Mode=OneWay, Path=FirstName}" />
<TextBox x:Name="tbLastName" Grid.Column="1" Grid.Row="1"
    Margin="10,5,10,5" HorizontalAlignment="Left" Height="30"
    Width="240" Text="{Binding Mode=OneWay, Path=LastName}" />
<TextBox x:Name="tbCompany" Grid.Column="1" Grid.Row="2"
    Margin="10,5,10,5" HorizontalAlignment="Left" Height="30"
    Width="240" Text="{Binding Mode=OneWay, Path=Company}" />
```

Notice that the binding markup has been created in the XAML with the `Path` property set to the appropriate property name for each `TextBox` control. Also notice that the `Mode` has been set to `OneWay`. This means the binding will flow in one direction, from the binding source (the inherited `DataContext`'s `Person` instance) to the binding target (each `TextBox` control's `Text` property).

 We will discuss the binding modes of `OneTime`, `OneWay`, and `TwoWay` in detail in Chapter 3.

You can create the entire design of the user control through Blend, and create its .NET code in Visual Studio 2008. When the user control is compiled and viewed, the data is bound and displayed in the user control, as shown in Figure 2-13.

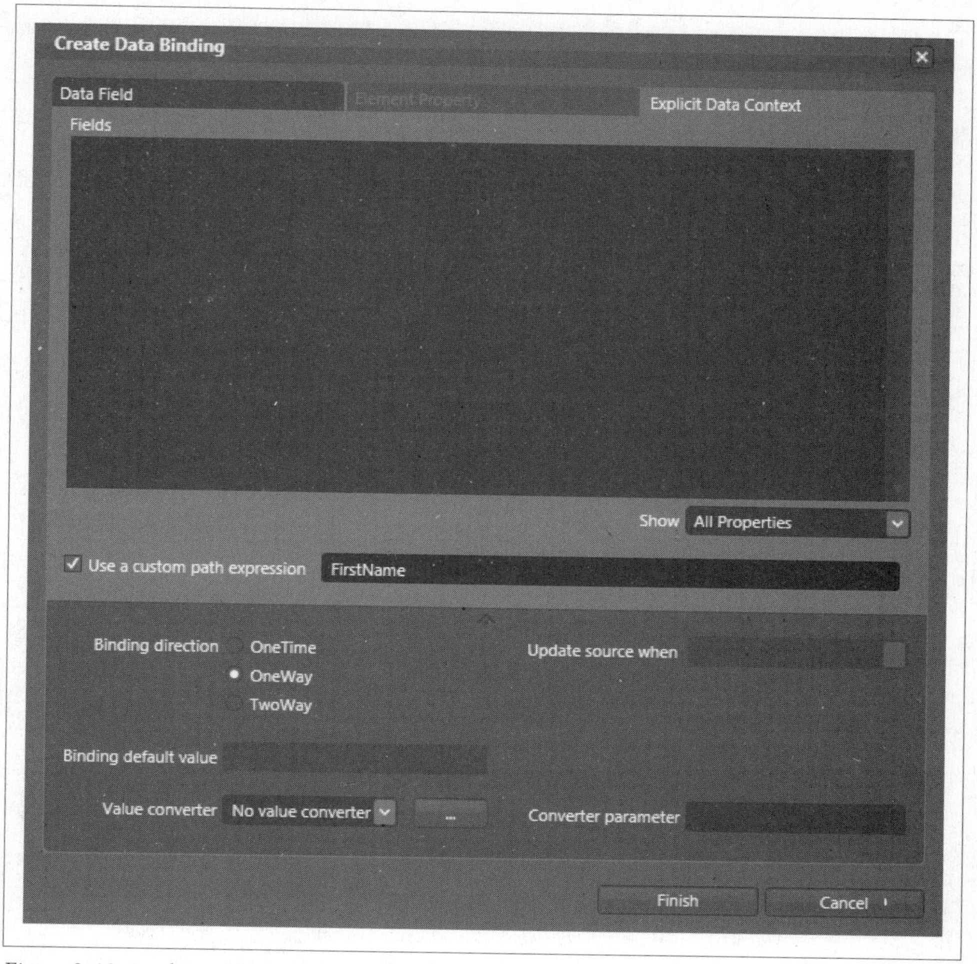

Figure 2-12. Binding a TextBox in Expression Blend

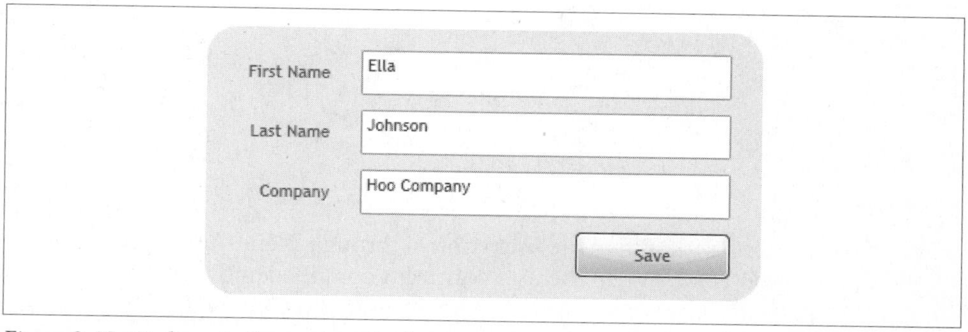

Figure 2-13. Binding via Expression Blend

Summary

This chapter discussed the foundations of the data-binding techniques in Silverlight 2, the features it supports, and how they work. Data binding is baked into Silverlight 2 and XAML, making it easy to create powerful and flexible binding solutions. The `DataContext`, binding markup extensions, and dependency property are the foundations of data binding with Silverlight 2 and its controls. Using these tools as a foundation, you can create applications with rich interfaces and very little .NET code, as shown previously in Example 2-13 through both Expression Blend and Visual Studio 2008.

CHAPTER 3

Modes and Notifications

Chapter 2 demonstrated the foundations of data-binding functionality in Silverlight 2 using the `DataContext` property and runtime binding techniques through both Visual Studio and Expression Blend. All of the examples in Chapter 2 used the default binding mode of `OneWay`, which tells the bindings to push values from the source to the target when the source values change. The binding modes and their related functionality are a critical piece of the data-binding component. The binding modes make it very easy to support the binding of a source to a target and a target back to a source, if appropriate. A control's binding can indicate that it should be bound source to the target, for read-only data, or the control can designate that the binding should flow in both directions, thus making the control and its data values user-editable.

Two of the key sources of the power of XAML-based data binding are the `INotifyPropertyChanged` interface and the `INotifyCollectionChanged` interface. These interfaces provide the means for data source objects to let data bindings know that something about the source has changed. The `ObservableCollection<T>` implements the `INotifyCollectionChanged` interface, which yields a collection class that is able to provide notifications when items in the collection change.

Chapter 2 demonstrated how to bind a single-entity object source to a series of Silverlight 2 controls through various means, including inheriting a `DataContext`. The controls were bound to the object source and each control indicated the property of the source object to which it was specifically bound. This property was set using the XAML binding markup extension's `Path` property (which is optional). You also can bind controls directly to an object source or to a list of objects, such as a `List<T>` or an `Observable Collection<T>`. This is especially useful for binding a list of objects to a list-based control such as `ItemsControl`, `ListBox`, or `DataGrid`, or to a third-party list-based control. Like the `INotifyPropertyChanged` interface, the `INotifyCollectionChanged` interface provides a way for the collection to notify the bindings when the contents have changed.

This chapter will delve into the binding modes as well as how to notify the bindings when a data-binding source changes. In addition to explaining binding modes and notifications for properties, this chapter also discusses best practices for using the different binding modes, and provides practical tips on implementing the

`INotifyPropertyChanged` interface and its `PropertyChanged` event. In Chapter 4, we will dive into list binding and the `INotifyCollectionChanged` interface, as well as a popular implementation of it, `ObservableCollection<T>`.

Binding Modes

Bindings exist between a source and a target. The binding extension's `Mode` property determines whether the target or the source will be updated, and when it will be updated. The default value for the `Mode` property is different depending on the control. The `Mode` property indicates that the source will update the target when the data binding is first established between the source and its target(s). The `OneWay` binding mode also indicates that any changes to the source data will update the target as long as the source entity implements the `INotifyPropertyChanged` interface and its source properties raise the `PropertyChanged` event. The values presented to the user will be updated when the binding first occurs and whenever the data source changes.

There are three valid binding mode settings: `OneTime`, `OneWay`, and `TwoWay`. Simply put, these modes determine how often and in which direction binding will occur between the target and its source. Along with the binding modes, Table 3-1 shows which events can cause the binding modes to jump into action, and whether the target or the source is ultimately updated as a result.

Table 3-1. Effect of binding modes and INotifyPropertyChanged

Event	What changes	OneTime	OneWay	TwoWay
Binding is set	Target	Yes	Yes	Yes
Source changes	Target	No	Yes	Yes
Target changes	Source	No	No	Yes

OneTime

Table 3-1 shows that when `OneTime` binding is used the target is updated only when the source is first bound to the target(s). For example, when a control's `DataContext` property is set to an object, the object becomes the source of a data-binding collaboration. When this occurs, all bindings for this source will receive the values from the corresponding properties of the source. Bindings with the `Mode` property set to `OneTime` will receive this value at this time and only at this time. Figure 3-1 shows that when the `Mode` is set to `OneTime`, the only action that causes the values to be pushed to the targets is setting the source object to the `DataContext`. Figure 3-1 also shows that with `OneTime` binding mode, the only time values are sent to the target controls is when the source object is set as the binding source.

The following XAML shows a `TextBlock` bound to a `CustomerId` property from an inherited `DataContext`. The binding mode is set to `OneTime` binding, so the `CustomerId` value will be pushed from the source object to the target `TextBlock`'s `Text` property just

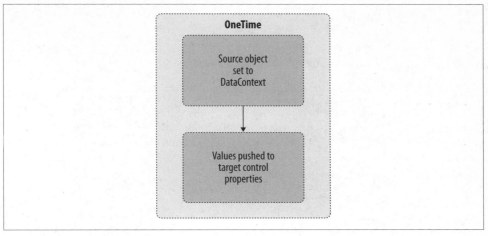

Figure 3-1. OneTime binding

once, when the source is set to the `DataContext`. This would be a good choice if the `CustomerId` is not expected to change at all:

```
<TextBlock
    Margin="10,5,10,5"
    HorizontalAlignment="Left" Height="30" Width="240"
    Text="{Binding Mode=OneTime, Path=CustomerId}" />
```

`OneTime` binding is ideal for binding a source object to a control to represent read-only information that is not expected to change in the source. (If it did change in the source, the new value would not be propagated to the target with `OneTime` binding.)

 Whether the binding mode is set to `OneWay` or `OneTime`, if the data source does not implement `INotifyPropertyChanged`, updates to the data source's property will not notify the target. The net effect would be that even with `OneWay` binding mode, the value would not be updated. So, without `INotifyPropertyChanged`, `OneWay` has the same behavior as `OneTime`.

In the preceding example, the `CustomerId` is the key property of the `Customer` entity. (The `Path` property is optional.) This is an ideal situation for a read-only control and read-only binding, because the user should not be able to change the `CustomerId`'s value. You could use `OneWay` binding in this situation and still be bound to a read-only type of control such as the `TextBlock`. Whether to use `OneTime` or `OneWay` binding mode depends entirely on the situation. If the source data is not expected to change, setting the mode to `OneTime` is best and incurs a little less overhead than setting it to `OneWay` binding. This is because `OneWay` binding listens for the `PropertyChanged` event notifications from the implementation of the `INotifyPropertyChanged` interface.

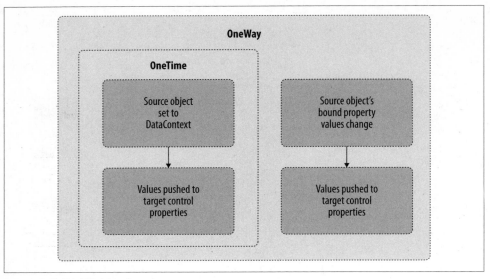

Figure 3-2. OneWay binding

In short, `OneTime` binding is an appropriate choice if you need a snapshot of the data and you expect no changes. `OneTime` binding is the simplest type of binding and has the best performance, as it does not listen for the `PropertyChanged` event, which is not true of the `OneWay` and `TwoWay` binding modes.

OneWay

`OneWay` binding builds off the `OneTime` binding features. `OneWay` binding sends the source values to the target when the source is set, but it also listens for any changes in the source object and sends those on to the target as well. If the source object implements the `INotifyPropertyChanged` interface and its property setters raise the `PropertyChanged` event, the target of the binding will listen for this event and will receive the updated value. Table 3-1 and Figure 3-2 reiterate this concept, showing that changes are sent from the source to the target either when the source is set or the source is changed.

`OneWay` binding is best reserved for cases when the user control does not allow the user to edit the data, but any changes from the source are expected to be pushed to the user control. The following example shows a `TextBlock` that is bound to an inherited `DataContext`. Assuming that the source is an instance of a `Customer` class that has a `CompanyName` property, the `TextBlock` will display the value for the `CompanyName` using `OneWay` binding. If the value changes in the source, the new value will be presented in the `TextBlock`.

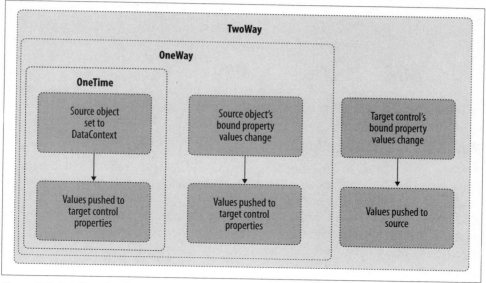

Figure 3-3. TwoWay binding

```
<TextBlock
    Margin="10,5,10,5"
    HorizontalAlignment="Left" Height="30" Width="240"
    Text="{Binding Mode=OneWay, Path=CompanyName}" />
```

TwoWay

TwoWay binding builds off OneWay binding by adding the ability to send changed data in the target back to the source. Both OneWay and TwoWay binding notify the target about changes if the source object implements the INotifyPropertyChanged interface and the source's property setters raise the PropertyChanged event. Table 3-1 and Figure 3-3 both demonstrate how TwoWay binding has everything OneWay binding offers, plus the ability to send changes back to the source.

The following example demonstrates how to create a TextBox that is bound to an inherited DataContext using the TwoWay binding mode:

```
<TextBox
    Margin="10,5,10,5"
    HorizontalAlignment="Left" Height="30" Width="240"
    Text="{Binding Mode=TwoWay, Path=CompanyName }" />
```

Figure 3-3 shows all three binding modes and how they build off each other. OneTime binding simply pushes values from the source to the target on binding. OneWay has all of OneTime's features, plus it updates the target when the source changes, provided that the INotifyPropertyChanged interface is implemented and its PropertyChanged event is raised. The TwoWay binding mode has the other modes' features, plus it allows the target to update the source.

Here are some good rules of thumb to determine when it is best to use each binding mode. OneTime binding is a great choice for read-only information and when the target needs to be updated when it is first bound to the source, creating a snapshot of the source in the target that will not change as the source changes. OneWay binding is great for read-only data that must reflect any changes to the binding source object. TwoWay binding is the best choice when the user must be able to change the data in a control and have that change reflected in the source object.

Modes Without Notifications

When you use OneTime binding the target controls will never send changes to the source, nor will they listen for changes from the source. However, with OneWay and TwoWay binding the target controls will be listening for any updates from the source. If the source does not raise the PropertyChanged event when its properties change, the binding mode is somewhat irrelevant.

The code in Example 3-1 demonstrates this reliance on the PropertyChanged event of the INotifyPropertyChanged interface (or of the INotifyCollectionChanged interface for list binding, which we'll discuss in Chapter 4). Example 3-1 shows the XAML of the ModeSimpleDemo user control in its entirety, except for the style resources that it references, which are in *app.xaml*. Notice the boldface sections of the code, which are the bindings for the various controls. All three binding modes are used where they are most appropriate. When the application is executed, the user control will present the data in the appropriate controls, showing the bound values (see Figure 3-4, later in this chapter).

The CustomerId property will never change, so its target control is a read-only Text Block control and it uses the OneTime binding mode. The CreatedDate property cannot be changed from this user control, so it is displayed in a TextBlock. The CreatedDate property could change in the data source, so this binding mode is set to OneWay. All other properties could change and this user control will allow the user to modify them, so their binding modes are all set to TwoWay.

Example 3-1. XAML for ModeSimpleDemo user control

```
<UserControl x:Class="AdvBindings.ModeSimpleDemo"
    xmlns="http://schemas.microsoft.com/winfx/2006/xaml/presentation"
    xmlns:x="http://schemas.microsoft.com/winfx/2006/xaml"
    Width="500" Height="360" mc:Ignorable="d"
    xmlns:d="http://schemas.microsoft.com/expression/blend/2008"
    xmlns:mc="http://schemas.openxmlformats.org/markup-compatibility/2006" >
    <Grid x:Name="LayoutRoot" Margin="10,10,10,10">
        ...
        ...
        ... grid rows and columns defined ...
        ...
        ...
            <TextBlock Text="Customer Id" Grid.Row="0" Grid.Column="0"
```

```xml
                    Margin="10,5,10,5"
                    Style="{StaticResource TextBlockCaptionStyle}"/>
    <TextBlock Text="Company" Grid.Row="1" Grid.Column="0"
                    Margin="10,5,10,5"
                    Style="{StaticResource TextBlockCaptionStyle}"/>
    <TextBlock Text="Contact First Name" Grid.Row="2" Grid.Column="0"
                    Margin="10,5,10,5"
                    Style="{StaticResource TextBlockCaptionStyle}"/>
    <TextBlock Text="Contact Last Name" Grid.Row="3" Grid.Column="0"
                    Margin="10,5,10,5"
                    Style="{StaticResource TextBlockCaptionStyle}"/>
    <TextBlock Text="Credit Limit" Grid.Row="4" Grid.Column="0"
                    Margin="10,5,10,5"
                    Style="{StaticResource TextBlockCaptionStyle}"/>
    <TextBlock Text="Created Date" Grid.Row="5" Grid.Column="0"
                    Margin="10,5,10,5"
                    Style="{StaticResource TextBlockCaptionStyle}"/>
    <TextBlock Text="Active" Grid.Row="6" Grid.Column="0"
                    Margin="10,5,10,5"
                    Style="{StaticResource TextBlockCaptionStyle}"/>
    <TextBlock x:Name="lbCustomerId" HorizontalAlignment="Left"
                    Grid.Row="0" Grid.Column="1" Margin="11,5,10,5"
                    Style="{StaticResource TextBlockReadOnlyStyle}"
                    Text="{Binding Path=CustomerId, Mode=OneTime}"/>
    <TextBox x:Name="tbCompany" Grid.Column="1" Grid.Row="1"
                    Margin="10,5,10,5" HorizontalAlignment="Left"
                    Height="30"  Width="240"
                    Style="{StaticResource TextBoxStyle}"
                    Text="{Binding Mode=TwoWay, Path=Company}"/>
    <TextBox x:Name="tbContactFirstName" Grid.Column="1" Grid.Row="2"
                    Margin="10,5,10,5" HorizontalAlignment="Left" Height="30"
                    Width="240" Style="{StaticResource TextBoxStyle}"
                    Text="{Binding Mode=TwoWay, Path=ContactFirstName}"/>
    <TextBox x:Name="tbContactLastName" Grid.Column="1" Grid.Row="3"
                    Margin="10,5,10,5" HorizontalAlignment="Left" Height="30"
                    Width="240" Style="{StaticResource TextBoxStyle}"
                    Text="{Binding Mode=TwoWay, Path=ContactLastName}"/>
    <TextBox x:Name="tbCreditLimit" Grid.Column="1" Grid.Row="4"
                    Margin="10,5,10,5" HorizontalAlignment="Left" Height="30"
                    Width="240" Style="{StaticResource TextBoxStyle}"
                    Text="{Binding Mode=TwoWay, Path=CreditLimit}"/>
    <TextBlock x:Name="lbCreatedDate" Grid.Column="1" Grid.Row="5"
                    Margin="10,5,10,5" HorizontalAlignment="Left" Height="30"
                    Width="240" Style="{StaticResource TextBlockReadOnlyStyle}"
                    Text="{Binding Mode=OneWay, Path=CreatedDate}" />
    <CheckBox x:Name="cbActive" Grid.Column="1" Grid.Row="6"
                    Margin="10,5,10,5" HorizontalAlignment="Left" Height="30"
                    Width="240" Style="{StaticResource CheckBoxStyle}"
                    IsChecked="{Binding Mode=TwoWay, Path=Active}"/>
    <StackPanel Orientation="Horizontal" Grid.Column="2" Grid.Row="7"
                    HorizontalAlignment="Right" >
        <Button x:Name="btnUpdateSource" Content="Update Source"
                    Margin="10,5,10,5" HorizontalAlignment="Right" Height="30"
                    Width="120" Style="{StaticResource ButtonStyle}"/>
        <Button x:Name="btnOK" Content="OK" Margin="10,5,10,5"
```

```
                    HorizontalAlignment="Right" Height="30" Width="100"
                    Style="{StaticResource ButtonStyle}"/>
            </StackPanel>
        </Grid>
    </Grid>
</UserControl>
```

All of the controls will be bound to an inherited `DataContext` which will be a `Customer`
class. Example 3-2 shows the code for the `Customer` class. The `Customer` class contains
seven properties of various scalar types. Each property is involved in a binding with the
XAML to a different target control, as shown in Example 3-1. Notice that the
`Customer` class does not implement an interface and does not raise any events. Therefore,
any property values are changed on an instance of a `Customer`, and no notifications will
be sent to the bindings.

Example 3-2. The Customer class

C#
```csharp
public class Customer
{
    public int CustomerId { get; set; }
    public string Company { get; set; }
    public string ContactFirstName { get; set; }
    public string ContactLastName { get; set; }
    public DateTime  CreatedDate { get; set; }
    public double CreditLimit { get; set; }
    public bool Active { get; set; }
}
```

VB
```vb
Public Class Customer
    Private privateCustomerId As Integer
    Public Property CustomerId() As Integer
        Get
            Return privateCustomerId
        End Get
        Set(ByVal value As Integer)
            privateCustomerId = value
        End Set
    End Property
    Private privateCompany As String
    Public Property Company() As String
        Get
            Return privateCompany
        End Get
        Set(ByVal value As String)
            privateCompany = value
        End Set
    End Property
    Private privateContactFirstName As String
    Public Property ContactFirstName() As String
        Get
            Return privateContactFirstName
        End Get
        Set(ByVal value As String)
            privateContactFirstName = value
```

```
        End Set
    End Property
    Private privateContactLastName As String
    Public Property ContactLastName() As String
        Get
            Return privateContactLastName
        End Get
        Set(ByVal value As String)
            privateContactLastName = value
        End Set
    End Property
    Private privateCreatedDate As DateTime
    Public Property CreatedDate() As DateTime
        Get
            Return privateCreatedDate
        End Get
        Set(ByVal value As DateTime)
            privateCreatedDate = value
        End Set
    End Property
    Private privateCreditLimit As Double
    Public Property CreditLimit() As Double
        Get
            Return privateCreditLimit
        End Get
        Set(ByVal value As Double)
            privateCreditLimit = value
        End Set
    End Property
    Private privateActive As Boolean
    Public Property Active() As Boolean
        Get
            Return privateActive
        End Get
        Set(ByVal value As Boolean)
            privateActive = value
        End Set
    End Property
End Class
```

It is easy to demonstrate this by creating a Customer instance, binding it to the target controls, and updating the source. When this happens, the target controls will not display the updated values from the source, regardless of the binding mode, as there is no INotifyPropertyChanged interface implementation. The code in Example 3-3 creates an instance of the Customer class, sets each of its properties to a value, and sets this Customer instance to the DataContext.

Example 3-3. Setting a Customer to the DataContext

```
private void ModeSimpleDemo_Loaded(object sender, RoutedEventArgs e)
{
    Customer customer = CreateCustomer();
    LayoutRoot.DataContext = customer;
}
```

```
private Customer CreateCustomer()
{
    var today = DateTime.Today;
    double creditLimit = 100000;
    return new Customer { CustomerId = 123, Company = "Hoo Company",
        ContactFirstName= "Ella", ContactLastName = "Johnson",
        CreatedDate=today, CreditLimit=creditLimit, Active=true };
}
```

VB
```
Private Sub ModeSimpleDemo_Loaded(ByVal sender As Object, _
        ByVal e As RoutedEventArgs)
    Dim customer As Customer = CreateCustomer()
    LayoutRoot.DataContext = customer
End Sub

Private Function CreateCustomer() As Customer
    Dim today = DateTime.Today
    Dim creditLimit As Double = 100000
    Return New Customer With {.CustomerId = 123, _
        .Company = "Hoo Company", _
        .ContactFirstName= "Ella", .ContactLastName = "Johnson", _
        .CreatedDate=today, .CreditLimit=creditLimit, .Active=True}
End Function
```

When the user clicks the Update Source button in the application (shown in Figure 3-4), the code in Example 3-4 executes. This code grabs the `Customer` instance from the `DataContext` and manually modifies all of its property values. Because the `Customer` class does not implement the `INotifyPropertyChanged` interface or its `PropertyChanged` events, the values in the target controls are left completely unchanged.

Example 3-4. Updating the source

C#
```
private void btnUpdateSource_Click(object sender, RoutedEventArgs e)
{
    // Manually force the entity data source to be updated
    Customer customer = (Customer)LayoutRoot.DataContext;
    customer.Company += " 1";
    customer.ContactFirstName += " 1";
    customer.ContactLastName += " 1";
    customer.CreditLimit += 1;
    customer.CreatedDate = customer.CreatedDate .AddDays(1);
    customer.Active = !customer.Active;
    customer.CustomerId += 1;
}
```

VB
```
Private Sub btnUpdateSource_Click(ByVal sender As Object, _
        ByVal e As RoutedEventArgs)
    ' Manually force the entity data source to be updated
    Dim customer As Customer = CType(LayoutRoot.DataContext, Customer)
    customer.Company &= " 1"
    customer.ContactFirstName &= " 1"
    customer.ContactLastName &= " 1"
    customer.CreditLimit += 1
    customer.CreatedDate = customer.CreatedDate.AddDays(1)
```

```
    customer.Active = Not customer.Active
    customer.CustomerId += 1
End Sub
```

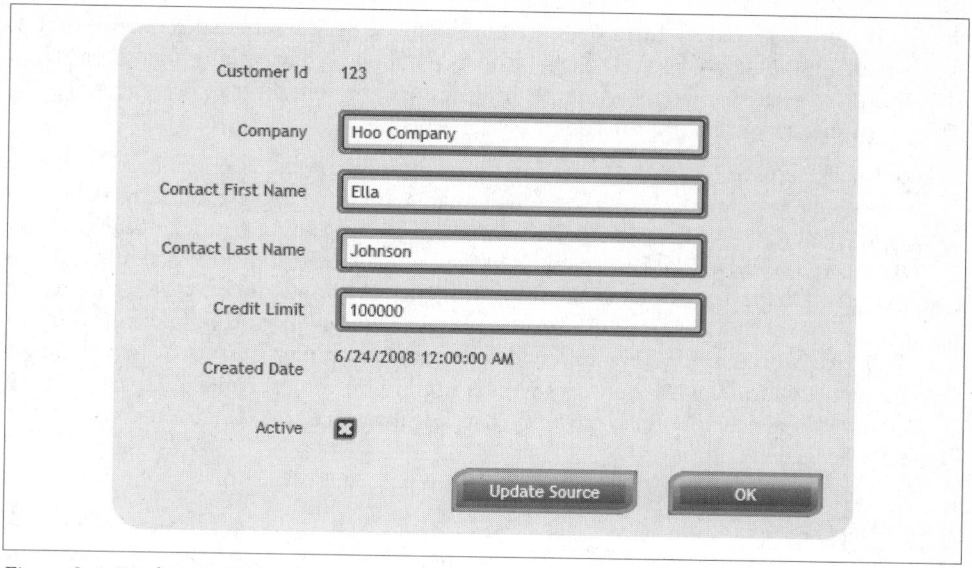

Figure 3-4. Bindings without change notifications from the source

It is a good idea to implement the INotifyPropertyChanged interface on any business entity that you expect will be used in data binding. It allows bound controls to be notified when the contents of the data source object are changed, which also keeps controls synchronized with each other and with the source.

The target controls that use TwoWay binding allow the user to change a value in the target controls, and the values are sent back to the source. However, if any changes occur in the source, they are not communicated to the target controls. In the next section, I will demonstrate how to modify this application so that it will notify the bindings when a property changes.

To Notify or Not to Notify

The previous examples demonstrate how the binding modes work when the INotifyPropertyChanged interface is not implemented on the data source entities. For read-only data, it is perfectly acceptable to not use this interface, thereby omitting its slight overhead. Silverlight applications that allow reading and writing of data through TwoWay binding can also skip using the INotifyPropertyChanged interface, as long as there is no chance the values will be updated and will need to be shown. However, it's important to note that this can be difficult to protect against, especially when considering future expansion of an application. For example, a new set of bound controls could be added to the same Silverlight user control with the intent that the bound controls be able to see updated changes from the existing read/write controls.

Although you do not have to use the INotifyPropertyChanged interface with bindings, doing so comes with very little overhead and can be very beneficial to applications. Implementing INotifyPropertyChanged can be trivial with a little planning. Later in this chapter, I will demonstrate some techniques to implement the INotifyProperty Changed interface and its required members.

I recommend creating a base class for the entities in your domain model so the base class can help consolidate and encapsulate the implementation of the INotifyPropertyChanged interface for all entities. Creating some entities in the domain model that implement INotifyPropertyChanged and others that do not could lead to confusion and disparity among the entities. Imagine an application in which this exists, and on one screen the entities raise the PropertyChanged event and on another they do not. This situation would likely leave a developer scratching his head. When building a domain entity model whose entities will be used in binding scenarios, a best practice is to implement the INotifyPropertyChanged interface on them and raise the PropertyChanged event.

Notifications

Classes that represent entities such as customer or product generally contain public properties that describe the entities. The Customer class in Example 3-2 shows a simple entity that has a handful of public properties describing the customer. When a property's value is changed, the entity does not communicate the change at all. If an instance of the entity is bound to a set of controls, the controls will not be notified or updated with the new values from the class instance.

Adding notifications to a class will enable the class to be able to raise events when its properties are changed, which in turn can be received by binding targets. The INotifyPropertyChanged interface is the device that carries out this mission.

Implementing the INotifyPropertyChanged Interface

The next set of examples will demonstrate how to make an entity support the INotifyPropertyChanged interface and hook into XAML-based binding modes. Example 3-5 shows the Product class written in C# using automatic properties. Using automatic properties restricts the property accessors to having the simplest getter and setter code that merely gets and sets the values. You would have to modify this code to use formal getters and setters to implement the INotifyPropertyChanged interface.

Example 3-5. The Product class

C#

```csharp
public class Product
{
    public int ProductId { get; set; }
    public string ProductName { get; set; }
    public int QuantityPerUnit { get; set; }
    public decimal UnitPrice { get; set; }
    public int UnitsInStock{ get; set; }
    public int UnitsOnOrder{ get; set; }
    public int ReorderLevel { get; set; }
    public bool Discontinued{ get; set; }
    public DateTime DiscontinuedDate{ get; set; }
    public List<Category> CategoryList { get; set; }
}
```

VB

```vbnet
Public Class Product
Private privateProductId As Integer
Public Property ProductId() As Integer
    Get
        Return privateProductId
    End Get
    Set(ByVal value As Integer)
        privateProductId = value
    End Set
End Property
Private privateProductName As String
Public Property ProductName() As String
    Get
        Return privateProductName
    End Get
    Set(ByVal value As String)
        privateProductName = value
    End Set
End Property
Private privateQuantityPerUnit As Integer
Public Property QuantityPerUnit() As Integer
    Get
        Return privateQuantityPerUnit
    End Get
    Set(ByVal value As Integer)
        privateQuantityPerUnit = value
    End Set
End Property
Private privateUnitPrice As Decimal
Public Property UnitPrice() As Decimal
    Get
        Return privateUnitPrice
    End Get
    Set(ByVal value As Decimal)
        privateUnitPrice = value
    End Set
End Property
Private privateUnitsInStock As Integer
Public Property UnitsInStock() As Integer
    Get
```

```
            Return privateUnitsInStock
        End Get
        Set(ByVal value As Integer)
            privateUnitsInStock = value
        End Set
    End Property
    Private privateUnitsOnOrder As Integer
    Public Property UnitsOnOrder() As Integer
        Get
            Return privateUnitsOnOrder
        End Get
        Set(ByVal value As Integer)
            privateUnitsOnOrder = value
        End Set
    End Property
    Private privateReorderLevel As Integer
    Public Property ReorderLevel() As Integer
        Get
            Return privateReorderLevel
        End Get
        Set(ByVal value As Integer)
            privateReorderLevel = value
        End Set
    End Property
    Private privateDiscontinued As Boolean
    Public Property Discontinued() As Boolean
        Get
            Return privateDiscontinued
        End Get
        Set(ByVal value As Boolean)
            privateDiscontinued = value
        End Set
    End Property
    Private privateDiscontinuedDate As DateTime
    Public Property DiscontinuedDate() As DateTime
        Get
            Return privateDiscontinuedDate
        End Get
        Set(ByVal value As DateTime)
            privateDiscontinuedDate = value
        End Set
    End Property
    Private privateCategoryList As List
    Public Property CategoryList() As List(Of Category)
        Get
            Return privateCategoryList
        End Get
        Set(ByVal value As List)
            privateCategoryList = value
        End Set
    End Property
End Class
```

In the sample application included in this chapter's code (the **AdvBindings** solution),
which is another custom Silverlight user control, **ProductDetailsView** will demonstrate

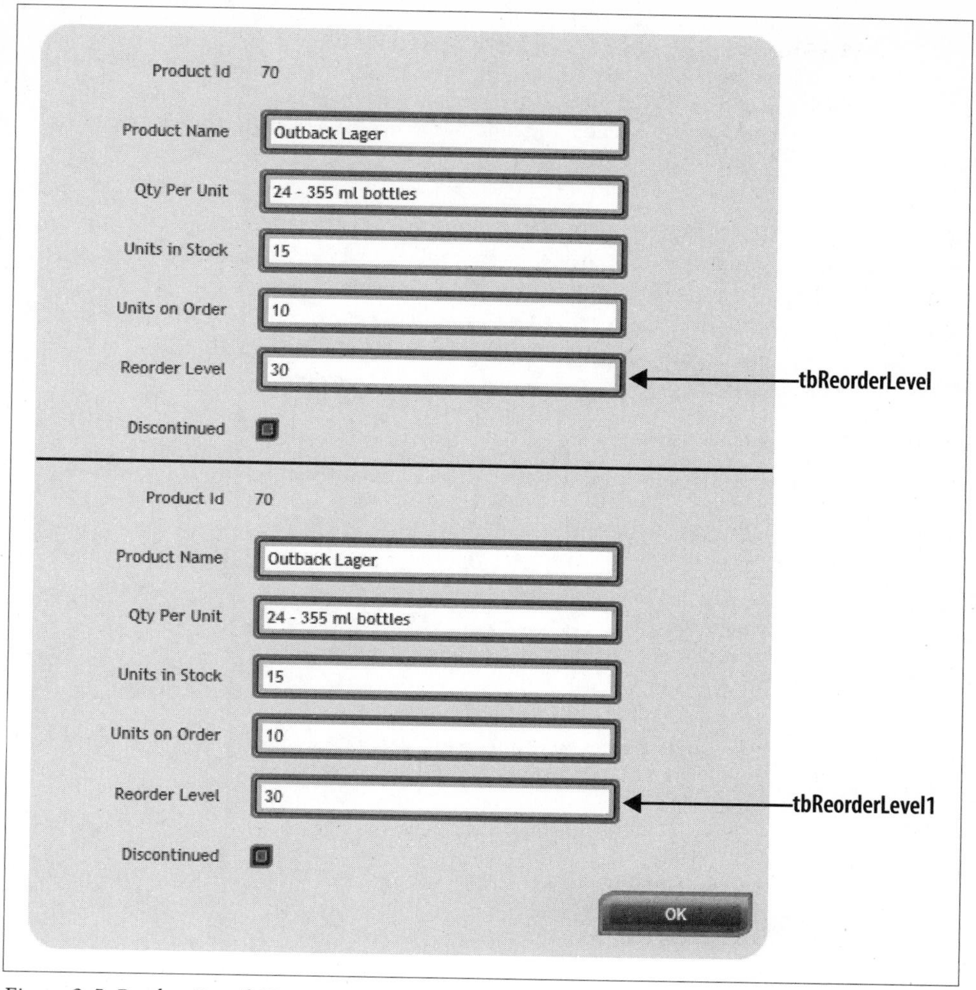

Figure 3-5. *ProductDetailsView at startup*

how the `INotifyPropertyChanged` interface can influence an application through bindings and event notifications. The `ProductDetailsView` sample user control is the next logical step in understanding binding and notification concepts. The `ProductDetailsView` user control will handle the notifications, but it will not provide a list of bound entities. The next iteration of the sample builds on this one as it shows how lists and detail sets of controls can be bound and can stay in sync.

The `ProductDetailsView` control shown in Figure 3-5 has two sets of controls to present product information to the user. The top and bottom sections are identical, other than the names of the controls. The point of this example is to demonstrate how the presence of notifications can affect this application.

Notice the tbReorderLevel and tbReorderLevel1 controls in Figure 3-5. When you copy sets of controls in Expression Blend and paste them, Blend copies everything exactly, except for the name. Blend copies the name and appends the number 1 to copies, which is how tbReorderLevel1 was named.

When the ProductDetailsView Silverlight user control loads, it creates an instance of a Product entity and binds it to the DataContext of the ProductDetailsLayout Grid control. Example 3-6 shows the code that loads this default Product instance. This Grid control contains all of the other TextBox, TextBlock, and CheckBox controls that are visible to the user. These child controls inherit the Product instance from the DataContext of the containing ProductDetailsLayout Grid control's DataContext.

Example 3-6. Binding the product on load

```
private void ProductDetailsView_Loaded(object sender, RoutedEventArgs e)
{
    Product product = CreateProduct();
    ProductDetailsLayout.DataContext = product;
}

private Product CreateProduct()
{
    return new Product {
        ProductId = 70, ProductName = "Outback Lager",
        QuantityPerUnit = "24 - 355 ml bottles", UnitsInStock = 15,
        UnitPrice = 15, UnitsOnOrder = 10, ReorderLevel = 30,
        Discontinued = false }
        ;
}
```

```
Private Sub ProductDetailsView_Loaded(ByVal sender As Object, _
        ByVal e As RoutedEventArgs)
    Dim product As Product = CreateProduct()
    ProductDetailsLayout.DataContext = product
End Sub

Private Function CreateProduct() As Product
    Return New Product With {.ProductId = 70, _
        .ProductName = "Outback Lager", _
        .QuantityPerUnit = "24 - 355 ml bottles", _
        .UnitsInStock = 15, .UnitPrice = 15, _
        .UnitsOnOrder = 10, .ReorderLevel = 30, _
        .Discontinued = False}
End Function
```

When this Silverlight user control runs, both sets of controls on the top and bottom are bound to the same Product class instance. However, neither set of controls is receiving change notifications. For example, say a user changes the product's reorder level from 30 to 7 using the top set of controls. The reorder level in the top is now 7, and in the bound Product instance (through the DataContext) it is also 7, because the tbReorderLevel control is using TwoWay binding. However, the tbReorderLevel1 control on the bottom half of the screen is still showing a value of 30 for the reorder level, even though it is also bound to the same Product instance that now has a ReorderLevel of 7. This out-of-sync state occurs because nobody told the controls that a property value changed. Fortunately, an easy fix will keep all of the controls in sync.

Adding Notifications

Part of the beauty of XAML-based data binding is that you can construct the user interface without explicitly tying the controls to an instance of a class at design time. The XAML does not define the Product class anywhere in its markup. However, the XAML does refer to the properties contained within the markup for its bindings. You can easily modify the ProductDetailsView user control example to keep its controls in sync by adding notifications to the Product class. You do not need to make any changes to the XAML or to the code in the ProductDetailsView user control. The bindings that are designated with OneWay and TwoWay binding modes will always listen for notifications. Without the INotifyPropertyChanged interface, there is nothing to listen to. Now it is time to add the notifications so that the bindings can receive the updates.

The Product class, shown in Example 3-5, is defined without any interfaces or base classes. The first step is to make the Product class implement the INotifyPropertyChanged interface. This interface is part of the System.ComponentModel namespace, which you can resolve by adding a using statement in the class file.

The INotifyPropertyChanged interface has a single member that must be implemented: the PropertyChanged event. The Product class's properties must raise this event in their setters. If automatic properties are used to create the Product's properties, this is a good time to convert them to use standard getters and setters so that you can invoke the additional functionality of raising the event when a property is changed.

Example 3-7 shows the inclusion of the System.ComponentModel namespace so that the INotifyPropertyChanged interface can be inherited by the Product class. Immediately inside the class's code the PropertyChanged event is implemented, thus fulfilling the interface's requirements. Example 3-7 also shows the first two properties of the Product class using the full getter and setter syntax to get and set their values. The setter code sets the value of the property's backing field, checks for the existence of the PropertyChanged event, and if it exists, raises the PropertyChanged event. (The complete code for Example 3-7 and the Product class are included in the Chapter 3 code that accompanies this book.)

Example 3-7. Adding the PropertyChanged event notifications

```
namespace AdvBindings
{
    public class Product : INotifyPropertyChanged
    {
        public event PropertyChangedEventHandler PropertyChanged;
```

```csharp
    private int _productId;
    public int ProductId
    {
        get { return _productId; }
        set
        {
            _productId = value;
            if (PropertyChanged != null)
                PropertyChanged(this,
                    new PropertyChangedEventArgs("ProductId"));
        }
    }

    private string _productName;
    public string ProductName
    {
        get { return _productName; }
        set
        {
            _productName = value;
            if (PropertyChanged != null)
                PropertyChanged(this,
                    new PropertyChangedEventArgs("ProductName"));
        }
    }
```

VB
```vbnet
Namespace AdvBindings
    Public Class Product
        Implements INotifyPropertyChanged

        Public Event PropertyChanged As PropertyChangedEventHandler

        Private _productId As Integer
        Public Property ProductId() As Integer
            Get
                Return _productId
            End Get
            Set(ByVal value As Integer)
                _productId = value
                If PropertyChanged IsNot Nothing Then
                    PropertyChanged(Me, New _
                        PropertyChangedEventArgs("ProductId"))
                End If
            End Set
        End Property

        Private _productName As String
        Public Property ProductName() As String
            Get
                Return _productName
            End Get
            Set(ByVal value As String)
                _productName = value
                If PropertyChanged IsNot Nothing Then
                    PropertyChanged(Me, _
```

```
                    New PropertyChangedEventArgs("ProductName"))
        End If
    End Set
End Property
```

Each property of the Product class needs to raise the PropertyChanged event, so you should repeat the coding pattern demonstrated in Example 3-7 for each property. Of course, you can refactor this to make it easier and more maintainable, but for now assume that the code is copied for each property with the name of the appropriate property set.

 It is important to first set the property value and then raise the event. In this sequence, when the PropertyChanged event is raised, any listeners to this event will want to know the value of the property. If the property value has already been updated, the listeners will receive the new property value, as they should. If the property value is set after the event is raised, the listeners will receive the event notifications but will get the old value of the property. Thus, the sequence of these few lines of code is very important.

This is the proper sequence:

1. Set the property value.
2. Make sure that the event is declared and is not null.
3. Raise the event:

```
set
{
    productName = value;
    if (PropertyChanged != null)
        PropertyChanged(this,
    new PropertyChangedEventArgs("ProductName"));
}
```

Once all of the properties raise the PropertyChanged event, the ProductDetailsView application behaves much better. Now when a user changes the reorder level from 30 to 7 in the bottom set of controls (and tabs out), the new value will be sent to the bound Product instance and to the other reorder level TextBox. The sequence of events is as follows:

1. The user clicks in the tbReorderLevel1 control on the bottom half of the screen.
2. The user changes the reorder level from 30 to 7 in tbReorderLevel1.
3. The TwoWay binding sends the new value of 7 to the bound Product instance.
4. The Product instance receives the new value of 7.
5. The Product instance's ReorderLevel property setter sets the value to 7 and raises the PropertyChanged event.
6. Both the tbReorderLevel and tbReorderLevel1 TextBox controls listen to the event.

7. The new value of 7 is displayed in both `TextBox` controls and all values are in sync.

Figure 3-6 shows the `ProductDetailsView` user control after adding the `INotifyPropertyChanged` interface and raising the `PropertyChanged` event in each property setter of the `Product` class. The reorder level uses a `TwoWay` binding mode, which is why the value is sent from the target control `tbReorderLevel1` to the `Product` instance's `ReorderLevel` property, and why the value is sent back up and received by both targets (`tbReorderLevel` and `tbReorderLevel1`). Controls that use the `OneWay` binding mode will not be able to send user changes from the target control to the data-bound source. However, `OneWay` controls will receive updates from the data-bound source. The `lbProductId` `TextBlock` uses a `OneTime` binding mode, so the only time a change is sent to the target is when the `DataContext` is first set. Silverlight applications will often use a combination of binding modes set on different controls, depending on which is most appropriate for each control.

Refactoring Options

The code in Example 3-7 shows each property setter raising the `PropertyChanged` event. However, applying this code to dozens of entities in a domain model would quickly become very tedious, which makes this code a prime candidate for some refactoring. The first step when refactoring is to put the common lines of code in an extracted method. For example, each property could call a method such as the `PropertyChangedHandler` method shown in Example 3-8.

Example 3-8. Extracting the PropertyChanged invocation code

```
private void PropertyChangedHandler(object sender, string propertyName)
{
    var handler = PropertyChanged;
    if (handler != null)
        handler(this, new PropertyChangedEventArgs(propertyName));
}
```

```
Private Sub PropertyChangedHandler(ByVal sender As Object, ByVal
  propertyName As String)
    Dim handler = PropertyChanged
    If handler IsNot Nothing Then
        handler(Me, New PropertyChangedEventArgs(propertyName))
    End If
End Sub
```

The `PropertyChangedHandler` method accepts the object that is raising the event and the name of the property that was changed. This instantly reduces the amount of code you need to write, and reduces some of the maintenance. However, if you place this code in the `Product` class, only the `Product` class's properties can use it. So the next step in the refactoring process is to find a way to make this code more accessible to those who need it. Each property getter and setter would look something like the code in Example 3-9.

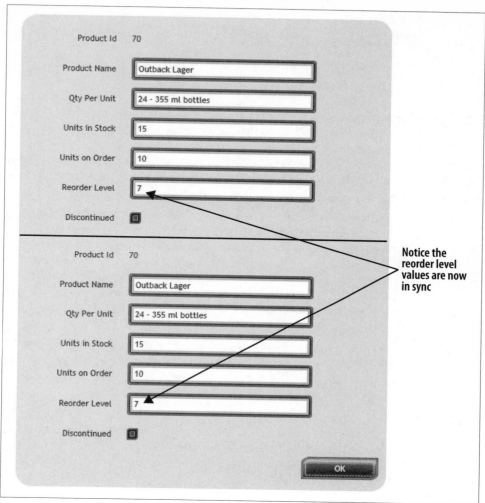

Notice the reorder level values are now in sync

Figure 3-6. *Notifications keep bindings in sync*

Example 3-9. *Raising the PropertyChanged event*

C#
```csharp
public string ProductName
{
    get { return _productName; }
    set
    {
        _productName = value;
        PropertyChangedHandler(this, "ProductName");
    }
}
```

VB
```vb
Public Property ProductName() As String
    Get
```

```
            Return _productName
        End Get
        Set(ByVal value As String)
            _productName = value
            PropertyChangedHandler(Me, "ProductName")
        End Set
    End Property
```

Another option is to place this method in a utility class and make the method static. This technique is somewhat of a catchall that has been used as a fallback when all other options fail. Although it will work, you should consider that good design principles should allow only entities in the domain model to have access to this method. Making this a static method in a utility class works, but there may be better ways to handle this.

The ideal solution is to find a way to minimize the code needed to raise the event and restrict which classes have access to the method to only those that are entities. One way to accomplish this is to create a base class for all entities and have it handle the heavy lifting. The base class could be called `EntityBase`, would implement the `INotifyPropertyChanged` interface, and would contain a protected method that handles raising the `PropertyChanged` event. This moves the code to a central location that is accessible to all entities that inherit from `EntityBase`, moves some of the `INotifyPropertyChanged` implementation out of the entities and to the `EntityBase` class, and reduces code maintenance.

Creating base classes for entities is not a new concept, and in most applications the entities already inherit from a base class. If that is the case, you could simply refactor the base class for the entities to include the code shown in Example 3-10. For argument's sake, Example 3-10 will assume there is no existing entity base class.

The `EntityBase` class in Example 3-10 is abstract, as no one should instantiate it directly. It implements the `INotifyPropertyChanged` interface and its `PropertyChanged` event. The `PropertyChangedHandler` method is a protected member, so it can be called by any class that inherits from `EntityBase`, thus limiting access to the entities.

Example 3-10. The EntityBase class

[C#]
```
public abstract class EntityBase : INotifyPropertyChanged
{
    public event PropertyChangedEventHandler PropertyChanged;
    protected void PropertyChangedHandler(string propertyName)
    {
        if (PropertyChanged != null)
            PropertyChanged(this, new PropertyChangedEventArgs(propertyName));
    }
}
```

[VB]
```
Public MustInherit Class EntityBase
    Implements INotifyPropertyChanged
    Public Event PropertyChanged As PropertyChangedEventHandler
    Protected Sub PropertyChangedHandler(ByVal propertyName As String)
        RaiseEvent PropertyChanged(Me, New PropertyChangedEventArgs(propertyName))
```

```
        End Sub
End Class
```

The `Product` class is then refactored to inherit from the `EntityBase` class. Also, the `Product` class no longer needs to implement the `INotifyPropertyChanged` interface, so this is removed along with the `Product` class's `PropertyChanged` event declaration. This code was refactored down to the base class, thus cleaning up a bit in the child `Product` class. Finally, in all of the setters, the code can be refactored to call the base class's `PropertyChangedHandler` method. All properties would then look something like the code in Example 3-9.

Summary

The binding modes and the `INotifyPropertyChanged` interface are important to building rich data-bound user controls with Silverlight 2. The target controls, entity source, binding modes, `DataContext` property, `INotifyPropertyChanged` interface, and `PropertyChanged` event all work in concert to create a loosely coupled but highly functional XAML-based binding experience. I will expand on this in the next chapter by reviewing `ObservableCollection<T>`, binding to `ListBox` controls, using templates, and presenting data with converters.

CHAPTER 4

Managing Lists, Templates, and Converters

Silverlight 2 supports binding lists of items to target controls through the same mechanisms as those you would use to bind to a single item, such as an entity. Binding to lists also is similar to binding to single entities. Entities can implement the `INotifyPropertyChanged` interface to communicate with the target controls to notify them when a property value has changed. List-based controls can also benefit from notifications if they are bound to lists created with the `ObservableCollection<T>` or collection classes that implement the `INotifyCollectionChanged` interface.

You can bind controls directly to an object source or to a list of objects. This is especially useful for binding a list of objects to a list-based control such as `ItemsControl`, `ListBox`, or `DataGrid`, or to a third-party list-based control. Like the `INotifyProperty Changed` interface, the `INotifyCollectionChanged` interface provides a way for the collection to notify the bindings when the contents have changed.

List-based controls in Silverlight 2 have an `ItemTemplate` property that defines how each row in a list-based control will be presented. The `ItemTemplate` can refer to a `DataTemplate` resource, which you can then reuse to apply the same template to different list-based controls. The template's contents can be data-binding targets so that they can benefit from the data-bound source's property values. This chapter will build on the binding techniques we've already discussed, and will show you how to bind to lists of entities, implement event notifications, and design item templates for lists.

Binding to List-Based Controls

List-based binding begins with a list of items. These items can be represented by, for example, a `List<T>` or any `IEnumerable` derived class. Once the list of items is obtained, the list can be bound to an appropriate target control such as a `ListBox`, `ItemsControl`, `ComboBox`, or `DataGrid`.

Because the concepts of binding apply to all of these types of list-based controls in much the same way, the examples in this chapter will use the ListBox control. ItemsControl is similar to ListBox, which inherits from ItemsControl.

The ListBox control can display items in a standard and straight list, or it can have its item template completely overridden and replaced with a custom set of XAML. Either way, a list of items that is bound to the ListBox control can be displayed item by item within the ListBox.

Setting the ItemsSource

Figure 4-1 shows a basic ListBox bound to a list of products. This ListBox is bound by setting the ListBox control's ItemsSource property to the List<Product>. The previous examples in this book bind a property of a target control to a source object's property. In the examples, the source object is set to the DataContext (either directly or through an inherited DataContext). The target controls in the previous examples had a value that they needed to display, and that value was derived from the data-binding source. For example, a TextBox control that displays a product's name from an entity has the TextBox's Text property bound to the source. A ListBox control differs from these examples in that the ListBox will display several items, and binding the source to a single property of the ListBox (the ItemsSource) is not enough to make the ListBox display the item values.

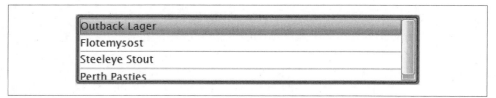

Figure 4-1. ListBox bound to basic list

The ListBox control in Figure 4-1 has its ItemsSource property bound to the DataContext. This associates the List<Product> to the ListBox, but the display of the items must also be set up. Otherwise, if the ItemsSource is bound and the contents of the ListBox are not established, the ListBox will display the ToString() contents of each item in the List<Product>, as shown in Figure 4-2.

The ListBox shown in Figure 4-2 does not display the contents of each item, because it is not being told what to display or how to display it. The "how to display it" part is determined by creating controls that will visually display the desired content. In this case, the ListBox's items can simply be displayed as a TextBlock that shows the name of each product. The display could also be much more elaborate, as you can represent the content of each ListBox item using templates of your own design. For the example

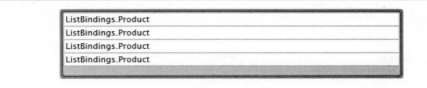

Figure 4-2. ListBox bound to ItemsSource

shown in Figure 4-1, the `ListBox` items (displayed via the `ItemTemplate` property) are represented by a `DataTemplate` that contains a single `TextBlock`.

Example 4-1 shows the XAML for the `ListBox` shown in Figure 4-1. Two main bindings are functioning here. First, the `List<Product>` is bound to the `ListBox`'s `ItemsSource` property. Second, each row in the `ListBox` is bound to a `Product` from the `ItemsSource` binding and will be displayed using the `DataTemplate`.

Example 4-1. ListBox with a template

```
<ListBox x:Name="lstProducts" Height="88" HorizontalAlignment="Left"
    VerticalAlignment="Bottom" Margin="20,20,20,5" Width="440"
    Style="{StaticResource ListBoxStyle}" ItemsSource="{Binding}" >
    <ListBox.ItemTemplate>
        <DataTemplate>
            <StackPanel Orientation="Horizontal">
                <TextBlock Text="{Binding ProductName, Mode=OneWay}"
                Style="{StaticResource TextBlockCaptionStyle}"
                FontSize="14"/>
            </StackPanel>
        </DataTemplate>
    </ListBox.ItemTemplate>
</ListBox>
```

Notice that the `TextBlock` is using data binding to bind the `Text` property to the `ProductName` property of the binding source. The binding source refers to the objects in the `ItemsSource`, which gets the data source from the `DataContext`. The `DataContext` will be set at runtime in the .NET code to a `List<Product>` which is bound to the `ItemsSource` property of the `ListBox`. Each row in the `ListBox` is bound to one instance of a `Product`. This symbiotic relationship between the source object, the `DataContext`, and the bound target control properties enables developers to declare what will be bound, and how, at design time in the XAML.

The `ListBox` control's `ItemsSource` shown in Example 4-1 is set to the `Binding` keyword. This indicates that the `ItemsSource` will be bound to the inherited `DataContext`. You could set the `DataContext` for the `ListBox` or a parent control of the `ListBox` to the `List<Product>`, and the `ItemsSource` would inherit that `List<Product>`. The code in Example 4-2 shows how to do this inside the `Loaded` event handler for the Silverlight control.

Example 4-2. Setting the DataContext

C#
```
List<Product> productList = CreateProductList();
lstProducts.DataContext = productList;
```

VB
```
Dim productList As List(Of Product) = CreateProductList()
lstProducts.DataContext = productList;
```

> The `CreateProductList` method creates a `List<Product>` inside the Silverlight 2 control. Chapters 5–11 will demonstrate how to retrieve records and fill them from server-based services using Windows Communication Foundation (WCF) and REST. You can find the source for `CreateProductList` and all of the source code for this chapter in the sample code in the `ListBindings` solution.

An alternative method is to set the `ItemsSource` directly in the code. Either way, the `ListBox` gets the collection of items, which then leaves it up to the template to determine how to display the `Product` entity information. The code in Example 4-3 shows how to do this inside the `Loaded` event handler for the Silverlight control.

Example 4-3. Setting the ItemsSource directly

C#
```
List<Product> productList = CreateProductList();
lstProducts.ItemsSource = productList;
```

VB
```
Dim productList As List(Of Product) = CreateProductList()
lstProducts.ItemsSource = productList
```

Whatever binding technique you use, it is important to be consistent throughout the application. For example, it is a poor coding practice to bind an `ItemsSource` property to the `DataContext` in one place and to bind an `ItemsSource` property directly to a specific `List<T>` someplace else. Consistency is a good rule to stick with in development. However, it could be argued that using the `DataContext` technique is a better approach, as all other nonlist-based bindings rely on it as well.

Binding Mode Considerations

Notice that the binding mode for the `TextBox` shown in Example 4-1 is set to `OneWay`. This indicates that the `TextBox` will listen for notifications that tell it when the value that it is bound to changes. This means that if the value changes in the source object, that new value will be presented in the `TextBox` immediately.

Consider that this application is extended so that a set of `TextBox` controls below the `ListBox` will represent the details of each product. These `TextBox` controls that represent the details are bound to the selected `Product` using the `TwoWay` binding mode. If you want the changes a user types to automatically update the `ListBox` contents, `OneWay` does the job. However, if you want the changes to never be updated in the `ListBox`, the `OneTime` binding mode might be better suited to this task.

Choosing the appropriate binding mode is important and depends on the application's requirements. A good rule of thumb to follow is to set the binding mode for ListBox items to OneTime when dealing with most master detail scenarios. Also, you should use OneWay binding for ListBox items only when you need to have the items updated, as the values in the source object change, which may be when another control loses focus. Often, ListBox items or DataGrid items are interpreted as representing what has come out of a data source, such as a database. Thus, if a user changes a value and has not yet clicked Save, and the value is changed in the ListBox (due to OneWay binding in the ListBox items), the user could become confused.

Templates and Rows

You can add items to ListBox controls declaratively, through code, or through data binding.

Adding ListBox items through declarative techniques requires simply adding items in the XAML either by typing them in or by using a designer such as Expression Blend. But although the declarative technique makes it easy to add items in a designer, it does not offer a way to add items from a database, because the values are not known at design time.

To set or modify items through code, you would access the object model for the ListBox. You would use this technique when employing a manual binding strategy. Manual binding involves pulling values from a data source and manually loading them into target controls in the ListBox. Then the values can be manually pulled from the controls and back to a data source when the user clicks a button, for example. Manual binding does not require a DataContext or any binding syntax. Instead, it simply loads property values into targets, one by one, for each row in the ListBox.

A ListBox can take advantage of data-binding techniques to eliminate the code that is required in the manual binding process. Using the binding syntax and the techniques shown in the previous examples in this chapter, you can easily make a ListBox push and pull data to and from a data source and a target.

The ListBox control uses a template to predetermine the layout of its item rows. You define this template using the ItemTemplate of the ListBox. The ItemTemplate can refer to a DataTemplate that defines the contents of the bound elements that you will use to present the values from the data-binding source. You can define the ItemTemplate directly inline, as shown in Example 4-1, or it can refer to a DataTemplate as a resource. Either way, the DataTemplate is a very useful technique for designing repetitive rows of information for controls such as the ListBox.

DataTemplates As Resources

Instead of creating a `DataTemplate` inline, you can create it as a resource. This approach allows you to use throughout the Silverlight 2 application the layout you used in the `DataTemplate`. For example, you could create a user control in the application that defines the layout of the same controls you will be using in a list-based control. You can reference this new user control as the `DataTemplate` source anywhere within the Silverlight 2 application. In this case, a `ListBox` control can refer to the resource by its `Key` property. You can remove the `DataTemplate` in Example 4-1 and create it as a resource, as shown in Example 4-4. The `DataTemplate` syntax itself is exactly the same, except for the addition of the `x:Key` attribute. The value of the `Key` property is referred to by the `ItemTemplate`, so it can use the exact `DataTemplate` it requires.

Example 4-4. DataTemplate as a resource

```
<UserControl.Resources>
    <DataTemplate x:Key="ProductTemplate">
        <StackPanel Orientation="Horizontal">
            <TextBlock Text="{Binding ProductName, Mode=OneWay}"
Style="{StaticResource TextBlockCaptionStyle}" FontSize="14"/>
        </StackPanel>
    </DataTemplate>
</UserControl.Resources>
```

You define the `DataTemplate` within the `UserControl`'s resource section, though you also could create it in any resource section the `ListBox` can obtain. For example, you could have created it as a resource of the container control of the `ListBox`, which in this case is a `StackPanel`. Creating the `DataTemplate` as a resource helps separate the declarative code and allows the template to be used by other controls, if needed. You can also create the `DataTemplate` as a resource in the *app.xaml* page. This would allow the template to be accessible from anywhere within the Silverlight application.

Changing an inline `DataTemplate` to a resource makes the `ListBox` control's XAML much cleaner. The `ListBox` control shown in Example 4-1 shows several lines of XAML that include the reference to the `DataTemplate` via the `ListBox`'s `ItemTemplate`. By removing all of the children elements of the `ListBox` element shown in Example 4-1, you could rewrite this as a single line of XAML.

Example 4-5 shows the modified version of this XAML. The `ItemTemplate` property is moved up into the `ListBox` element and refers to a `StaticResource` named `ProductTemplate`. You can replace the XAML in Example 4-1 with the combination of the XAML in Examples 4-4 and 4-5 to yield the same effect shown in Figure 4-1.

Example 4-5. ListBox referring to a DataTemplate resource

```
<ListBox x:Name="lstProducts" Height="88" HorizontalAlignment="Left"
    VerticalAlignment="Bottom" Margin="20,20,20,5" Width="440"
    Style="{StaticResource ListBoxStyle}"
    ItemsSource="{Binding}"
    ItemTemplate="{StaticResource ProductTemplate}"/>
```

Complex DataTemplates

DataTemplates do not need to contain merely columns of information. Instead, they can contain any creative combination of elements that are required to present the data. For example, you could define a DataTemplate as a Grid container control that contains a table of values, or a Canvas layout control that contains images and text from the data source, or a StackPanel layout control with a series of horizontally and vertically stacked controls.

Figure 4-3 shows a ListBox that uses a DataTemplate that contains a slightly more complicated presentation. The template contains a horizontally oriented StackPanel, which contains a nested, vertically oriented StackPanel and a Grid layout control, for a side-by-side effect. The nested StackPanel contains two TextBlocks that are used to display the ProductName and UnitPrice properties from the data source. These TextBlocks use some custom styles to give them the gradient effect shown in Figure 4-3. The Grid layout control appears to the right. It contains three rows of property names and values, which display a summary of the product information. This is a very simple demonstration of how to create DataTemplates that contain nested controls for presentation. You can modify this in many ways and with a variety of controls to present a more aesthetically pleasing look based on the application.

 The UnitPrice shown in Figure 4-3 is not formatted as a currency value. The value for UnitPrice is a decimal value that must be converted to represent the currency value. You can do this using a converter class, which I will explain later in this chapter.

Outback Lager	Product ID	70
15	Price	15
	Units	15
Flotemysost	Product ID	71
21.5	Price	21.5
	Units	25
Steeleye Stout	Product ID	35
18	Price	18
	Units	20

Figure 4-3. ListBox's DataTemplate with nested controls

The XAML that creates the ListBox shown in Figure 4-3 appears in Example 4-6. All of the styles are defined as local resources to the Silverlight control named ListBoxTemplate. Notice that the DataTemplate ListBoxTemplate is contained as a local

named resource and that the `ListBox` `lstProducts` references the `DataTemplate` in its
`ItemTemplate` property.

Example 4-6. Stacked DataTemplate

```xml
<UserControl x:Class="ListBindings.ListBoxTemplate"
    xmlns="http://schemas.microsoft.com/winfx/2006/xaml/presentation"
    xmlns:x="http://schemas.microsoft.com/winfx/2006/xaml"
    Width="510" Height="500">
    <UserControl.Resources>
        <Style x:Key="TitlePanel" TargetType="StackPanel">
            <Setter Property="Margin" Value="3,3,3,3"/>
            <Setter Property="Width" Value="260"/>
            <Setter Property="Height" Value="50"/>
            <Setter Property="Background">
                <Setter.Value>
                    <LinearGradientBrush EndPoint="0.5,1" StartPoint="0.5,0">
                        <GradientStop Color="#FF2A3557" Offset="0.004"/>
                        <GradientStop Color="#FFFFFFFF" Offset="1"/>
                        <GradientStop Color="#FF6199CD" Offset="0.388"/>
                        <GradientStop Color="#FF4480A0" Offset="0.737"/>
                    </LinearGradientBrush>
                </Setter.Value>
            </Setter>
        </Style>
        <Style x:Key="TitleTextBlock" TargetType="TextBlock">
            <Setter Property="HorizontalAlignment" Value="Center"/>
            <Setter Property="FontWeight" Value="Bold"/>
            <Setter Property="Foreground" Value="#BBFFFFFF"/>
            <Setter Property="FontFamily" Value="Verdana"/>
        </Style>
        <Style x:Key="SubTitleTextBlock" TargetType="TextBlock">
            <Setter Property="HorizontalAlignment" Value="Center"/>
            <Setter Property="FontFamily" Value="Trebuchet MS"/>
            <Setter Property="Foreground" Value="#BBFFFFFF"/>
        </Style>
        <Style x:Key="TextBlockStyle" TargetType="TextBlock">
            <Setter Property="Margin" Value="3,3,3,3"/>
            <Setter Property="FontFamily" Value="Trebuchet MS"/>
            <Setter Property="TextAlignment" Value="Left"/>
            <Setter Property="FontSize" Value="12"/>
            <Setter Property="VerticalAlignment" Value="Center"/>
        </Style>
        <DataTemplate x:Key="StackedProductTemplate">
            <StackPanel Orientation="Horizontal">
                <StackPanel Style="{StaticResource TitlePanel}"
                    Orientation="Vertical">
                    <TextBlock Text="{Binding ProductName, Mode=OneWay}"
                    Style="{StaticResource TitleTextBlock}"
                    FontSize="14"/>
                <TextBlock Text="{Binding UnitPrice,
                    Mode=OneWay}"
                    Style="{StaticResource SubTitleTextBlock}" />
                </StackPanel>
                <Grid>
```

```
<Grid.RowDefinitions>
    <RowDefinition></RowDefinition>
    <RowDefinition></RowDefinition>
    <RowDefinition></RowDefinition>
</Grid.RowDefinitions>
<Grid.ColumnDefinitions>
    <ColumnDefinition></ColumnDefinition>
    <ColumnDefinition></ColumnDefinition>
</Grid.ColumnDefinitions>
<TextBlock Text="Product ID"
Style="{StaticResource TextBlockStyle}"
Grid.Row="0" Grid.Column="0"/>
<TextBlock Text="{Binding ProductId, Mode=OneWay}"
Style="{StaticResource TextBlockStyle}"
Foreground="#FF001070" Grid.Row="0" Grid.Column="1"/>
<TextBlock Text="Price"
Style="{StaticResource TextBlockStyle}" Grid.Row="1"
Grid.Column="0"/>
<TextBlock Text="{Binding UnitPrice, Mode=OneWay}"
Foreground="#FF001070"
Style="{StaticResource TextBlockStyle}"
Grid.Row="1" Grid.Column="1"/>
<TextBlock Text="Units"
Style="{StaticResource TextBlockStyle}" Grid.Row="2"
Grid.Column="0"/>
<TextBlock Text="{Binding UnitsInStock, Mode=OneWay}"
Foreground="#FF001070"
Style="{StaticResource TextBlockStyle}" Grid.Row="2"
Grid.Column="1"/>
            </Grid>
        </StackPanel>
    </DataTemplate>
</UserControl.Resources>
<Grid x:Name="LayoutRoot" Background="White">
    <ListBox x:Name="lstProducts" Height="220" HorizontalAlignment="Left"
    VerticalAlignment="Bottom" Margin="10,10,10,10" Width="480"
    Style="{StaticResource ListBoxStyle}"
    ItemsSource="{Binding}"
    ItemTemplate="{StaticResource StackedProductTemplate}">
    </ListBox>
</Grid>
</UserControl>
```

Named templates are easy to set up as resources and to reuse, if needed. If you intend to use a DataTemplate in multiple Silverlight controls, it would be beneficial to put the DataTemplate in the *app.xaml* file as an application global resource. If the template is designed specifically for a control, it would be better to put the resource in the local file, as shown in Example 4-6. You also could create the resource as a resource of any container control of the ListBox, such as the LayoutRoot Grid. However, it is a better practice to keep resources at the user control level unless there is a specific reason to move the resource closer to where it will be used.

Item Selection

User interfaces often display a list of items to a user in a control such as a `ListBox` and allow the user to select one of the items. Once he makes the selection, the user may be brought to another screen, another control may appear with detailed information about the selected item, or the selected item's details may appear in a series of controls below the `ListBox`. Generally, this is a good design practice, as it is often impossible to effectively display all of the information about an item in a list-based control. For example, if an entity such as a `Product` has more than 50 properties, displaying all of those properties in a list-based control would be problematic and likely would not be very user-friendly. Though with Silverlight 2 and XAML, you can alleviate this somewhat by creating a `DataTemplate` that contains several rows of information within each row of the `ListBox`. However, even this solution has its limits.

One possible solution to this type of problem is to display a list of items that contains a summary of the items in a control such as a `ListBox`. Then when the user selects an item from the `ListBox`, the details of all of the properties for the `Product` are displayed in a series of controls. The code in Example 4-7 shows how to implement this type of scenario.

Example 4-7. Setting the DataContext for the selected product

```C#
private void lstProducts_SelectionChanged(object sender,
        SelectionChangedEventArgs e)
{
    Product product = (Product) lstProducts.SelectedItem;
    ProductDetailsLayout.DataContext = product;
}
```

```VB
Private Sub lstProducts_SelectionChanged(ByVal sender As Object, _
        ByVal e As SelectionChangedEventArgs)
    Dim product As Product = CType(lstProducts.SelectedItem, Product)
    ProductDetailsLayout.DataContext = product
End Sub
```

When a user selects an item from a `ListBox`, the `SelectionChanged` event is raised. You can write an event handler for this event that retrieves the selected item and sets the `DataContext` of a series of detailed controls that are bound to a `DataContext` that is expecting a product instance. For example, the following code shows the `lstProducts_SelectionChanged` event handler getting a reference to the `lstProducts` `ListBox`'s `SelectedItem` property. The `SelectedItem` contains either null or a `Product` instance. The `Product` instance is then set to the `DataContext` of a `Grid` layout control named `ProductDetailsLayout`.

Example 4-8 shows the XAML that contains the `ListBox` and the details controls that will present the `Product` information. The details controls are contained within the `Grid` layout control named `ProductsDetailsLayout`, shown in bold in Example 4-8. When the `lstProducts_SelectionChanged` event handler executes, it sets the

`DataContext` for this `Grid` control to the selected product from the `lstProducts` `ListBox`. The controls contained within the `ProductDetailsLayout` `Grid` control inherit this `DataContext`, as none of their `DataContext` properties are set. This allows each of them to bind to the selected item in the `ListBox` and have the values displayed whenever a user selects a different item.

Example 4-8. XAML for product ListBox and details controls

```
<Grid x:Name="LayoutRoot" Margin="10,10,10,10">
    <Rectangle Fill="#FFDEE6FB" Grid.Column="0" Grid.Row="0"
        Grid.RowSpan="2" RadiusX="20" RadiusY="20" Opacity="0.8"
        StrokeThickness="0" />
    <StackPanel Grid.Column="0" Grid.Row="0">
        <ListBox x:Name="lstProducts" Height="88" HorizontalAlignment="Left"
            VerticalAlignment="Bottom" Margin="20,20,20,5" Width="440"
            Style="{StaticResource ListBoxStyle}"
            ItemTemplate="{StaticResource ProductTemplate}"
            ItemsSource="{Binding}"/>
        <StackPanel Orientation="Horizontal" x:Name="buttonPanel"
            HorizontalAlignment="Right" Margin="10,0,10,0" >
            <Button x:Name="btnAddProduct" Content="Add Product" Margin="10,5,10,5"
            HorizontalAlignment="Right" Height="30" Width="120"
                Style="{StaticResource ButtonStyle}"/>
            <Button x:Name="btnRemoveProduct" Content="Remove Product"
                Height="30" Width="120" Style="{StaticResource ButtonStyle}"/>
        </StackPanel>
        <Grid Margin="10,10,10,10" x:Name="ProductDetailsLayout">
            <Grid.ColumnDefinitions>
                <ColumnDefinition Width="123"/>
                <ColumnDefinition Width="Auto" MinWidth="337"/>
            </Grid.ColumnDefinitions>
            <Grid.RowDefinitions>
                <RowDefinition Height="40"/>
                <RowDefinition Height="40"/>
                <RowDefinition Height="40"/>
                <RowDefinition Height="40"/>
                <RowDefinition Height="40"/>
                <RowDefinition Height="40"/>
                <RowDefinition Height="40"/>
                <RowDefinition Height="40"/>
            </Grid.RowDefinitions>
            <TextBlock Text="Product Id" Grid.Row="0" Grid.Column="0"
            Margin="10,5,10,5" Style="{StaticResource TextBlockCaptionStyle}"/>
            <TextBlock Text="Product Name" Grid.Row="1" Grid.Column="0"
            Margin="10,5,10,5" Style="{StaticResource TextBlockCaptionStyle}"/>
            <TextBlock Text="Qty Per Unit" Grid.Row="2" Grid.Column="0"
            Margin="10,5,10,5" Style="{StaticResource TextBlockCaptionStyle}"/>
            <TextBlock Text="Units in Stock" Grid.Row="3" Grid.Column="0"
            Margin="10,5,10,5" Style="{StaticResource TextBlockCaptionStyle}"/>
            <TextBlock Text="Units on Order" Grid.Row="4" Grid.Column="0"
            Margin="10,5,10,5" Style="{StaticResource TextBlockCaptionStyle}"/>
            <TextBlock Text="Reorder Level" Grid.Column="0" Grid.Row="5"
            Margin="10,5,10,5" Style="{StaticResource TextBlockCaptionStyle}"/>
            <TextBlock Text="Discontinued" Grid.Row="6" Grid.Column="0"
```

```
Margin="10,5,10,5" Style="{StaticResource TextBlockCaptionStyle}"/>
<TextBlock Text="Discontinued Date" Grid.Row="7" Grid.Column="0"
Margin="10,5,10,5" Style="{StaticResource TextBlockCaptionStyle}"/>

<TextBlock Text="{Binding Path=ProductId, Mode=OneTime}" Grid.Row="0"
Grid.Column="1" Margin="11,5,10,5"
Style="{StaticResource TextBlockReadOnlyStyle}"
x:Name="lbProductId" HorizontalAlignment="Left"/>
<TextBox x:Name="tbProductName" Grid.Column="1" Grid.Row="1"
Margin="10,5,10,5" HorizontalAlignment="Left"
Height="30"   Width="240"
  Style="{StaticResource TextBoxStyle}"
Text="{Binding Mode=TwoWay, Path=ProductName}"/>
<TextBox x:Name="tbQtyPerUnit" Grid.Column="1" Grid.Row="2"
Margin="10,5,10,5" HorizontalAlignment="Left"
Height="30" Width="240"
  Style="{StaticResource TextBoxStyle}"
Text="{Binding Mode=TwoWay, Path=QuantityPerUnit}"/>
<StackPanel Grid.Row="3" Grid.Column="1" Orientation="Horizontal">
    <Slider HorizontalAlignment="Left" Margin="10,5,10,5"
    x:Name="sliUnitsInStock" VerticalAlignment="Stretch"
    LargeChange="10" Maximum="150" SmallChange="1" Width="240"
      Value="{Binding Mode=TwoWay, Path=UnitsInStock}"
    Style="{StaticResource SliderStyle}" />
    <TextBlock Text="{Binding Path=UnitsInStock, Mode=OneWay}"
    Margin="5,5,10,5"
    Style="{StaticResource TextBlockReadOnlyStyle}"
    x:Name="lbUnitsInStock" HorizontalAlignment="Left"/>
</StackPanel>
<StackPanel Grid.Row="4" Grid.Column="1" Orientation="Horizontal">
    <Slider HorizontalAlignment="Left" Margin="10,5,10,5"
    x:Name="sliUnitsOnOrder" VerticalAlignment="Stretch"
    LargeChange="10" Maximum="150" SmallChange="1" Width="240"
    Value="{Binding Mode=TwoWay, Path=UnitsOnOrder}"
    Style="{StaticResource SliderStyle}" />
    <TextBlock Text="{Binding Path=UnitsOnOrder, Mode=OneWay}"
    Margin="5,5,10,5"
    Style="{StaticResource TextBlockReadOnlyStyle}"
    x:Name="lbUnitsOnOrder" HorizontalAlignment="Left"/>
</StackPanel>
<StackPanel Grid.Row="5" Grid.Column="1" Orientation="Horizontal">
    <Slider Margin="10,5,10,5" HorizontalAlignment="Left"
    Style="{StaticResource SliderStyle}"
    Value="{Binding Mode=TwoWay, Path=ReorderLevel}"
    VerticalAlignment="Stretch" x:Name="sliReorderLevel"
    LargeChange="10" Maximum="150" SmallChange="1" Width="240" />
    <TextBlock Text="{Binding Path=ReorderLevel, Mode=OneWay}"
    Margin="5,5,10,5"
    Style="{StaticResource TextBlockReadOnlyStyle}"
    x:Name="lbReorderLevel" HorizontalAlignment="Left"/>
</StackPanel>
<CheckBox x:Name="cbDiscontinued" Grid.Column="1" Grid.Row="6"
Margin="10,5,10,5" HorizontalAlignment="Left" Height="30" Width="240"
  Style="{StaticResource CheckBoxStyle}"
IsChecked="{Binding Mode=TwoWay, Path=Discontinued}"/>
```

```
    <TextBlock x:Name="lbDiscontinuedDate" Grid.Column="1" Grid.Row="7"
        Margin="10,5,10,5" HorizontalAlignment="Left" Height="13" Width="240"
          Style="{StaticResource TextBlockReadOnlyStyle}"
        Text="{Binding Mode=OneWay, Path=DiscontinuedDate}"
        VerticalAlignment="Center" />
    </Grid>
      <StackPanel Orientation="Horizontal" x:Name="bottomButtonPanel"
          Height="40" HorizontalAlignment="Right" Margin="10,0,10,0" >
          <Button x:Name="btnOK" Content="OK" Height="30" Width="120"
          Style="{StaticResource ButtonStyle}"/>
      </StackPanel>
    </StackPanel>
</Grid>
```

Using Different Binding Modes

Each details control in Example 4-8 uses a different binding mode. The `ProductId` property is the identifier for the `Product` entity and it will not be changed. This property value is displayed in a `TextBlock`, because it is read-only and the binding mode is set to `OneTime`. `OneTime` tells the target property that it need not listen for change notifications on this property, as the property will never change. Therefore, the only time this `TextBlock`'s value will be updated is when the `DataContext` is set.

The `ProductName` property is bound to a `TextBox` target control, because the user may decide to change this value. The binding mode is set to `TwoWay` for this and many other controls. `TwoWay` allows the user to change the value in the target control and have the new value sent automatically to the bound data source. It also tells the target control to listen for property change notifications so that it can update the contents of the `TextBox` if this event is raised for its bound property.

The `UnitsInStock`, `ReorderLevel`, and `UnitsOnOrder` properties are bound to two different controls. Each property is bound to a `Slider` and to a `TextBlock` control. The `Slider` is bound using the `TwoWay` binding mode to the corresponding property so that when the user moves the `Slider` left or right, the value is sent automatically back to the bound data source. The `Slider` control does not display a value, however, so a `TextBlock` has been placed to the right of each `Slider` control to display the `Slider`'s value. In Example 4-8, this is implemented entirely through declarative code using XAML. The `TextBlock`'s `Text` property and the `Slider`'s `Value` property are both bound to the same property of the `Product` data source. The `Slider`'s binding uses the `TwoWay` binding mode and the `TextBlock` uses the `OneWay` binding mode. The `TextBlock` cannot be updated, so it need not use the `TwoWay` binding mode. The `TextBlock` must listen for `PropertyChanged` events so that it knows when to display the updated value.

For example, when the user slides the `Slider` named `sliReorderLevel` (shown in bold in the middle of Example 4-8) to the right, increasing the value to 50, that value is sent to the `Product` instance, which calls the setter code for the `ReorderLevel` property, which raises the `PropertyChanged` event, which notifies anyone listening (in this case, the `TextBlock` named `lbReorderLevel`) and updates the target control's value. The bindings

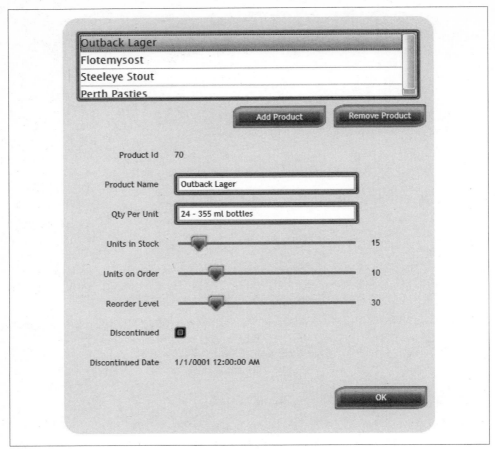

Figure 4-4. ProductView Silverlight control

shown in Example 4-8 demonstrate that all three types of binding modes can be valuable assets when used in the same Silverlight control. The presentation of the XAML in Example 4-8 appears in Figure 4-4. (Refer to Figure 4-5 in the next section for a look at the updated reorder level.)

Lists and Notifications

Entities can implement the INotifyPropertyChanged interface to communicate with the target controls to notify them when a property value has changed. Lists of items can also receive notifications when the contents of the list have changed. The ObservableCollection<T> is a special collection that works well with XAML-based bindings to notify binding targets when a change has been made to a list of items in the ObservableCollection<T>.

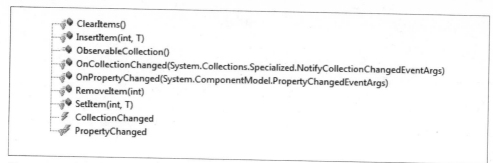

Figure 4-5. ObservableCollection<T> members

ObservableCollection<T>

The ObservableCollection<T>, part of the System.Collections.ObjectModel namespace, implements both the INotifyPropertyChanged and INotifyCollectionChanged interfaces. When a class inherits from the ObservableCollection<T>, the derived class also gets the benefit of the INotifyPropertyChanged interface. This allows the derived class to raise the PropertyChanged event for the ObservableCollection<T>-derived class when a property on the collection has changed.

 Although this section of the chapter focuses on using the Observable Collection<T> for list-based binding and notifications, any collection class that implements the INotifyCollectionChanged interface will also reap the benefits discussed here.

Notice that in Figure 4-5, where the members of ObservableCollection<T> are displayed, the PropertyChanged event is listed as a protected event, which allows classes that inherit from ObservableCollection<T> to implement the event. In fact, most of the members of the ObservableCollection<T> collection are protected, as they exist to help a derived class implement and manage the list of items using the ObservableCollection<T>. The only two public members are the constructor and the CollectionChanged event.

The ObservableCollection<T> also implements the INotifyCollectionChanged interface. This interface contains a single member which is the CollectionChanged event. The ObservableCollection<T> raises this event automatically whenever an item in the ObservableCollection<T> is added or removed from the list. Binding targets in Silverlight receive these notifications and allow list-based controls to update themselves upon receiving a change notification from one of these interfaces when one of their change events fires.

Changing a List<T>

You can bind list-based controls directly to an object source or a list of objects, such as a List<T> or an ObservableCollection<T>. This is especially useful for binding a list of objects to a list-based control, such as the ListBox or DataGrid, or a third-party list-based control, when these controls must be updated when their bound lists change. The ObservableCollection<T> exists to help fill in the gaps of notifying binding targets where a regular list-based object does not notify the binding targets of changes.

For example, Figure 4-6 shows a list of products contained within a List<T>. This List<Product> is set to the DataContext for the ListBox's container control (in this case, the grid layout control). The ListBox is loaded with a List<Product> containing four Product objects. Example 4-9 shows the four Product objects created in the *ProductView.xaml.cs* code file. When items are added to this List<Product>, no notifications are sent and the data-bound targets never update the ListBox contents.

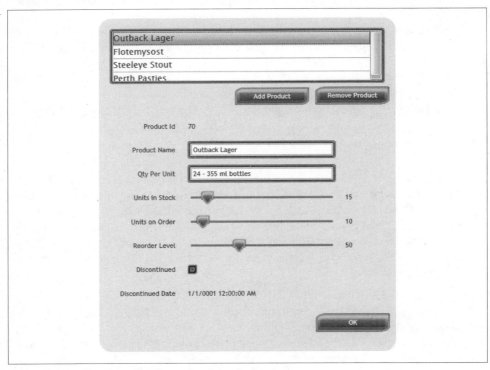

Figure 4-6. ProductView showing updated reorder level

Example 4-9. Creating a list of product entities

```csharp
private List<Product> CreateProductList()
{
    List<Product> products = new List<Product>
```

```csharp
        {
            new Product
            {
                ProductId = 70, ProductName = "Outback Lager",
                QuantityPerUnit = "24 - 355 ml bottles",
                UnitsInStock = 15,  UnitPrice = 15,
                UnitsOnOrder = 10,  ReorderLevel = 30,
                Discontinued = false
            },
            new Product
            {
                ProductId = 71, ProductName = "Flotemysost",
                QuantityPerUnit = "10 - 500 g pkgs.",
                UnitsInStock = 25, UnitPrice = (decimal)21.5,
                UnitsOnOrder = 0, ReorderLevel = 0,
                Discontinued = false
            },
            new Product
            {
                ProductId = 35, ProductName = "Steeleye Stout",
                QuantityPerUnit = "24 - 12 oz bottles",
                UnitsInStock = 20, UnitPrice = (decimal)18,
                UnitsOnOrder = 0, ReorderLevel = 15,
                Discontinued = false
            },
            new Product
            {
                ProductId = 53, ProductName = "Perth Pasties",
                QuantityPerUnit = "48 pieces",
                UnitsInStock = 0, UnitPrice = (decimal)32.80,
                UnitsOnOrder = 0, ReorderLevel = 0,
                Discontinued = true,
                DiscontinuedDate = new DateTime(1996, 7, 4)
            }
        };
    return products;
}
```

```vbnet
Private Function CreateProductList() As List(Of Product)
    Dim products As List(Of Product) = New List(Of Product) _
    (New Product() {New Product With _
        {.ProductId = 70, .ProductName = "Outback Lager", _
        .QuantityPerUnit = "24 - 355 ml bottles", .UnitsInStock = 15, _
        .UnitPrice = 15, .UnitsOnOrder = 10, .ReorderLevel = 30, _
        .Discontinued = False}, _
    New Product With {.ProductId = 71, .ProductName = "Flotemysost", _
        .QuantityPerUnit = "10 - 500 g pkgs.", .UnitsInStock = 25, _
        .UnitPrice = CDec(21.5), .UnitsOnOrder = 0, .ReorderLevel = 0, _
        .Discontinued = False}, _
    New Product With {.ProductId = 35, .ProductName = "Steeleye Stout", _
        .QuantityPerUnit = "24 - 12 oz bottles", .UnitsInStock = 20, _
        .UnitPrice = CDec(18), .UnitsOnOrder = 0, .ReorderLevel = 15, _
        .Discontinued = False}, _
    New Product With {.ProductId = 53, .ProductName = "Perth Pasties", _
        .QuantityPerUnit = "48 pieces", .UnitsInStock = 0, _
        .UnitPrice = CDec(32.80), .UnitsOnOrder = 0, .ReorderLevel = 0, _
```

```
        .Discontinued = True, .DiscontinuedDate = New DateTime(1996, 7, 4)} _
    })
    Return products
End Function
```

When a user clicks the Add Product button, a new `Product` instance is created and is added to the `List<Product>` that is bound to the `DataContext`. When this new `Product` instance is created the `List<Product>` expands to contain it; however, the `ListBox` whose `ItemsSource` is bound to the same `DataContext` does not add the new `Product` to its items collection. As far as the user can tell, the Add Product button did not add a new `Product` instance at all. The code for adding a new `Product` instance simply creates a fake new `Product` with some dummy values, as shown in Example 4-10.

When the `Product` is added to the `productList`, which is set to the `DataContext` of the `ListBox`, the `ListBox` is not made aware of the newly added item. The `ListBox` is fully capable of adding the new item to its contents without refreshing the list. However, for the `ListBox` to add the new item to its list of items, the data source list must raise the `CollectionChanged` event. The `CollectionChanged` event is a member of the `INotifyCollectionChanged` interface, which the `ObservableCollection<T>` implements inherently. The `List<T>` does not implement any notifications on its own.

 The complete code for `List<T>` is in *ProductView.xaml.cs* in the sample code for this chapter.

Example 4-10. Adding a product to the list

C#
```
private void btnAddProduct_Click(object sender, RoutedEventArgs e)
{
    Product product = new Product { Discontinued = false,
        DiscontinuedDate = new DateTime(2008, 7, 11), ProductId = 1111,
        ProductName = "Test Product", QuantityPerUnit = "1",
        ReorderLevel = 10, UnitPrice = 5, UnitsInStock = 20,
        UnitsOnOrder = 0 };
    productList.Add(product);
}
```

VB
```
Private Sub btnAddProduct_Click(ByVal sender As Object, ByVal e As RoutedEventArgs)
    Dim product As Product = New Product With {.Discontinued = False, _
        .DiscontinuedDate = New DateTime(2008, 7, 11), _
        .ProductId = 1111, .ProductName = "Test Product", _
        .QuantityPerUnit = "1", .ReorderLevel = 10, .UnitPrice = 5, _
        .UnitsInStock = 20, .UnitsOnOrder = 0}
    productList.Add(product)
End Sub
```

When a user selects an item from the `ListBox` and clicks the Remove Product button, the item is indeed removed from the data source `List<Product>` that is set to the `DataContext`. However, once again the `List<Product>` does not raise the

CollectionChanged event, so the ListBox does not remove the selected item from its items collection. The ListBox's ItemsSource property is the target of a binding operation. The bound item has been changed (an item was removed from the List<Product>). However, the data source in this case does not raise the Collection Changed event, so the ListBox is never told that one of its items should be removed.

Changing an ObservableCollection<T>

You can modify this example by using an ObservableCollection<T> instead of a List<T> to contain the set of products. You could modify the code in Example 4-9 slightly to create an instance of an ObservableCollection<Product> and to return that instance from the CreateProductList method. The code in Example 4-11 shows the first few lines of the newly revised CreateProductList method to handle the ObservableCollection<Product>.

Example 4-11. Creating an ObservableCollection

```
private ObservableCollection<Product> CreateProductOC()
{
    ObservableCollection<Product> products = new ObservableCollection<Product>
```

```
Private Function CreateProductOC() As ObservableCollection(Of Product)
    Dim products As ObservableCollection(Of Product) = _
        New ObservableCollection(Of Product)
```

The ObservableCollection<T> implements the INotifyCollectionChanged interface, which automatically raises the CollectionChanged event when an item is added or removed from the ObservableCollection<T>'s internal collection. List-based data-bound targets listen for the event. When you change the code for this example to use an ObservableCollection<Product> instead of a List<Product> and the user adds or removes an item from the ListBox, the ListBox listens for the event and adds or removes the item as directed. For example, if the user clicks on the Add Product button several times, the ObservableCollection<Product> will add several new Product instances to the collection, each raising the CollectionChanged event, which causes the ListBox to add the new items to its items collection. To the user, it simply looks like the Add Product button works.

When the user selects an item from the ListBox and clicks the Remove Product button, the code in Example 4-12 is executed and the item is removed from the ObservableCollection<Product>. The ListBox listens for the CollectionChanged event once again and updates the ListBox's items collection. To the user, the ListBox simply removed the selected item. As you can see, it is very easy to implement the ObservableCollection<T> and take advantage of its notifications.

You can find the complete code for `ObservableCollection<T>` in *ProductViewOC.xaml.cs* in the sample code for this chapter.

Example 4-12. Removing a product

```csharp
private void btnRemoveProduct_Click(object sender, RoutedEventArgs e)
{
    Product product = lstProducts.SelectedItem as Product;
    if (product == null)
        return;

    if (productList.Contains(product))
        productList.Remove(product);
}
```

```vbnet
Private Sub btnRemoveProduct_Click(ByVal sender As Object, _
        ByVal e As RoutedEventArgs)
    Dim product As Product = TryCast(lstProducts.SelectedItem, Product)
    If product Is Nothing Then
        Return
    End If

    If productList.Contains(product) Then
        productList.Remove(product)
    End If
End Sub
```

Converters

When binding an entity object source to Silverlight 2 controls, it is often desirable to present the values in the target in a different format from the source. For example, when a date value is stored in a database, you almost always must format the value when you're displaying it in a user interface. You might need to convert this value to an MM/DD/YYYY format to be displayed in a Silverlight user control. Another example might be a string property of an entity that represents a color, such as blue. You might intend to use this value as a `Brush` for a Silverlight 2 control. You must convert these types of values from their native format into a format that is appropriate. Type conversions are common and you can tackle them by creating a class that implements the `IValueConverter` interface.

IValueConverter

The `IValueConverter` interface exposes two methods that must be implemented. The `Convert` and `ConvertBack` methods handle converting a value to and from the target and source of a binding. The `Convert` method morphs the data on its way from *the source to* the target. The `ConvertBack` method morphs the data from the target and back to the source.

Using a converter requires the following steps. First, you must create a converter class that implements the `IValueConverter` interface. Next, you must implement both the `Convert` and `ConvertBack` methods. The `Convert` method converts the value from the source to the target. This conversion is required for all binding modes. The `ConvertBack` method is called in `TwoWay` binding when the value in the target is sent back to the source. If the binding mode is `OneWay` or `OneTime`, the value is never sent from the target back to the source, so the `ConvertBack` method is not used.

Once you have created the converter class and implemented the `IValueConverter` methods, you can apply the converter in an appropriate binding scenario. You must declare an instance of the converter as a resource in the XAML page in order to do this. Then you can set the `Converter` property in the binding syntax to use the converter class instance. For example, the following code snippet declares a converter class instance as a `UserControl` resource:

```
<UserControl.Resources>
    <ListBindings:DateTimeConverter x:Key="myDateTimeConverter" />
</UserControl.Resources>
```

The following applies this converter in a binding operation:

```
Text="{Binding Mode=OneWay, Path=DiscontinuedDate,
        Converter={StaticResource myDateTimeConverter}}"
```

Conversions

Figure 4-6 shows the `ProductView` Silverlight control with its Discontinued Date using the default `DateTime` format. You could convert this value to use a different format to display in the Silverlight control if it applies a class that implements the `IValueConverter` interface. The `Product` class also has a `UnitPrice` property, which is not displayed on the Silverlight control. The `UnitPrice` is stored as a decimal value, but it should be displayed as a currency value with exactly two decimal places. Once you have added the `UnitPrice` to the Silverlight control, along with the conversions, the data will be formatted properly for the user. Example 4-13, which appears in the following section, will build on the `ProductView` control by adding the `UnitPrice` property and using the converters for the `DateTime` and the `Decimal` values. You can find the code for this control, named *ProductViewWithConverter.xaml*, in the code for this chapter.

DateTime conversions

Example 4-13 shows the `DateTimeConverter` class that converts a `DateTime` value to a string value using a specific date format of MM/DD/YYYY. The `Convert` method is implemented and grabs the value parameter which represents the `DateTime` value that is being sent from the source to the target. The `Convert` method intercepts the `DateTime` value and converts it to a formatted string. The `ConvertBack` method is not implemented, because the date value will not be involved in a TwoWay binding operation in this example.

You can use the `targetType` parameter to make sure the binding is operating on the appropriate target type. For example, in this case the target should be a property that is looking for a string value. The `targetType` is especially valuable when converting a value to a specific property type, such as a `Brush` or an enumeration.

Example 4-13. DateTimeConverter

C#
```csharp
public class DateTimeConverter : IValueConverter
{
    public object Convert(object value, Type targetType,
        object parameter, CultureInfo culture)
    {
        DateTime theDate = (DateTime)value;
        string formattedDate = string.Empty;

        if (parameter == null)
            formattedDate = theDate.ToString(culture);
        else
            formattedDate = theDate.ToString(parameter as string, culture);

        return formattedDate;
    }

    public object ConvertBack(object value, Type targetType,
        object parameter, CultureInfo culture)
    {
        throw new System.NotImplementedException();
    }
}
```

VB
```vb
Public Class DateTimeConverter
    Implements IValueConverter
    Public Function Convert(ByVal value As Object, ByVal targetType As Type, _
            ByVal parameter As Object, ByVal culture As CultureInfo) As Object
        Dim theDate As DateTime = CDate(value)
        Dim formattedDate As String = String.Empty

        If parameter Is Nothing Then
            formattedDate = theDate.ToString(culture)
        Else
            formattedDate = theDate.ToString(TryCast(parameter, String), culture)
        End If

        Return formattedDate
    End Function

    Public Function ConvertBack(ByVal value As Object, ByVal targetType As Type, _
            ByVal parameter As Object, ByVal culture As CultureInfo) As Object
        Throw New System.NotImplementedException()
    End Function
End Class
```

The following line adds an instance of the converter to the `UserControl`'s resource section:

```
<ListBindings:DateTimeConverter x:Key="myDateTimeConverter" />
```

The XAML for the `lbDiscontinuedDate` `TextBlock` is modified to include the converter in the binding operation. The resultant XAML for this `TextBlock` will look like the XAML snippet in Example 4-14.

Example 4-14. Using a converter in XAML

```
<TextBlock x:Name="lbDiscontinuedDate" Grid.Column="1" Grid.Row="8"
    Margin="10,5,10,5" HorizontalAlignment="Left" Height="13" Width="240"
    Style="{StaticResource TextBlockReadOnlyStyle}"
    Text="{Binding Mode=OneWay, Path=DiscontinuedDate,
        Converter={StaticResource myDateTimeConverter}}"
        VerticalAlignment="Center" />
```

Currency conversions

The `Grid` panel in Example 4-13 is adjusted to contain the new `tbUnitPrice` `TextBox`. The value must be converted from a decimal to a guaranteed two-decimal value string. The `Convert` method intercepts the decimal value on its way from the source to the target `TextBox`'s `Text` property. Because this `TextBox` is involved in a `TwoWay` binding operation, the `ConvertBack` method intercepts the value on its way back from the target to the source. The XAML snippet in Example 4-15 shows the `tbUnitPrice` `TextBox` code.

Example 4-15. Setting a ConverterParameter

```
<TextBox x:Name="tbUnitPrice" Grid.Column="1" Grid.Row="2"
    Margin="10,5,10,5" HorizontalAlignment="Left" Height="30" Width="240"
    Style="{StaticResource TextBoxStyle}"
    Text="{Binding Mode=TwoWay, Path=UnitPrice,
        Converter={StaticResource myCurrencyConverter}},
        ConverterParameter=C}"/>
```

Notice that a parameter is passed to the converter through the `ConverterParameter` property in the XAML. The `ConverterParameter` property allows XAML to influence how the converter class handles the conversion. In this case, the currency format is passed to the converter.

The following XAML snippet creates the instance of the `CurrencyConverter` class in the resource section of the `UserControl`:

```
<ListBindings:CurrencyConverter x:Key="myCurrencyConverter" />
```

The `CurrencyConverter` class code in Example 4-16 shows the simple conversion from the decimal value to the formatted string value in the `Convert` method. Once these changes are made, the `ProductViewWithConverter` control will display the values, as shown in Figure 4-7.

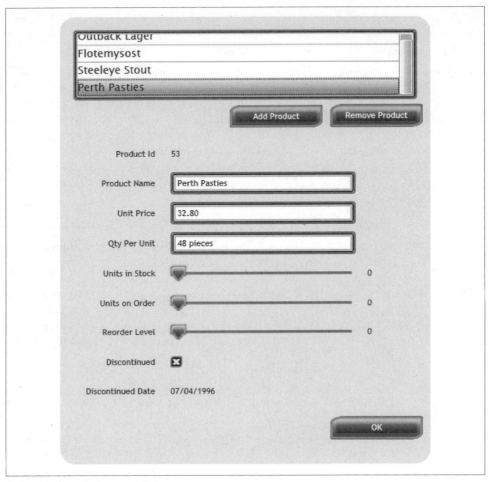

Figure 4-7. ProductViewWithConverter—using converters

Example 4-16. CurrencyConverter

```
public class CurrencyConverter : IValueConverter
{
    public object Convert(object value, Type targetType,
        object parameter, CultureInfo culture)
    {
        decimal amount = System.Convert.ToDecimal(value);
        string c = amount.ToString(parameter as string, culture);
        return c;
    }

    public object ConvertBack(object value, Type targetType,
        object parameter, CultureInfo culture)
    {
```

```
                        throw new System.NotImplementedException();
                    }
                }

  VB    Public Class CurrencyConverter
            Implements IValueConverter
            Public Function Convert(ByVal value As Object, ByVal targetType As Type, _
                    ByVal parameter As Object, ByVal culture As CultureInfo) As Object
                Dim amount As Decimal = System.Convert.ToDecimal(value)
                Dim c As String = amount.ToString(TryCast(parameter, String), culture)
                Return c
            End Function

            Public Function ConvertBack(ByVal value As Object, ByVal targetType As Type, _
                ByVal parameter As Object, ByVal culture As CultureInfo) As Object
                Throw New System.NotImplementedException()
            End Function
        End Class
```

This example shows how you can use converters to intercept and morph values on their way from a source to a target and vice versa. You can use converters to convert from any type of source value to any type of target value, as long as the conversion follows common-sense rules. For example, it would make sense in some cases to convert an enumeration value that represents a color to a `Brush`. However, it would not make sense to convert a `DateTime` value to a slider control's value property. If you use converters appropriately, though, you can use them throughout an application to achieve consistent data conversion to and from bindings.

Summary

Two of the key sources of the power of XAML-based data binding are the `INotifyPropertyChanged` interface and the `ObservableCollection<T>`. These classes provide the means for data source objects to notify data bindings that something about the source has changed. Converters are integral components of the binding process, as they can seamlessly convert values involved in both one-way and two-way binding operations.

CHAPTER 5

WCF, Web Services, and Cross-Domain Policies

Silverlight 2 brings a tremendous number of tools to the client for creation of rich user interfaces. It also has the ability to consume a variety of services across a network or the Internet. The ability to communicate with different types of web services in different ways (through RESTful services, syndicated feeds, and SOAP services, to name a few) allows Silverlight 2 applications to take advantage of the features these services expose. Silverlight 2 clients provide a robust user experience, and the ability to interact with a variety of services makes Silverlight 2 a great choice for interactive and service-based applications.

This chapter will discuss and demonstrate how to create ASMX web services and Windows Communication Foundation (WCF) web services, and how to communicate with them from a Silverlight 2 client application. First you will create a SOAP-based ASMX service, referenced and consumed from a Silverlight 2 application. I will demonstrate several aspects of service-based communication, including how to set up asynchronous communication from Silverlight 2 clients to ASMX and WCF services, implement handlers, consume results, and handle exceptions. This chapter will also discuss how Silverlight 2 clients can create and consume WCF services, and will demonstrate some of the ways in which data can be passed to and from these services. Figure 5-1 shows the discoverable services and that Silverlight 2 can communicate with them.

All services should protect themselves against unintended clients using their services. Cross-domain policies handle this level of protection for ASMX and WCF services as well as for services that do not describe themselves, including REST, RSS, and Plain Old XML (POX)-based services. Both Flash and Silverlight provide an XML file schema that you can design in such a way as to allow and deny clients from using these types of services. This chapter will review how these files work and will provide some tips for creating them.

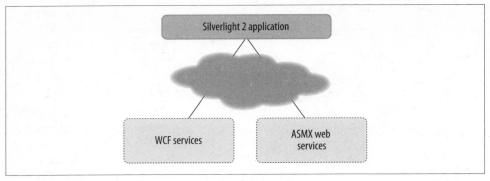

Figure 5-1. Discoverable web services and Silverlight

ASMX Web Services

Interacting with ASMX web services is commonplace today. If you are familiar with creating and consuming ASMX web services, apart from making a few minor adjustments it should be straightforward to create an ASMX web service that a Silverlight 2 client application can consume. For example, consuming an ASMX web service from an ASP.NET client involves adding a reference to the ASMX web service, creating a proxy for it, and making a call to the service either synchronously or asynchronously. One difference is that a Silverlight 2 client can call a web service only asynchronously.

 Some restrictions define which types of services you can use from Silverlight 2 client applications. For example, WCF services must use the `basicHttpBinding` binding, and services supporting custom SOAP headers are not supported.

To use an ASMX web service, first you have to create the service (if one does not exist). Then you must define the service's purpose (the actions or methods that it exposes). Next, the Silverlight 2 client application must reference the service. Once the Silverlight 2 application has a reference to the service, it creates a proxy for the service and handlers for the asynchronous invocation of its methods. Finally, the Silverlight 2 application can invoke the service and consume its results.

Creating an ASMX Web Service

Generally, developers will either communicate with an existing web service or create a web service for their own purposes. This chapter will demonstrate a few variations of web services and how you can communicate with them from Silverlight 2 clients. First, we'll examine what you need in order to create an ASMX web service and communicate with it from a Silverlight 2 client application.

The example Silverlight 2 application we'll create will allow a user to send an email message. Because the Silverlight client does not have access to the `System.Net.Mail` namespace, it must communicate with a server that allows it to send email messages. Otherwise, the client could invoke the default mail application and use it to send a message. However, a server-based solution is often more advantageous, as it allows for far more customization.

The Silverlight 2 application shown in Figure 5-2 simply allows the user to enter the basic information for sending an email message. When the user enters the information for the email message and clicks the Send via ASMX button, the Silverlight application creates a proxy to the ASMX web service, adds an event handler to handle the return of the ASMX web service call, and invokes the web service asynchronously. The web service is passed the information from the Silverlight client application, which the service then uses to send the email to the recipient(s).

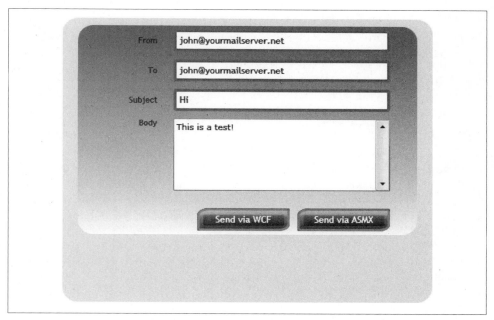

Figure 5-2. Silverlight email client

Getting Started with the Example

The example solution is contained in the Chapter 5 code folder. The solution is named `EmailServiceSample` and it contains five projects, as shown in Figure 5-3. The `SilverlightEmailClient` project is a Silverlight 2 project that contains the Silverlight client shown in Figure 5-2. The `SilverlightEmailClientWeb` project is a web application project that hosts the Silverlight application; you'll use it simply for testing the

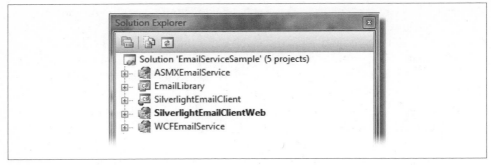

Figure 5-3. The EmailServiceSample solution

Silverlight client. The `ASMXEmailService` project contains the ASMX web service that will be called from the `SilverlightEmailClient` project. The `EmailLibrary` project contains a simple .NET class named `Mail` that the sample code uses to send an email message using the `System.Net.Mail` namespace's `MailMessage` class.

The final project is the `WCFEmailService` project. This project contains the WCF web service that provides functionality equivalent to that of the `ASMXEmailService`, but instead of using ASMX, it uses WCF. We will discuss the `WCFEmailService` project later in this chapter.

Creating the ASMX Web Service

The `ASMXEmailService` project is an ASP.NET Web Application project that will use IIS to host the ASMX service. It could be a website, too, but for this example it uses the Cassini web server to host the service. The project contains a single ASMX web service named `EmailService.asmx`. Example 5-1 shows the contents of the `EmailService` class, which simply defines a web service method named `SendMailMessage` that accepts the required mail message information. The `EmailService` web service defines its namespace as *http://www.silverlight-data.com* and decorates the `SendMailMessage` method with the `WebMethod` attribute. This attribute declares that this method will be accessible from clients that reference the `EmailService` web service.

I've separated the `EmailLibrary.Mail` class into its own project, because it will also be called by the WCF web service used later in this chapter.

Example 5-1. The EmailService class

```
using System.Web.Services;
using EmailLibrary;

namespace ASMXEmailService
{
```

```
[WebService(Namespace = "http://www.silverlight-data.com/")]
[WebServiceBinding(ConformsTo = WsiProfiles.BasicProfile1_1)]
[System.ComponentModel.ToolboxItem(false)]
public class EmailService : System.Web.Services.WebService
{
    [WebMethod]
    public void SendMailMessage(string from, string to,
        string subject, string body)
    {
        new Mail().SendMessage(from, to, subject, body);
    }
}
}
```

```
Imports System.Web.Services
Imports EmailLibrary

Namespace ASMXEmailService
    <WebService(Namespace := "http://www.silverlight-data.com/"), _
        WebServiceBinding(ConformsTo := WsiProfiles.BasicProfile1_1), _
        System.ComponentModel.ToolboxItem(False)> _
    Public Class EmailService
        Inherits System.Web.Services.WebService
        <WebMethod> _
        Public Sub SendMailMessage(ByVal from As String, _
            ByVal [to] As String, ByVal subject As String, _
            ByVal body As String)
            CType(New Mail(), Mail).SendMessage(From, [to], subject, body)
        End Sub
    End Class
End Namespace
```

The SendMailMessage method calls the EmailLibrary.Mail class's SendMessage method.
Example 5-2 shows the contents of the Mail class and its SendMessage method, which
sends the message to a list of recipients. This code lacks some easy-to-add exception
handling and sophistication, but that is not the focus of this chapter.

Notice that this code requires that the SMTP port and host be set to the
appropriate settings for the SMTP server that will be used. You must
change these to the correct settings before trying the sample code.

Example 5-2. The Mail class

```
using System;
using System.Net.Mail;

namespace EmailLibrary
{
    public class Mail
    {
        private readonly char[] separator = { ';' };
        private readonly string host = "mail.yoursmtpserver.net";
```

```csharp
        private readonly int port = 25;

        public void SendMessage(string from, string to,
            string subject, string body)
        {
            using (MailMessage message =
            new MailMessage { From = new MailAddress(from),
                          Body = body, Subject = subject })
            {
                string[] addresses = to.Split(separator,
                        StringSplitOptions.RemoveEmptyEntries);
                foreach (string t in addresses)
                    message.To.Add(new MailAddress(t));
                SmtpClient smtpClient = new SmtpClient(host, port);
                smtpClient.Send(message);
            }
        }
    }
}
```

VB
```vbnet
Imports System
Imports System.Net.Mail

Namespace EmailLibrary
    Public Class Mail
        Private ReadOnly separator() As Char = { ";"c }
        Private ReadOnly host As String = "mail.yourmailserver.net"
        Private ReadOnly port As Integer = 25

        Public Sub SendMessage(ByVal from As String, ByVal [to] As String, _
                ByVal subject As String, ByVal body As String)
            Using message As MailMessage = New MailMessage _
                With {.From = New MailAddress(From), .Body = body, _
                .Subject = subject}
                Dim addresses() As String = [to].Split(separator, _
                        StringSplitOptions.RemoveEmptyEntries)
                For Each t As String In addresses
                    message.To.Add(New MailAddress(t))
                Next t
                Dim smtpClient As New SmtpClient(host, port)
                smtpClient.Send(message)
            End Using
        End Sub
    End Class
End Namespace
```

This is all you need to create an ASMX web service that a Silverlight application can consume. The next step is to reference the service.

Referencing an ASMX Web Service

Before you can use the service, the Silverlight client application must add a service reference to the ASMX web service that was created. You can add a service reference by going to the Project Explorer, right-clicking the Service Reference node for the `SilverlightEmailClient` project, and selecting the Add Service Reference menu option. A window will open, which you can use to search for (or discover) any services available on the computer. Alternatively, you can enter a URL to a specific web service. Because the `EmailService.asmx` service is on the same computer as this solution, you can click the Discover button. After a few moments, the Silverlight 2 client application will find the `EmailService.asmx` service and you can select it. This window will search for any service that exposes Web Services Description Language (WSDL), which makes it discoverable. Both WCF web services and ASMX web services support SOAP 1.1 and are discoverable, so you can find them through this window.

You can add as a service reference from a Silverlight 2 application any SOAP service that is discoverable and supports the basic profile of SOAP 1.1. Discoverable services are those that support WSDL. These include both WCF services and ASMX services, as shown in this chapter. You can access services that do not describe themselves (such as REST, POX, and RSS) via `WebClient` and `HttpWebRequest`, which we will discuss in later chapters.

Figure 5-4 shows the `EmailService.asmx` service selected, and its services and methods expanded to show the `SendMailMessage` web method that was just created. The service is renamed to `ASMXEmailService`, which will become the namespace for the proxy class we will create to invoke the ASMX web service.

 Notice that the address of the web service shown in Figure 5-4 indicates that it is using the Cassini web server on port 8242. Cassini is the ASP.NET Development Web Server. When you're creating a web application using Cassini, the port number may vary.

The `ASMXEmailService` is a web application that runs under Cassini and assigns a port automatically. If the service was created under a website instead, it would run under IIS and not Cassini.

Returning ObservableCollection<T>

The Advanced button (shown in the bottom left of Figure 5-4) allows you to customize the reference to the web service. Figure 5-5 shows how this option allows you to customize the `Collection` type that we will use for collection-based return values. This means that if a web service returns a `List<T>`, you can configure the service reference to convert the `List<T>` automatically to an `ObservableCollection<T>` if you want. You can configure several options, including `Array`, `List`, `Collection`, and `ObservableCollection`. This is important, because it makes it easy to use services that return lists of entities with the data-binding features of an `ObservableCollection`.

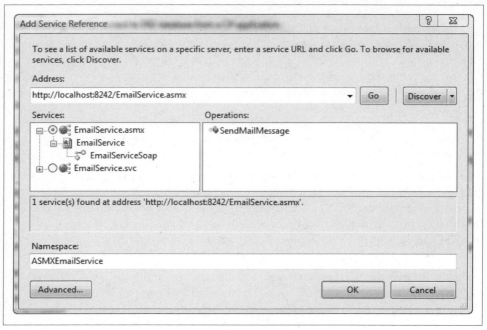

Figure 5-4. Adding the ASMX email service reference

Consuming an ASMX Web Service

Once a Silverlight application has a service reference to an ASMX web service, it can invoke the web service through a proxy object. The basic steps for invoking a web service are to add the service reference, create the instance of the proxy object, add an event handler for its completion event, and invoke the web service asynchronously.

Bindings Again

The Silverlight application contains four TextBox controls that represent the To address, From address, Subject, and Body of the email message. The To address can contain a series of email addresses delimited by a semicolon.

You can manually load the default values into the TextBox controls by setting each TextBox's Text property value. After the user has entered the values, you can retrieve the values from the TextBox controls to pass them to the web service's web method by manually pulling the values from the controls and into local variables.

Although this technique works, another option is to take advantage of the XAML-based binding techniques. A MessageInfo class exists in the example code for the purpose of storing the values from these fields and acting as a mediator for the TextBox controls. Example 5-3 shows the code for the MessageInfo class. An instance of the

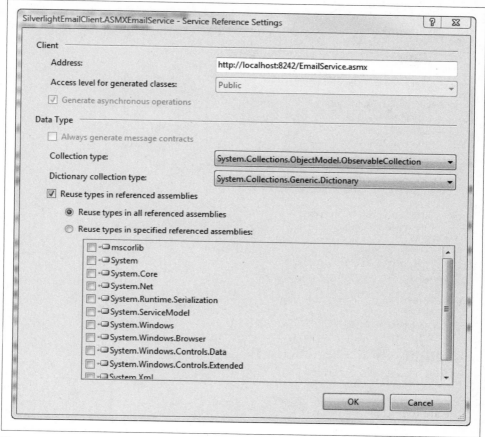

Figure 5-5. Service reference settings

`MessageInfo` class is created and the default values are initialized in the constructor of the `EmailClient` Silverlight 2 control. Example 5-4 shows a snippet of the control's XAML and its bindings.

Example 5-3. MessageInfo class

```C#
public class MessageInfo
{
    public string FromAddress { get; set; }
    public string ToAddress { get; set; }
    public string Subject { get; set; }
    public string Body  { get; set; }

    public string BodyWithDateTag
    {
        get { return string.Format("{0}\n\nSent on: {1}",
            this.Body, DateTime.Now.ToString("yyyy-MM-dd HH:mm:ss")); }
```

```vb
        }
    }
```

VB
```vb
    Public Class MessageInfo
        Private privateFromAddress As String
        Public Property FromAddress () As String
            Get
                Return privateFromAddress
            End Get
            Set(ByVal value As String)
                privateFromAddress = value
            End Set
        End Property
        Private privateToAddress As String
        Public Property ToAddress() As String
            Get
                Return privateToAddress
            End Get
            Set(ByVal value As String)
                privateToAddress = value
            End Set
        End Property
        Private privateSubject As String
        Public Property Subject() As String
            Get
                Return privateSubject
            End Get
            Set(ByVal value As String)
                privateSubject = value
            End Set
        End Property
        Private privateBody As String
        Public Property Body() As String
            Get
                Return privateBody
            End Get
            Set(ByVal value As String)
                privateBody = value
            End Set
        End Property

        Public ReadOnly Property BodyWithDateTag() As String
            Get
                Return String.Format("{0}" & Constants.vbLf + Constants.vbLf & _
                    "Sent on: {1}", Me.Body, _
                    DateTime.Now.ToString("yyyy-MM-dd HH:mm:ss"))
            End Get
        End Property
    End Class
```

Once the instance is created, it is set to the DataContext of the Grid layout panel that contains the four TextBox controls. Each TextBox control's Text property is bound to the corresponding property of the MessageInfo instance using TwoWay binding. This setup eliminates the need to manually push or pull the values into and out of the

TextBox controls. Instead, you can use the `messageInfo` instance variable to grab or set the values.

Example 5-4. Silverlight 2 EmailClient control XAML

```
<TextBox Grid.Row="0" Grid.Column="1" Margin="11,5,45,5"
    Style="{StaticResource TextBoxStyle}" x:Name="tbFrom"
    HorizontalAlignment="Stretch"
    Text="{Binding Mode=TwoWay, Path=FromAddress}"/>

<TextBox Grid.Row="1" Grid.Column="1" Margin="11,5,45,5"
    Style="{StaticResource TextBoxStyle}"
    x:Name="tbTo" HorizontalAlignment="Stretch"
    Text="{Binding Mode=TwoWay, Path=ToAddress}"/>

<TextBox Grid.Row="2" Grid.Column="1" Margin="11,5,45,5"
    Style="{StaticResource TextBoxStyle}" x:Name="tbSubject"
    HorizontalAlignment="Stretch"
    Text="{Binding Mode=TwoWay, Path=Subject}"/>

<TextBox Grid.Row="3" Grid.Column="1" Margin="11,5,45,5"
    Style="{StaticResource TextBoxStyle}" x:Name="tbBody"
    HorizontalAlignment="Stretch" VerticalAlignment="Top" Height="100"
    VerticalScrollBarVisibility="Visible" AcceptsReturn="True" TextWrapping="Wrap"
    Text="{Binding Mode=TwoWay, Path=Body}"/>
```

The `MessageInfo` class contains a read-only public property named `BodyWithDateTag`, which does not refer directly to a backing property. Instead, the `BodyWithDateTag` returns the message's `Body` property along with a date and timestamp, mostly for debugging purposes.

The `EmailClient` constructor (shown in Example 5-5) also adds the `Click` event handler for the `Button` named `btnSendViaASMX`. The `btnSendViaASMX_Click` method handles the click event when the user is ready to send the message. This method will create the proxy and make the call to the web service.

Example 5-5. Binding setup

```csharp
public partial class EmailClient : UserControl
{
    private MessageInfo messageInfo;

    public EmailClient()
    {
        InitializeComponent();
        btnSendViaASMX.Click += new RoutedEventHandler(btnSendViaASMX_Click);
        messageInfo = new MessageInfo
            { FromAddress = "john@yourmailserver.net",
            ToAddress = "john@yourmailserver.net" };
```

```
        EmailClientLayout.DataContext = messageInfo;
    }
```

VB
```
Partial Public Class EmailClient
    Inherits UserControl
    Private messageInfo As MessageInfo

    Public Sub New()
        InitializeComponent()
        AddHandler btnSendViaASMX.Click, AddressOf btnSendViaASMX_Click
        messageInfo = New MessageInfo With _
            {.FromAddress = "john@yourmailserver.net", _
            .ToAddress = "john@yourmailserver.net"}
        EmailClientLayout.DataContext = messageInfo
    End Sub
End Sub
```

Creating a Proxy

The proxy object is the portal to the web service and all of the methods that it exposes. Example 5-6 shows the btnSendViaASMX_Click method, which handles the click event when the user sends the email. After a quick check to make sure the fields are filled in, an instance of the proxy class EmailServiceSoapClient is created. This class allows access to the methods in the web service asynchronously. The two key members of the proxy class are the SendMailMessageCompleted event and the SendMailMessageAsync method. Notice that there is no method named SendMailMessage. This is because no synchronous web service invocations are allowed from Silverlight 2 applications. All calls are asynchronous so that the user is not frozen from the application while waiting for the call to return. Each web method will get an event and an asynchronous method in the proxy class.

Example 5-6. ASMX web method invocation

C#
```
private void btnSendViaASMX_Click(object sender, RoutedEventArgs e)
{
    lbMessage.Text = string.Empty;
    if (!ValidInfo()) return;

    EmailServiceSoapClient proxy = new EmailServiceSoapClient();
    proxy.SendMailMessageCompleted += proxy_SendMailMessageCompleted_viaASMX;
    proxy.SendMailMessageAsync(messageInfo.FromAddress, messageInfo.ToAddress,
        messageInfo.Subject, messageInfo.BodyWithDateTag);
}
```

VB
```
Private Sub btnSendViaASMX_Click(ByVal sender As Object, _
        ByVal e As RoutedEventArgs)
    lbMessage.Text = String.Empty
    If (Not ValidInfo()) Then
        Return
    End If

    Dim proxy As New EmailServiceSoapClient()
    AddHandler proxy.SendMailMessageCompleted, _
        AddressOf proxy_SendMailMessageCompleted_viaASMX
```

```
    proxy.SendMailMessageAsync(messageInfo.FromAddress, messageInfo.ToAddress, _
        messageInfo.Subject, messageInfo.BodyWithDateTag)
End Sub
```

Asynchronous Invocation

Once the proxy has been created, the next step is to add an event handler for the SendMailMessageCompleted event. This event handler will be called when the asynchronous call to the web service's server-side SendMailMessage method returns. Once the handler is defined, the call to SendMailMessageAsync is executed. This method passes the values from the messageInfo instance's property values to the web service. Because the binding technique was used, there is no need to pull the values manually from the TextBox controls. The binding already sent the values to the messageInfo instance when the user changed the values in the TextBox controls.

Asynchronous Completion

When the ASMX web service has completed its task, the SendMailCompleted_viaASMX method is executed. It receives the sender and a set of AsyncCompletedEventArgs in an instance named e. The AsyncCompletedEventArgs contains the result if the web method has a return value. The result's type is the same type that the web method returns. The returned value can be accessed through the Result property of the e instance. This is useful when performing searches for one or more items from a web service, for example.

Our example called a web method that has no return value, so the code does not check for the Result property. However, another important AsyncCompletedEventArgs property is the Error property. You can check the Error property to see whether anything went wrong during the call. In Example 5-7, the code checks the e.Error property value to see whether an error occurred. If one did, a message is formatted and displayed in a TextBlock on the Silverlight control.

Example 5-7. ASMX completion event handler

`C#`
```
private void proxy_SendMailMessageCompleted_viaASMX(
        object sender, AsyncCompletedEventArgs e)
{
    string msg = "Message was ";
    if (e.Error != null)
        msg += string.Format("not sent.\n\n{0}", e.Error.Message);
    else
        msg += "sent using ASMX";
    lbMessage.Text = msg;
}
```

`VB`
```
Private Sub proxy_SendMailMessageCompleted_viaASMX(ByVal sender As Object, _
        ByVal e As AsyncCompletedEventArgs)
    Dim msg As String = "Message was "
    If e.Error IsNot Nothing Then
        msg &= String.Format("not sent." & Constants.vbLf + Constants.vbLf & _
            "{0}", e.Error.Message)
```

```
        Else
            msg &= "sent using ASMX"
        End If
        lbMessage.Text = msg
End Sub
```

Running the ASMX Web Service

The example code has an ASMX web service that contains a web method that sends an email message. The Silverlight control has a service reference to the ASMX web service, an instance of the proxy class, and the code to send the message. The Silverlight application is now ready to be compiled and executed. When the application is run and the user enters valid email addresses, a subject, and a message body and then clicks the Send via ASMX button, the expected result is a success message. However, an error occurs, as shown in Figure 5-6.

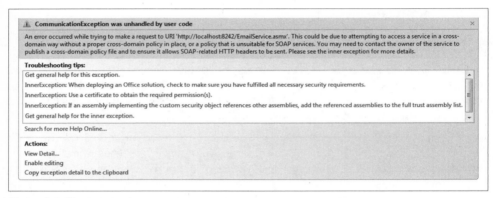

Figure 5-6. Communication error

In this case, the error is indicating that a file was not found on the server. The remote server that the error message refers to is the server that is hosting the ASMX web service. This error message may sound like Silverlight 2 cannot find the web service; however, this is not the case. The error is occurring because Silverlight cannot find the cross-domain policy file on the web service's server. To fix this problem, first you need to understand why the problem occurred and how to diagnose it; then you can solve the cross-domain access issues.

Cross-Domain Calls and Policies

Silverlight enforces a level of protection so that it cannot be used to invoke web services that are on a different domain than the server that hosts the Silverlight application. For example, a Silverlight 2 application that is hosted on *silverlight-data.com* can request services that are also hosted on *silverlight-data.com*. However, if a Silverlight 2

---

application that is hosted on *yourmailserver.net* requests a service that is hosted on *silverlight-data.com*, by default the application's request will not be permitted (see Figure 5-7).

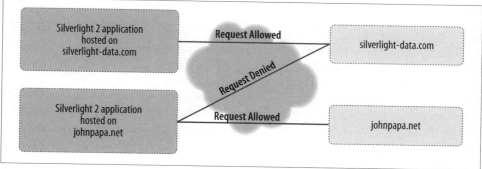

Figure 5-7. Cross-domain access

Understanding Cross-Domain Restrictions

As a security precaution, Silverlight does not allow calls across domain boundaries. By default, this measure prevents Silverlight applications from accessing any web service that is hosted on a domain or domain-and-port combination that is different from the domain that hosts the Silverlight application. The target site can specify which domains can access its services if it implements the Silverlight policy file (*clientaccesspolicy.xml*) or the Flash policy file (*crossdomain.xml*) at the website's root. At least one of these files must exist in the website's root. It is important to remember that the policy file must be placed at the website's root, and not at the web application's root.

Silverlight is a browser plug-in, so it adheres to the same standards as browsers, in that it enforces the site-of-origin restriction across all Silverlight web requests. This means Silverlight is aware that cross-domain HTTP requests can be harmful if the target server does not want them. Silverlight enforces the site-of-origin restriction for ASMX web services, WCF web services, and all `WebClient` and `HttpWebRequest` calls.

Crossing the Boundary

Getting back to the error in the `EmailClient` Silverlight application, the problem is occurring because the `EmailClient` Silverlight application is trying to access a web service on a different domain. In this case, both domains are on the *http://localhost* server; however, both use a different port number (since both projects were set up to use the Cassini web server). The `EmailClient` Silverlight application is hosted on the *http://localhost:8249* server and the `ASMXEmailService` is hosted on *http://localhost:8242*. If the Silverlight application and the web service were hosted on the same domain, the error would not have occurred.

The ports that the Cassini web server assigns are not always consistent. For example, when you run the EmailClient application, you may have a different port number assigned.

One solution is to move the Silverlight application and the web service to the same domain and not to use Cassini. A more practical solution is to implement one of the cross-domain policy files. When a Silverlight application makes a request across a domain boundary, Silverlight requests the *clientaccesspolicy.xml* file from the target server. If it does not find this file, it then requests the *crossdomain.xml* file from the target server. If it doesn't find this file either, an exception is thrown and the resultant 404 error will likely appear to the user (as shown earlier in Figure 5-6).

Watching the Requests

Debugging cross-domain issues is much easier using a tool such as Fiddler2 (for all browsers), Firebug (a plug-in for Firefox), or the Web Development Helper (an Internet Explorer plug-in) to track the network traffic of the requests. These tools show the requests the client application made and the status of those requests. For the EmailClient Silverlight application that threw the error shown in Figure 5-6, these tools can help clarify the error. The communication error refers to a file that is not found. The files that are not found are the *clientaccesspolicy.xml* file and the *crossdomain.xml* file.

Figure 5-8 shows the EmailClient Silverlight application running the Web Development Helper tool with logging turned on. Notice that the first request is made for the *clientaccesspolicy.xml* file and it results in a status of 404 (File Not Found). The next request is for the *crossdomain.xml* file and again the status is 404. After both of these files are not found, Silverlight throws an exception and the web service request is halted.

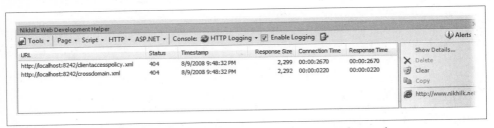

Figure 5-8. Watching network requests with the Web Development Helper tool

Again, it is important to remember that the policy file must be placed at the website's root, not at the web application's root. If a Silverlight application returns a 404 error during a web service call, using the Web Development Helper tool or Fiddler2 to watch the requests can help you debug the problem. These tools will show the exact location where Silverlight is looking for the files, which can clarify whether the file was placed in the wrong location (perhaps incorrectly at the web application root instead of the at appropriate website root).

Silverlight Policy File

The solution to the 404 problem with the `EmailClient` Silverlight application is to create a *clientaccesspolicy.xml* file in the website's root. Because the website is hosted in Cassini, you cannot simply place the file at the *http://localhost* server. Instead, you must place the file at the root of the combination of the server and the port number. The easiest way to do this is to place the file in the root of the web application project through Visual Studio. This solves the problem of where to place the file. The next step is to determine what the file should contain.

Example 5-8 shows a *clientaccesspolicy.xml* file that allows all requests from all domains to all services on the website that hosts the *clientaccesspolicy.xml* file. This is a completely relaxed permission set and you should not use it in production. You should tighten the *clientaccesspolicy.xml* file's settings so that unwanted requests are denied.

Example 5-8. The clientaccesspolicy.xml file for ASMXEmailService's website

```
<?xml version="1.0" encoding="utf-8"?>
<access-policy>
  <cross-domain-access>
    <policy>
      <allow-from http-request-headers="*">
        <domain uri="*"/>
      </allow-from>
      <grant-to>
        <resource path="/" include-subpaths="true"/>
      </grant-to>
    </policy>
  </cross-domain-access>
</access-policy>
```

You can enforce four basic restrictions in the *clientaccesspolicy.xml* file:

- Requesting domain's URI
- Request headers
- Path on the target website
- Allow subpaths on the target website (`boolean` value)

The `uri` property of the `domain` element is set to allow all domains access to any services on the target website. Also, a list of domains can be specified. Example 5-8 shows a *clientaccesspolicy.xml* file that allows requests to come only from the *silverlight-data .com* domain. You can add additional domains if you want by adding additional domain elements.

Example 5-9 shows that only services in the `MyAwesomeServices` path will be allowed and that all subpaths under `MyAwesomeServices` are also allowed. You can add additional paths if needed. The request headers can also be restricted, as shown in Example 5-9, through the `http-request-headers` property.

Example 5-9. A more restrictive clientaccesspolicy.xml

```xml
<?xml version="1.0" encoding="utf-8"?>
<access-policy>
  <cross-domain-access>
    <policy>
      <allow-from http-request-headers="SOAPAction, Content-Type">
        <domain uri="http://silverlight-data.com "/>
      </allow-from>
      <grant-to>
        <resource path="/MyAwesomeServices/" include-subpaths="true"/>
      </grant-to>
    </policy>
  </cross-domain-access>
</access-policy>
```

Once the policy file is created and added to the website's root (as shown in Figure 5-9), the `EmailClient` Silverlight application can access the ASMX web service and send the email message. A quick look at the Web Development Helper tool when running the application shows that the *clientaccesspolicy.xml* file is found and the status is good, as shown in Figure 5-10.

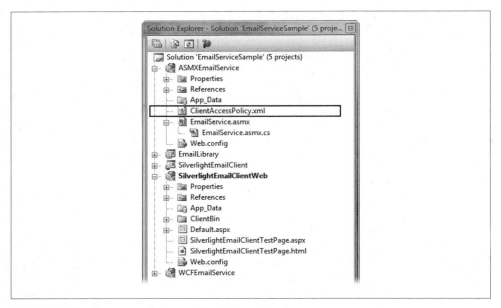

Figure 5-9. The clientaccesspolicy.xml file in the web's root

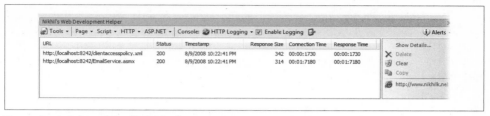

Figure 5-10. Successful call of EmailService.asmx

The crossdomain.xml File

If Silverlight sees that the call to a web service is on a different domain or on a different port, it will first look for the *clientaccesspolicy.xml* or *crossdomain.xml* file. The *crossdomain.xml* file is an older format that was introduced for Flash. The *crossdomain.xml* file shown in Example 5-10 is located at *http://www.amazon.com/crossdomain.xml* and restricts its services to be callable only by the Amazon.com websites listed in the file.

Example 5-10. A crossdomain.xml file example

```
<?xml version="1.0" ?>
  <!DOCTYPE cross-domain-policy (View Source for full doctype...)>
  <cross-domain-policy>
 <allow-access-from domain="*.amazon.com" secure="true" />
   <allow-access-from domain="amazon.com" secure="true" />
   <allow-access-from domain="www.amazon.com" secure="true" />
   <allow-access-from domain="pre-prod.amazon.com" secure="true" />
   <allow-access-from domain="devo.amazon.com" secure="true" />
   <allow-access-from domain="anon.amazon.speedera.net" secure="true" />
   <allow-access-from domain="*.images-amazon.com" secure="true" />
   <allow-access-from domain="*.ssl-images-amazon.com" secure="true" />
   <allow-access-from domain="*.amazon.ca" secure="true" />
   <allow-access-from domain="*.amazon.de" secure="true" />
   <allow-access-from domain="*.amazon.fr" secure="true" />
   <allow-access-from domain="*.amazon.jp" secure="true" />
   <allow-access-from domain="*.amazon.co.jp" secure="true" />
   <allow-access-from domain="*.amazon.uk" secure="true" />
   <allow-access-from domain="*.amazon.co.uk" secure="true" />
  </cross-domain-policy>
```

Silverlight 2 looks for both the *clientaccesspolicy.xml* and *crossdomain.xml* files, because many sites such as Amazon.com, Flickr.com, and Ebay.com use *crossdomain.xml* already but do not implement *clientaccesspolicy.xml*. This allows developers of the trusted domains listed in *crossdomain.xml* to use the services of these sites without having to wait for the sites to implement *clientaccesspolicy.xml*.

Cross-Domain Summary

If a cross-domain service request is made and an error is thrown, a number of things could have caused that error. To rectify the situation, first make sure the *clientaccesspolicy.xml* file contains the appropriate access. Second, use a tool such as the Web Development Helper to determine whether the *clientaccesspolicy.xml* file is found. If it is not found, verify the location in which Silverlight is looking for the file. It will be looking for the file in the website's root. Third, if the file does exist but it is not in the location that Silverlight is looking, move the file to the website's root.

A common mistake is to place the *clientaccesspolicy.xml* file in the web application's root instead of in the website's root. For example, *http://silverlight-data.com* is the website root (the proper place for the *clientaccesspolicy.xml* file), whereas *http://silver light-data.com/samples* is a web application root (not the proper place for *clientaccesspolicy.xml*).

Silverlight checks for the cross-domain policy files on any request to a service on a domain other than the domain that hosts the Silverlight application. This is not limited to ASMX web service requests. Any request for any service, including ASMX web services, WCF web services, REST services, POX services, and any other service, triggers Silverlight to look for the *clientaccesspolicy.xml* file on the target website.

Creating a Silverlight-Enabled WCF Service

You can modify the sample application shown throughout this chapter to use a WCF web service instead of an ASMX web service. In this section, I will demonstrate a few of the differences in setting up a WCF web service and invoking it from a Silverlight 2 client application.

Creating the WCF Web Service

You can create WCF web services that Silverlight 2 clients can consume either by creating a WCF web service using the default WCF service file template, or by using a Silverlight-enabled WCF Service file template. A standard WCF service file template uses the `wsHttpBinding` binding. You must change this to `basicHttpBinding` for Silverlight 2 to be able to communicate with the WCF web service, because Silverlight 2 supports only `basicHttpBinding`. If a WCF web service is created using the Silverlight-enabled WCF Service file template, `basicHttpBinding` is set by default.

You can modify the `EmailClient` application to call a WCF web service. The first step is to create the new WCF web service. The sample code for this chapter contains an IIS web application running under Cassini, named `WCFEmailService` (an IIS website would also work). You can create a new WCF web service by right-clicking the `WCFEmailService` project's node in the Project Explorer, choosing Add New Item, and selecting "Silverlight-enabled WCF Service". Figure 5-11 shows the WCF web service being named *EmailService.svc*.

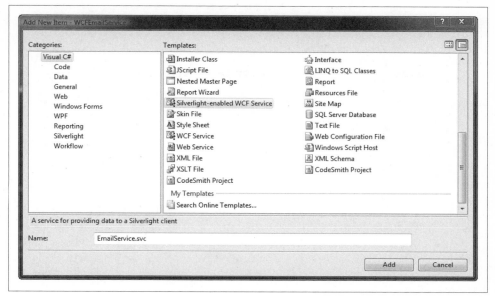

Figure 5-11. Creating EmailService.svc

Bindings

The Silverlight-enabled WCF Service file template sets up a few items automatically that are geared for WCF web services that Silverlight clients will consume. First, the binding for the endpoints is set by default to basicHttpBinding. A WCF web service that is created using the standard WCF service file template (also shown but not selected in Figure 5-11) will set the binding of the endpoints to wsHttpBinding. Currently, Silverlight 2 does not support any binding other than basicHttpbinding, so if a WCF service is created using the standard file template, you must change the binding to basicHttpBinding.

Example 5-11 shows the WCF section of the *web.config* file for the WCFEmailService project. Notice that the binding is set to basicHttpBinding for the service named WCFEmailService.EmailService.

Example 5-11. The web.config configuration for the WCF service

```
<system.serviceModel>
    <behaviors>
        <serviceBehaviors>
            <behavior name="WCFEmailService.EmailServiceBehavior">
                <serviceMetadata httpGetEnabled="true" />
                <serviceDebug includeExceptionDetailInFaults="false" />
            </behavior>
        </serviceBehaviors>
    </behaviors>
    <serviceHostingEnvironment aspNetCompatibilityEnabled="true" />
```

```
    <services>
        <service behaviorConfiguration="WCFEmailService.EmailServiceBehavior"
            name="WCFEmailService.EmailService">
            <endpoint address="" binding="basicHttpBinding"
            contract="WCFEmailService.IEmailService" />
            <endpoint address="mex" binding="mexHttpBinding"
            contract="IMetadataExchange" />
        </service>
    </services>
</system.serviceModel>
</configuration>
```

WCF Service Setup

Example 5-12 shows the WCF service that is created from the Silverlight-enabled WCF Service file template. The `Service1` class is created and properly decorated with a `ServiceContract` attribute which designates this class as being a service that can be requested. All public methods that are intended to be called for a service must be decorated with the `OperationContract` attribute. Where ASMX web services designate public methods with the `WebMethod` attribute, WCF services use the `OperationContract` attribute.

Example 5-12. Starting point for Silverlight-enabled WCF service

C#
```
using System;
using System.Linq;
using System.Runtime.Serialization;
using System.ServiceModel;
using System.ServiceModel.Activation;

namespace WCFEmailService
{
    [ServiceContract(Namespace = "")]
    [AspNetCompatibilityRequirements
        (RequirementsMode = AspNetCompatibilityRequirementsMode.Allowed)]
    public class Service1
    {
        [OperationContract]
        public void DoWork()
        {
            // Add your operation implementation here
            return;
        }

        // Add more operations here and mark them with [OperationContract]
    }
}
```

VB
```
Imports System
Imports System.Linq
Imports System.Runtime.Serialization
Imports System.ServiceModel
Imports System.ServiceModel.Activation
```

```
Namespace WCFEmailService
    <ServiceContract(Namespace := ""), _
        AspNetCompatibilityRequirements( _
        RequirementsMode := AspNetCompatibilityRequirementsMode.Allowed)> _
    Public Class Service1
        <OperationContract> _
        Public Sub DoWork()
            ' Add your operation implementation here
            Return
        End Sub

        ' Add more operations here and mark them with [OperationContract]
    End Class
End Namespace
```

The template also sets up the configuration for the WCF service and its contract in the
web.config file. One side effect of using the Silverlight-enabled WCF Service file template that is worth noting is that it does not create an interface for the
`ServiceContract` by default. You can do this easily, however, by manually creating an
interface (e.g., `IService1`) and decorating the `IService1` interface with the
`ServiceContract` attribute instead of decorating the `Service1` class.

For example, when the `EmailService` WCF service is created from the
Silverlight-enabled WCF Service file template, you can modify it to use an interface
called `IEmailService`. Example 5-13 shows that the `EmailService` class is not decorated
with the `ServiceContract` attribute, nor is its `SendMailMessage` method decorated with
the `OperationContract` attribute. Instead, the `EmailService` class implements the
`IEmailService` interface, which is decorated with the attributes (shown in Example 5-14).

Example 5-13. EmailService class

C#
```
using System.ServiceModel.Activation;
using EmailLibrary;

namespace WCFEmailService
{
    [AspNetCompatibilityRequirements(RequirementsMode =
        AspNetCompatibilityRequirementsMode.Allowed)]
    public class EmailService : IEmailService
    {
        public void SendMailMessage(
        string from, string to, string subject, string body)
        {
            new Mail().SendMessage(from, to, subject, body);
        }
    }
}
```

VB
```
Imports System.ServiceModel.Activation
Imports EmailLibrary
```

```vb
Namespace WCFEmailService
    <AspNetCompatibilityRequirements( _
        RequirementsMode := AspNetCompatibilityRequirementsMode.Allowed)> _
    Public Class EmailService
        Implements IEmailService

        Public Sub SendMailMessage(ByVal from As String, _
            ByVal [to] As String, ByVal subject As String, _
        ByVal body As String)
            CType(New Mail(), Mail).SendMessage(From, [to], subject, body)
        End Sub
    End Class
End Namespace
```

Example 5-14. IEmailService interface

C#
```csharp
using System.ServiceModel;

namespace WCFEmailService
{
    [ServiceContract(Namespace = "http://www.silverlight-data.com")]
    public interface IEmailService
    {
        [OperationContract]
        void SendMailMessage(string from, string to, string subject, string body);
    }
}
```

VB
```vb
Imports System.ServiceModel

Namespace WCFEmailService
    <ServiceContract(Namespace := "http://www.silverlight-data.com")> _
    Public Interface IEmailService
        <OperationContract> _
        Sub SendMailMessage(ByVal from As String, _
            ByVal [to] As String, ByVal subject As String, _
            ByVal body As String)
    End Interface
End Namespace
```

Notice that the `IEmailService` interface is decorated with the `ServiceContract` and the `SendMailMessage` interface method is decorated with the `OperationContract` attribute. Although it is not necessary to use interfaces for the services, it can be beneficial to use interfaces so that you can isolate the contracts for the services in the interfaces and identify them easily.

If you modify the service and create the interface as shown in Examples 5-13 and 5-14, you must also modify the configuration to update the contract name. The `ServiceContract` attribute was moved from the `EmailService` class to the `IEmailService` interface. Therefore, you must modify the name of the contract in the *web.config* file to reflect this change. Example 5-15 shows the updated *web.config* WCF service section for the sample project.

Example 5-15. Configuration for IEmailService contract

```
<system.serviceModel>
    <behaviors>
        <serviceBehaviors>
            <behavior name="WCFEmailService.EmailServiceBehavior">
                <serviceMetadata httpGetEnabled="true" />
                <serviceDebug includeExceptionDetailInFaults="false" />
            </behavior>
        </serviceBehaviors>
    </behaviors>
    <serviceHostingEnvironment aspNetCompatibilityEnabled="true" />
    <services>
        <service behaviorConfiguration="WCFEmailService.EmailServiceBehavior"
            name="WCFEmailService.EmailService">
            <endpoint address="" binding="basicHttpBinding"
            contract="WCFEmailService.IEmailService" />
            <endpoint address="mex" binding="mexHttpBinding"
            contract="IMetadataExchange" />
        </service>
    </services>
</system.serviceModel>
```

Invoking the WCF Service

Once the WCF service has been created, the Silverlight 2 client application can reference the service using the same technique it used to reference the `ASMXEMailService` ASMX web service. Figure 5-12 shows the Add Service Reference window after it has discovered the ASMX web service and the WCF web service. The Discover button found both services, because they both expose a WSDL file and thus are self-describing and discoverable.

Figure 5-12 also shows the WCF web service being named `WCFEMailService`, for clarity, as both the ASMX web service and the WCF web service are referenced by the same Silverlight client application. If the WCF service changes at any point, you can update the service reference by selecting the service, right-clicking it, and choosing the Update Reference menu option.

The technique you use to invoke a WCF service is very similar to the technique you use to invoke an ASMX service from a Silverlight client application. Both require a proxy object, both only make the web requests asynchronously, and both use the same signature for the completion event handler.

Example 5-16 shows the newly created `btnSendViaWCF_Click` event handler that executes when the corresponding button is clicked in the Silverlight application's user interface. An instance of `EmailServiceClient` is created as the proxy for the web requests. Then the `proxy_SendMailMessageCompleted_viaWCF` method is set to be the event handler for the `SendMailMessageCompleted` event. Finally, the `SendMailMessageAsync` method is invoked, which calls the web service's

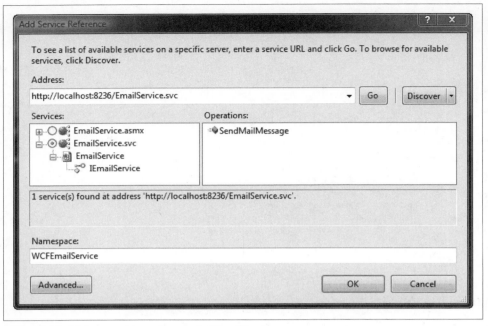

Figure 5-12. Adding a service reference for EmailService.svc

`SendMailMessage` method on the server using WCF. When the request has finished, the event handler (shown in Example 5-17) executes.

Example 5-16. Invoking the WCF service

C#

```csharp
private void btnSendViaWCF_Click(object sender, RoutedEventArgs e)
{
    lbMessage.Text = string.Empty;
    if (!ValidInfo()) return;

    EmailServiceClient proxy = new EmailServiceClient();
    proxy.SendMailMessageCompleted += new proxy_SendMailMessageCompleted_viaWCF;
    proxy.SendMailMessageAsync(messageInfo.From, messageInfo.To,
        messageInfo.Subject, messageInfo.BodyWithDateTag);
}
```

VB

```vbnet
Private Sub btnSendViaWCF_Click(ByVal sender As Object, ByVal e As RoutedEventArgs)
    lbMessage.Text = String.Empty
    If (Not ValidInfo()) Then
        Return
    End If

    Dim proxy As New EmailServiceClient()
    AddHandler proxy.SendMailMessageCompleted, _
        AddressOf proxy_SendMailMessageCompleted_viaWCF
    proxy.SendMailMessageAsync(messageInfo.From, messageInfo.To, _
        messageInfo.Subject, messageInfo.BodyWithDateTag)
End Sub
```

Example 5-17. The callback for the WCF service

```csharp
private void proxy_SendMailMessageCompleted_viaWCF(
        object sender, AsyncCompletedEventArgs e)
{
    string msg = "Message was ";
    if (e.Error != null)
        msg += string.Format("not sent.\n\n{0}", e.Error.Message);
    else
        msg += "sent using WCF";
    lbMessage.Text = msg;
}
```

```vb
Private Sub proxy_SendMailMessageCompleted_viaWCF(ByVal sender As Object, _
        ByVal e As AsyncCompletedEventArgs)
    Dim msg As String = "Message was "
    If e.Error IsNot Nothing Then
        msg &= String.Format("not sent." & Constants.vbLf + _
            Constants.vbLf & "{0}", e.Error.Message)
    Else
        msg &= "sent using WCF"
    End If
    lbMessage.Text = msg
End Sub
```

Once the *clientaccesspolicy.xml* file is placed in the root of the website, you can run the application and both the ASMX web service and the WCF web service will function properly from the Silverlight client application. The *clientaccesspolicy.xml* file must go in the website's root. Because this example creates the WCF service in a web application hosted in the Cassini web server, which will automatically assign a port number to the local domain, the easiest way to add the *clientaccesspolicy.xml* file in the right place is to put it in the root of the project in Visual Studio.

You also can host the WCF web service or the ASMX web service in IIS. Figure 5-13 shows how you could set the service to be hosted in IIS instead of Cassini. If this were the case, the URL for the WCF web service might be *http://localhost/WCFEmailSer vice*. This URL is the web application's root and is not the appropriate place for the *clientaccesspolicy.xml* file to reside. The appropriate place for *clientaccesspolicy.xml* to reside in this case would be *http://localhost*, which of course is the website's root. The website's root is always where Silverlight looks for the *clientaccesspolicy.xml* and *crossdomain.xml* files.

Calling Services Written by Other Developers

Many callable services are available on the Web. Some of these web services are discoverable, such as Live Search, and others are not and use REST, such as Amazon ECS. Most of these services require that a unique key be sent to the service so that the request can be tied back to whoever the key belongs to. Live Search calls its key an AppID.

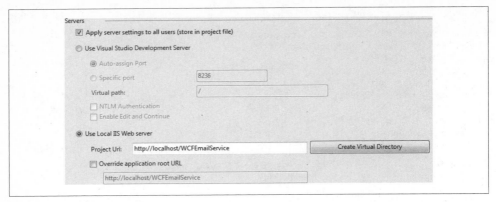

Figure 5-13. Hosting the service in IIS

 You can find instructions for creating an AppID for Live Search at *http: //msdn.microsoft.com/en-us/library/bb266187.aspx*. You can find instructions for using the Live Search service at *http://msdn.microsoft .com/en-us/library/bb251808.aspx*.

The following example shows how you can conduct a simple search using a SOAP-based web service provided by Live Search. First, you must request and use the AppID in the LiveSearchClient sample program included with this chapter. Next, you need to add a service reference to the Live Search service. (You can find this service at *http:// soap.search.msn.com/webservices.asmx?wsdl*.) The sample names the service LiveSearchService, as shown in Figure 5-14.

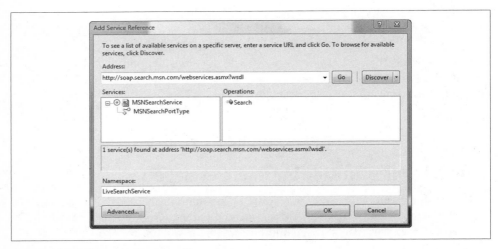

Figure 5-14. Referencing Live Search

Once the service has been referenced, you can create a proxy to the service and invoke its SearchAsync method. This method requires a SearchRequest parameter, which can include a lot of intricate parameters defining the type of search. This example will keep the search parameters simple and return only the first 10 hits (shown by the Offset property in Example 5-18). Example 5-18 also shows the creation of the proxy object, the setup of the search parameters, the addition of the event handler for the completion of the search, and the asynchronous SearchAsync method call to the web service.

Example 5-18. Searching asynchronously

```
private void btnSearch_Click(object sender, RoutedEventArgs e)
{
    MSNSearchPortTypeClient proxy = new MSNSearchPortTypeClient();
    proxy.SearchCompleted += new
        EventHandler<SearchCompletedEventArgs>(proxy_SearchCompleted);

    SourceRequest[] sourceRequests = new SourceRequest[1];
    sourceRequests[0] = new SourceRequest();
    sourceRequests[0].Source = SourceType.Web;
    sourceRequests[0].ResultFields = ResultFieldMask.All |
        ResultFieldMask.SearchTagsArray;
    sourceRequests[0].Count = 10;
    sourceRequests[0].Offset = 0;

    SearchRequest searchRequest = new SearchRequest();
    searchRequest.AppID = appID;
    searchRequest.Query = tbSearch.Text;
    searchRequest.CultureInfo = "en-US";
    searchRequest.Requests = sourceRequests;
    searchRequest.SafeSearch = SafeSearchOptions.Moderate;
    searchRequest.Flags = SearchFlags.None;

    proxy.SearchAsync(searchRequest);
}
```

```
Private Sub btnSearch_Click(ByVal sender As Object, ByVal e As RoutedEventArgs)
    Dim proxy As New MSNSearchPortTypeClient()
    AddHandler proxy.SearchCompleted, AddressOf proxy_SearchCompleted

    Dim sourceRequests(0) As SourceRequest
    sourceRequests(0) = New SourceRequest()
    sourceRequests(0).Source = SourceType.Web
    sourceRequests(0).ResultFields = ResultFieldMask.All Or _
        ResultFieldMask.SearchTagsArray
    sourceRequests(0).Count = 10
    sourceRequests(0).Offset = 0

    Dim searchRequest As New SearchRequest()
    searchRequest.AppID = appID
    searchRequest.Query = tbSearch.Text
    searchRequest.CultureInfo = "en-US"
    searchRequest.Requests = sourceRequests
    searchRequest.SafeSearch = SafeSearchOptions.Moderate
    searchRequest.Flags = SearchFlags.None
```

```
    proxy.SearchAsync(searchRequest)
End Sub
```

Once the search has been completed, the `proxy_SearchCompleted` event handler in Example 5-18 executes and binds the result to the `ListBox` control. A `DataTemplate` simply displays the `Title`, `Url`, and `Description` of each search result in the `ListBox`. Figure 5-15 shows the results of a sample search.

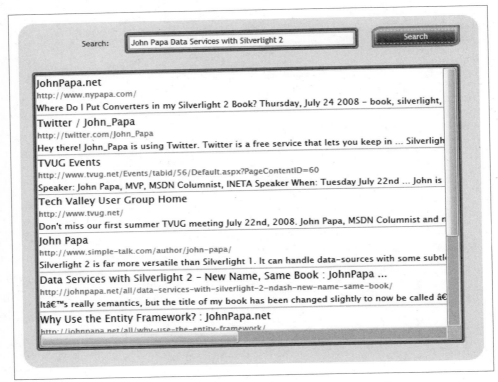

Figure 5-15. Live Search results

When the Silverlight 2 client makes the web service request, the call originates from the local website that hosts the Silverlight 2 application and is sent to the Live Search domain. This call crosses the domain boundary. Silverlight will request the *clientaccesspolicy.xml* file and will find it, as shown in Example 5-19.

Example 5-19. Binding the Live Search results

```csharp
private void proxy_SearchCompleted(object sender, SearchCompletedEventArgs e)
{
    SearchResponse searchResponse = e.Result;
    var resultsList = searchResponse.Responses[0].Results;
```

```
            lstResults.DataContext = resultsList;
    }
```
VB
```
    Private Sub proxy_SearchCompleted(ByVal sender As Object, ByVal e As
      SearchCompletedEventArgs)
        Dim searchResponse As SearchResponse = e.Result
        Dim resultsList = searchResponse.Responses(0).Results
        lstResults.DataContext = resultsList
    End Sub
```

The *clientaccesspolicy.xml* file shown in Example 5-20 indicates that Silverlight 2 will allow any SOAP request from any domain to use the web services located anywhere on the website, which is *http://soap.search.msn.com*.

Example 5-20. The clientaccesspolicy.xml file for Live Search

```
<?xml version="1.0" encoding="utf-8" ?>
<access-policy>
    <cross-domain-access>
        <policy>
            <allow-from http-request-headers="SOAPAction,Content-Type">
                <domain uri="*" />
            </allow-from>
            <grant-to>
                <resource path="/" include-subpaths="true" />
            </grant-to>
        </policy>
    </cross-domain-access>
  </access-policy>
```

Summary

Silverlight 2 clients can call any discoverable web services using ASMX web services and WCF web services, as shown in this chapter. Although Silverlight can also call services that do not describe themselves, such as REST services, self-describing services such as WCF services are beneficial because they can tell the client application exactly how they should be called and what type of data they will return (if any). In the next chapter, we will review how to create WCF services that send and receive complex data using domain model entities.

It is critical to remember that cross-domain calls are restricted unless the target server allows the client's domain access to the target server's services. Using a tool such as Fiddler2, Firebug, or Web Development Helper can make the debugging process much simpler.

CHAPTER 6

Passing Entities via WCF

Silverlight 2 can communicate with SOAP-based web services such as ASMX web services and WCF web services using `basicHttpBinding`, as you learned in Chapter 5. That chapter shows how to create SOAP-based services with .NET and communicate with them from a Silverlight application. The examples create simple services that pass scalar type values. Web services can also pass complex structures such as instances of classes, lists of classes, and even *graphs* (classes that contain other classes as part of a hierarchy). These classes often are part of a domain model that contains class entities.

Whether the entities are created through custom code or through a generation tool such as LINQ to SQL or NHibernate, the entities can be passed across physical tiers to a Silverlight client application. This chapter discusses multitiered architecture with Silverlight applications and the role of domain model entities. It also demonstrates how to pass entities between Silverlight applications and WCF services, and provides tips on how to configure the services and their data models to work well and be consumable by Silverlight.

Passing Entities Between Physical Tiers

Passing complex structures such as entities or lists of entities using Web Communication Foundation (WCF) is a common request and is easily handled using WCF and Silverlight. The following scenarios describe the process and demonstrate how to return entities gathered from custom class models, and entities derived from custom tools such as LINQ to SQL.

Figure 6-1 shows a model of a multitiered architecture with a Silverlight client application taking on the role of the presentation layer. In this architecture, the WCF services act as the traffic cop between the Silverlight client application and the lower layers. The business layer is composed of rule classes; the data layer maps the data from the database into the entity models for data retrieval. The data layer also maps data from the entities back into the database when data is saved. The entity model represents the structure of the application's data model. The entities are filled in the lower layers and

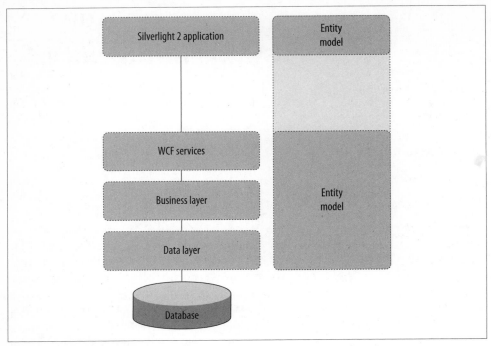

Figure 6-1. A multitiered Silverlight 2 application

are passed up through WCF services to the Silverlight client application. They can also be passed through regular SOAP services using an ASMX web service.

These SOAP-based services are ideal for passing domain model entities because these services describe themselves and what they return through WSDL. The Silverlight client application can reference the SOAP services and generate a proxy class to call the services and classes to represent the entities. The entities that are passed up through the SOAP-based services are serialized and then deserialized back into the entities (from the service-generated classes) on the Silverlight client.

Domain Model Entities

You can use domain model entities to represent an application's data using a class structure. The entities are the classes that represent the objects used in the application that can store data in memory, perform business operations, and be used as a means to pass data between tiers of an application. There are several ways to create and pass domain model entities (hereafter known as *entities*). You can create them and map them using the ADO.NET API directly, or you can generate and map them using a tool such as LINQ to SQL, the Entity Framework, NHibernate, or other ORM tools. As long as the entities can be serialized properly, you can pass them between the physical tiers of an application.

Silverlight and Entities

The entity model is defined in the lower tier on the server, so without some help the Silverlight application is not aware of the domain entity model. A Silverlight application can add a service reference to a WCF web service that exposes service methods that return entities. Chapter 5 demonstrated how the service reference generates a proxy class that describes the methods. The service reference also describes any classes that the WCF web service exposes.

Serialization by Default

The classes in the lower tier should be serializable, as this allows the Silverlight 2 client application to be aware of the class structure. The Silverlight application can create instances of the classes, pass them to the web service, or retrieve them from a web service.

You can indicate that a class should be exposed by the WCF service and be serializable in a few ways. The first way is to use the default behavior of .NET 3.5 SP 1. Starting with .NET 3.5 SP 1, all classes are automatically serializable as long as they have a zero argument default constructor. If a class does not have a constructor, .NET will automatically generate a zero-argument default constructor for it. If a .NET class has a constructor with one or more arguments already and no zero argument constructor, .NET will not automatically generate a zero argument constructor. Also, all properties of a class that have both a public setter and a public getter accessor will be serialized.

Starting with .NET 3.5 SP 1, Plain Old CLR Object (POCO) classes can be serialized as long as they have a zero-argument constructor. Example 6-1 shows a demonstration of a `Customer` POCO class that has three properties. The `CustomerId` property has only a public getter and no setter. This property will not be serialized, because it lacks the combination of the getter and the setter. The `CompanyName` and `City` properties both have a getter and a setter, so they will both be serialized. The C# example shows that the `City` property was created using automatic properties. This is still serialized, because .NET generates the getter and the setter for this property, as both were indicated in the automatic property declaration.

Example 6-1. POCO class

```
public class Customer
{
    private int _customerId;
    public int CustomerId
    {
        get { return _customerId; }
    }

    private string _companyName;
    public string CompanyName
```

```
    {
        get { return _companyName; }
        set { _companyName = value; }
    }

    public string City { get; set; }
}
```

```
Public Class Customer
    Private _customerId As Integer
    Public ReadOnly Property CustomerId() As Integer
        Get
            Return _customerId
        End Get
    End Property

    Private _companyName As String
    Public Property CompanyName() As String
        Get
            Return _companyName
        End Get
        Set(ByVal value As String)
            _companyName = value
        End Set
    End Property

    Private privateCity As String
    Public Property City() As String
        Get
            Return privateCity
        End Get
        Set(ByVal value As String)
            privateCity = value
        End Set
    End Property
End Class
```

After you add a POCO class to a WCF project and add a service reference to it from a Silverlight client application, a proxy class for `Customer` is generated in the Silverlight client application. The contents of this class (shown later in Example 6-3) show that only the `CompanyName` and `City` properties were serialized. Notice that the proxy class tagged the properties as having the `DataMember` attributes and tagged the `Customer` class as having the `DataContract` attribute. This is part of the automatic serialization that started with .NET 3.5 SP 1. Any code run in previous versions of .NET will serialize the entities only if they are explicitly marked with serialization attributes.

The service contract shown in Example 6-2 will work with .NET 3.5 SP 1 and with the POCO class of Example 6-1. The `Customer` class is not decorated with any attributes, yet it will be serialized, so it is usable from this service contract.

Example 6-2. Service contract

C#
```
[ServiceContract]
public interface INorthwindService
```

```
    {
        [OperationContract]
        Customer GetCustomer();
    }
```

VB
```
<ServiceContract> _
Public Interface INorthwindService
    <OperationContract> _
    Function GetCustomer() As Customer
End Interface
```

Example 6-3. The service reference's proxy product class

C#
```
[System.Diagnostics.DebuggerStepThroughAttribute()]
[System.Runtime.Serialization.DataContractAttribute(Name="Customer",
 Namespace="http://schemas.datacontract.org/2004/07/NorthwindModel")]
public partial class Customer :
    PassingEntities.NorthwindServiceReference.EntityBase {

    private string CityField;

    private string CompanyNameField;

    [System.Runtime.Serialization.DataMemberAttribute()]
    public string City {
        get {
            return this.CityField;
        }
        set {
            if ((object.ReferenceEquals(this.CityField, value) != true)) {
                this.CityField = value;
                this.RaisePropertyChanged("City");
            }
        }
    }

    [System.Runtime.Serialization.DataMemberAttribute()]
    public string CompanyName {
        get {
            return this.CompanyNameField;
        }
        set {
            if ((object.ReferenceEquals(this.CompanyNameField, value) != true)) {
                this.CompanyNameField = value;
                this.RaisePropertyChanged("CompanyName");
            }
        }
    }
}
```

VB
```
<System.Diagnostics.DebuggerStepThroughAttribute(), _
 System.Runtime.Serialization.DataContractAttribute(Name:="Customer", _
 Namespace:="http://schemas.datacontract.org/2004/07/NorthwindModel")> _
Partial Public Class Customer
    Inherits PassingEntities.NorthwindServiceReference.EntityBase
```

```
        Private CityField As String

        Private CompanyNameField As String

        <System.Runtime.Serialization.DataMemberAttribute()> _
        Public Property City() As String
            Get
                Return Me.CityField
            End Get
            Set(ByVal value As String)
                If (Object.ReferenceEquals(Me.CityField, value) <> True) Then
                    Me.CityField = value
                    Me.RaisePropertyChanged("City")
                End If
            End Set
        End Property

        <System.Runtime.Serialization.DataMemberAttribute()> _
        Public Property CompanyName() As String
            Get
                Return Me.CompanyNameField
            End Get
            Set(ByVal value As String)
                If (Object.ReferenceEquals(Me.CompanyNameField, value) <> True) Then
                    Me.CompanyNameField = value
                    Me.RaisePropertyChanged("CompanyName")
                End If
            End Set
        End Property
End Class
```

Serialization Attributes

Another way to serialize a class is to use the `Serializable` attribute on the class itself. This marks the entire class and all of its member properties to be serialized. This is a common approach to tagging classes to be serialized, but it offers less control over which properties are serialized.

Another option is to use the `DataContract` attribute. The `DataContract` attribute decorates a class that will be serialized. Only members of this class that are decorated with the `DataMember` attribute and have both a public getter and setter will be serialized. If a public property is decorated with the `DataMember` attribute and that property does not have both a getter and a setter accessor, an exception will be thrown when the service reference is added or updated.

Example 6-4 shows a different `Customer` class that has been decorated with the `DataContract` attribute. The `Customer` class has two of its three public properties decorated with the `DataMember` attribute, which marks them as being serializable and exposed to any client that adds a service reference. The `CustomerId` and `CompanyName` properties both have a getter and a setter and are decorated with the `DataMember` attribute.

However, the `City` property is not decorated with the `DataMember` attribute and will not be serialized.

Example 6-4. Using DataContract and DataMember

C#

```csharp
[DataContract]
public class Customer
{
    private int _customerId;
    public int CustomerId
    {
        get { return _customerId; }
        set { _customerId = value; }
    }

    [DataMember]
    private string _companyName;
    public string CompanyName
    {
        get { return _companyName; }
        set { _companyName = value; }
    }

    private string _city;
    public string City
    {
        get { return _city; }
        set { _city = value; }
    }
}
```

VB

```vb
<DataContract> _
Public Class Customer
    Private _customerId As Integer
    Public Property CustomerId() As Integer
        Get
            Return _customerId
        End Get
        Set(ByVal value As Integer)
            _customerId = value
        End Set
    End Property

    <DataMember> _
    Private _companyName As String
    Public Property CompanyName() As String
        Get
            Return _companyName
        End Get
        Set(ByVal value As String)
            _companyName = value
        End Set
    End Property

    Private _city As String
```

```
      Public Property City() As String
        Get
            Return _city
        End Get
        Set(ByVal value As String)
            _city = value
        End Set
    End Property
End Class
```

When decorating a class with the DataContract attribute, only public properties that are decorated with the DataMember attribute will be serialized. Generally, it is a good idea to use the DataContract attribute on classes that will be exposed if you want to control which properties will be exposed.

As mentioned before, prior to .NET 3.5 SP 1, any base class must also be decorated with the DataContract attribute. This is important because it changed the way entities can be designed. For example, a Customer class is decorated with the DataContract attribute. The Customer inherits from an EntityBase class. Even though the Customer class is the only class that the service contract will return, the EntityBase class must still be decorated with the DataContract attribute because it is partially exposed through the Customer class (since it inherits from EntityBase). Starting with .NET 3.5 SP 1, this is not necessary. However, it is recommended that you use a single scheme for exposing classes. In other words, you should either use DataContract to mark all classes that will be exposed, or not use DataContract at all. For the sake of maintainability and readability, do not mark only some classes with DataContract and not others.

Putting It Together

This section demonstrates an example that consumes an entity from a Silverlight 2 application. The example uses a WCF web service to expose the functionality to retrieve and save instances of a Product class through a Silverlight 2 client application. You can find the sample code for this application with the samples for this chapter.

The first step is to create a Silverlight 2 application named PassingEntities. This application will show a list of products in a ListBox control and will allow the user to select a product to edit. The edited fields of a product will be saved to the database when the user clicks the OK button. Figure 6-2 shows the Silverlight 2 user interface for this example with a product selected and displayed in the bound controls.

The TextBox, Slider, CheckBox, and TextBlock controls in Figure 6-2 are bound to the selected item in the ListBox. The ListBox is bound to a List<Product> through its ItemsSource property, which in turn is bound to the DataContext.

 For details on the layout of this UI, see Chapter 4, where I demonstrate how to bind this type of master detail section using the DataContext and the different binding modes.

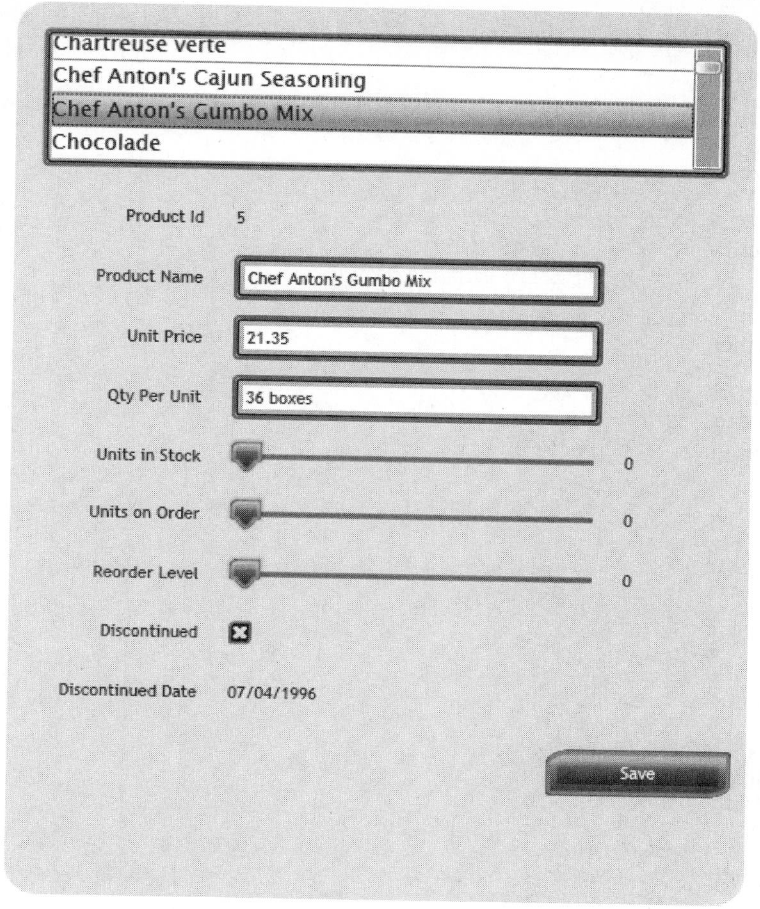

Figure 6-2. PassingEntities example UI

The Silverlight 2 client project uses a WCF web service to retrieve and save product information. A web application named NorthwindWCF hosts the WCF web service for this sample. A WCF service class named NorthwindService was created to detail the service methods that will be exposed. Example 6-5 shows the code for the Northwind service file.

The NorthwindWCF service project refers to a NorthwindBusiness namespace and a NorthwindModel namespace. Both of these are contained in separate projects in the same solution with the sample code for this chapter. The NorthwindModel project contains the classes that define the domain model entity. The NorthwindBusiness project contains the code that will map the data into and out of the entities.

Example 6-5. NorthwindService class

```csharp
using System.Collections.Generic;
using System.ServiceModel.Activation;
using NorthwindBusiness;
using NorthwindModel;

namespace NorthwindWCF
{
    [AspNetCompatibilityRequirements(RequirementsMode =
        AspNetCompatibilityRequirementsMode.Allowed)]
    public class NorthwindService : INorthwindService
    {
        public Product FindProduct(int productId)
        {
            return new ProductMgr().FindProduct(productId);
        }

        public List<Product> FindProductList()
        {
            return new ProductMgr().FindProductList();
        }

        public void SaveProduct(Product product)
        {
            new ProductMgr().SaveProduct(product);
        }
    }
}
```

```vbnet
Imports System.Collections.Generic
Imports System.ServiceModel.Activation
Imports NorthwindBusiness
Imports NorthwindModel

Namespace NorthwindWCF
    <AspNetCompatibilityRequirements(RequirementsMode := _
        AspNetCompatibilityRequirementsMode.Allowed)> _
    Public Class NorthwindService
        Implements INorthwindService
        Public Function FindProduct(ByVal productId As Integer) As Product
            Return New ProductMgr().FindProduct(productId)
        End Function

        Public Function FindProductList() As List(Of Product)
            Return New ProductMgr().FindProductList()
        End Function

        Public Sub SaveProduct(ByVal product As Product)
            CType(New ProductMgr(), ProductMgr).SaveProduct(product)
        End Sub
    End Class
End Namespace
```

Notice that the NorthwindService class implements the INorthwindService interface. This is the service contract that is exposed via WCF to any clients that will subscribe to it. The INorthwindService interface contains the method definitions for the service. The INorthwindService interface is decorated with the ServiceContract attribute and its methods are decorated with the OperationContract attribute. Example 6-6 shows the INorthwindService interface.

Example 6-6. INorthwindService interface

```csharp
using System.Collections.Generic;
using System.ServiceModel;
using NorthwindModel;

namespace NorthwindWCF
{
    [ServiceContract(Namespace = "")]
    public interface INorthwindService
    {
        [OperationContract]
        Product FindProduct(int productId);
        [OperationContract]
        List<Product> FindProductList();
        [OperationContract]
        void SaveProduct(Product product);
    }
}
```

```vb
Imports System.Collections.Generic
Imports System.ServiceModel
Imports NorthwindModel

Namespace NorthwindWCF
    <ServiceContract(Namespace := "")> _
    Public Interface INorthwindService
        <OperationContract> _
        Function FindProduct(ByVal productId As Integer) As Product
        <OperationContract> _
        Function FindProductList() As List(Of Product)
        <OperationContract> _
        Sub SaveProduct(ByVal product As Product)
    End Interface
End Namespace
```

The Product class and its EntityBase base class exist in the NorthwindModel project. This project contains only the domain model entities for the application. It is a common practice for entities to remain in an isolated project so that multiple projects can refer to them without any dependencies. The Product and EntityBase classes are decorated with the DataContract attribute and their public properties are decorated with the DataMember attribute.

Configuration changes

Sometimes it is necessary to change the configuration of a service contract in the *web.config* file. The NorthwindService was generated using the Silverlight-enabled WCF Service file template, which creates the class but not the interface. The interface was extracted from the NorthwindService class; along with it the ServiceContract attribute was moved from the class to the INorthwindService interface (see Example 6-6). The contract that WCF will expose was originally named NorthwindService, after the class. However, the contract has been changed to be the name of the interface, as that is where the ServiceContract attribute exists.

This means that you must modify the configuration file with the revised name of the contract. Otherwise, although the project will compile when you try to create an instance of the proxy class, it will throw an exception because it cannot find the old contract name.

The name of the contract is in the WCF section of the *web.config* file under the system.serviceModel element. The contract name is defined in the endpoint element, shown in bold in Example 6-7. The name of the contract in Example 6-7 has correctly been changed to match the name of the INorthwindService contract interface.

Example 6-7. Service contract section of web.config

```
<system.serviceModel>
    <behaviors>
        <serviceBehaviors>
            <behavior name="NorthwindWCF.NorthwindServiceBehavior" >
                <serviceMetadata httpGetEnabled="true"/>
                <serviceDebug includeExceptionDetailInFaults="true"/>
            </behavior>
        </serviceBehaviors>
    </behaviors>
    <serviceHostingEnvironment aspNetCompatibilityEnabled="true"/>
    <services>
        <service behaviorConfiguration="NorthwindWCF.NorthwindServiceBehavior"
            name="NorthwindWCF.NorthwindService">
            <endpoint address="" binding="basicHttpBinding"
                contract="NorthwindWCF.INorthwindService"/>
            <endpoint address="mex" binding="mexHttpBinding"
                contract="IMetadataExchange"/>
        </service>
    </services>
</system.serviceModel>
```

> When debugging WCF services it is a good idea to set the includeExceptionDetailsInFaults attribute to true. This attribute is located in the system.serviceModel element in the WCF configuration file under the serviceBehaviors section. When you set this to true, detailed exception messages will be sent to the Silverlight client application, which can help considerably when you're debugging problems.

Getting and saving

The `ProductMgr` data mapper class handles the task of filling the entity lists. The `FindProductList` method hits the SQL Server database using ADO.NET and its `SqlClient` library, as shown in Example 6-8. A `SqlConnection` object is used to connect to the database and the `SqlCommand` object queries the database for the products. Once the query is done executing, the results are iterated using a `SqlDataReader`. This is where each product result is mapped into a `Product` entity.

Example 6-8. Getting a product

```csharp
public List<Product> FindProductList()
{
    var productList = new List<Product>();
    using (var cn = new SqlConnection(nwCn))
    {
        const string sql = @"SELECT p.ProductID, p.ProductName, p.SupplierID, " +
        "p.CategoryID, p.QuantityPerUnit, p.UnitPrice, p.UnitsInStock, " +
        "p.UnitsOnOrder, p.ReorderLevel, p.Discontinued, p.DiscontinuedDate, " +
        "p.RowVersionStamp FROM Products p ORDER BY p.ProductName";
        cn.Open();
        using (var cmd = new SqlCommand(sql, cn))
        {
            SqlDataReader rdr = cmd.ExecuteReader(CommandBehavior.CloseConnection);
            if (rdr != null)
                while (rdr.Read())
                {
                    var product = CreateProduct(rdr);
                    productList.Add(product);
                }
            return productList;
        }
    }
}
```

```vbnet
Public Function FindProductList() As List(Of Product)
    Dim productList = New List(Of Product)()
    Using cn = New SqlConnection(nwCn)
        Const sql As String = "SELECT p.ProductID, p.ProductName,p.SupplierID," & _
        "p.CategoryID, p.QuantityPerUnit, p.UnitPrice, p.UnitsInStock, " & _
        "p.UnitsOnOrder, p.ReorderLevel, p.Discontinued, p.DiscontinuedDate, " & _
        "p.RowVersionStamp FROM Products p ORDER BY p.ProductName"
        cn.Open()
        Using cmd = New SqlCommand(sql, cn)
            Dim rdr As SqlDataReader = _
                cmd.ExecuteReader(CommandBehavior.CloseConnection)
            If rdr IsNot Nothing Then
                Do While rdr.Read()
                    Dim product = CreateProduct(rdr)
                    productList.Add(product)
                Loop
            End If
            Return productList
        End Using
```

```
        End Using
    End Function
```

Once the data is retrieved, it is mapped into a List<Product>, as shown in Example 6-9. The CreateProduct method examines the values in the SqlDataReader and maps them to the corresponding properties of the Product class.

Example 6-9. Mapping the data into entities

C#
```csharp
private Product CreateProduct(SqlDataReader rdr)
{
    var product = new Product
    {
        ProductId = Convert.ToInt32(rdr["ProductID"]),
        ProductName = rdr["ProductName"].ToString(),
        QuantityPerUnit = rdr["QuantityPerUnit"].ToString(),
        Discontinued = Convert.ToBoolean(rdr["Discontinued"])
    };
    if (rdr["UnitPrice"] != DBNull.Value) product.UnitPrice =
        Convert.ToDecimal(rdr["UnitPrice"]);
    if (rdr["UnitsInStock"] != DBNull.Value) product.UnitsInStock =
        Convert.ToInt32(rdr["UnitsInStock"]);
    if (rdr["UnitsOnOrder"] != DBNull.Value) product.UnitsOnOrder =
        Convert.ToInt32(rdr["UnitsOnOrder"]);
    if (rdr["ReorderLevel"] != DBNull.Value) product.ReorderLevel =
        Convert.ToInt32(rdr["ReorderLevel"]);
    if (rdr["DiscontinuedDate"] != DBNull.Value) product.DiscontinuedDate =
        Convert.ToDateTime(rdr["DiscontinuedDate"]);
    return product;
}
```

VB
```vb
Private Function CreateProduct(ByVal rdr As SqlDataReader) As Product
    Dim product = New Product With _
        { _
        .ProductId = Convert.ToInt32(rdr("ProductID")), _
        .ProductName = rdr("ProductName").ToString(), _
        .QuantityPerUnit = rdr("QuantityPerUnit").ToString(), _
        .Discontinued = Convert.ToBoolean(rdr("Discontinued")) _
        }

    If rdr("UnitPrice") IsNot DBNull.Value Then
        product.UnitPrice = Convert.ToDecimal(rdr("UnitPrice"))
    End If
    If rdr("UnitsInStock") IsNot DBNull.Value Then
        product.UnitsInStock = Convert.ToInt32(rdr("UnitsInStock"))
    End If
    If rdr("UnitsOnOrder") IsNot DBNull.Value Then
        product.UnitsOnOrder = Convert.ToInt32(rdr("UnitsOnOrder"))
    End If
    If rdr("ReorderLevel") IsNot DBNull.Value Then
        product.ReorderLevel = Convert.ToInt32(rdr("ReorderLevel"))
    End If
    If rdr("DiscontinuedDate") IsNot DBNull.Value Then
        product.DiscontinuedDate = Convert.ToDateTime(rdr("DiscontinuedDate"))
    End If
```

```
    Return product
End Function
```

The call to the service will be made from Silverlight asynchronously. But first you must add a service reference to the Silverlight client application. Figure 6-3 shows this reference being added and named `NorthwindServiceReference`. This generates the `NorthwindServiceClient` proxy class, which can then be used to call the methods exposed by the service contract.

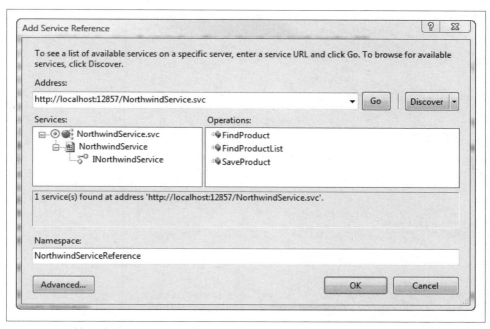

Figure 6-3. Adding the WCF service reference

Once the instance of the proxy is created, the `FindProductListCompleted` event handler is set and the asynchronous call to the `FindProductListAsync` method is executed. When the data is retrieved, the event handler binds the data to the `DataContext` of the `ListBox`, as shown in Example 6-10.

Example 6-10. Calling for the list of products from Silverlight

```C#
private void LoadProductList()
{
    NorthwindServiceClient proxy = new NorthwindServiceClient();
    proxy.FindProductListCompleted += new (proxy_FindProductListCompleted);
    proxy.FindProductListAsync();
}

public void proxy_FindProductListCompleted(object sender, FindProductList
CompletedEventArgs e)
```

```
{
    productList = e.Result;
    lstProducts.DataContext = productList;
}
```

```
Private Sub LoadProductList()
    Dim proxy As New NorthwindServiceClient()
    AddHandler proxy.FindProductListCompleted, _
            AddressOf proxy_FindProductListCompleted
End Sub

Public Sub proxy_FindProductListCompleted(ByVal sender As Object, _
        ByVal e As FindProductListCompletedEventArgs)
    productList = e.Result
    lstProducts.DataContext = productList
End Sub
```

When the user saves, the process of saving the data in an entity and passing it through a WCF web service is quite simple once the foundation is set up. In this sample, the WCF service and its entities are defined and the service reference has been made from the Silverlight client application. Thus, all that is left to do to save the data is to grab the entity from the DataContext and pass it to the SaveProduct method asynchronously. Example 6-11 shows how to grab the Product instance from the DataContext of the Silverlight user control's product details section.

Example 6-11. Saving asynchronously

```
private void btnSave_Click(object sender, RoutedEventArgs e)
{
    Product product = ProductDetailsLayout.DataContext as Product;
    if (product == null) return;

    NorthwindServiceClient proxy = new NorthwindServiceClient();
    proxy.SaveProductCompleted += new proxy_SaveProductCompleted;
    proxy.SaveProductAsync(product);
}

private void proxy_SaveProductCompleted(object sender, System.
ComponentModel.AsyncCompletedEventArgs e)
{
    LoadProductList();
}
```

```
Private Sub btnSave_Click(ByVal sender As Object, ByVal e As RoutedEventArgs)
    Dim product As Product = TryCast(ProductDetailsLayout.DataContext, Product)
    If product Is Nothing Then
        Return
    End If

    Dim proxy As New NorthwindServiceClient()
    proxy.SaveProductCompleted += New proxy_SaveProductCompleted
    proxy.SaveProductAsync(product)
End Sub

Private Sub proxy_SaveProductCompleted(ByVal sender As Object, ByVal e As
```

```
System.ComponentModel.AsyncCompletedEventArgs)
    LoadProductList()
End Sub
```

Using LINQ to SQL with Silverlight

The previous sections described how Silverlight 2 client applications can serialize and consume POCO classes and classes decorated with the `DataContract` attribute. It is quite common to use a custom class and consume it from a Silverlight application. However, it is also common to use tools such as LINQ to SQL to act as a data layer for your application.

Building applications that use LINQ to SQL and WCF web services is not part of Silverlight 2, but it requires skills that intersect with Silverlight applications. These types of tools that gather data, process business logic, and provide a means of communication between the Silverlight client and a server are important pieces of a Silverlight application. This section will describe how to pass entities built with LINQ to SQL to and from a Silverlight application. The purpose of this section is to show how you can use object relational tools such as LINQ to SQL with Silverlight applications. Therefore, we will discuss only aspects that are critical to learning how to integrate LINQ to SQL with Silverlight.

LINQ to SQL Entity Serialization

When server objects are dragged to the designer, LINQ to SQL generates entities from them. The generated class can be serialized by default (now that it is no longer required that a `DataContract` attribute explicitly decorate a class, as discussed earlier in this chapter). Alternatively, the generated classes and their properties can be serialized out of the box by LINQ to SQL. In these subsections, I will show how entities are created from LINQ to SQL, serialized, passed to a Silverlight client application, and bound to target controls. The entities will then be modified on the client and passed back to the server via WCF, and saved to the database using LINQ to SQL's API.

Creating Entities with LINQ to SQL

The example in this subsection demonstrates how LINQ to SQL-generated entities can be passed between a WCF service and a Silverlight client application. The first step is to create a Silverlight client application, which in the example solution is a Silverlight project named `LINQtoSQL`. Then a web application project named `NWService` is added to respond to the WCF service requests made from the Silverlight client. The `NWService` web application runs under the Cassini web server, though it could easily run under IIS if desired.

You can find this example code and database in the `LINQtoSQL` solution in the code for this chapter. The code uses a variation of the Northwind database with a few additional features to help clarify certain topics in this book.

A new file is added to the `NWService` web application LINQ to SQL file, and it is named *NWDataClasses.dbml*, as shown in Figure 6-4. This file is the core of the LINQ to SQL entity model that will be created for this example solution. When the file opens a designer is displayed.

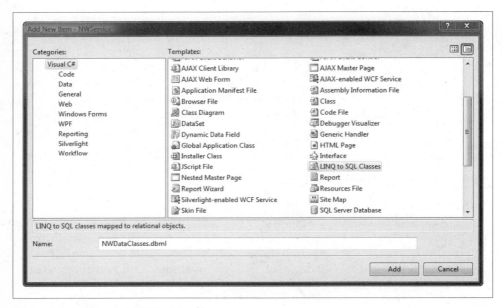

Figure 6-4. Creating a LINQ to SQL file

You can drag server objects from a SQL Server database to the designer; these objects will represent the entities in the model, and you can browse the objects from the Server Explorer window. For example, Figure 6-5 shows that the `Products` table is selected in the Server Explorer and is about to be dragged into the designer.

When you drag the `Products` table onto the surface of the open designer of the *NWDataClasses.dbml* file, the designer displays a class representation of the `Products` table (shown in Figure 6-6). The `Product` class contains a property for every column in the table by default, and indicates which property of the `Product` entity is mapped to the primary key column in the `Products` table. LINQ to SQL generates the class code for the `Product` entity for all of its members.

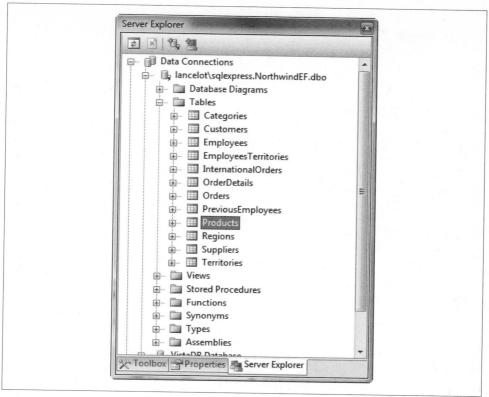

Figure 6-5. Selecting a table from the Server Explorer

Cyclical Serialization with LINQ to SQL

Currently, LINQ to SQL does not support object graph serialization out of the box. This means classes that contain references to other classes which contain a cyclical reference back to the first class cannot be serialized without some help. For example, a `Product` class that has a `Category` property of type `Category` refers to a `Category` class instance. The `Category` class has a `Products` property of type `List<Product>` that refers to zero or more instances of a `Product` class. This relationship is cyclical and cannot be serialized by default with LINQ to SQL.

Objects can be serialized in LINQ to SQL if the context object's serialization mode is set to Unidirectional. This means that only references in the object graph that go from parent to child will be serialized (thus ignoring child-to-parent references). The upside is, of course, that the objects can be serialized, whereas the downside is that the serialized version of the objects cannot travel from child to parent. Another option is to set the relationship between a parent and child object in the designer to have its `ChildProperty` set to `false`. Both of these options make the object model that is serialized be an object tree (hierarchical) instead of an object graph (cyclical). I fully expect that full object graph serialization for LINQ to SQL objects will be allowed in a future release of LINQ to SQL.

LINQ to SQL generates the classes without marking them with the `DataContract` or marking them with the `DataMember` attributes. Starting with .NET 3.5 SP 1, the entities will still be serialized using the `DataContractSerializer` by default. As LINQ to SQL-generated object graphs cannot be serialized with cyclical references at this time, one option to serialize the entities is to have the serialization process remove the cyclical references and make the serialized model a hierarchical object tree, which can be serialized easily. You can do this by clicking in the whitespace of the designer, going to the Properties window, and setting the Serialization Mode property of the data context to Unidirectional. (See the "Cyclical Serialization with LINQ to SQL" sidebar for more information on this topic.)

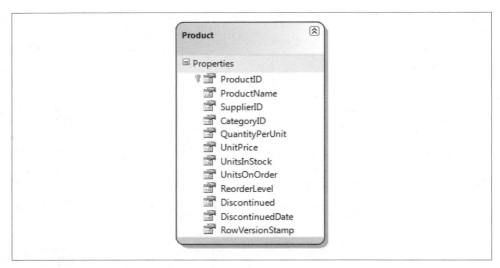

Figure 6-6. Product entity in LINQ to SQL

Serving the LINQ to SQL Model

The LINQ to SQL model for this example solution is exposed by a WCF web service named `NWService`, which is in the web application project of the same name. `NWService` is a Silverlight-enabled WCF web service that has a handful of public methods that allow the entities to be passed via WCF. The service contract for `NWService` is defined in the `INWService` interface, shown in Example 6-12. The example includes some methods for returning a `List<Product>` and a `SaveProduct` method, which accepts a `Product` instance from the Silverlight client application to be saved.

Example 6-12. INWService service contract

```csharp
[ServiceContract]
public interface INWService
{
    [OperationContract]
    List<Product> FindProductList();

    [OperationContract]
    List<Product> FindProductListByInventory(bool inStock);

    [OperationContract]
    void SaveProduct(Product product);
}
```

```vbnet
<ServiceContract> _
Public Interface INWService
    <OperationContract> _
    Function FindProductList() As List(Of Product)

    <OperationContract> _
    Function FindProductListByInventory(ByVal inStock As Boolean) _
        As List(Of Product)

    <OperationContract> _
    Sub SaveProduct(ByVal product As Product)
End Interface
```

The FindProductList method is shown in Example 6-13. This method uses the DataContext created by LINQ to SQL to access the Northwind database. A LINQ query is created that will grab all of the Product entities when executed. The query is executed when the ToList() method is executed on the query. This causes the SQL statement to grab the products to be generated and executed against the SQL Server Northwind database. The query's results will populate a List<Product>, which will then be returned from this WCF service method. The FindProductListByInventory method, also shown in Example 6-13, performs a similar query. The difference is that it adds a filtering condition to the LINQ to SQL query to retrieve either all products in inventory or products that are currently out of stock. When the Silverlight client application makes a request to either of these WCF web service methods, the List<Product> will be serialized and returned to the client application.

Example 6-13. Finding products with LINQ to SQL

```csharp
public List<Product> FindProductList()
{
    NWDataClassesDataContext ctx = new NWDataClassesDataContext();
    var productQuery = from p in ctx.Products
                        orderby p.ProductName ascending
                        select p;
    return productQuery.ToList();
}

public List<Product> FindProductListByInventory(bool inStock)
```

```
{
    NWDataClassesDataContext ctx = new NWDataClassesDataContext();
    var productQuery = from p in
        ctx.Products.Where(p =>
        (inStock ? p.UnitsInStock > 0 : p.UnitsInStock <= 0))
                    orderby p.ProductName ascending
                    select p;
    List<Product> list = productQuery.ToList();
    return list;
}

public void SaveProduct(Product product)
{
    NWDataClassesDataContext ctx = new NWDataClassesDataContext();
    if (product.ProductID == 0)
        ctx.Products.InsertOnSubmit(product);
    else
        ctx.Products.Attach(product, true);
    ctx.SubmitChanges();
}
```

VB
```
Public Function FindProductList() As List(Of Product)
    Dim ctx As New NWDataClassesDataContext()
    Dim productQuery = From p In ctx.Products _
                    Order By p.ProductName Ascending _
                    Select p
    Return productQuery.ToList()
End Function

Public Function FindProductListByInventory(ByVal inStock As Boolean) _
        As List(Of Product)
    Dim ctx As New NWDataClassesDataContext()
    Dim productQuery = From p In _
        ctx.Products.Where(Function(p) _
        (If(inStock, p.UnitsInStock > 0, p.UnitsInStock <= 0))) _
                    Order By p.ProductName Ascending _
                    Select p
    Dim list As List(Of Product) = productQuery.ToList()
    Return list
End Function

Public Sub SaveProduct(ByVal product As Product)
    Dim ctx As New NWDataClassesDataContext()
    If product.ProductID = 0 Then
        ctx.Products.InsertOnSubmit(product)
    Else
        ctx.Products.Attach(product, True)
    End If
    ctx.SubmitChanges()
End Sub
```

Consuming LINQ to SQL Entities from Silverlight

Once the WCF web service is compiled, the Silverlight client application can hook into the services and consume the entities as though they were custom entities (as in the previous examples in this chapter). The entities that are returned to the Silverlight client application through the WCF web service come to the Silverlight client application deserialized into an `ObservableCollection<Product>`.

The UI for the Silverlight 2 client for this example is similar to the one in the previous example solution, `PassingEntities`. They use a similar UI but hook into a different web service. A proxy class is created for the WCF web service, the methods are invoked asynchronously, and the results are retrieved through the completed event handler. The entities retrieved are bound to the target controls, and when their values are modified and the user clicks the Save button, the bound instance of the modified `Product` is passed to the `SaveProduct` method (shown in Example 6-13) in the WCF web service. When the completed `LINQtoSQL` solution for this example is executed, it will retrieve products and allow the user to save changes using the LINQ to SQL-based WCF web services. Figure 6-7 shows the Silverlight application.

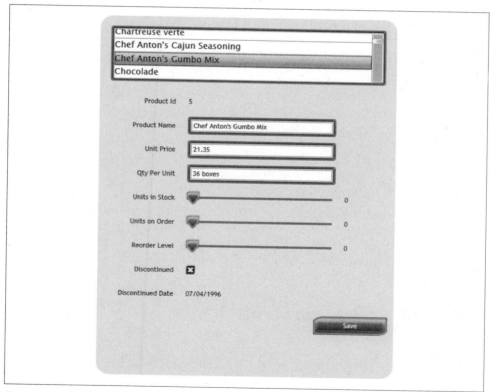

Figure 6-7. LINQ to SQL-based application

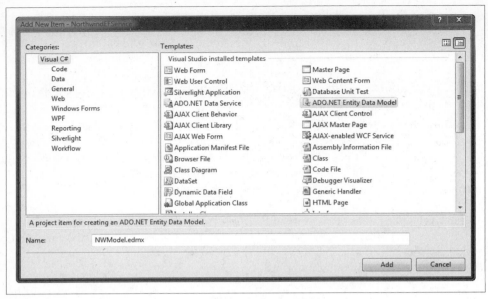

Figure 6-8. Creating an Entity Framework model EDMX file

Silverlight and the Entity Framework

As shown in the previous section, it is easy to consume domain entity models generated or created from an ORM such as LINQ to SQL. The ADO.NET Entity Framework is a far more powerful tool that LINQ to SQL, and it can easily create a domain entity model that is mapped to a database. The Entity Framework can easily create a domain entity model that is mapped to a database. The entities can be serialized, including full object graph serialization, using WCF and the `DataContractSerializer`. This section will demonstrate how to use the Entity Framework as it pertains directly to communications with WCF and Silverlight.

The `EFClient` sample application included in this chapter's code contains a Silverlight client application that communicates with a WCF web service that returns and accepts Entity Framework entities. The setup of this example solution is similar to the previous ones in this chapter; the only difference is that an Entity Framework model must be created.

Creating the Entity Framework Model

The WCF web services are served from the Cassini web server hosting the `NWEFService` web application. Figure 6-8 shows the creation of the *NWModel.edmx* file in the `NWEFService` web application. When this file is created the designer opens and a wizard dialog window appears that walks you through the process of creating the initial state of the Entity Framework model.

You can generate the model from an existing database or create it from scratch. For this sample, I selected the "Generate from database" option (see Figure 6-9) and chose the connection string to be stored in the configuration file (see Figure 6-10).

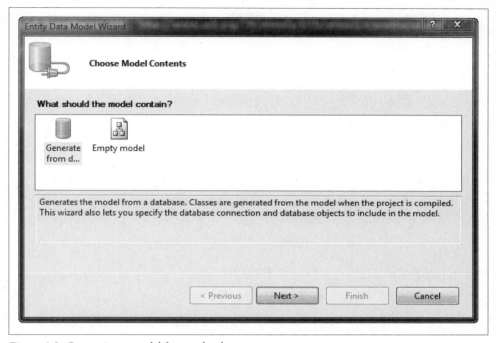

Figure 6-9. Generating a model from a database

The next page of the wizard, shown in Figure 6-11, allows you to select database objects to be included or excluded from the model. The Entity Framework will include in the initial model the tables, views, and stored procedures that are selected. For this sample, only the tables are selected for the model, as shown in Figure 6-12.

Once the model is created, you can write the services that interact with it. The syntax for consuming entities from the Entity Framework with LINQ to Entities is similar to that of LINQ to SQL. For instance, Example 6-14 shows the `FindProductList` method of the WCF service named `NWEFService`. This method creates an instance of the Entity Framework model's data context object. The `NorthwindEFEntities` data context is created and provides access to the sets of entities within the model. This allows queries to be written using LINQ to Entities which, when executed, will generate SQL to hit the underlying database to which the model is mapped.

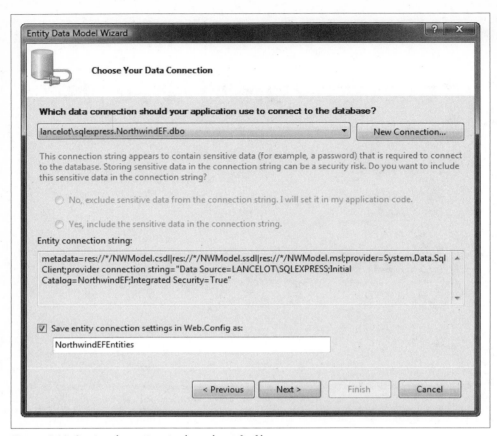

Figure 6-10. Storing the settings in the web.config file

Example 6-14. FindProductList

C#
```csharp
public List<Product> FindProductList()
{
    using (NorthwindEFEntities ctx = new NorthwindEFEntities())
    {
        var productQuery = from p in ctx.ProductSet
                           orderby p.ProductName
                           select p;
        var productList = productQuery.ToList();
        return productList;
    }
}
```

VB
```vb
Public Function FindProductList() As List(Of Product)
    Using ctx As New NorthwindEFEntities()
        Dim productQuery = From p In ctx.ProductSet _
                           Order By p.ProductName _
                           Select p
        Dim productList = productQuery.ToList()
```

```
        Return productList
    End Using
End Function
```

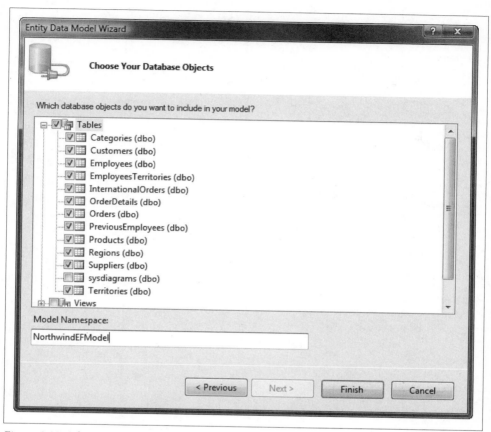

Figure 6-11. Selecting the objects to include in the model

The UpdateProduct method shown in Example 6-15 creates an instance of the data context for the model and saves the Product instance passed in via the method's argument. The data context handles all interaction between the model and the database. Therefore, the context first must reattach the Product instance that was passed into the method to the data context.

Because the data context does not travel to the Silverlight 2 client application, the data context is unaware of any changes that may have been made to the Product. This situation where the entity becomes detached from the data context occurs when entities are serialized and sent across a web service, as the data context is not serializable. The UpdateProduct method must pass the changes in the Product instance to the database. The first step in this process is to reattach the Product instance to the data context and

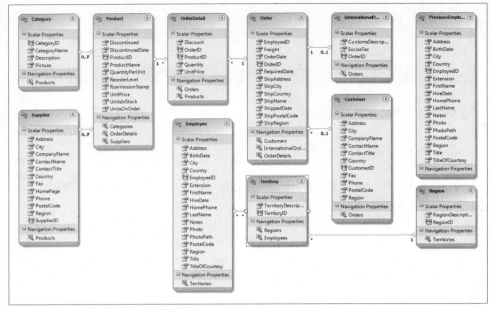

Figure 6-12. Designer view of the model

then to tell the data context explicitly that the `Product` instance has changes. One way to do this is to create a method that sets all the modified flags for the entity. This sample uses a custom extension method named `SetAllModified` to make this process easier. Once the `Product` instance is attached, the data context's `SaveChanges` method is invoked.

 You can find the complete source code for this sample, including the `SetAllModified` extension method, in this chapter's solution.

Example 6-15. Saving a product with the Entity Framework

```csharp
public void UpdateProduct(Product Product)
{
    using (NorthwindEFEntities ctx = new NorthwindEFEntities())
    {
        ctx.Attach(Product);
        Product.SetAllModified(ctx); // custom extension method

        try
        {
            ctx.SaveChanges();
        }
        catch (OptimisticConcurrencyException e)
        {
```

```
            ctx.Refresh(RefreshMode.ClientWins, Product); // Last in wins
            ctx.SaveChanges();
        }
    }
}
```

```vb
Public Sub UpdateProduct(ByVal Product As Product)
    Using ctx As New NorthwindEFEntities()
        ctx.Attach(Product)
        Product.SetAllModified(ctx) ' custom extension method

        Try
            ctx.SaveChanges()
        Catch e As OptimisticConcurrencyException
            ctx.Refresh(RefreshMode.ClientWins, Product) ' Last in wins
            ctx.SaveChanges()
        End Try
    End Using
End Sub
```

Consuming Entity Framework Entities from Silverlight

Once the WCF web service is compiled, the Silverlight client application can hook into the services and consume the entities as though they were custom entities, from LINQ to SQL, the ADO.NET Entity Framework, or from any other ORM tool. As the entities that are returned to the Silverlight client application through the WCF web service come to the Silverlight client application, they are deserialized into an `ObservableCollection<Product>`.

The Silverlight client adds a service reference to the WCF web service, a proxy class is created to the WCF web service, the methods are invoked asynchronously, and the results are retrieved through the completed event handler. The entities retrieved are bound to the target controls, and when their values are modified and the user clicks the Save button, the bound instance of the modified `Product` is passed to the `UpdateProduct` method in the WCF web service. The Silverlight application looks exactly like the user interface shown in Figure 6-7 for the previous example.

Summary

This chapter showed that individual ORM tools can expose domain entity models to Silverlight through WCF web services with relative ease. Although the models differ in how they work, Silverlight can interact with them all as plain entities as long as the objects can be serialized and sent through a web service.

Custom entities as well as entities created from LINQ to SQL, the Entity Framework, and many other ORM tools can be serialized and passed between WCF web services and Silverlight client applications. Web services and data contract serialization bridge the gap between the Silverlight client application and robust web services. This ability to reach web services that describe themselves (those that use SOAP, such as WCF web services and ASMX web services) by consuming and passing entities back and forth allows Silverlight applications to take advantage of complex data structures without having to parse results from a stream or XML.

Although this chapter showed how to expose entities through SOAP-based web services, you also can expose entities using REST services. Later chapters will demonstrate how to do this using the ADO.NET Data Services framework.

CHAPTER 7

Consuming RESTful Services with WebClient and HttpWebRequest

You have many options to consider when working with web services, including the design of a web service, how to pass data between an application and a web service, how to define what type of data is passed, how to invoke the web service, and how to consume the results. An important feature of Silverlight applications is their ability to communicate with web services to send and receive data. Understanding what the options are, how to use them, and how to build custom HTTP-based web services can bring a wide array of flexibility to a Silverlight application.

The previous chapters discussed how to send and receive data with services that describe themselves using SOAP via ASMX and WCF web services. Other variations of HTTP-based web services do not use SOAP, but rather the features inherent to HTTP. This chapter provides a brief but important overview of HTTP web services, their relationship to SOAP-based web services, and the architectural nature of REST-style web services as they relate to being consumed by Silverlight applications. Once these foundations of web services are laid out, the chapter provides examples of how to communicate with them and how they differ.

This chapter also demonstrates how to invoke third-party HTTP web services using `WebClient` and `HttpWebRequest`. Once the information has been retrieved from a service, it must be consumed so that it can be used in the Silverlight application. These services do not describe themselves, so you must take steps to put the data in a construct that allows it to be readily consumed. This chapter discusses these options and shows you how to get the data into an appropriate format using LINQ to XML.

RESTful Primer

Silverlight applications can easily access RESTful web services exposed by third parties, or custom REST (REpresentational State Transfer) services created using Windows Communication Foundation (WCF). It is important to understand how REST services work in order to communicate with them from Silverlight applications. This section provides a primer on RESTful web services and how to consume them.

The .NET Framework supports the creation of SOAP-based web services to be written through ASMX or WCF. These SOAP-based web services describe themselves by exposing Web Services Description Language (WSDL), which allows them to be referenced by adding a service reference to the web service from an application. SOAP supports the packaging of a message that is sent over HTTP via a POST to a web service. For example, a SOAP message that contains a serialized Customer object can be sent to the service *http://samples.silverlight-data.com/MyService.svc* to update a customer. SOAP is one of the most common ways to send data between disconnected applications over HTTP in modern applications. SOAP-based web services are very popular and are commonly used in many applications, primarily because it's easy to add them as a service reference which then generates a proxy class for the service and any returned entities.

You also can design web services without SOAP, and instead use HTTP to perform operations and pass data. Many languages support the creation of HTTP-based web services, which client applications can then consume over the Internet. Several available third-party services expose APIs to their HTTP-based web services that accept requests over HTTP and often return data as XML or JSON. Some popular third-party services that expose HTTP-based services are Google, Amazon, Digg, Flickr, and Twitter. This chapter demonstrates how to communicate with third-party web services over HTTP using both WebClient and HttpWebRequest.

Basic HTTP Web Requests

One of the most basic examples of a web service that can return Plain Old XML (POX) over HTTP without SOAP is a basic ASP.NET page. For example, you can write a service as a basic ASP.NET page (e.g., *http://samples.silverlight-data.com/MyPOXSer vice.aspx*) to return a list of Customers as XML in its response. When the URL for the ASP.NET page is invoked, the page will write the list of Customers as pure XML. If this ASP.NET page is called from an application such as Silverlight, the XML can be consumed using LINQ to XML, stored in a class instance, and bound to a DataContext for representation in some target controls. This is a very basic way to return XML that can be consumed over HTTP without SOAP. However, there are richer ways to create services over HTTP that return XML or JSON without using SOAP.

HTTP does not require SOAP in order to make rich web requests that pass complex data. HTTP web services can allow an operation to be performed on a resource. For instance, the following sample HTTP web service request might allow a list of customers to be retrieved:

```
http://samples.silverlight-data.com/MyService.asmx?op=GetCustomerList()
```

The request is made to a service that exposes a method called `GetCustomerList`, which performs an operation that returns a list of customers. The style of this web request is designed with the action in mind (i.e., get the customers). There might also be a service that performs a delete or some other action, as well.

RESTful Web Services Provide Resources

REST is an architectural style that embraces the web programming model. In a RESTful-style service, everything is treated as a resource and representations of resources can be uniquely addressed by a unique URI. Unlike SOAP, which primarily uses `POST`, RESTful services take advantage of various HTTP verbs such as `GET`, `POST`, `PUT`, and `DELETE`. This differs greatly from SOAP-style services in that you can glean the intent of a RESTful service call from the HTTP verb, whereas you can identify the target of the call by the unique URI. Take, for example, an HTTP `GET` to the URI *http://www.silverlight-data.com/book/dataserviceswithsilverlight*. It would be clear that we intend to fetch the resource with that unique URI. Had we issued a `DELETE` to that same resource, it would be clear that we intended to delete that same resource. Within a SOAP call, both the intent and the context are contained in the SOAP envelope.

So, what is a resource? Every page contains a collection of items; these may include HTML content, XML data, or images, as shown in Figure 7-1. The web pages are simply containers of information, or resources. A web browser such as Internet Explorer or Firefox consumes those resources and displays them. The RESTful style works with a representation of an entity that is mapped to the actual entity. A client application can consume a representation of a resource too, and can perform other operations with the data derived from a resource.

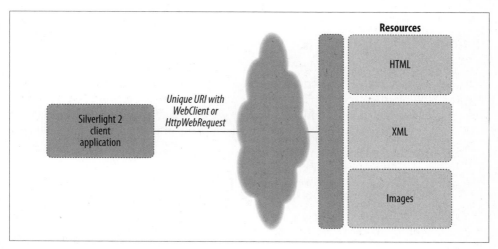

Figure 7-1. Consuming resources

Unique URIs

It is helpful to think of web pages as resources to fully understand the RESTful architectural style. A Silverlight 2 client could make a request to a web page (a resource) and receive a representation of the resource's data. Each resource has a unique URI that represents that resource. For example, the following URI represents a standard HTTP SOAP web request that can perform different actions based on the SOAP message's content:

http://samples.silverlight-data.com/MyService.asmx

You can modify this URI to call multiple methods to perform operations and act upon different resource representations (i.e., `Product`, `Customer`, and `Order`). A RESTful-style web service would have a unique URI mapped to each resource, as shown here:

http://samples.silverlight-data.com/MyRESTService.svc/Product
http://samples.silverlight-data.com/MyRESTService.svc/Customer
http://samples.silverlight-data.com/MyRESTService.svc/Order

Each of these represents a unique URI to a specific resource, allowing us to reference that resource unambiguously. Combining a URI such as this with an appropriate HTTP verb provides both the intent of the call as well as the context regarding the resource upon which to act. The URI could be mapped to a resource, an action to perform (`GET`, `POST`, `PUT`, or `DELETE`), and a response format (XML or JSON) to help pass information into the web service.

 "Creating RESTful Services from WCF" in Chapter 9 explains how to create RESTful web services and set all of the attributes that are required to customize them to be consumed by Silverlight 2 applications.

Anatomy of a RESTful Service

Now that you have a better understanding of RESTful services, it makes sense to take a closer look at some of their common characteristics. The rest of this chapter (pun intended) follows the RESTful primer with examples of how to consume RESTful services from Silverlight applications. Examples will use publicly available third-party RESTful web services from places such as Amazon.com and Digg.com.

A RESTful web service has several attributes that you can configure. Some of the more important ones are:

- URI template
- Parameters
- Format of the request and response messages
- Action

URI templates and parameters (as created through WCF)

When a RESTful web service is defined it uses a URI template to match a unique URI to a web method. A template contains a path, an optional query, and an optional fragment. The path and query may contain a combination of literals and variables. For example, the following URI template maps the relative path `Product` from the service's URL:

http://samples.silverlight-data.com/MyRESTService.svc/Product/1

Parameter names must match the name of a parameter in the method. So, the `productId` parameter in the URI template must also be a parameter in the method. Also, the mapped parameters in the path segment must be defined as strings in the method. For example, values such as integers must be defined as a string and then mapped to an integer in the method. Simple type conversion will take place on variables in the query string, as of .NET 3.5 SP 1.

Example 7-1 shows a sample of a basic RESTful web method that maps a URI using a parameterized template.

Example 7-1. RESTful web method built with WCF

```
[OperationContract]
[WebGet(UriTemplate = "Product/{productIdString}",
    ResponseFormat = WebMessageFormat.Json)]
public Product FindProduct(string productIdString)
{
    int productId = int.Parse(productIdString);
    return GetProduct(productId);
}
```

```
<OperationContract, WebGet(UriTemplate := "Product/{productIdString}", _
        ResponseFormat := WebMessageFormat.Json)> _
Public Function FindProduct(ByVal productIdString As String) As Product
    Dim productId As Integer = Integer.Parse(productIdString)
    Return GetProduct(productId)
End Function
```

Notice that the name of the parameter is the same in the template and in the web method's signature. Any subsequent parameters in the web method that are not mapped in the URI template are deserialized. This allows an entity, such as a product, to be passed in via a `POST`. In Chapter 9, I'll demonstrate detailed examples of building RESTful services that Silverlight can consume.

Prior to .NET 3.5 SP 1, you had to define variables in an entire path segment or as a query string value. Support was added for compound path segments starting with .NET 3.5 SP 1. The basic rules are that variables need to be named and must be separated by a literal. Some examples are `/mydoc.{ext}`, `/{docname}.{ext}`, and `/Product({productId})`. The following example shows two different ways you can map a URI template to accept the `productId` parameter. You could use either one of these URI templates with the method in Example 7-1. The key factor is that the matching engine for the RESTful service must be able to latch a URI to a method without any ambiguity.

> *http://samples.silverlight-data.com/MyRESTService.svc/Product({productId})*
> *http://samples.silverlight-data.com/MyRESTService.svc/Product/{productId}*

An example of an invalid URI template mapping would be any URI that combines a parameter and a resource mapping in the same segment, such as this:

> *http://samples.silverlight-data.com/MyRESTService.svc/{productId}{categoryId}/*

These templates can also continue to drill down into resources by appending more items to the URI template. For example, the following URI template might map to an employee's address:

> *http://samples.silverlight-data.com/MyRESTService.svc/Employee/{employeeId}/Address*

Actions and responses

RESTful web services, such as the one shown in Example 7-1 that is created with .NET code, accept an action in the request. The action is defined as an HTTP method, such as POST, PUT, DELETE, or GET. Example 7-1 uses the HTTP GET action, as the web service method is decorated with the WebGetAttribute. If the method were decorated with the WebInvokeAttribute, the action parameter could be set to POST by default. You can configure it to use any other valid HTTP verb by setting the Method parameter. Example 7-2 shows a RESTful web service method that accepts a Product instance as XML from the POST request.

Example 7-2. RESTful POST

C#
```
[OperationContract]
[WebInvoke(UriTemplate = "Product", Method = "POST",
        RequestFormat= WebMessageFormat.Xml)]
public void AddProduct(Product product)
{
    SaveIt(product);
}
```

VB
```
<OperationContract, WebInvoke(UriTemplate := "Product", _
        Method := "POST", RequestFormat:= WebMessageFormat.Xml)> _
Public Sub AddProduct(ByVal product As Product)
    SaveIt(product)
End Sub
```

You can set the RequestFormat and ResponseFormat properties of the WebGetAttribute and WebInvokeAttribute classes to either WebMessageFormat.Xml *or* WebMessageFormat.Json. The response format for the method shown in Example 7-1 is defined as JSON, whereas the request format from Figure 7-2 is defined as XML. It is a good practice to either stick with a single format for the web methods in a RESTful service instead of swapping back and forth, or design the web services to be able to return either JSON or XML depending on the request. In environments where the RESTful services will be consumed by services (such as Ajax) that require JSON and services that require XML, it is a good practice to expose both XML and JSON.

REST SERVICE

REST Definitions

There seem to be various perspectives regarding what defines a RESTful service. Even some of the third-party REST-based web services discussed in this chapter have slightly differing perspectives regarding REST. This can be confusing. Some definite characteristics influence whether a web service is RESTful. Also, some gray areas exist where RESTful web service publishers have taken some liberties in creating REST-style web services.

For example, REST services make the use of the HTTP verbs GET, PUT, POST, and DELETE perform actions on resources. However, some REST services will use a POST to handle inserts, updates, and deletes (often referred to as *Lo-REST*) instead of using the corresponding HTTP verbs of POST, PUT, and DELETE, respectively (often referred to as *High-REST*). Either way, the service can be called RESTful. There are varying definitions of REST-style web services. REST is a style and not a cut-and-dry pattern.

Also, some RESTful web services use parameter-driven query strings more so than a resource-driven URI, instead of sticking with the school of thought that says that a URI should be purely resource-driven. For example, the following URI defines a RESTful service exposed by Amazon.com:

> *http://webservices.amazon.com/onca/xml?Service=AWSECommerceService&AWSAccessKeyId=YourKeyGoesHere&Operation=ItemSearch&SearchIndex=Books&ResponseGroup=Medium*

This URI uses a series of parameters to define both the action and the parameters to call a RESTful web service method. Notice that most of the service is defined through query string parameters. A more resource-driven version of that URI might look something like this:

> *http://webservices.amazon.com/onca/AWSECommerceService/Books/KeyWords=Silverlight?AWSAccessKeyId=YourKeyGoesHere&ResponseGroup=Medium*

This fictitious example shows a URI that references the service and the Books resource explicitly. A parameter is passed in to indicate the keywords to search for when finding Books, while other parameters can be used to further qualify any information needed beyond resolving the resource.

RESTful services focus on providing access to resources through the common HTTP verbs. Whether a web service follows the definition of REST in a strict or loose sense, as long as the web service falls somewhere in the range of being RESTful it should not matter.

WebClient

Unlike SOAP services, you cannot create a service reference for a RESTful web service since most RESTful services do not expose a contract, nor do they have WSDL definitions. This means a Silverlight 2 client application cannot simply add a service reference to a RESTful web service. Instead, Silverlight 2 client applications must make use of the `WebClient` and `HttpWebRequest` classes to communicate with RESTful web services.

 One of the RESTful tenets is that a resource is self-describing. An HTTP request using `OPTIONS` will discover what can be done with a resource and the formats supported by it.

In a nutshell, `WebClient` is a simpler API that can communicate with an HTTP-based web service. It can send `GET` and `POST` requests (but not `PUT` or `DELETE` requests) to a service to send and receive data. `HttpWebRequest` also provides the means to communicate with HTTP-based web services. It accepts a URI, just like the `WebClient` library, but allows greater customization of the information sent to the web service, such as more control over headers than with `WebClient`. The `WebClient` class uses the `HttpWebRequest` class under the covers, but `WebClient` is a much simpler API and often is all that is required. As with any remote web service invocation from Silverlight, a cross-domain policy file must exist on the root of the remote server's domain to allow Silverlight to call the service.

 Silverlight 2 applications allow communication with remote web services on a domain that is different from the domain hosting the Silverlight client application. These are often called *cross-domain services*. Cross-domain communication through any communication library requires a policy file. This means that whether `WebClient`, `HttpWebRequest`, ASMX, or WCF with SOAP is used to communicate to a remote web service, a cross-domain policy file is required.

You can find more information about cross-domain services in Chapter 5, including how to debug cross-domain issues and how to configure cross-domain policy files.

Preparing to Consume a RESTful Service with WebClient

Both `WebClient` and `HttpWebRequest` are part of the `System.Net` namespace. You can use both very effectively to communicate with RESTful (and other) web services. `WebClient` has a simpler API, whereas `HttpWebRequest` allows more granular control over remote service calls. When invoking a remote web service to retrieve data, it is important that you follow these steps:

1. Reference `System.Net.dll` and create the `WebClient` instance.
2. Add an event handler to the `WebClient` instance's `DownloadStringCompleted` event.
3. Format the URI to pass to the remote web service, including any parameters.
4. Invoke the `WebClient` instance's `DownloadStringAsync` method.
5. In the event handler for `DownloadStringCompleted`, handle any errors resulting from the web service appropriately.
6. In the event handler for `DownloadStringCompleted`, consume the response (usually XML or JSON) and process it accordingly.

These steps are good guidelines to follow when using the `WebClient` class to talk to a remote web service. Before you can implement these guidelines in a RESTful example, however, you need a web service URI. The following URI is from the Digg.com RESTful API, which exposes a set of RESTful web services that provide access to the Digg.com content:

> *http://services.digg.com/stories/topic/Microsoft?appkey=http%3A%2F%2Fwww.sil verlight2data.com&count=10*

 You can find more information on the Digg.com API on Digg's website, at *http://apidoc.digg.com*.

This URI consists of some basic components. It begins with *http://services.digg.com/ stories/topic*, which resolves to a story's topic resource. The next part of the URI is a parameter that represents the topic to find. The parameter becomes part of the URI as it is qualifying the resource that will be identified. The query string parameters in this example are `appkey` and `count`. The `appkey` parameter is a required parameter that the Digg.com API uses to identify where the call originated. Digg.com does not require any registration to obtain an `appkey`; however, some other third-party APIs, such as Amazon.com, do require registration to obtain an `appkey` so that they can identify any purchases made through their RESTful API. The `count` parameter tells the web service method how many items to return from the request. If access to the Digg.com API were made transparent, the definition for the URI template for this service might look something like the following:

> *http://services.digg.com/stories/topic/{Topic}?{appKey}&{count*

This example uses an `appkey` with a value of *http://www.silverlight-data.com* to identify that it came from this book's domain. You can test the URI in this example by simply copying it into a browser and viewing the XML results, as shown in Figure 7-2 using the Firefox web browser.

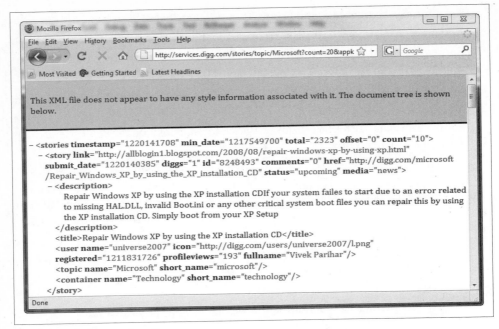

Figure 7-2. Calling services.digg.com

Testing RESTful Services with Fiddler2

It is often helpful to test calls to HTTP-based web services outside the code, to make sure the calls are formatted properly. This eliminates any problems that may arise from the structure of the .NET code. A great tool for testing HTTP-based web services is Fiddler2. Fiddler2 can sniff network traffic, and make remote web service calls, format requests, and display responses and any HTTP status codes.

You can download Fiddler2 from *http://www.fiddlertool.com/fiddler/*.

Fiddler2 has a Request Builder tab where you can enter a URI, specify an HTTP action, and optionally specify any request headers. Figure 7-3 shows Fiddler2's Request Builder section invoking the Digg RESTful web service. When the request has completed, it will show up in the Web Sessions section of Fiddler2 along with the HTTP status code from the request. From here it is easy to identify whether the request succeeded. If it did not succeed, you can view the HTTP status code and any message associated with it to help debug the problem.

You can find the response from a successful call in the Session Inspector tab of Fiddler2. After successfully calling the Digg.com web service with the following URI, the XML response is shown (see Figure 7-4):

> *http://services.digg.com/stories/topic/Microsoft?appkey=http%3A%2F%2Fwww .silverlight-data.com&count=10*

Appendix B discusses how to use Fiddler2 as well as other debugging tools such as Firebug and Web Development Helper to identify and resolve communication issues.

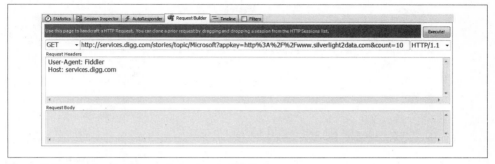

Figure 7-3. Invoking the Digg web service via Fiddler2

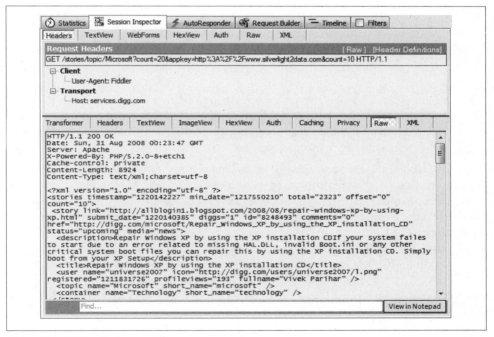

Figure 7-4. Fiddler2's Session Inspector

Invoking a RESTful Service with WebClient

The following example will demonstrate the steps required to invoke a RESTful web service using WebClient. You can find the complete example code in the book's code folder for this chapter. The sample displays a Silverlight 2 client application's *DiggStoryView.xaml* control, shown in Figure 7-5, which allows the user to retrieve the most recent stories from the RESTful Digg.com web service.

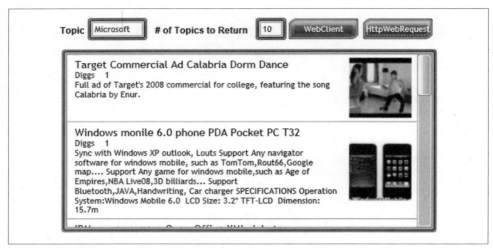

Figure 7-5. The DiggStoryView.xaml control

The `WebClient` class invokes asynchronous operations that fire off events when they have completed their respective tasks. Some of the asynchronous operations also fire events that contain information regarding the progress of the asynchronous operations. `WebClient` contains the asynchronous operations shown in Table 7-1.

Only one request can be made to an asynchronous operation at a time using `WebClient`. If a second asynchronous operation is invoked, an exception will be thrown. When event handlers are added to the `WebClient` class's events, the code in the handler executes in the UI thread, not in the background thread. This is significant because by operating on the UI thread, any code executing in the event handler can get values, set values, and interact with controls in the Silverlight client application's UI without any special coding. The `WebClient` API has a very simple interface that makes it easy to use. It also is very effective at making web service calls for most situations. For scenarios that involve more control over the request, such as specialized headers, the `HttpWebRequest` class is a good alternative.

Table 7-1. Key methods and events of WebClient

Methods and events	Type	Description
CancelAsync	Method	Cancels the active asynchronous operation.
DownloadStringAsync	Method	Performs an HTTP GET and begins the download of data via the response. The value is returned as a string.
OpenReadAsync	Method	Opens a readable stream.

Methods and events	Type	Description
OpenWriteAsync	Method	Opens a writable stream.
UploadStringAsync	Method	Performs an HTTP POST and begins the upload of data via the request.
DownloadProgressChanged	Event	Fires when some or all of the data has been downloaded from the web service request. You can use it to indicate the progress of the download.
DownloadStringCompleted	Event	Fires when all of the data has been downloaded from the web service request and the response is available.
OpenReadCompleted	Event	Fires when the OpenReadAsync method has completed.
OpenWriteCompleted	Event	Fires when the OpenWriteAsync method has completed.
UploadProgressChanged	Event	Fires when some or all of the data has been uploaded to the web service. You can use it to indicate the progress of the upload.
UploadStringCompleted	Event	Fires when all of the data has been uploaded to the web service.

Creating the XAML for the UI

The XAML contains a TextBox named txtTopic that is passed to the web service so that it can find the most recent stories for that topic. The XAML also contains a TextBox named txtCount to quantify how many recent stories should be retrieved. Finally, the XAML includes a ListBox control which contains a data-bound DataTemplate that formats the response from the web service. In the preceding section, Figure 7-5 shows the DiggStoryView.xaml application.

Example 7-3 shows the complete XAML for the DiggStoryView control. Notice that the lstResults ListBox's ItemsSource property is bound to the DataContext. The results from the response of the WebClient call will be collected and bound to the ListBox's ItemsSource. The items within the ItemTemplate's DataTemplate are bound to the individual items.

Example 7-3. DiggStoryView XAML

```
<UserControl x:Class="RemoteServices.DiggStoryView"
    xmlns="http://schemas.microsoft.com/winfx/2006/xaml/presentation"
    xmlns:x="http://schemas.microsoft.com/winfx/2006/xaml"
    Width="Auto" Height="Auto">
    <Grid x:Name="LayoutRoot" Background="White">
        <Grid.RowDefinitions>
            <RowDefinition Height="40"/>
            <RowDefinition Height="*"/>
        </Grid.RowDefinitions>
        <Grid.ColumnDefinitions>
            <ColumnDefinition Width="500"/>
        </Grid.ColumnDefinitions>
        <StackPanel Grid.Column="0" Grid.Row="0" Orientation="Horizontal">
            <TextBlock Text="Topic" Style="{StaticResource TextBlockCaptionStyle}"
            Width="36" Margin="0,0,5,0" />
            <TextBox x:Name="txtTopic" Width="77" Height="30" Grid.Column="0"
            Grid.Row="0" Text="Microsoft"
```

```
                    Style="{StaticResource TextBoxStyle}"></TextBox>
                    <TextBlock Text="# of Topics to Return"
                    Style="{StaticResource TextBlockCaptionStyle}" />
                    <TextBox x:Name="txtTopicCount" Width="40" Height="30" Grid.Column="0"
                    Grid.Row="0" Text="10"
                    Style="{StaticResource TextBoxStyle}"></TextBox>
                    <Button x:Name="btnUseWebClient" Width="90" Height="28"
                    Content="WebClient" Grid.Column="1" Grid.Row="0"
                    Style="{StaticResource ButtonStyle}" Margin="3,0,3,0"></Button>
                    <Button x:Name="btnUseHttpWebRequest" Width="90"
                    Content="HttpWebRequest" Style="{StaticResource ButtonStyle}"
                    Height="28" Margin="3,0,3,0"/>
                </StackPanel>
                <ListBox x:Name="lstResults" Grid.ColumnSpan="2" Grid.Column="0"
                    Grid.Row="1" Width="480" HorizontalAlignment="Left" Height="240"
                       Margin="10,10,10,10" VerticalAlignment="Top"
                    Style="{StaticResource ListBoxStyle}" ItemsSource="{Binding}">
                    <ListBox.ItemTemplate>
                        <DataTemplate>
                            <StackPanel Orientation="Horizontal">
                                <StackPanel Orientation="Vertical" Width="350"
                                Margin="5,5,5,5">
                                    <TextBlock Text="{Binding Title}"
                                FontFamily="Trebuchet MS" FontSize="14"
                                Margin="5,0,5,0" Width="Auto" TextWrapping="Wrap"/>
                                    <StackPanel Orientation="Horizontal">
                                        <TextBlock Text="Diggs " FontFamily="Trebuchet MS"
                                    FontSize="11" Margin="5,0,5,0"></TextBlock>
                                        <TextBlock Text="{Binding DiggCount}"
                                    FontFamily="Trebuchet MS" FontSize="11"
                                    Margin="5,0,5,0" />
                                    </StackPanel>
                                    <TextBlock Text="{Binding Description}"
                                    FontFamily="Trebuchet MS" FontSize="11"
                                    Margin="5,0,5,0" Width="Auto"
                                    TextWrapping="Wrap"/>
                                </StackPanel>
                                <Image Source="{Binding ThumbNail}" Margin="5,5,5,5" />
                            </StackPanel>
                        </DataTemplate>
                    </ListBox.ItemTemplate>
                </ListBox>
        </Grid>
</UserControl>
```

Invoking the Service with WebClient

The Digg web service for this sample is executed using the WebClient class. When the user clicks the WebClient button, an instance of WebClient is created, an event handler is added to its DownloadStringCompleted event, and then the DownloadStringAsync method is executed, as shown later in Example 7-5. The DownloadStringAsync method invokes the web service using the URI and its query string parameters. You can test this web service call by pasting the URI into the address bar of a web browser such as

Internet Explorer or Firefox. You can also test and debug it using the Fiddler2 tool (see the "Testing RESTful Services with Fiddler2" sidebar).

When the `WebClient` is used to invoke a web service through the `DownloadStringAsync` method, the service is passed an HTTP action of `GET`. `WebClient` can also send an action of `POST`, which I will demonstrate in Chapter 9. However, `WebClient` in Silverlight 2 cannot send a `PUT` or a `DELETE` HTTP action verb.

The web service is invoked asynchronously, so the user can go about his business until the web service has returned a response. When the web service sends a response, the event handler for the `DownloadStringCompleted` method will execute. This method receives a `DownloadStringCompletedEventArgs` parameter that contains error information as well as the response from the web service.

The `Error` property of the `DownloadStringCompletedEventArgs` parameter will be null if the service completed successfully. If an error occurred, this property will contain the information about the error which can then be logged, displayed, or translated to the user. If the service completes successfully, the `DownloadStringCompletedEventArgs` `Result` property will contain the web service's response, shown in part in Example 7-4.

Example 7-4. Digg web service response

```
<?xml version="1.0" encoding="utf-8" ?>
<stories timestamp="1222283588" min_date="1219691580" total="2681"
    offset="0" count="10">
 <story link="http://cyberst0rm.blogspot.com/2008/09/7-reasons-why-not-to-use-
    internet.html" submit_date="1222283542" diggs="1" id="8672002"
    comments="0"
    href="http://digg.com/microsoft/7_reasons_why_NOT_to_use_Internet_Explorer"
    status="upcoming" media="news">
  <description>So what are some concrete reasons behind my recommendation
        against Internet Explorer in general? Without further ado they
        are:</description>
  <title>7 reasons why NOT to use Internet Explorer</title>
  <user name="uganr" icon="http://digg.com/img/udl.png" registered="1176558229"
        profileviews="878" />
  <topic name="Microsoft" short_name="microsoft" />
  <container name="Technology" short_name="technology" />
  <thumbnail originalwidth="400" originalheight="300" contentType="image/png"
   src="http://digg.com/microsoft/7_reasons_why_NOT_to_use_Internet_Explorer/t.png"
   width="80" height="80" />
 </story>
...
...
```

The sample service returns XML containing the list of stories that meet the criteria passed into the web service. When consuming HTTP-based web services, it is critical to examine the API documentation of the remote web service to understand both how to send a request to the web service and the expected format of the web service's response. The API will define the structure of the response for a specific request so that it can be consumed accordingly.

Example 7-5. Invoking the web service call

C#
```csharp
WebClient svc = new WebClient();
private string appKey = "http%3A%2F%2Fwww.silverlight-data.com";
private string baseUri = "http://services.digg.com/stories/topic";

private void btnUseWebClient_Click(object sender, RoutedEventArgs e)
{
    string topic = txtTopic.Text;
    int count = int.Parse(txtTopicCount.Text);
    string url = String.Format("{0}/{1}?appkey={2}&count={3}",
        baseUri, topic, appKey, count);
    svc.DownloadStringCompleted += svc_DownloadStringCompleted;
    svc.DownloadStringAsync(new Uri(url));
}
```

VB
```vbnet
Private svc As New WebClient()
Private appKey As String = "http%3A%2F%2Fwww.silverlight-data.com"
Private baseUri As String = "http://services.digg.com/stories/topic"

Private Sub btnUseWebClient_Click(ByVal sender As Object, _
    ByVal e As RoutedEventArgs)
    Dim topic As String = txtTopic.Text
    Dim count As Integer = Integer.Parse(txtTopicCount.Text)
    Dim url As String = String.Format("{0}/{1}?appkey={2}&count={3}", _


    svc.DownloadStringCompleted += svc_DownloadStringCompleted
    svc.DownloadStringAsync(New Uri(url))
End Sub
```

Consuming the Response with LINQ to XML

When a service response comes back as XML, any XML parsing library can consume it. The `System.Linq.dll` assembly is added to a Silverlight application by default. This library provides the basic features of LINQ to the Silverlight client, including the `select` and `from` syntax. You must reference the `System.Xml.Linq.dll` assembly to add the LINQ to XML features to the application.

The code in Example 7-6 gathers the XML and uses LINQ to XML to put the response into a class structure so that it can easily be bound to the `ListBox`'s `DataContext` property. The `XDocument` class instance parses the XML response and puts it in a format that can easily be queried using LINQ to XML.

 Some web services allow their content to be returned in either XML or JSON. This chapter demonstrates how to consume XML from a response. Chapter 9 demonstrates how to consume JSON from a RESTful web service call.

Example 7-6. Using LINQ to XML on the response

```csharp
private void svc_DownloadStringCompleted(object sender, DownloadStringCompletedEventArgs e)
{
    if (e.Error == null)
    {
        string rawXml = e.Result;
        List<DiggStory> list = CreateStoryList(rawXml);
        lstResults.DataContext = list;
    }
}

private List<DiggStory> CreateStoryList(string rawXml)
{
    XDocument xml = XDocument.Parse(rawXml);

    var storiesQuery = from story in xml.Descendants("story")
                select new DiggStory
                {
                  Id = (int) story.Attribute("id"),
                  Title = ((string) story.Element("title")).Trim(),
                  Description = ((string) story.Element("description")).Trim(),
                  ThumbNail =
                      (story.Element("thumbnail") == null
                            ? string.Empty
                            : story.Element("thumbnail").Attribute("src").Value),
                  Link = new Uri((string) story.Attribute("link")),
                  DiggCount = (int) story.Attribute("diggs")
                };

    lstResults.SelectedIndex = -1;
    return storiesQuery.ToList();
}
```

```vbnet
Private Sub svc_DownloadStringCompleted(ByVal sender As Object, _
        ByVal e As DownloadStringCompletedEventArgs)
    If e.Error Is Nothing Then
        Dim rawXml As String = e.Result
        Dim list As List(Of DiggStory) = CreateStoryList(rawXml)
        lstResults.DataContext = list
    End If
End Sub

Private Function CreateStoryList(ByVal rawXml As String) As List(Of DiggStory)
    Dim xml As XDocument = XDocument.Parse(rawXml)

    Dim storiesQuery = From story In xml.Descendants("story") _
                    Select New DiggStory With { _
        .Id = CInt(Fix(story.Attribute("id"))), _
        .Title = (CStr(story.Element("title"))).Trim(), _
        .Description = (CStr(story.Element("description"))).Trim(), _
        .ThumbNail = (If(story.Element("thumbnail") Is Nothing, _
            String.Empty, story.Element("thumbnail").Attribute("src").Value)), _
        .Link = New Uri(CStr(story.Attribute("link"))), _
        .DiggCount = CInt(Fix(story.Attribute("diggs"))) _
        }
```

```
    lstResults.SelectedIndex = -1
    Return storiesQuery.ToList()
End Function
```

The XML from the response has a root object named <stories>, which contains a number of <story> elements. The <story> elements contain information about each story from the Digg web service. Example 7-7 shows a sample of how the response is formatted from the web service. I have removed the attributes from the XML to make the structure more readable.

Example 7-7. Sample XML response

```
<stories>
    <story>
        <description>
        </description>
        <title></title>
        <user/>
        <topic name="Microsoft" short_name="microsoft"/>
        <container name="Technology" short_name="technology"/>
    </story>
</stories>
```

Once the XDocument class parses the XML, a query is created with LINQ to XML that puts the contents into an instance of a custom DiggStory class (shown in Example 7-8). The query begins by querying each <story> element within the root of the XML response using the XDocument's IEnumerable Descendents collection. Each <story> element is then translated into a format that the DiggStory class can accept. The values for each <story> element are used to initialize an instance of a DiggStory class, being careful to convert datatypes and check for null values where appropriate.

Example 7-8. DiggStory class

C#
```
public class DiggStory
{
    public int Id { get; set; }
    public string Title { get; set; }
    public string Description { get; set; }
    public int DiggCount { get; set; }
    public Uri Link { get; set; }
    public string ThumbNail { get; set; }
}
```

VB
```
Public Class DiggStory
    Private privateId As Integer
    Public Property Id() As Integer
        Get
            Return privateId
        End Get
        Set(ByVal value As Integer)
            privateId = value
        End Set
```

```vb
        End Property
        Private privateTitle As String
        Public Property Title() As String
            Get
                Return privateTitle
            End Get
            Set(ByVal value As String)
                privateTitle = value
            End Set
        End Property
        Private privateDescription As String
        Public Property Description() As String
            Get
                Return privateDescription
            End Get
            Set(ByVal value As String)
                privateDescription = value
            End Set
        End Property
        Private privateDiggCount As Integer
        Public Property DiggCount() As Integer
            Get
                Return privateDiggCount
            End Get
            Set(ByVal value As Integer)
                privateDiggCount = value
            End Set
        End Property
        Private privateLink As Uri
        Public Property Link() As Uri
            Get
                Return privateLink
            End Get
            Set(ByVal value As Uri)
                privateLink = value
            End Set
        End Property
        Private privateThumbNail As String
        Public Property ThumbNail() As String
            Get
                Return privateThumbNail
            End Get
            Set(ByVal value As String)
                privateThumbNail = value
            End Set
        End Property
End Class
```

LINQ to XML is certainly not the only XML parsing library available to Silverlight 2. Another technique is to use the XmlReader to read a stream of XML from a response and parse it. The XmlReader allows for parsing XML elements and attributes as it reads the XML content. Although this is an effective way to parse XML, LINQ to XML is a much cleaner, more manageable way to parse XML. In Silverlight, even if a stream is returned that contains the XML content, the stream could be converted into a string and then parsed using LINQ to XML. I recommend using LINQ to XML to consume XML content in Silverlight over other techniques.

In Example 7-7 the `<story>` element is represented by the `story` variable, which is then used in the object initializer for each `DiggStory` class to get at each XML attribute for the `<story>` element. For example, you can initialize the `Title` property of the `DiggStory` class by using the following code snippet from Example 7-7:

```
Title = ((string)story.Element("title")).Trim(),
```

This uses the `story` variable that represents the `<story>` element to get the child element `<title>`. Some of the `DiggStory` class's properties are set using elements and others are set using attributes. For example, the number of diggs for a story is set by accessing the `diggs` attribute of the `<story>` element.

When the `storiesQuery` query created using LINQ to XML is executed, its results are converted to a `List<DiggStory>` and are bound to the `DataContext` of the `ListBox`. You can use other standard LINQ query constructs, including filters and sequences, with LINQ to XML, too. For instance, you could modify the query in Example 7-5 to include a filter using the `where` keyword, and filter out any stories that do not contain a photo. Figure 7-5, earlier in this chapter, shows the results of running this sample and passing it the topic of "Microsoft".

Measuring Progress

The time it takes for a web service request to complete its task and send a response back to the Silverlight client application may vary from instantaneous to several seconds in many cases. For example, a web service may be returning a lot of data over a slow connection. This is when it is nice to put a progress indicator on the screen to let the user know how the web service is progressing. The main steps to create a progress indicator when using `WebClient` are as follows:

1. Create the XAML.
2. Add an event handler to receive progress notification events.
3. Increment the progress indicator values.

The first step is to create a progress indicator in XAML to visually show the progress (as shown in Figure 7-6). This is an excellent case for creating a separate user control, as the progress indicator will likely be used in multiple areas of the application.

Example 7-9 shows the additional XAML that was added to *DiggStoryView.xaml* below the `ListBox`. This XAML creates a `Border` panel named `brdProgressBoundary` that is set to the maximum width of the area that should be filled. The nested `Border` panel named `brdProgressMeter` contains a `Border` background using a `LinearGradientBrush`. The width of the `brdProgressMeter` begins at 0, its starting point. This width will be incremented and a text message showing the percentage complete will be displayed to show progress.

Example 7-9. Adding a progress indicator

```
<Border x:Name="brdProgressBoundary" CornerRadius="5" Width="250" Height="25"
        BorderThickness="1" BorderBrush="#FF00135B" Margin="10,5,10,10"
        VerticalAlignment="Top" Grid.Row="2">
    <Grid HorizontalAlignment="Stretch">
        <Border x:Name="brdProgressMeter" Opacity="0.6" CornerRadius="5"
            HorizontalAlignment="Left" Width="250">
            <Border.Background>
                <LinearGradientBrush StartPoint="0,0.5" EndPoint="1,0.5">
                    <GradientStop Color="#FEBDE2F4" Offset="0.0"/>
                    <GradientStop Color="#FF00135B" Offset="0.75"/>
                </LinearGradientBrush>
            </Border.Background>
        </Border>
        <TextBlock x:Name="lbProgressValue" HorizontalAlignment="Center"
            VerticalAlignment="Center" FontSize="10"/>
    </Grid>
</Border>
```

The `WebClient` class has a `DownloadProgressChanged` event, which `WebClient` raises at intervals as the web service is working. The code in Example 7-10 shows the `svc_DownloadProgressChanged` handler being added. Since the `WebClient` is a field member in the class and is always accessible, you can add this code to the `DiggStoryView` constructor.

Example 7-10. Handling progress change events

C#
```
HideProgressBar();
svc.DownloadProgressChanged += svc_DownloadProgressChanged;
```

VB
```
HideProgressBar()
svc.DownloadProgressChanged += svc_DownloadProgressChanged
```

When the constructor code executes, this causes the `HideProgressBar` method to fire, which simply makes the progress indicator invisible since it is not needed yet. Example 7-11 shows the event handler where the progress is updated. This example also shows the code that hides and resets the progress indicator. The `HideProgressBar` method is also called in the event handler for the `DownloadStringCompleted` event.

When the event is raised, the handler receives a `DownloadProgressChangedEventArgs` parameter that contains information about the progress of the web service request's response message transfer. The `ProgressPercentage` property returns an integer value that represents the percentage of the download that is complete. The code converts this value to a percentage by multiplying it by 0.01 to set the width of the brdProgressBoundary. The width of the brdProgressBoundary is set at design time to 250. This value will not change, as it is used to set the boundaries of the progress bar. As the events are raised and the ProgressPercentage value increases, the width of the brdProgressMeter will expand to fill the outer brdProgressBoundary Border. When the application runs and a user clicks on the WebClient button to call the web service, the progress indicator will increase and will display as shown in Figure 7-6.

Example 7-11. Setting the progress indicator

```csharp
private void svc_DownloadProgressChanged(object sender,
        DownloadProgressChangedEventArgs e)
{
    int pct = e.ProgressPercentage;
    lbProgressValue.Text = pct.ToString() + "%";
    brdProgressMeter.Width = pct * 0.01 * brdProgressBoundary.Width;
}

private void HideProgressBar()
{
    brdProgressBoundary.Visibility = System.Windows.Visibility.Collapsed;
}

private void ResetProgressBar()
{
    brdProgressMeter.Width = 0;
    lbProgressValue.Text = "0 %";
    brdProgressBoundary.Visibility = System.Windows.Visibility.Visible;
}
```

```vbnet
Private Sub svc_DownloadProgressChanged(ByVal sender As Object, _
        ByVal e As DownloadProgressChangedEventArgs)
    Dim pct As Integer = e.ProgressPercentage
    lbProgressValue.Text = pct.ToString() & "%"
    brdProgressMeter.Width = pct * 0.01 * brdProgressBoundary.Width
End Sub

Private Sub HideProgressBar()
    brdProgressBoundary.Visibility = System.Windows.Visibility.Collapsed
End Sub

Private Sub ResetProgressBar()
    brdProgressMeter.Width = 0
    lbProgressValue.Text = "0 %"
    brdProgressBoundary.Visibility = System.Windows.Visibility.Visible
End Sub
```

If the operation is taking a long time, it might be a good idea to allow the user to click a button to cancel the asynchronous operation. To do that, first you must check whether the WebClient is involved in an asynchronous operation by checking the value of the IsBusy property. If it is involved in an asynchronous operation, you can invoke

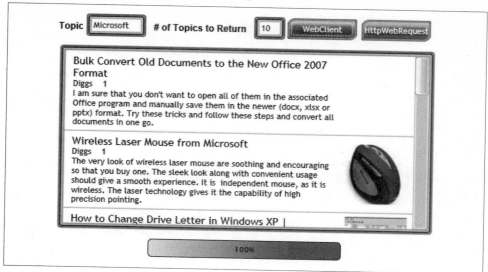

Figure 7-6. Showing the progress

the `CancelAsync` method on the `WebClient` class to cancel the active asynchronous operation. The code snippet in Example 7-12 shows how to cancel an active asynchronous operation on an instance of the `WebClient` called `svc`.

Example 7-12. Canceling the service request

C#
```
if (svc.IsBusy)
    svc.CancelAsync();
```

VB
```
If svc.IsBusy Then
    svc.CancelAsync()
End If
```

HttpWebRequest

Besides `WebClient`, the `HttpWebRequest` class is another option that allows web service requests to be made. `WebClient` offers a simple yet effective API to invoke and consume web services from Silverlight applications. All calls made through `WebClient` are actually passed through the `HttpWebRequest` class under the covers. `WebClient` is basically a simplified wrapper on top of `HttpWebRequest`. You should use the `HttpWebRequest` class when you require more granular control over the web service call.

`HttpWebRequest` exposes properties that allow customization of the web service call by including headers through the `Headers` property and setting the content type through the `ContentType` property. Table 7-2 lists some of the most important members of `HttpWebRequest` used in invoking web services.

Table 7-2. *Key methods and properties of HttpWebRequest*

Methods and events	Type	Description
Abort	Method	Cancels a request made with HttpWebRequest.
BeginGetRequestStream	Method	Begins the asynchronous request for a stream to send HTTP request data to a service.
BeginGetResponseStream	Method	Begins the asynchronous request for a stream to receive an HTTP response from a service.
Create	Method	Method of the base class WebRequest. It creates an instance of a WebRequest given a URI.
EndGetRequestStream	Method	Ends the asynchronous request to obtain a stream to send an HTTP request.
EndGetResponse	Method	Ends the asynchronous request to obtain a stream to receive an HTTP response.
ContentType	Property	Gets or sets the ContentType in an HTTP header.
Headers	Property	Collection of HTTP headers. You can add and set name/value pairs. These are sent as HTTP headers to a request.
Method	Property	The HTTP verb to be sent in the request (i.e., GET or POST).

HttpWebRequest inherits from the WebRequest base class. WebRequest exposes a Create method that accepts a URI and returns an instance of a WebRequest that can be used to invoke web services asynchronously. For example, the following code will create an instance of a WebRequest that can invoke a web service given a string representing a URL:

C#
```
WebRequest request = HttpWebRequest.Create(new Uri(url));
```

VB
```
Dim request As WebRequest = HttpWebRequest.Create(New Uri(url))
```

Once the WebRequest instance has been created, you can invoke a web service request using the BeginGetResponse method and passing it a callback method and the instance of the WebRequest. The callback method is an AsyncCallback instance, which is a method that receives an IAsyncResult parameter.

C#
```
request.BeginGetResponse(new AsyncCallback(ReadCallback), request);
```

VB
```
request.BeginGetResponse(New AsyncCallback(AddressOf ReadCallback), request)
```

When the web service has completed, the callback method will execute. It receives the IAsyncResult instance, which contains information about the web service results. You can examine the AsyncResult to retrieve the web service's response. The callback code casts the IAsyncResult instance's AsyncState property to an HttpWebRequest class and stores it in the request variable. From here the HttpWebRequest's EndGetResponse method is invoked. It retrieves an HttpWebResponse class, which in turn is used to invoke the GetResponseStream method of the HttpWebResponse. This returns a StreamReader instance which can easily be read to its end to access the response, which in this case contains XML.

In review, the steps to retrieve the response in a string format are as follows:

1. Convert the IAsyncResult parameter's AsyncState to an HttpWebRequest instance.

```
C#   HttpWebRequest request = (HttpWebRequest)ar.AsyncState;
```

```
VB   Dim request As HttpWebRequest = CType(ar.AsyncState, HttpWebRequest)
```

2. Use the EndGetResponse method on the HttpWebRequest to obtain the HttpWebResponse instance.

```
C#   HttpWebResponse response = (HttpWebResponse)request.EndGetResponse(ar);
```

```
VB   Dim response As HttpWebResponse = _
         CType(request.EndGetResponse(ar), HttpWebResponse)
```

3. Use the GetResponseStream method on the HttpWebResponse to read the response contents using a StreamReader.

```
C#   StreamReader streamReader = new StreamReader(response.GetResponseStream());
```

```
VB   Dim streamReader As New StreamReader(response.GetResponseStream())
```

4. Using the StreamReader, read the stream to its end and dump its contents into a string.

```
C#   string rawXml = streamReader.ReadToEnd();
```

```
VB   Dim rawXml As String = streamReader.ReadToEnd()
```

HttpWebRequest in Action

The DiggStoryView sample application in this chapter allows the user to retrieve stories from the Digg.com RESTful web service using either the WebClient class or the HttpWebRequest class. When the user clicks the HttpWebRequest button, shown in Figure 7-6, the Digg.com web service is invoked using the code shown in Example 7-13.

The URI for the Digg.com RESTful web service is formatted and passed to the HttpWebRequest's Create method. You can use the same URI for the HttpWebRequest technique and the WebClient technique in the previous examples. The web service is then invoked asynchronously, passing along the request. The request carries along with it any customizations that may have been made to the request, including any headers or the content type, if needed.

Example 7-13. Invoking a RESTful web service through HttpWebRequest

```
C#   private void btnUseHttpWebRequest_Click(object sender, RoutedEventArgs e)
     {
         string topic = txtTopic.Text;
         int count = int.Parse(txtTopicCount.Text);
         string url = String.Format("{0}/{1}?appkey={2}&count={3}",
             baseUri, topic, appKey, count);

         WebRequest request = HttpWebRequest.Create(new Uri(url));
         request.BeginGetResponse(new AsyncCallback(ReadCallback), request);
     }
```

```
VB   Private Sub btnUseHttpWebRequest_Click(ByVal sender As Object, _
             ByVal e As RoutedEventArgs)
         Dim topic As String = txtTopic.Text
```

```
      Dim count As Integer = Integer.Parse(txtTopicCount.Text)
      Dim url As String = String.Format("{0}/{1}?appkey={2}&count={3}", _
          baseUri, topic, appKey, count)

      Dim request As WebRequest = HttpWebRequest.Create(New Uri(url))
      request.BeginGetResponse(New AsyncCallback(AddressOf ReadCallback), request)
End Sub
```

In addition to passing the request, the `BeginGetResponse` method also indicates the callback method that will be executed when the web service has responded. The callback method must match the signature of the delegate for the `AsyncCallback`, which has a single parameter of type `IAsyncResult`, as shown here:

[C#]
```
      public delegate void AsyncCallback(System.IAsyncResult ar)
```

[VB]
```
      Public Delegate Sub AsyncCallback(ByVal ar As System.IAsyncResult)
```

Working with the Callback

The `ReadCallback` method, shown in Example 7-14, retrieves the response from the web service call and converts it to a string. The string contains the response from the Digg.com RESTful web service, which can be consumed using any of the XML libraries, including LINQ to XML. The XML is passed to the `CreateStoryList` method, which uses LINQ to XML to parse the data and put it into a `List<DiggStory>`. This is the same `CreateStoryList` method that the `WebClient` uses. You can use the same method, because the response's XML content uses the identical schema whether it is called from `WebClient` or `HttpWebRequest`.

The `List<DiggStory>` that is created from the web service's response must then be data-bound to the `lstResults` `ListBox`. When the `HttpWebRequest` asynchronous web service calls invoke their callback methods, the callback method operates on the background worker thread and not the UI thread. This means that code in the callback method cannot access and update controls in the UI, because they are operating on a different thread. Obviously, this causes a problem since the likely intention of calling a web service using an HTTP `GET` is to retrieve the web service's response and use it to do something to the UI.

Example 7-14. HttpWebRequest's callback method

[C#]
```
private void ReadCallback(IAsyncResult ar)
{
    HttpWebRequest request = (HttpWebRequest)ar.AsyncState;
    HttpWebResponse response = (HttpWebResponse)request.EndGetResponse(ar);
    Stream stream = response.GetResponseStream();

    using (StreamReader streamReader = new StreamReader(stream))
    {
        string rawXml = streamReader.ReadToEnd();
        List<DiggStory> list = CreateStoryList(rawXml);

        // Method 1: delegate
```

```
            this.Dispatcher.BeginInvoke(new dBindTheList(this.BindTheList), list);
        }
```

VB
```
Private Sub ReadCallback(ByVal ar As IAsyncResult)
    Dim request As HttpWebRequest = CType(ar.AsyncState, HttpWebRequest)
    Dim response As HttpWebResponse = _
        CType(request.EndGetResponse(ar), HttpWebResponse)
    Dim stream As Stream = response.GetResponseStream()

    Using streamReader As New StreamReader(stream)
        Dim rawXml As String = streamReader.ReadToEnd()
        Dim list As List(Of DiggStory) = CreateStoryList(rawXml)

        ' Method 1: delegate
        Me.Dispatcher.BeginInvoke(New dBindTheList(Me.BindTheList), list)
    End Using
End Sub
```

Crossing Threads

The code in Example 7-14 cannot simply bind the List<DiggStory> to a ListBox in the
UI, because the code is operating in the background thread and the UI is in the UI
thread. (The UI thread is the only thread that can communicate with the UI elements.)
However, you can use the Dispatcher class to send a request to execute a method on
the UI thread.

The Dispatcher class is available on a DependencyObject; in the case of Example 7-14,
the DependencyObject is the DiggStoryView Silverlight user control. The Dispatcher class
exposes a BeginInvoke method that executes a delegate asynchronously on the thread
of the DependencyObject. This means that the callback code from the
HttpWebRequest, which operates in the background worker thread, can use the
Dispatcher.BeginInvoke method to execute code that will run on the UI thread. In other
words, the response can be consumed and bound to the UI. The callback method in
Example 7-14 uses the delegate and method shown in Example 7-15 to bind the
List<DiggStory> to the DataContext of the ListBox.

Example 7-15. Delegate to bind a List<T> to the UI

C#
```
private delegate void dBindTheList(List<DiggStory> list);
private void BindTheList(List<DiggStory> list)
{
    lstResults.DataContext = list;
}
```

VB
```
Private Delegate Sub dBindTheList(ByVal list As List(Of DiggStory))
Private Sub BindTheList(ByVal list As List(Of DiggStory))
    lstResults.DataContext = list
End Sub
```

As the code in the callback shown in Example 7-14 implies, there is more than one way
to use a delegate in the Dispatcher.BeginInvoke method. The example shows an explicit
implementation of the dBindTheList delegate using the BindTheList method. However,

```
```

you can avoid the explicit delegate by using an anonymous delegate, as shown in Example 7-16.

Example 7-16. Executing an anonymous delegate on the UI thread

```
// Method 2: anonymous delegate
this.Dispatcher.BeginInvoke(delegate()
    {
        lstResults.DataContext = list;
    });
```

Yet a more concise version does the same job as the other two techniques. You can use lambda expressions as a form of shorthand for the anonymous delegate. This technique embeds all of the code in a single line, as shown in Example 7-17.

Example 7-17. Executing a lambda on the UI thread

C#
```
// Method 3: lambda expression
Deployment.Current.Dispatcher.BeginInvoke(() => lstResults.DataContext = list);
```

VB
```
' Method 3: lambda expression
Deployment.Current.Dispatcher.BeginInvoke(Function() lstResults.DataContext = list)
```

Threading with WebClient and HttpWebRequest

The example in this chapter demonstrates that when using HttpWebRequest to invoke web services, callbacks are sent on a worker thread rather than the UI thread. This means the callback will not have access to the UI thread implicitly. While it is in an HttpWebRequest callback, the code is on a background worker thread, so although the callback may receive the response content from the web service, it will not be able to directly set the content to a control in the user interface.

There are two ways to work around this. One way is to use WebClient to invoke the web service, as WebClient invokes the callbacks on the UI thread automatically. Example 7-6 uses this technique. Another way is to explicitly set the content to the UI thread using the Dispatcher.BeginInvoke method, which is what the code in Example 7-12 uses.

When a web service call is invoked using WebClient's DownloadStringAsync method (or any of its asynchronous web service invocation methods), the event handler assigned to the DownloadStringCompleted event is automatically placed on the UI thread. This makes using the WebClient class a good choice for making web requests to retrieve results via a response, and using XAML-based data binding to bind them to a control in the UI.

Summary

RESTful web services are growing in number and are providing opportunities for Silverlight 2 applications to reach out to a variety of third-party and custom services. Using the `WebClient` and `HttpWebRequest` libraries, you can make requests to these RESTful services and consume their responses. In addition to making HTTP `GET` requests, Silverlight 2 applications can issue `POST` HTTP actions. Some solid techniques are available for creating through WCF web services a custom RESTful service that a Silverlight 2 application will consume. Chapters 8 and 9 explore these topics more deeply via demonstrations of interactions with the Amazon.com and Twitter.com RESTful service APIs.

CHAPTER 8

Consuming Amazon's RESTful Services with Silverlight 2

Chapter 7 provided a primer on REST and how to consume RESTful web services from Silverlight 2 using LINQ to XML with both `WebClient` and `HttpWebRequest`. RESTful services can be highly interactive with third-party RESTful APIs. These RESTful services can enhance a Silverlight application by adding their functionality into the robust user experience that Silverlight 2 provides. To demonstrate this symbiosis, this chapter shows how to build a Silverlight 2 application that searches the Amazon book database and allows a user to manage her shopping cart and purchase books using the Amazon RESTful API.

Data in the Cloud

Many third parties have opened the doors of their applications to developers through SOAP and RESTful APIs. Amazon, Google, Flickr, Live Search, Digg, and Twitter (to name a few) all allow developers to communicate with their systems through an open API. Today there is a growing trend to build web applications that communicate with each other. Silverlight 2 is ideal for building these types of applications because it brings a robust user experience to rich Internet applications (RIAs) and has the ability to communicate with remote web services. For example, you can build a single Silverlight 2 application that communicates with several different web service libraries from multiple third parties and custom web services. The boundaries between applications are breaking down and are bringing a cloud of services within reach of applications.

The popularity of these services works well for both the consumer and the publisher of the service. The consumer gains the features and information of the third-party publisher. Often, you cannot obtain these features without these third-party services (at least not without investing some serious time in development). For example, it is much easier to use the Amazon RESTful web service library to search for books to purchase than it is to create a searchable book library.

The publisher of the service also benefits from offering its services and access to its data through the cloud. For example, if a publisher sells a product and opens an API to allow client applications to also sell its products, this is a win for the publisher. In this case, the publisher has increased its visibility and the likelihood of getting a sale. Publishers that do not sell products but offer services or social community networking, such as Twitter, Flickr, or even Live Search, get the added visibility of being in additional client applications. The incentives are high for both publishers and consumers to work together through the cloud.

Creating an Amazon Shopping Cart

The previous chapters demonstrated the basic concepts of communicating with a RESTful remote web service using `WebClient` and `HttpWebRequest`, using LINQ to XML to consume a response, conquering cross-domain policies, and creating rich data-bound applications. Although it is great to talk about what RESTful services are and how to consume them, the power behind opening applications to these services is more obvious when you can see it demonstrated in an example with an existing RESTful API. In this chapter, we'll do just that with Amazon's E-Commerce Services (Amazon ECS). The example will show you how many of the capabilities we've discussed work together in a real application that allows a user to search the Amazon book database, create a shopping cart stored at Amazon, add and remove items from the cart, accumulate an order total, and begin the checkout process, all from a Silverlight 2 client application.

The architecture of this example involves a few moving parts. First the Silverlight 2 application provides the interface for the user and the communication between the user interface and the shopping services at Amazon. The Amazon E-Commerce Service has a RESTful API that makes it easy to plug into the Amazon product database. This example will focus on shopping for books at Amazon to keep the example focused; however, it is possible to do much more with the API. The Silverlight 2 client application will use the `WebClient` library to communicate with Amazon's RESTful web services to both send and receive information in building a shopping cart. Figure 8-1 shows the architecture of the example. You can find the complete source code for the example with the code for this chpater.

Before jumping into the code, it is important to establish an account with the Amazon ECS to be an approved Amazon Web Services developer. Registration for this service is free. You can find more information about registering for the Amazon ECS on the Amazon site using the following link:

http://docs.amazonwebservices.com/AWSEcommerceService/2005-03-23/

Amazon ECS creates and assigns a unique access key to each registered user. This access key is required in every call to all of the web service methods exposed by the Amazon ECS API. The access key included in the example code has been replaced with a

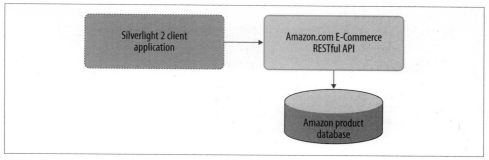

Figure 8-1. Amazon Services example architecture

placeholder. Before running any of the examples, you must obtain this access key and copy it to the source code.

RESTful Actions

The next step in building the example application is to define what operations the application will support. The user interface will allow the user to search for books from the Amazon ECS database using a set of keywords to filter the search. From the results, the user will be able to select books and add them to a shopping cart. If the shopping cart has not been created yet, the application should automatically create a shopping cart first, and then add the items to the shopping cart. Features should also allow the user to remove items from the shopping cart, add items to the cart, and clear the cart entirely. In summary, the following operations are required to interact with the Amazon ECS RESTful API:

- Search for books, using keywords for filtering
- Create a cart
- Add items to the cart
- Remove items from the cart
- Empty the cart

You could easily enhance the application by adding other features that the Amazon ECS RESTful API supports, such as submitting the cart for purchase or retrieving an existing cart. But to keep this focused, we'll stick with these basic operations. You can map these operations to some of the operations found in the Amazon ECS documentation. Figure 8-2 shows some of the Amazon ECS RESTful web service methods that the example application uses to support these features.

You can configure the `ItemSearch` method to search a specific Amazon product store, provide filtering criteria for the search, and return a specific response containing as much or as little information as required by the consumer of the service. Example 8-1 shows the syntax of the sample `ItemSearch` method. Breaking down the parts of the

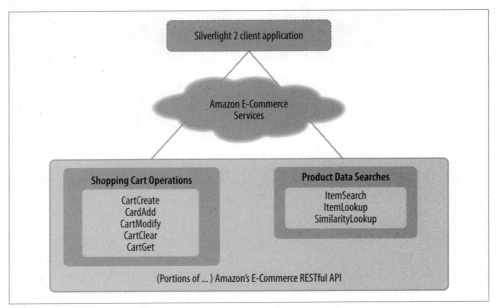

Figure 8-2. RESTful operations

syntax, you can see that some key elements are required when calling the `ItemSearch` method:

- The service URI
- The `Service` to communicate with
- The `SubscriptionId` (a.k.a. the unique access key)
- The `Operation` (a.k.a. the action to perform)
- The `Keywords` used to filter the request
- The store to search (`SearchIndex`)
- The information set that should be returned (`ResponseGroup`)

Example 8-1. ItemSearch syntax

```
http://webservices.amazon.com/onca/xml?Service=AWSECommerceService&SubscriptionId=[
Your Subscription ID Here]&Operation=ItemSearch&Keywords=[A Keywords
String]&SearchIndex=[A Search Index String]&ResonseGroup=[A Response Group]
```

The `SubscriptionId` parameter is where the unique access key goes that Amazon ECS assigns to each user. The examples in this chapter leave this parameter open. When running the application for this chapter, be sure to replace this with a unique Amazon access key. You can replace the operation with whatever operation is required. The example application uses the following operations:

- `ItemSearch` (search for books)

- **CartCreate** (create a cart and add the first book to it)
- **CartAdd** (add additional books to the existing cart)
- **CartModify** (modify the quantity of books in the cart)
- **CartClear** (remove all books from the cart)

These operations, also shown in Example 8-2, are a subset of the operations exposed by Amazon ECS that this example application uses. To keep things focused, the example application will allow the user to add only one of each item to the cart. This is a limitation of the example in this chapter, not of Amazon ECS. Amazon ECS provides the CartModify operation that allows you to change the quantity of an item in the cart. For this example, we will use the CartModify operation to remove a book from the cart by setting its quantity to 0.

The user of the example application will enter the keywords, which will be used to filter the search results for the ItemSearch operation. The SearchIndex parameter indicates the type of search—whether for toys, books, or DVDs, for instance. In this example, the search will look for books, so the parameter will be Books. The ResponseGroup parameter defines the set (or sets) of information that the ItemSearch operation will return. Amazon ECS offers several predefined response groups that can be requested and returned as XML to the consumer application. Some response groups return very limited information, which is ideal for simply getting back a list of the items. Other response groups return much more detailed information about each item that was found. A good practice is to use the response group that yields the information that is needed, and little more. The larger the response group, the larger the size of the response from the web service method. The larger the response size, the slower the operation could become. The definitions of what each response group returns are in the Amazon ECS documentation. For this example application, the ResponseGroup is set to Medium, which returns a good balance of detail for each book, including the price, an image, the title, the publisher, and other required information.

Example 8-2 shows a sample request to the Amazon ECS RESTful API to find all books that have the keywords Silverlight 2 and Data. Again, notice that there is a placeholder for the access key. As mentioned earlier, you must replace this with a unique access key obtained from the Amazon ECS registration process.

 You can find more information on formatting RESTful requests to the Amazon ECS services in the Amazon documentation, and on the Amazon ECS website at *http://docs.amazonwebservices.com/AWSECom merceService/2007-10-29/DG/MakingRESTRequests.html*.

Example 8-2. ItemSearch sample request

```
http://webservices.amazon.com/onca/xml?Service=AWSECommerceService&AWSAccessKeyId=[
YourAccessKeyGoesHere]&Operation=ItemSearch&SearchIndex=Books&ResponseGroup=Medium&
Keywords=Silverlight%202%20Data
```

Figure 8-3. Search results for ItemSearch operation

Example 8-3 shows the completed application, where the HTTP GET request in Example 8-2 has been invoked and its response has been gathered. The response includes five books, which are shown in Figure 8-3. The next steps are to write the application that will perform the search, bind the results, and create the shopping cart experience.

DEBUGGING SERVICE REQUESTS

Examining the Request with Fiddler2

Fiddler2 is a great tool that reveals a lot of information about a request, including any headers for the request, status codes, and its response. This tool can save you a ton of time debugging requests and responses as it highlights the operations and what is happening with them. However, not only is it a great tool for debugging; it also helps you to clarify what is happening during the request and response process. Fiddler2 watches the traffic during the HTTP request and displays the HTTP status codes, the request, and the response. Figure 8-4 shows the results of invoking the HTTP GET request to the Amazon ECS RESTful API in Fiddler2. The left window pane of Fiddler2 shows all of the requests made for this operation.

Notice that Figure 8-4 shows three web requests when the HTTP request from Example 8-2 is performed. Before the Amazon ECS service can be invoked, Silverlight 2 realizes that this is a call from one domain to another. Because this is a cross-domain call, it requests the cross-domain policy files. First it requests the *clientaccesspolicy.xml* file from the *webservice.amazon.com* host. This file does not exist, so a 404 HTTP status code is returned signifying that the file is not found. Silverlight 2 then moves on to request the *crossdomain.xml* file from the host. This file is found and contains permissions that allow requests from all domains, as shown in Example 8-3. Now that permission has been granted to access the Amazon ECS service, the actual request is performed.

You also can use Fiddler2 to view the response, as shown in Example 8-3. You can view the response for the `ItemSearch` operation in Fiddler2 by double-clicking the request in the left pane (shown in Figure 8-4), which displays the Session Inspector tab of Fiddler2 (shown in Figure 8-5). You can view the raw response in the bottom pane in the Session Inspector. The response includes the original request parameters and the `Medium` response group. A good practice is to return the original request in the response when debugging. This helps you to pinpoint problems in the request and response process as it may point out any discrepancies between what was intended to be sent and what was actually sent to the request.

#	Re...	Pro...	Host	URL	Body	C.	Content-Type	Proces
⚠ 1	404	HTTP	webservices.amazon.com	/clientaccesspolicy.xml	191		text/html; charset...	iexplor
2	200	HTTP	webservices.amazon.com	/crossdomain.xml	152		text/xml	iexplor
3	200	HTTP	webservices.amazon.com	/onca/xml?Service=AWS...	4,299		text/xml; charset=...	iexplor

Figure 8-4. Watching the request in Fiddler2

Example 8-3. The response from crossdomain.xml

```
HTTP/1.1 200 OK
Date: Mon, 08 Sep 2008 15:31:09 GMT
Server: Server
Last-Modified: Tue, 20 Apr 2004 04:20:54 GMT
ETag: "1400018-ca-f71580"
Accept-Ranges: bytes
nnCoection: close
Content-Type: text/xml
Vary: Accept-Encoding,User-Agent
Content-Length: 202
Cneonction: close

<?xml version="1.0"?>
<!DOCTYPE cross-domain-policy SYSTEM "http://www.macromedia.com/xml/dtds/
cross-domain-policy.dtd">
<cross-domain-policy>
```

```
    <allow-access-from domain="*" />
</cross-domain-policy>
```

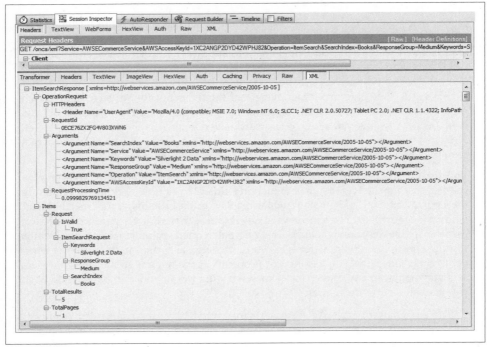

Figure 8-5. Response for ItemSearch in Fiddler2

Searching for Books

The example Silverlight 2 client application allows the user to search the Amazon database for books. As the Silverlight 2 client application may call several different operations, the parts of the request that do not change are represented by constants. Example 8-4 shows the three constants that are used by the example application. Be sure to replace the `ACCESS_KEY` constant's value with the key value that Amazon ECS provides to you after you register with the Amazon service. This is the unique value that identifies the registered user who makes a request to the Amazon ECS service. The `ServiceUrlBase` read-only property puts these base components together to create the base URL for each web service call.

Example 8-4. Constants and base URL for BookSearch

```csharp
private const string NAMESPACE_AWSECommerceService =
    "http://webservices.amazon.com/AWSECommerceService/2005-10-05";
private const string SERVICE_URL = "http://webservices.amazon.com/onca/xml";
private const string ACCESS_KEY = "PutYourAccessKeyHere";
private const string SERVICE_NAME = "AWSECommerceService";
```

```
    private string ServiceUrlBase
    {
        get { return string.Format("{0}?Service={1}&AWSAccessKeyId={2}",
            SERVICE_URL, SERVICE_NAME, ACCESS_KEY); }
    }
```

VB
```
Private Const NAMESPACE_AWSECommerceService As String = _
    "http://webservices.amazon.com/AWSECommerceService/2005-10-05"
Private Const SERVICE_URL As String = "http://webservices.amazon.com/onca/xml"
Private Const ACCESS_KEY As String = "PutYourAccessKeyHere"
Private Const SERVICE_NAME As String = "AWSECommerceService"

Private ReadOnly Property ServiceUrlBase() As String
    Get
        Return String.Format("{0}?Service={1}&AWSAccessKeyId={2}", _
            SERVICE_URL, SERVICE_NAME, ACCESS_KEY)
    End Get
End Property
```

You can divide the pieces of the HTTP request into two categories: the parts that stay the same in each request, and the parts that vary from call to call. The constant values shown in Example 8-4 represent the consistent aspects of each HTTP request. The aspects that change depend on the operation (i.e., the action to perform) and any parameters required by that operation.

When performing the `ItemSearch` operation, the `DataContext` for the `ListBox` named `lstBooks` is set to null to clear any binding with the `lstBooks` search results. The `SearchAsync` method shown in Example 8-5 sets up the call to the `ItemSearch` operation. The keywords that the user entered are retrieved, the `ResponseGroup` is set to `Medium`, and the operation is set to `ItemSearch`. These aspects of the URI are then put together with the static aspects of the URL to form the URI for the web service request that performs the book search.

An instance of `WebClient` is created to communicate with the HTTP-based web service. Because all calls to web services from Silverlight 2 are asynchronous operations, before invoking the web service an event handler is set to the `DownloadStringCompleted` event. This event handler, `SearchAsyncCompleted`, will execute when the web service has completed and sends its response back to the Silverlight 2 client application. You can watch the call to the web service in Fiddler2, where the requests for the cross-domain policy files and the actual web service request will be displayed.

Example 8-5. Asynchronous search

C#
```
private void SearchAsync()
{
    string filter = txtFilter.Text;
    string searchIndex = "Books";
    string responseGroup = "Medium";
    string operation = "ItemSearch";
    string url =
string.Format("{0}&Operation={1}&SearchIndex={2}&ResponseGroup={3}&Keywords={4}",
```

```
            ServiceUrlBase, operation, searchIndex, responseGroup, filter);
        var service = new WebClient();
        service.DownloadStringCompleted += AmazonService_SearchAsyncCompleted;
        service.DownloadStringAsync(new Uri(url));
    }
```

VB
```
    Private Sub SearchAsync()
        Dim filter As String = txtFilter.Text
        Dim searchIndex As String = "Books"
        Dim responseGroup As String = "Medium"
        Dim operation As String = "ItemSearch"
        Dim url As String = _
String.Format("{0}&Operation={1}&SearchIndex={2}&ResponseGroup={3}&Keywords={4}", _
            ServiceUrlBase, operation, searchIndex, responseGroup, filter)
        Dim service = New WebClient()
        service.DownloadStringCompleted += AmazonService_SearchAsyncCompleted
        service.DownloadStringAsync(New Uri(url))
    End Sub
```

Once the web service has completed, the `AmazonService_SearchAsyncCompleted` event handler is executed. This event handler receives the response as a string in the `e.Result` parameter. If an error occurred during the request, `e.Error` will contain an error that you can examine. If `e.Result` is null (or `Nothing` in VB) the operation completed and you can retrieve the `e.Result` value. Example 8-6 shows the event handler code grabbing the result, which in this case is an XML string containing the `Medium ResponseGroup` from the Amazon ECS service. The results are then parsed and translated into a `List<Book>` and displayed in the `lstBooks ListBox`.

Example 8-6. Asynchronous completion handler

C#
```
    private void AmazonService_SearchAsyncCompleted(object sender,
        DownloadStringCompletedEventArgs e)
    {
        if (e.Error == null)
        {
            string result = e.Result;
            List<Book> bookList = GetBooks(result);
            DisplayBooks(bookList);
        }
    }
```

VB
```
    Private Sub AmazonService_SearchAsyncCompleted(ByVal sender As Object, _
        ByVal e As DownloadStringCompletedEventArgs)
        If e.Error Is Nothing Then
            Dim result As String = e.Result
            Dim bookList As List(Of Book) = GetBooks(result)
            DisplayBooks(bookList)
        End If
    End Sub
```

A few important aspects in Example 8-6 warrant closer inspection. First, the `GetBooks` method accepts the XML in string format. You can parse this XML response using `XmlReader`, LINQ to XML, or any other XML parsing utility available to the .NET

CLR for Silverlight 2. `GetBooks` uses LINQ to XML to parse the results and create the `List<Book>`. Creation of the `List<Book>` happens inside the LINQ to XML query. The second important aspect to examine in Example 8-6 is that the `List<Book>` is displayed in the `lstBooks ListBox`. Because the XML is translated into a `List<Book>`, it is easily bound to target controls and displayed in the Silverlight 2 client application.

Parsing Books with LINQ to XML

The `GetBooks` method accepts an XML string through the `result` parameter. The Amazon ECS documentation publishes the shape of the XML response, so using LINQ to XML on the response is a relatively straightforward process of querying the elements and attributes by name. First, the XML contained in the `result` parameter is parsed into an instance of the `XDocument` object. The `XDocument` object will then represent the XML document, and you can query it using LINQ to XML to pull out the values needed to create the `List<Book>`.

When querying using LINQ to XML it is important to specify the namespace of the elements, if one exists. Otherwise, without the namespace being indicated, the query will not find the elements. A good practice is to create a variable in the method that creates the LINQ to XML query to represent the namespace. This namespace must precede every name of each element and attribute that will be queried. Example 8-7 shows how to parse the XML string into an `XDocument` and specify a short name to represent the namespace for the XML.

Example 8-7. Parsing into an XDocument

[C#]
```
XDocument bookXml = XDocument.Parse(result);
XNamespace ns = NAMESPACE_AWSECommerceService;
```

[VB]
```
Dim bookXml As XDocument = XDocument.Parse(result)
Dim ns As XNamespace = NAMESPACE_AWSECommerceService
```

The purpose of the LINQ to XML query is to translate the XML into a `List<Book>` so that it can be bound to the Silverlight 2 target controls. Example 8-8 shows the full LINQ to XML query, but there are many important pieces to examine and break down.

The XML response contains a list of items. The items represent books in this case, because the `SearchIndex` parameter was set to `books`. The query begins by accessing the list of items in the `from` clause of the LINQ query definition. The `book` parameter in the LINQ query now represents each individual book item from the response.

There is more than one way to grab a value from an element or attribute using LINQ to XML. The `let` statement is one way that you can set a value to a placeholder variable in a LINQ query. The advantage of using a `let` statement to set a variable is that other statements can then use the variable repeatedly throughout the LINQ query definition. For example, the `attributes` variable is set to the `ItemAttributes` element from the XML. Many of the values that are retrieved from this LINQ query definition are contained in child elements and attributes of the `ItemAttributes` element. Once the `attributes` variable is set, this makes retrieval of any child elements or attributes much simpler:

```
let attributes = book.Element(ns + "ItemAttributes")
```
```
Let attributes = book.Element(ns + "ItemAttributes") _
```

Another advantage of using the `let` statement is that you can use it to physically put all of the variable setting logic in one location in the query. For instance, in Example 8-8, all of the `let` statements are adjacent to each other. These statements handle the logic for getting the values out of the XML, checking for null values, and checking for the existence of values and any logic that may be needed to calculate the values. Putting all of this logic in the `let` statements and keeping them adjacent to each other makes the `select` statement of the query much cleaner and simpler to read and maintain.

Example 8-8. LINQ to XML on the books

```csharp
private List<Book> GetBooks(string result)
{
    XDocument bookXml = XDocument.Parse(result);
    XNamespace ns = NAMESPACE_AWSECommerceService;

    var bookQuery = from book in bookXml.Descendants(ns + "Item")

                    let attributes = book.Element(ns + "ItemAttributes")
                    let price = Decimal.Parse(
                        (book.Elements(ns + "OfferSummary").Any()
                         && book.Element(ns + "OfferSummary").Elements(
                        ns + "LowestNewPrice").Any()
                            ? book.Element(ns + "OfferSummary").Element(
                            ns + "LowestNewPrice").Element(
                            ns + "Amount").Value
                            : (attributes.Elements(ns + "ListPrice").Any()
                                    ? attributes.Element(
                                ns + "ListPrice").Element(
                                ns + "Amount").Value
                                    : "0"))
                        ) / 100
                    let pageCount =
                        (attributes.Elements(ns + "NumberOfPages").Any()
                            ? Int32.Parse(attributes.Element(
                            ns + "NumberOfPages").Value)
                            : 0)
                    let imageSource =
                        (book.Elements(ns + "SmallImage").Any()
                            ? book.Element(ns + "SmallImage").Element(
                            ns + "URL").Value
                            : string.Empty)
                    let year = Int32.Parse((attributes.Element(
                    ns + "PublicationDate").Value).Substring(0, 4))

                    where attributes.Elements(ns + "ISBN").Any()
                        && price > 0
```

```
                    orderby attributes.Element(ns + "Title").Value ascending

                    select new Book
                    {
                        AmazonASIN = ((string)book.Element(ns + "ASIN")).Trim(),
                        ISBN = attributes.Element(ns + "ISBN").Value,
                        Title = attributes.Element(ns + "Title").Value,
                        PageCount = pageCount,
                        Price = price,
                        Publisher = attributes.Element(ns + "Publisher").Value,
                        Year = year,
                        HrefLink = new Uri(book.Element(
                        ns + "DetailPageURL").Value),
                        Authors = (
                                    from author in book.Descendants(
                                ns + "Author")
                                        select author.Value
                                    ).ToList(),
                        ImageSource = imageSource
                    };

        List<Book> bookList = bookQuery.ToList<Book>();
        return bookList;
    }

Private Function GetBooks(ByVal result As String) As List(Of Book)
    Dim bookXml As XDocument = XDocument.Parse(result)
    Dim ns As XNamespace = NAMESPACE_AWSECommerceService

    Dim bookQuery = _
        From book In bookXml.Descendants(ns + "Item") _

        Let attributes = book.Element(ns + "ItemAttributes") _
        Let price = Decimal.Parse((If(book.Elements(ns + "OfferSummary").Any() _
        AndAlso book.Element(ns + "OfferSummary").Elements( _
        ns + "LowestNewPrice").Any(), _
        book.Element(ns + "OfferSummary").Element( _
        ns + "LowestNewPrice").Element(ns + "Amount").Value, _
        (If(attributes.Elements(ns + "ListPrice").Any(), _
        attributes.Element(ns + "ListPrice").Element(ns + "Amount").Value, _
        "0"))))) / 100 _
        Let pageCount = (If(attributes.Elements(ns + "NumberOfPages").Any(), _
        Int32.Parse(attributes.Element(ns + "NumberOfPages").Value), 0)) _
        Let imageSource = (If(book.Elements(ns + "SmallImage").Any(), _
        book.Element(ns + "SmallImage").Element(ns + "URL").Value, _
        String.Empty)) _
        Let year = Int32.Parse((attributes.Element( _
        ns + "PublicationDate").Value).Substring(0, 4)) _

        Where attributes.Elements(ns + "ISBN").Any() AndAlso price > 0 _

        Order By attributes.Element(ns + "Title").Value Ascending _

        Select New Book With { _
        .AmazonASIN = (CStr(book.Element(ns + "ASIN"))).Trim(), _
```

```
            .ISBN = attributes.Element(ns + "ISBN").Value, _
            .Title = attributes.Element(ns + "Title").Value, _
            .PageCount = pageCount, .Price = price, _
            .Publisher = attributes.Element(ns + "Publisher").Value, _
            .Year = year, _
            .HrefLink = New Uri(book.Element(ns + "DetailPageURL").Value), _
            .Authors = ( _
                    From author In book.Descendants(ns + "Author") _
                    Select author.Value).ToList(), .ImageSource = imageSource}

        Dim bookList As List(Of Book) = bookQuery.ToList(Of Book)()
        Return bookList
End Function
```

One of the things you must do when writing a LINQ query definition is check for the existence of nonrequired elements and attributes before using them. For instance, the example Silverlight 2 client application displays an image of the book in the `ListBox` control's `ItemTemplate`. The source URL of the image is grabbed from the `SmallImage` element's URL element. If the `SmallImage` element does not exist, which is certainly a possibility if there is no image on record at Amazon for the item, the LINQ query definition must account for this. If the `SmallImage` element does exist, it will be shaped as shown in Example 8-9.

Example 8-9. Image XML from Amazon

```
<Item>
    <SmallImage>
        <URL>
            http://www.silverlight-data.com/images/someImage.png
        </URL>
    </SmallImage>
</Item>
```

Before grabbing a value, you can perform a simple check to make sure the element exists; you do this by checking the `Elements` collection's `Any` method. The `Any` method returns a `Boolean` value that indicates whether the collection contains elements. If the element exists, you can grab the value of the element. If the element does not exist you can set alternatives. For the image, there may not be an alternative. Example 8-8 shows the logic that checks for the existence of the image's URL; if it is found it grabs the value and sets it to the `imageSource` variable, as shown in Example 8-10.

Example 8-10. LINQ to XML to set the image's source

C#
```
let imageSource = (book.Elements(ns + "SmallImage").Any()
    ? book.Element(ns + "SmallImage").Element(ns + "URL").Value
    : string.Empty)
```

VB
```
Let imageSource =
    (If(book.Elements(ns + "SmallImage").Any(), _
    book.Element(ns + "SmallImage").Element(ns + "URL").Value, _
    String.Empty)) _
```

It may be that only one place in the XML contains the image source URL, but the price of the book could be located in several places to account for discount, special offer, used item, and retail pricing. If the book is available at a special price, the XML elements might go through an `OfferSummary` element to get the current lowest price. If there is no current special offer, the price of the book could fall back to the original list price. If there is no list price, perhaps because the book has not yet been released for sale, the code can check for that and set the price to 0. Example 8-11 shows in bold the shape of the XML that would contain the lowest price for a promotional offer.

Example 8-11. ItemSearch operation response sample

```
<ItemSearchResponse
    xmlns="http://webservices.amazon.com/AWSECommerceService/2005-10-05">
  <Items>
    <Request>
      <IsValid>True</IsValid>
      <ItemSearchRequest>
        <Keywords>Silverlight 2 Data</Keywords>
        <ResponseGroup>Medium</ResponseGroup>
        <SearchIndex>Books</SearchIndex>
      </ItemSearchRequest>
    </Request>
    <TotalResults>5</TotalResults>
    <TotalPages>1</TotalPages>
    <Item>
      <ASIN>0596523092</ASIN>
      <DetailPageURL>http://www.amazon.com/Data-Services-Silverlight-John-
Papa/dp/0596523092%3FSubscriptionId%3D[YourAmazonKeyGoesHere]%26tag%3Dws%26linkCode
%3Dxm2%26camp%3D2025%26creative%3D165953%26</DetailPageURL>
      <SalesRank>50009</SalesRank>
      <SmallImage>
        <URL>http://ecx.images-amazon.com/images/I/51pTT41KsyL._SL75_.jpg</URL>
        <Height Units="pixels">75</Height>
        <Width Units="pixels">57</Width>
      </SmallImage>
      <MediumImage>
        <URL>http://ecx.images-amazon.com/images/I/51pTT41KsyL._SL160_.jpg</URL>
        <Height Units="pixels">160</Height>
        <Width Units="pixels">122</Width>
      </MediumImage>
      <LargeImage>
        <URL>http://ecx.images-amazon.com/images/I/51pTT41KsyL._SL500_.jpg</URL>
        <Height Units="pixels">500</Height>
        <Width Units="pixels">381</Width>
      </LargeImage>
      <ImageSets>
        <ImageSet Category="primary">
          <SwatchImage>
            <URL>http://ecx.images-amazon.com/images/I/51pTT41KsyL._SL30_.jpg</URL>
            <Height Units="pixels">30</Height>
            <Width Units="pixels">23</Width>
          </SwatchImage>
          <SmallImage>
```

```xml
          <URL>http://ecx.images-amazon.com/images/I/51pTT41KsyL._SL75_.jpg</URL>
          <Height Units="pixels">75</Height>
          <Width Units="pixels">57</Width>
        </SmallImage>
        <MediumImage>
          <URL>
          http://ecx.images-amazon.com/images/I/51pTT41KsyL._SL160_.jpg</URL>
          <Height Units="pixels">160</Height>
          <Width Units="pixels">122</Width>
        </MediumImage>
        <LargeImage>
          <URL>
          http://ecx.images-amazon.com/images/I/51pTT41KsyL._SL500_.jpg</URL>
          <Height Units="pixels">500</Height>
          <Width Units="pixels">381</Width>
        </LargeImage>
      </ImageSet>
    </ImageSets>
    <ItemAttributes>
      <Author>John Papa</Author>
      <Binding>Paperback</Binding>
      <DeweyDecimalNumber>005</DeweyDecimalNumber>
      <EAN>9780596523091</EAN>
      <Edition>1st</Edition>
      <ISBN>0596523092</ISBN>
      <Label>O'Reilly Media, Inc.</Label>
      <ListPrice>
        <Amount>4499</Amount>
        <CurrencyCode>USD</CurrencyCode>
        <FormattedPrice>$44.99</FormattedPrice>
      </ListPrice>
      <Manufacturer>O'Reilly Media, Inc.</Manufacturer>
      <NumberOfItems>1</NumberOfItems>
      <NumberOfPages>250</NumberOfPages>
      <ProductGroup>Book</ProductGroup>
      <PublicationDate>2008-12-01</PublicationDate>
      <Publisher>O'Reilly Media, Inc.</Publisher>
      <Studio>O'Reilly Media, Inc.</Studio>
      <Title>Data Services with Silverlight 2</Title>
    </ItemAttributes>
    <OfferSummary>
      <LowestNewPrice>
        <Amount>2969</Amount>
        <CurrencyCode>USD</CurrencyCode>
        <FormattedPrice>$29.69</FormattedPrice>
      </LowestNewPrice>
      <TotalNew>1</TotalNew>
      <TotalUsed>0</TotalUsed>
      <TotalCollectible>0</TotalCollectible>
      <TotalRefurbished>0</TotalRefurbished>
    </OfferSummary>
  </Item>
 </Items>
</ItemSearchResponse>
```

The existence of both the `OfferSummary` and the `LowestNewPrice` elements is checked. If both elements exist, the value for the `Amount` element is retrieved. Both elements must be checked because there may be an offer for a used item, but the example application may be interested in retrieving only new items. These types of checks are critical when parsing XML to avoid null reference exceptions at runtime. Only where it is guaranteed that the elements and attributes will exist should this type of logic be skipped. Once the price has been determined, the value is divided by 100 to get the actual price, because Amazon returns the values without the decimal point. This makes it easier to convert to a specific culture, if required. (Figure 8-7, later in this chapter, shows the results of the full code.)

Once the range variables have been set using the `let` keyword, the `where` clause filters out any books that do not have an ISBN and any books that do not yet have a price greater than 0. The query defines that the items are sorted by title and then gathers the values for each book, creates an instance of a `Book` class, and sets the values of all of the class's properties using an object initializer.

The `Book` class has an `Authors` property which is of type `List<string>`. This property is filled using a nested LINQ query definition that gets the name of each author. Figure 8-6 shows the details of the `Book` class. Once the query is executed and converted to a `List<Book>`, the result is returned from the `GetBooks` method. The ASIN is the unique identifier that Amazon uses to identify every item it stores in its database. The application will use this value when creating the shopping cart to indicate which items will be included in the cart.

Binding the Search Results

Once the `List<Book>` has been created from the XML response, it is now in a form that you can use in a XAML-based data-binding operation. When the `List<Book>` is created, the next step is to call the `DisplayBooks` method (shown in Example 8-12). `DisplayBooks` sets the `DataContext` for the `StackPanel` named `panelSearchResults` to the `List<Book>`.

The list could have been bound directly to the `lstBooks.DataContext`, since `lstBooks.ItemsSource` has already been set to `{Binding}`. However, in this case more than one control must be involved in the data-binding operation to the `List<Book>`. The Silverlight 2 client application displays the total number of books that were returned from the search in a `TextBlock` above the `ListBox`. Instead of setting the `DataContext` for both the `TextBlock` and the `ListBox`, the code sets the `DataContext` for the `StackPanel` that is the immediate parent of both of these controls. This is a common practice with XAML-based data binding when all controls involved in a binding operation are contained within a parent control or panel.

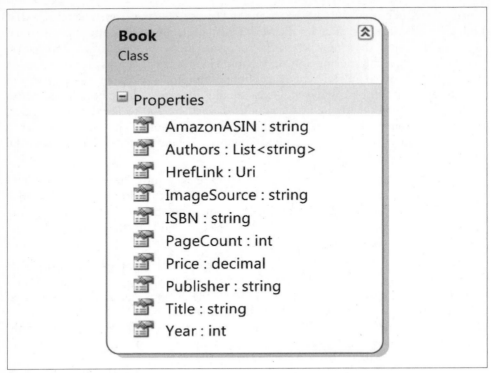

Figure 8-6. The Book class

Example 8-12. Book binding

```csharp
private void DisplayBooks(List<Book> books)
{
    lstBooks.SelectedIndex = -1;
    panelSearchResults.DataContext = books;
}
```

```vb
Private Sub DisplayBooks(ByVal books As List(Of Book))
    lstBooks.SelectedIndex = -1
    panelSearchResults.DataContext = books
End Sub
```

Example 8-13 shows the XAML that displays the search results, with all of the binding XAML in bold. Since all of the search results are contained within the panelSearchResults StackPanel and the DataContext of panelSearchResults is set to the List<Book>, each child element can access the List<Book>. The lblResultsCount TextBlock has its Text property bound to the Count property of the List<Book> and the lstBooks ListBox has its ItemsSource property bound to the List<Book> itself.

All of the bindings use the OneTime binding Mode setting, because they need to be updated when the List<Book> that is bound to them changes. The binding changes when the entire List<Book> is replaced with a new search result. As this effectively replaces the binding, there is no need for the Mode to be OneWay. The OneWay binding mode would be ideal if the List<Book> and its contents were updated.

Example 8-13. StackPanel containing the search results

```
<StackPanel Orientation="Vertical" Grid.Row="2" Margin="10,0,10,0"
    x:Name="panelSearchResults">
    <StackPanel Orientation="Horizontal" Margin="0,0,0,5">
        <TextBlock Text="# Items Found:"
        Style="{StaticResource TextBlockSimpleStyle}" />
        <TextBlock x:Name="lblResultsCount"
        Text="{Binding Path=Count, Mode=OneTime}"
        Style="{StaticResource TextBlockSimpleStyle}"/>
    </StackPanel>
    <ListBox x:Name="lstBooks" Width="480" HorizontalAlignment="Left"
        Height="230" VerticalAlignment="Top"
         Style="{StaticResource ListBoxStyle}"
        ItemsSource="{Binding Mode=OneTime}">
        <ListBox.ItemTemplate>
            <DataTemplate>
                <Grid x:Name="BookItemLayout" Height="110" Width="450">
                    <Grid.ColumnDefinitions>
                        <ColumnDefinition Width="90"/>
                        <ColumnDefinition Width="*"/>
                    </Grid.ColumnDefinitions>
                    <HyperlinkButton HorizontalAlignment="Stretch"
                    NavigateUri="{Binding Mode=OneTime, Path=HrefLink}"
                    FontFamily="Trebuchet MS" FontSize="10" Margin="0,0,0,0"
                    VerticalAlignment="Stretch" Grid.Column="0" Grid.Row="0" >
                    <Image Source="{Binding Mode=OneTime,
                        Path=ImageSource}" Margin="3,3,3,3"/>
                    </HyperlinkButton>
                    <Grid Grid.Column="1" x:Name="DetailsLayout" Margin="3,3,3,3">
                        <Grid.RowDefinitions>
                            <RowDefinition Height="30"/>
                            <RowDefinition Height="15"/>
                            <RowDefinition Height="15"/>
                            <RowDefinition Height="15"/>
                            <RowDefinition Height="15"/>
                            <RowDefinition Height="15"/>
                        </Grid.RowDefinitions>
                        <TextBlock Text="{Binding Mode=OneTime, Path=Title}"
                        Style="{StaticResource TextBlockSimpleStyle}"
                            Width="Auto" TextWrapping="Wrap" Grid.Row="0"/>
                        <TextBlock
                        Text="{Binding Converter={StaticResource
                        myAuthorConverter}, Mode=OneTime, Path=Authors}"
                            Style="{StaticResource TextBlockSimpleStyle}"
                        Grid.Row="1" />
                        <TextBlock Text="{Binding Mode=OneTime,
                        Path=Publisher}"
                        Style="{StaticResource TextBlockSimpleStyle}"
                        Grid.Row="2"/>
                        <StackPanel Orientation="Horizontal" Grid.Row="3">
                            <TextBlock Text="ISBN: "
```

```
                            Style="{StaticResource TextBlockSimpleStyle}" />
                        <TextBlock Text="{Binding Mode=OneTime, Path=ISBN}"
                            Style="{StaticResource TextBlockSimpleStyle}"
                            Grid.Row="1" />
                    </StackPanel>
                    <StackPanel Orientation="Horizontal" Grid.Row="4">
                        <TextBlock Text="Price: "
                        Style="{StaticResource TextBlockSimpleStyle}" />
                        <TextBlock Text="{Binding Converter={StaticResource
                        myCurrencyConverter}, Mode=OneTime, Path=Price}"
                            Style="{StaticResource TextBlockSimpleStyle}" />
                    </StackPanel>
                    <StackPanel Orientation="Horizontal" Grid.Row="5">
                        <TextBlock Text="Pub Year:"
                        Style="{StaticResource TextBlockSimpleStyle}" />
                        <TextBlock Text="{Binding Mode=OneTime, Path=Year}"
                        Style="{StaticResource TextBlockSimpleStyle}" />
                    </StackPanel>
                </Grid>
            </Grid>
        </DataTemplate>
    </ListBox.ItemTemplate>
  </ListBox>
</StackPanel>
<?xml version="1.0" encoding="UTF-8"?>
```

Cart Operations

Five operations help to build and manage a shopping cart with the Amazon RESTful
web services, which are shown again in Figure 8-7. When a user of the Silverlight 2
client application clicks the button to add a book to the shopping cart, a few things
happen to initialize the cart. First, the logic shown in Example 8-14 checks to make
sure there is no cart already. It does this by examining the BookSearch class's
_shoppingCart field through its ShoppingCart public property. If the shopping cart's
Id property has a value, the cart exists and a new item will be added to it. If the
cart's Id property is null, a new cart will be created and the item will be added to it.

Example 8-14. Adding an item to the cart

```csharp
private void AddToCart(Book book)
{
    // If cart does not exist, create it and add the book. Then get out.
    if (ShoppingCart.Id == null)
    {
        CreateCartAsync(book);
        return;
    }

    // Cart exists already, so check to see if the book is
    // already in the cart. Otherwise get out
    CartItem cartItem = ShoppingCart.CartItemList.FirstOrDefault(
        i => i.AmazonASIN == book.AmazonASIN);
```

```
            if (cartItem == null)
                AddToCartAsync(book);
            else
                return;
    }
```
```
[VB]  Private Sub AddToCart(ByVal book As Book)
          ' If cart does not exist, create it and add the book. Then get out.
          If ShoppingCart.Id Is Nothing Then
              CreateCartAsync(book)
              Return
          End If

          ' Cart exists already, so check to see if the
          ' book is already in the cart. Otherwise get out
          Dim cartItem As CartItem = ShoppingCart.CartItemList.FirstOrDefault( _
              Function(i) i.AmazonASIN = book.AmazonASIN)

          If cartItem Is Nothing Then
              AddToCartAsync(book)
          Else
              Return
          End If
      End Sub
```

Amazon exposes the **CartCreate** operation to handle creating a shopping cart. The cart itself is stored on Amazon's server for 90 days. Each cart gets a **CartId** and an HMAC code, which uniquely identify the cart with Amazon. When items are added or removed, when the cart is cleared entirely, or when the contents of a cart are simply being retrieved, these values must be passed to the Amazon services.

Figure 8-7. Shopping cart operations

The **CartCreate** operation is invoked from the **CreateCartAsync** method, shown in Example 8-15. The method (**request, cart**) indicates that both the original request and the cart response groups should be returned in the response. The original request is always beneficial to examine during debugging; however, you can omit this once you no longer need it for testing or debugging. The smaller the response, the less bandwidth it will take, which can help to improve performance on a larger scale.

The `CartCreate` operation expects parameters for an item's ASIN, a quantity, and the response groups. You cannot create a cart without at least one item. As noted earlier, the ASIN is the Amazon unique identifier for each item in the Amazon database. Each item is indicated using the syntax in the URI:

```
Item.[sequential number].ASIN=[ASIN Value]&Item.[sequential number].
Quantity=[Quantity]
```

(As a reminder, the sequential number allows the operation to accept several items in a single call. For this example application, only one item can be added to the cart at a time and only one of each item can be added. These are limitations of the example application and not of the web service.)

The `CartCreate`, `CartAdd`, `CartRemove`, and `CartGet` operations call the same event handler at the completion of their asynchronous event. The `AmazonService_CartOperation Completed` method is called when each of these operations completes. Each operation performs an action on the cart and returns the contents of the cart once again. The handler calls the `GetCart` method, which extracts the cart contents using LINQ to XML into an instance of a `ShoppingCart` object.

Example 8-15. Creating a cart asynchronously

```csharp
private void CreateCartAsync(Book book)
{
    string operation = "CartCreate";
    string responseGroup = "Request,Cart";
    string url = string.Format(
        "{0}&Operation={1}&Item.1.ASIN={2}&Item.1.Quantity=1&ResponseGroup={3}",
        ServiceUrlBase, operation, book.AmazonASIN, responseGroup);

    var service = new WebClient();
    service.DownloadStringCompleted += AmazonService_CartOperationCompleted;
    service.DownloadStringAsync(new Uri(url));
}
```

```vbnet
Private Sub CreateCartAsync(ByVal book As Book)
    Dim operation As String = "CartCreate"
    Dim responseGroup As String = "Request,Cart"
    Dim url As String = String.Format( _
        "{0}&Operation={1}&Item.1.ASIN={2}&Item.1.Quantity=1&ResponseGroup={3}", _
        ServiceUrlBase, operation, book.AmazonASIN, responseGroup)

    Dim service = New WebClient()
    service.DownloadStringCompleted += AmazonService_CartOperationCompleted
    service.DownloadStringAsync(New Uri(url))
End Sub
```

The response from the cart operations is parsed using the code shown in Example 8-16. First the XML string is loaded into an instance of an `XDocument` object, which is then queried using LINQ to XML. The query definition searches the response for the values for the ShoppingCart object. Figure 8-8 shows the definition of the Cart and CartItem classes that are loaded from the LINQ to XML query execution.

Example 8-16. Parsing the cart contents

```csharp
XDocument cartXml = XDocument.Parse(result);
XNamespace ns = NAMESPACE_AWSECommerceService;

var cartQuery = from cart in cartXml.Descendants(ns + "Cart")
    let subTotal = (cart.Elements(ns + "SubTotal").Any()
        ? cart.Element(ns + "SubTotal").Element(ns + "Amount").Value : "0")
    select new Cart
    {
        Id = cart.Element(ns + "CartId").Value.Trim(),
        HMAC = cart.Element(ns + "HMAC").Value.Trim(),
        URLEncodedHMAC = cart.Element(ns + "URLEncodedHMAC").Value.Trim(),
        SubTotal = Decimal.Parse(subTotal) / 100,
        CartItemList = (
            from item in cart.Descendants(ns + "CartItems").Descendants(
              ns + "CartItem")
            let price = (item.Elements(ns + "Price").Any()
                ? item.Element(ns + "Price").Element(ns + "Amount").Value : "0")
            select new CartItem
            {
                Id = item.Element(ns + "CartItemId").Value.Trim(),
                AmazonASIN = item.Element(ns + "ASIN").Value.Trim(),
                Title = item.Element(ns + "Title").Value.Trim(),
                Price = Decimal.Parse(price) / 100
            }
        ).ToList()
    };

ShoppingCart = cartQuery.SingleOrDefault();
```

```vbnet
Dim cartXml As XDocument = XDocument.Parse(result)
Dim ns As XNamespace = NAMESPACE_AWSECommerceService

Dim cartQuery = _
    From cart In cartXml.Descendants(ns + "Cart") _
    Let subTotal = (If(cart.Elements(ns + "SubTotal").Any(), _
        cart.Element(ns + "SubTotal").Element(ns + "Amount").Value, "0")) _
    Select New Cart With {.Id = cart.Element(ns + "CartId").Value.Trim(), _
        .HMAC = cart.Element(ns + "HMAC").Value.Trim(), _
        .URLEncodedHMAC = cart.Element(ns + "URLEncodedHMAC").Value.Trim(), _
        .SubTotal = Decimal.Parse(subTotal) / 100, _
        .CartItemList = ( _
            From item In cart.Descendants(ns + "CartItems").Descendants( _
            ns + "CartItem") _
            Let price = (If(item.Elements(ns + "Price").Any(), _
            item.Element(ns + "Price").Element(ns + "Amount").Value, "0")) _
            Select New CartItem With { _
            .Id = item.Element(ns + "CartItemId").Value.Trim(), _
            .AmazonASIN = item.Element(ns + "ASIN").Value.Trim(), _
            .Title = item.Element(ns + "Title").Value.Trim(), _
            .Price = Decimal.Parse(price) / 100}).ToList() _
```

```
    }
ShoppingCart = cartQuery.SingleOrDefault()
```

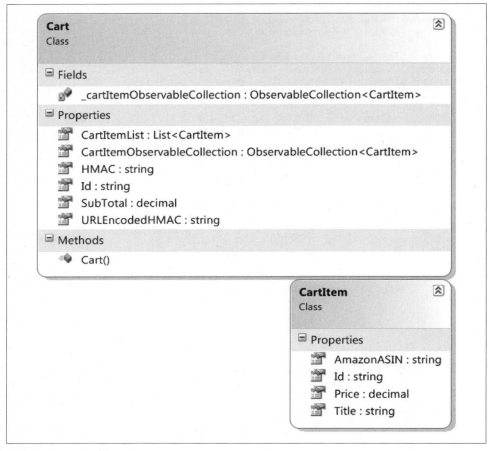

Figure 8-8. Cart and CartItem entities

As items are added and removed from the cart (shown in Figure 8-9), the items are displayed in the `lstCart ListBox` on the bottom of the Silverlight 2 client application. When the cart is modified, the `ShoppingCart` instance is set to the `panelCart StackPanel`'s `DataContext`. The `panelCart StackPanel` contains the `lstCart ListBox` as well as a few `TextBlock` controls that display the total number of items in the cart and the total price for those items. All of these values are data-bound to the properties of the `Cart` object. Setting the `DataContext` of this container control makes it easier to update the bindings for all of the bound controls for the cart, instead of having to set the `DataContext` for each individual control.

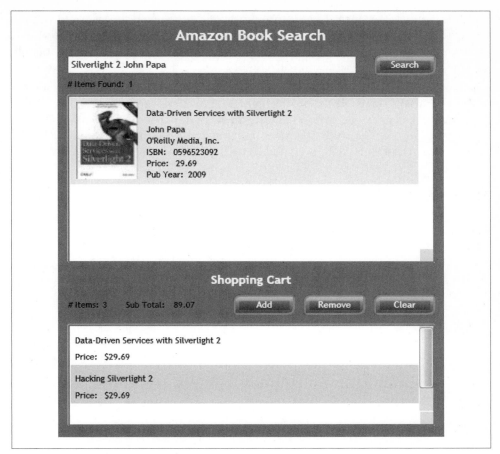

Figure 8-9. Full shopping cart

This is all you need to create a Silverlight 2 client application that searches and shops for books using the Amazon RESTful web services. The response from each cart operation includes a `PurchaseUrl` element which contains a URL that can be used to purchase the contents of the cart. For example, the Silverlight 2 client application can use this URL via a `HyperLinkbutton` control to bring the user to the Amazon website, where the user will be prompted to log in with her credentials before being brought to a page where she can purchase the contents of the cart.

Summary

This chapter demonstrated how to pull together several features of Silverlight 2, XAML, and RESTful services to create a powerful application that taps into a third party's shopping engine. You use XAML-based data binding to bind the *responses* to the controls, you use `WebClient` to asynchronously invoke the web services, and you use LINQ to XML to parse the responses into local entity structures. All of these aspects are a great example of how these features can work together to create a robust application through RESTful services in Silverlight 2.

The next chapter discusses how to create RESTful services that perform `POST` and `GET` HTTP operations using .NET that Silverlight 2 applications can consume. The chapter will show several examples of how to create the RESTful services and then will tie them all together with a case study that uses both custom RESTful services and RESTful services from the Twitter API.

CHAPTER 9

Creating RESTful Services and Introducing SilverTwit

The preceding chapter showed how you can take advantage of the RESTful services exposed by the Amazon web services API to create a robust Silverlight 2 client that allows a user to search through and shop on Amazon.com. The case study demonstrated how to request data using the HTTP GET method, but of course there are ways to submit data using HTTP through POST, PUT, DELETE, and other HTTP methods, as well. This chapter will expand on these topics by demonstrating how to build custom REST web services using Windows Communication Foundation (WCF), support HTTP actions, customize URI templates, and return data as either XML or JSON.

When you are designing web services to expose functionality and resources to client applications, in many cases RESTful web services are a good alternative to using SOAP-based web services. You can build custom RESTful services in a variety of ways; however, WCF provides a lot of the plumbing that you need to create RESTful services out of the box. This chapter shows how to build custom RESTful services using WCF that send and receive requests and responses. The chapter also demonstrates various HTTP methods, and shows how to implement status codes and define URI templates.

You can design a RESTful service to return data in different formats. Two common data formats are XML and JSON. This chapter demonstrates how to design services that send responses as JSON or XML, and shows how to consume the response using tools such as LINQ to XML, LINQ to JSON, and `DataContractJsonSerializer`. I will demonstrate these topics through simple examples that build Silverlight 2 applications that invoke custom WCF RESTful web services.

Following these examples is a walkthrough of building a Silverlight 2 Twitter client that reads and posts messages from the Twitter RESTful API using both GET and POST HTTP actions. The example builds on the topics we've discussed throughout this book in creating a Silverlight 2 client, creating a RESTful service designed with WCF, handling cross-domain issues, and LINQ. This chapter will discuss server-side (the RESTful services) and client-side code (to consume the services), jumping back and forth between them to drive the points home.

Creating RESTful Services from WCF

Chapter 7 discussed the anatomy of a RESTful service and how the main tenets of a RESTful service include a unique URI and services that are resource-driven. This section will demonstrate how to create a RESTful service using WCF that Silverlight 2 can consume.

Before creating a RESTful service, it is important to consider the differences between the characteristics of a RESTful web service and a SOAP-based web service. WCF services generally focus on performing an action, such as getting a list of products (`FindProducts()`), adding customers (`AddCustomer(Customer cust)`), or searching for orders (`FindOrders(int year)`). Some developers like to think of these types of services as *verbs*, as they are action-based. REST-based web services generally focus on the resource and not the action; as such, you can think of REST-based services as revolving around *nouns* (the resources).

For example, whereas in WCF a service method may be `FindProducts()`, in a RESTful web service operation the URI might be a `GET` HTTP method call to *http://silverlight -data.com/MyService.svc/Product*. Although a WCF service method may be `AddCustomer(Customer cust)`, its RESTful counterpart might be an HTTP `POST` method to the URI *http://silverlight-data.com/MyService.svc/Customer*. The styles of these services are clearly different in both implementation and design. The latter causes the developer to think more about working with resources, and the former about the action to be performed.

Creating a RESTful Service

Creating a REST-friendly WCF web service that is hosted in IIS or Windows Process Activation Service (WAS) involves completing the following steps:

1. Create a *RESTfulService.svc* file in the project root.
2. Create an accompanying *RESTfulService.cs* code file.
3. Configure the RESTful service in a **.config* file or declare a factory in your *.svc* file. Optionally, create an *IRESTfulService.cs* interface.
4. Define the characteristics of the individual operations.

The first step in creating a RESTful service using WCF is to add a new WCF service file to a project that can be hosted. The example code uses a web application project to host RESTful WCF web services. You can create a WCF service by using the WCF service file template or by creating the Silverlight-enabled WCF Service file template.

Regardless of which service file template you choose, you must modify the service configuration to support a RESTful service.

Creating the Service Interface

The code in the example application created a WCF service using the WCF service file template. This service, named *RESTfulService.svc*, defines its service contract and its operations in the *RESTfulService.cs* file by default. Optionally, you can move the service and operation contracts to an interface.

Defining an interface is an optional exercise that allows the publicly exposed web service methods to be clearly and succinctly defined in a single place. The web service methods (also referred to as *operations*) are defined in the interface along with the attributes that define the characteristics (such as the URI template and HTTP action) of each operation. The example code has a service implemented in the `RESTfulService` class, which implements the interface named `IRESTfulService`. The `IRESTfulService` interface defines the service's contract and its operations.

Configuring a RESTful Service

The configuration for a REST-friendly WCF web service requires different aspects than a SOAP-friendly WCF web service. A RESTful service does not need to publish metadata about itself, and therefore does not need to create a specific service behavior. This means you can omit from the configuration file the `serviceBehaviors` child element of the `system.serviceModel` section for the REST-friendly service.

SOAP-friendly services consumed by Silverlight 2 applications must use the `basicHttpBinding` binding. However, REST-friendly WCF web services use the `webHttpBinding` binding. No metadata is published for services exposed using `webHttpBinding`, which is why you do not need the `serviceBehavior` section for REST-friendly services. Although you do not need a `serviceBehavior` section, a RESTful web service does require an endpoint behavior. Example 9-1 shows the proper configuration for the RESTful WCF web service, including the `webHttp` setting in the endpoint behavior named `webBehavior`.

> You can find the complete set of code for all of the samples in this chapter in the `RESTfulClient` solution in this chapter's code folder.

Example 9-1. RESTful configuration

```
<system.serviceModel>
    <behaviors>
     <endpointBehaviors>
         <behavior name="webBehavior">
```

```
            <webHttp/>
        </behavior>
    </endpointBehaviors>
</behaviors>
<serviceHostingEnvironment aspNetCompatibilityEnabled="true"/>
<services>
    <service name="RESTfulServices.RESTfulService">
        <endpoint address="" behaviorConfiguration="webBehavior"
         binding="webHttpBinding"
         bindingConfiguration=""
         contract="RESTfulServices.IRESTfulService"/>
    </service>
</services>
</system.serviceModel>
```

The **service** section of the configuration defines the name of the service, and its child element **endpoint** defines the details of the RESTful endpoint of the web service. The **name** attribute in the **service** element is the fully qualified type name of the service implementation. The **address** attribute is left blank in Example 9-1. This means the endpoint will be used when a URI points to the root of the service. If multiple endpoints are defined—possibly one for a RESTful service and another for a SOAP-based service—the **address** attribute can differentiate them. For example, a RESTful endpoint might have an address setting of **rest** and a SOAP-based endpoint might have an address of **soap**. This would allow you to call both types of services simply by changing the URI to include the addition of one of these addresses. Sticking with this example, the following URI would refer to the REST-based web service:

http://silverlight-data.com/MyService.svc/rest/

This URI would refer to the SOAP-based web service:

http://silverlight-data.com/MyService.svc/soap/

The **behaviorConfiguration** attribute refers to the **webBehavior** endpoint behavior. In this case, this allows the service to support the REST characteristics. No binding configuration is needed for this REST-friendly endpoint.

The **contract** attribute refers to the name of the class or interface that defines the service contract. In this example, the contract is an interface named **IRESTfulService**. When you use the Silverlight-enabled WCF Service file template to create the service, the template does not create the interface. If an interface is added or refactored (as with this example), it is critical to change the contract name in the configuration to point to the interface and not to the class. Basically, the contract must be the name of the object that has the **ServiceContract** attribute.

The final attribute in the endpoint is the binding. The default binding for a WCF service is **wsHttpBinding**, which Silverlight 2 clients cannot consume. The binding that is set when a Silverlight-enabled WCF Service file template is used is **basicHttpBinding**. You use the **basicHttpBinding** setting when a SOAP-based WCF service is created and consumed—in this case, by a Silverlight 2 application. Neither of these binding settings supports RESTful services, so the REST-friendly `webHttpBinding` binding is set.

Defining the Contract

Once you have created and configured the RESTful WCF web service so that it can be consumed, the next step is to expose the individual operations that the service will perform. These operations are decorated with the `OperationContract` attribute in the `System.ServiceModel` namespace and are located in the `IRESTfulService` interface.

You can make the operations REST-friendly by decorating each operation with an additional attribute. The `System.ServiceModel.Web` namespace contains both the `WebGet` and the `WebInvoke` attributes. These attributes declare that a web service operation will support one of the HTTP methods, such as `GET`, `POST`, `PUT`, or `DELETE`. If an operation in the service contract is not decorated with `WebGet` or `WebInvoke`, the operation will default to a method of `POST` where the `UriTemplate` is the name of the operation. However, it is a good practice to decorate all of the operations with the `WebGet` or `WebInvoke` attribute explicitly for clarity.

 The project must reference the `System.ServiceModel.Web.dll` assembly before you can use the `WebGet` and `WebInvoke` attributes.

Figure 9-1 shows several of the characteristics of REST-friendly web service operations that you can set, including using the `WebGet` or `WebInvoke` attribute. The `WebGet` attribute indicates that an HTTP `GET` request will be made and a response may be required. The `WebInvoke` attribute indicates that an HTTP method such as `POST`, `PUT`, or `DELETE` will be issued. Although RESTful services created with WCF support `PUT` and `DELETE`, Silverlight 2 can only issue an HTTP `GET` or an HTTP `POST` through either the `WebClient` or the `HttpWebRequest` class. However, it is possible to issue a `PUT` or a `DELETE` through Silverlight 2 by using the JavaScript API and calling through the `XmlHttpRequest` object.

Example 9-2 shows the service contract and the first operation for the `IRESTfulService` interface. The `UriTemplate` in Example 9-2 indicates that the combination of the service path and the `UriTemplate` will create a unique path that will invoke the `FindProduct1` operation. The service is hosted at *http://localhost/RESTfulServices/RESTfulService.svc*. The full path to invoke this operation and pass a value for the `productIdString` parameter is *http://localhost/RESTfulServices/RESTfulService.svc/Product/1001*.

The `WebGet` attributes indicates that an HTTP `GET` request will be made. The `UriTemplate` defines that the `Product` resource will be requested for a specific product ID. The `ResponseFormat` indicates that the response will be sent back to the client as XML and the `BodyStyle` indicates that the request and response will be bare instead of

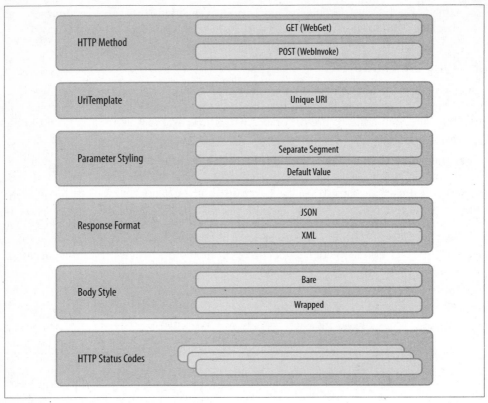

Figure 9-1. RESTful service design considerations

being wrapped. You can wrap requests and responses in a container element if needed. The requests and responses used in the following examples will not need to be wrapped, so Bare is indicated. Wrapped requests and responses are ideal when the content of the message requires a container element. For example, the response message may be an XML fragment with no root element. The XML fragment could be automatically wrapped with an outer XML element if you use WebMessageBodyStyle.Wrapped.

Example 9-2. Service contract and operation

```
[ServiceContract(Namespace = "http://www.silverlight-data.com")]
public interface IRESTfulService
{
    // #1
    [OperationContract]
    [WebGet(UriTemplate = "Product/{productIdString}",
        ResponseFormat = WebMessageFormat.Xml,
        BodyStyle = WebMessageBodyStyle.Bare)]
    Product FindProduct1(string productIdString);
```

```
      // More contracts defined here ...
}
```

VB
```vbnet
<ServiceContract(Namespace := "http://www.silverlight-data.com")> _
Public Interface IRESTfulService
    ' #1
    <OperationContract, WebGet(UriTemplate := "Product/{productIdString}", _
        ResponseFormat := WebMessageFormat.Xml, _
        BodyStyle := WebMessageBodyStyle.Bare)> _
    Function FindProduct1(ByVal productIdString As String) As Product

    ' More contracts defined here ...

End Interface
```

The implementation of the `FindProduct1` method in Example 9-3 shows that the `productIdString` parameter in the `UriTemplate` matches the name of the parameter in the `FindProduct1` method. You must enclose any parameter defined in the `UriTemplate` with curly braces, and the parameter must match the name of a parameter in the method. If the parameter is part of the URI path it must be a `string`. If the parameter is part of the query string, primitive type conversion is supported. Because the `ProductId` property of the `Product` class is an integer, you must convert the `produc tIdString` parameter to an integer first, as shown in Example 9-3.

You also can define the parameter as part of a compound segment; in a compound segment the path and the parameter exist in the same segment of the URI. For example, a `UriTemplate` of `Product({productIdString})` contains a compound segment where the parameter is being passed (inside parentheses) in the same segment as the `Product` literal. An example of this might be:

```
/somepath/some.svc/Product(123)
```

Once the appropriate product has been gathered using LINQ to Objects in the `FindProduct1` method, the `Product` is returned to the client via the `Response`. As the `ResponseFormat` is set to `WebMessageFormat.Xml`, the `Product` is serialized to XML before being sent back in the `Response`. Prior to .NET 3.5 SP 1 the class and its properties had to be decorated with the `DataMember` and `DataContract` attributes. However, starting with .NET 3.5 SP 1, the `Product` class can be decorated with the `DataContract` attribute and its properties decorated with the `DataMember` attributes if specific properties should be included and others excluded from the serialization process.

Example 9-3. Simple GET request for a product

C#
```csharp
public Product FindProduct1(string productIdString)
{
    int productId = int.Parse(productIdString);
    List<Product> products = GetProductList();
    var query = from p in products
                where p.ProductId == productId
                select p;
    Product product = query.FirstOrDefault() as Product;
```

```
        return product;
    }
```

```vb
Public Function FindProduct1(ByVal productIdString As String) As Product
    Dim productId As Integer = Integer.Parse(productIdString)
    Dim products As List(Of Product) = GetProductList()
    Dim query = _
        From p In products _
        Where p.ProductId = productId _
        Select p
    Dim product As Product = TryCast(query.FirstOrDefault(), Product)
    Return product End Function
```

Consuming the REST-Friendly Service

Once the service is defined, the client can be set up to consume the service. The Silverlight 2 client application named `RESTfulClient` (shown in Figure 9-2) in the sample code calls the RESTful service shown in Example 9-3 using the `WebClient` class and the unique URI that matches the `FindProduct1` operation. The application displays a list of operations that will invoke different web service methods from the `RESTfulService` project. Example 9-4 shows how the Silverlight 2 client application consumes the `FindProduct1` web service method.

Each invocation method has the same number in the comments as its corresponding web service method to make it easier to see which invocation methods call which web service methods.

Example 9-4. Invoking the RESTful service from Silverlight 2

C#
```csharp
private readonly string _domain = "localhost:9726";

public string BaseUri
{
    get { return string.Format("http://{0}/RESTfulService.svc", _domain); }
}

private void GetProductAsync_AsXml_IdInSegment()
{
    WebClient wc = new WebClient();
    wc.DownloadStringCompleted += ParseProducts_AsXml;
    int productId = 1001;
    string urlString = string.Format("{0}/Product/{1}", BaseUri, productId);
    Uri uri = new Uri(urlString);
    wc.DownloadStringAsync(uri);
}
```

VB
```vb
Private ReadOnly _domain As String = "localhost:9726"

Public ReadOnly Property BaseUri() As String
    Get
        Return String.Format("http://{0}/RESTfulService.svc", _domain)
```

```
        End Get
    End Property

    Private Sub GetProductAsync_AsXml_IdInSegment()
        Dim wc As New WebClient()
        wc.DownloadStringCompleted += ParseProducts_AsXml
        Dim productId As Integer = 1001
        Dim urlString As String = String.Format("{0}/Product/{1}", BaseUri, productId)
        Dim uri As New Uri(urlString)
        wc.DownloadStringAsync(uri)
    End Sub
```

The ParseProducts_AsXml method handles the DownloadStringCompleted event for the sample code's methods that retrieve one or more products as XML. It parses the XML to find the ProductId, UnitPrice, and ProductName property values and creates an instance of a Product class for each of them. The ToInt and ToDecimal methods are extension methods on the string class that simply parse a string value into an integer and a decimal, respectively. They are defined in the ConversionExtensions class in the RESTfulClient project. This LINQ to XML query definition works whether the web service returns a single product or multiple products.

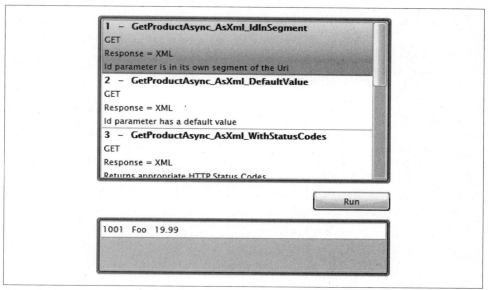

Figure 9-2. Getting a product from the RESTful service

The Silverlight 2 client application is hosted on a different domain than the web service (as is likely in a real-world application). Since this is a cross-domain request, a cross-domain file is required in the web root of the web service's domain that allows access to the services. The example code for this chapter has a copy of a *clientaccesspolicy.xml* file in the domain's root. Example 9-5 shows how the Silverlight 2 client application parses the response's XML using LINQ to XML.

Example 9-5. Parsing the response with LINQ to XML

```csharp
private void ParseProducts_AsXml(object sender, DownloadStringCompletedEventArgs e)
{
    string ns = "";
    string rawXml = e.Result;
    XDocument xdoc = XDocument.Parse(rawXml);
    var query = from product in xdoc.Descendants(ns + "Product")
        select new Product
            {
                ProductId = product.Element("ProductId").Value.ToInt(),
                ProductName = product.Element("ProductName").Value,
                UnitPrice = product.Element("UnitPrice").Value.ToDecimal()
            };
    List<Product> products = query.ToList() as List<Product>;
    lstProducts.DataContext = products;
}
```

```vbnet
Private Sub ParseProducts_AsXml(ByVal sender As Object, _
        ByVal e As DownloadStringCompletedEventArgs)
    Dim ns As String = ""
    Dim rawXml As String = e.Result
    Dim xdoc As XDocument = XDocument.Parse(rawXml)
    Dim query = _
        From product In xdoc.Descendants(ns & "Product") _
        Select New Product With _
        { _
        .ProductId = product.Element("ProductId").Value.ToInt(), _
        .ProductName = product.Element("ProductName").Value, _
        .UnitPrice = product.Element("UnitPrice").Value.ToDecimal() _
        }
    Dim products As List(Of Product) = TryCast(query.ToList(), List(Of Product))
    lstProducts.DataContext = products End Sub
```

Default Values

The code in Example 9-6 shows how you can modify the URI to allow the productId
String parameter to have a default value. If a URI is invoked that matches the
UriTemplate but omits the productIdString parameter, the following operation's
UriTemplate would match this request.

Example 9-6. Modified URI template on the service

```csharp
// #2
[OperationContract]
[WebGet(UriTemplate = "Product2/{productIdString=1011}",
    ResponseFormat = WebMessageFormat.Xml,
    BodyStyle = WebMessageBodyStyle.Bare)]
Product FindProduct2(string productIdString);
```

```vbnet
' #2
<OperationContract, _
    WebGet(UriTemplate := "Product2/{productIdString=1011}", _
    ResponseFormat := WebMessageFormat.Xml, _
```

```
            BodyStyle := WebMessageBodyStyle.Bare)> _
Product FindProduct2(String productIdString)¯
```

The code for the `FindProduct2` method is the same as the code for `FindProduct1` (shown in Example 9-3). The `Product` instance is serialized to XML and sent back to the Silverlight 2 client in the `Response`, where it is parsed with LINQ to XML in the `ParseProducts_AsXml` method (shown in Example 9-5). The results are then bound to a `ListBox` and are displayed to the user.

HTTP Status Codes

The status code provides a way to communicate the status of the operation to the invoking application over HTTP.

When developing RESTful web services, it is a good practice to return HTTP status codes when the operation has completed. The HTTP status codes can indicate common success and failure messages from the web service operation. For example, if a parameter contains an unexpected value, you can set the HTTP status code to the enumerator value `HttpStatusCode.BadRequest`, which translates to HTTP status 400. If the method finds the product and returns it successfully, you can set the HTTP status code to `HttpStatusCode.OK`, which returns an HTTP status of 200.

The default status codes are 200 (OK) and 500 (Internal Server Error). If no exception is thrown in a method and no status code is explicitly set in the method, the status code of 200 is returned. If an exception occurs and no status code is set, the status code of 500 will be returned.

You can find the `HttpStatusCode` enumeration in the `System.Net` namespace. The codes map directly to the standard HTTP status codes, such as 400 for `bad request`, 404 for `not found`, and 201 for `created`. The code in Example 9-7 finds a product and sets the HTTP status code to the appropriate enumerator value. These values become readily apparent when you run the service through a tool such as Fiddler2, as shown in Figure 9-3.

#	Result	Pro...	Host	URL	Body	Caching	Content-Type	Process
▣27	200	HTTP	localhost	/RESTfulServices/RESTfulService.svc/Product3/1001	354	private	application/xml; ...	

Figure 9-3. HTTP status 200

Example 9-7. Assigning HTTP status codes

```csharp
// # 3
public Product FindProduct3(string productIdString)
{
    if (productIdString.Length == 0)
    {
        WebOperationContext.Current.OutgoingResponse.StatusCode =
            HttpStatusCode.BadRequest;
```

```
            return null;
    }

    int productId = int.Parse(productIdString);
    List<Product> products = GetProductList();
    var query = from p in products
                where p.ProductId == productId
                select p;
    Product product = query.FirstOrDefault() as Product;
    WebOperationContext.Current.OutgoingResponse.StatusCode =
            HttpStatusCode.OK;
    return product;
}
```

VB

```
' # 3
Public Function FindProduct3(ByVal productIdString As String) As Product
    If productIdString.Length = 0 Then
        WebOperationContext.Current.OutgoingResponse.StatusCode = _
            HttpStatusCode.BadRequest
        Return Nothing
    End If

    Dim productId As Integer = Integer.Parse(productIdString)
    Dim products As List(Of Product) = GetProductList()
    Dim query = _
        From p In products _
        Where p.ProductId = productId _
        Select p
    Dim product As Product = TryCast(query.FirstOrDefault(), Product)
    WebOperationContext.Current.OutgoingResponse.StatusCode = _
        HttpStatusCode.OK
    Return product
End Function
```

Servicing JSON

Sometimes it is beneficial to create a RESTful service that can return a response message as either XML or JSON. Data formatted using JSON usually results in a smaller message size than data formatted as XML. JSON uses array structures to define the name and value pairs, whereas XML uses hierarchical elements. Although XML is much easier to read visually, JSON can be smaller and, thus, quicker to pass across a network.

 JSON is commonly used as a response format for services that Ajax clients consume.

Defining a JSON Response

Defining a set of operations that can perform the same operation but return the data as JSON or XML is very straightforward with WCF. You can set the ResponseFormat

---

attribute to either `WebMessageFormat.Xml` or `WebMessageFormat.Json` to indicate the format of the response message. Example 9-8 shows two operations that return a `Product` as XML or as JSON, respectively.

Notice that the `UriTemplate` for the `FindProductByNameAsXml` method is slightly different from the `UriTemplate` for the `FindProductbyNameAsJson` method. The slight difference is enough to make the `UriTemplate` find a match if `?json` is appended to the URI.

Example 9-8. Setting the response format

```csharp
// #4
[OperationContract]
[WebGet(UriTemplate = "Product/Name/{productName}",
    ResponseFormat = WebMessageFormat.Xml,
    BodyStyle = WebMessageBodyStyle.Bare)]
Product FindProductByNameAsXml(string productName);

// #5
[OperationContract]
[WebGet(UriTemplate = "Product/Name/{productName}?json",
    ResponseFormat = WebMessageFormat.Json,
    BodyStyle = WebMessageBodyStyle.Bare)]
Product FindProductByNameAsJson(string productName);
```

```vbnet
' #4
<OperationContract, _
    WebGet(UriTemplate := "Product/Name/{productName}", _
    ResponseFormat := WebMessageFormat.Xml, _
    BodyStyle := WebMessageBodyStyle.Bare)> _
Product FindProductByNameAsXml(String productName)

' #5
<OperationContract, _
    WebGet(UriTemplate := "Product/Name/{productName}?json", _
    ResponseFormat := WebMessageFormat.Json, _
    BodyStyle := WebMessageBodyStyle.Bare)> _
Product FindProductByNameAsJson(String productName)
```

When a `Product` is returned from the request to *http://localhost/RESTfulServices/REST fulService.svc/Product/Name/Hoo* it is returned as XML. Example 9-9 shows the XML response, which contains 355 bytes. When the request is made to *http://localhost/RESTfulServices/RESTfulService.svc/Product/Name/Hoo?json* the same `Product` instance is returned as JSON. Although both responses represent the same object, the XML version is much more readable than the JSON version. However, the XML response is 355 bytes, whereas the JSON response is only 202 bytes, as shown in Example 9-10. The process of allowing the caller to indicate the version of the resource being XML or JSON is called *content negotiation*.

Example 9-9. Product response as XML

```xml
<Product xmlns:i="http://www.w3.org/2001/XMLSchema-instance">
    <Discontinued>false</Discontinued>
    <DiscontinuedDate>0001-01-01T00:00:00</DiscontinuedDate>
```

```
    <ProductId>1003</ProductId>
    <ProductName>Hoo</ProductName>
    <QuantityPerUnit/>
    <ReorderLevel>0</ReorderLevel>
    <UnitPrice>109.99</UnitPrice>
    <UnitsInStock>0</UnitsInStock>
    <UnitsOnOrder>0</UnitsOnOrder>
</Product>
```

The samples use a set of 20 predefined `Product` instances that are created in *RESTfulService.cs*. These class instances are used for demonstration purposes only, instead of for hitting a database. To see the full list of products, visit the sample code for this chapter.

Example 9-10. Product response as JSON

```
{"Discontinued":false,"DiscontinuedDate":"\/Date(-62135578800000-
0500)\/","ProductId":1003,"ProductName":"Hoo","QuantityPerUnit":"","ReorderLevel":0
,"UnitPrice":109.99,"UnitsInStock":0,"UnitsOnOrder":0}
```

LINQ to JSON

Although JSON is a compact format, consuming JSON by iterating through its elements can be difficult without a library that targets JSON. LINQ to JSON makes it possible to parse and query JSON-formatted data using the familiar LINQ syntax. You can load a string or stream of JSON data into a `JsonObject` and then define a query using `JsonObject` at the root of the query.

The JSON features are available through the `System.Json` namespace by referencing the `System.Json.dll` assembly. The `System.Json` namespace contains the objects shown in Table 9-1.

Table 9-1. Key System.Json classes

Class	Description
JsonValue	Represents all JSON values; it is also the base class for JsonObject
JsonObject	Represents an object instance in JSON; it is also the base class for JsonArray
JsonArray	Represents an array of JsonObject instances

When a string or a stream of JSON data is passed to the `Parse` or `Load` method, respectively, the JSON data is loaded into the object. `JsonValue`, `JsonObject`, and `JsonArray` classes can load JSON data using these methods. Once the object is loaded with data, you can define a query using LINQ to JSON to extract and filter the data into another format.

For example, assume that the following JSON is returned as a response from a RESTful web service operation:

```
{"employees":[{"Id":107,"FullName":"John Papa"},{"Id":108,"FullName":"Kadi Papa"}]}
```

You could parse the JSON into a `JsonObject` instance and query it using the LINQ to JSON query definition in Example 9-11. Notice that the `emp` variable in the LINQ query definition is cast to a `JsonValue`, the base type for the `System.Json` objects. This query pulls the values out of the JSON data and creates instances of an anonymous type from the `Id` and `Name` properties. The values extracted from the query are of type `JsonValue`. You must convert them to the appropriate types, which in this case are `int` and `string`. The code in Example 9-11 shows how the Silverlight 2 client application parses the JSON with LINQ to JSON.

Example 9-11. Parsing JSON with LINQ to JSON

C#
```csharp
JsonObject employees = JsonObject.Parse(jsonString) as JsonObject;
var qry = from JsonValue emp in employees["employees"]
        select new {
            Id = (int)emp["Id"],
            Name = (string)emp["FullName"]
        };
foreach (var person in qry)
    Console.WriteLine(person.Name);
```

VB
```vb
Dim employees As JsonObject = TryCast(JsonObject.Parse(jsonString), JsonObject)
Dim qry = _
    From emp As JsonValue In employees("employees") _
    Select New With { _
        Key .Id = CInt(Fix(emp("Id"))), _
        Key .Name = CStr(emp("FullName")) _
        }
For Each person In qry
    Console.WriteLine(person.Name)
Next personSilverTwit
```

Consuming Products Using LINQ to JSON

The sample Silverlight 2 client application `RESTfulClient` invokes the operation shown in Example 9-8 using the URI *http://localhost/RESTfulServices/RESTfulService.svc/Product/Name/Hoo?json* to retrieve the JSON data shown in Example 9-10. The code to invoke the web service operation, shown in Example 9-12, adds the `json` parameter to the URI to indicate that the operation with the matching `UriTemplate` should be invoked.

Example 9-12. Invoking the JSON services from Silverlight

C#
```csharp
// # 5
private void GetProductByNameAsync_AsJson()
{
    WebClient wc = new WebClient();
    wc.DownloadStringCompleted += ParseProducts_AsJson;
```

```csharp
    string productName = "Hoo";
    string urlString =
        string.Format("{0}/Product/Name/{1}?json", BaseUri, productName);
    Uri uri = new Uri(urlString);
    wc.DownloadStringAsync(uri);
}
```

VB ' # 5
```vb
Private Sub GetProductByNameAsync_AsJson()
    Dim wc As New WebClient()
    AddHandler wc.DownloadStringCompleted, AddressOf ParseProducts_AsJson
    Dim productName As String = "Hoo"
    Dim urlString As String = _
        String.Format("{0}/Product/Name/{1}?json", BaseUri, productName)
    Dim uri As New Uri(urlString)
    wc.DownloadStringAsync(uri)
End Sub
```

The `ParseProducts_AsJson` method is added to handle the `DownloadStringCompleted` event for the asynchronous web service call. `ParseProducts_AsJson`, shown in Example 9-13, first creates an instance of a `JsonArray` object named `json`. The `json` object will be queried using LINQ to JSON to find all of the products.

Next, the method pulls the JSON data out of `e.Result` and loads it into a `JsonArray` object using the `Parse` method. If the JSON can be parsed into the `JsonArray`, the data is parsed into the `json` variable. If the data cannot be parsed into the `JsonArray`, it is parsed into a `JsonObject` and added to an instance of a `JsonArray`. Either way, the result is a `JsonArray` variable named `json` that contains one or more products contained in `JsonObject` instances.

By pulling the product data into a `JsonArray`, you can use the same query for a method that returns a single product (as in Example 9-12) or a method that returns a list of products (as in Example 9-13).

The product data is queried from the `JsonArray` `json` variable using LINQ to JSON. The results are selected into instances of the local `Product` class, loaded into a `List<Product>`, and bound to the `lstProducts` `ListBox`.

Example 9-13. Querying products with LINQ to JSON

C#
```csharp
private void ParseProducts_AsJson(object sender,
        DownloadStringCompletedEventArgs e)
{
    string raw = e.Result;

    JsonArray json;
    if (JsonArray.Parse(raw) as JsonArray == null)
        json = new JsonArray { JsonObject.Parse(raw) as JsonObject };
    else
        json = JsonArray.Parse(raw) as JsonArray;

    var query = from product in json
        select new Product
```

```
            {
                ProductId = (int)product["ProductId"],
                ProductName = (string)product["ProductName"],
                UnitPrice = (decimal)product["UnitPrice"]
            };
        List<Product> products = query.ToList() as List<Product>;
        lstProducts.DataContext = products;
}
```

VB
```
Private Sub ParseProducts_AsJson(ByVal sender As Object, _
        ByVal e As DownloadStringCompletedEventArgs)
    Dim raw As String = e.Result

    Dim json As JsonArray
    If TryCast(JsonArray.Parse(raw), JsonArray) Is Nothing Then
        json = New JsonArray With { TryCast(JsonObject.Parse(raw), JsonObject) }
    Else
        json = TryCast(JsonArray.Parse(raw), JsonArray)
    End If

    Dim query = _
        From product In json _
        Select New Product With _
        { _
            .ProductId = CInt(Fix(product("ProductId"))), _
            .ProductName = CStr(product("ProductName")), _
            .UnitPrice = CDec(product("UnitPrice")) _
        }
    Dim products As List(Of Product) = TryCast(query.ToList(), List(Of Product))
    lstProducts.DataContext = products
End Sub
```

When a web service operation returns more than one product, the JSON is formatted
slightly differently than a method that returns a single product. The JSON shown in
Example 9-10 represents a single product, whereas the JSON shown in Example 9-14
represents 10 products. The JSON in Example 9-14 is enclosed with square brackets
and each product instance is separated by a comma. Despite the slight differences in
format, the same event handler, ParseProducts_AsJson, parses the JSON in both
examples. The list of products is bound and the results are displayed, as shown in
Figure 9-4.

Example 9-14. List of products as JSON

```
[{"Discontinued":false,"DiscontinuedDate":"\/Date(-62135578800000-
0500)\/","ProductId":1017,"ProductName":"Zoo","QuantityPerUnit":"","ReorderLevel":0
,"UnitPrice":0.99,"UnitsInStock":0,"UnitsOnOrder":0},{"Discontinued":false,"Discont
inuedDate":"\/Date(-62135578800000-
0500)\/","ProductId":1005,"ProductName":"Loo","QuantityPerUnit":"","ReorderLevel":0
,"UnitPrice":1.99,"UnitsInStock":0,"UnitsOnOrder":0},{"Discontinued":false,"Discont
inuedDate":"\/Date(-62135578800000-
0500)\/","ProductId":1006,"ProductName":"Moo","QuantityPerUnit":"","ReorderLevel":0
,"UnitPrice":2.99,"UnitsInStock":0,"UnitsOnOrder":0},{"Discontinued":false,"Discont
inuedDate":"\/Date(-62135578800000-
0500)\/","ProductId":1016,"ProductName":"Coo","QuantityPerUnit":"","ReorderLevel":0
```

,"UnitPrice":4.99,"UnitsInStock":0,"UnitsOnOrder":0},{"Discontinued":false,"Discont
inuedDate":"\/Date(-62135578800000-
0500)\/","ProductId":1011,"ProductName":"Soo","QuantityPerUnit":"","ReorderLevel":0
,"UnitPrice":4.99,"UnitsInStock":0,"UnitsOnOrder":0},{"Discontinued":false,"Discont
inuedDate":"\/Date(-62135578800000-
0500)\/","ProductId":1016,"ProductName":"Boo","QuantityPerUnit":"","ReorderLevel":0
,"UnitPrice":9.99,"UnitsInStock":0,"UnitsOnOrder":0},{"Discontinued":false,"Discont
inuedDate":"\/Date(-62135578800000-
0500)\/","ProductId":1013,"ProductName":"Voo","QuantityPerUnit":"","ReorderLevel":0
,"UnitPrice":11.99,"UnitsInStock":0,"UnitsOnOrder":0},{"Discontinued":false,"Discon
tinuedDate":"\/Date(-62135578800000-
0500)\/","ProductId":1014,"ProductName":"Woo","QuantityPerUnit":"","ReorderLevel":0
,"UnitPrice":13.99,"UnitsInStock":0,"UnitsOnOrder":0},{"Discontinued":false,"Discon
tinuedDate":"\/Date(-62135578800000-
0500)\/","ProductId":1016,"ProductName":"Doo","QuantityPerUnit":"","ReorderLevel":0
,"UnitPrice":13.99,"UnitsInStock":0,"UnitsOnOrder":0},{"Discontinued":false,"Discon
tinuedDate":"\/Date(-62135578800000-
0500)\/","ProductId":1001,"ProductName":"Foo","QuantityPerUnit":"","ReorderLevel":0
,"UnitPrice":19.99,"UnitsInStock":0,"UnitsOnOrder":0}]

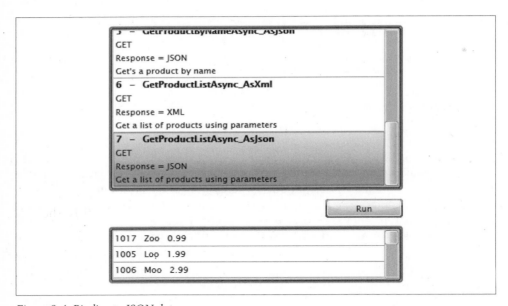

Figure 9-4. Binding to JSON data

Serialized JSON

Another option for managing JSON data besides using LINQ to JSON is to use the
System.Runtime.Serialization.Json.DataContractJsonSerializer class. Before you
use this class, you must make a reference to the System.ServiceModel.Web.dll assembly
for Silverlight 2. Like LINQ to JSON, the DataContractJsonSerializer class can help
to consume JSON and push the data elements into a known entity type.

`DataContractJsonSerializer` can deserialize JSON data into an object instance and can also serialize an object into JSON.

LINQ to JSON offers a great deal of flexibility for querying a data structure and pulling values out and into a new object. This makes LINQ ideal for parsing and querying XML, JSON, and other data structures. However, when a situation merely warrants converting a stream or string of JSON into a known entity, the `DataContractJsonSerializer` class is a good choice. For instance, Example 9-15 takes JSON data that represents a single product, reads the JSON into a `MemoryStream`, and converts the stream into a `Product` instance. This provides another option to consume JSON in a Silverlight 2 client application as it returns from a RESTful web service call.

Example 9-15. Reading JSON

```
string jsonSerializedProduct = "{\"Id\":201,\"ProductName\":\"Some Thing\"}";
DataContractJsonSerializer serializer =
    new DataContractJsonSerializer(typeof (Product));
MemoryStream stream = new
MemoryStream(Encoding.UTF8.GetBytes(jsonSerializedProduct));
Product product = serializer.ReadObject(stream) as Product;
stream.Close();

var name = product.ProductName;
```

```
Dim jsonSerializedProduct As String = "{""Id"":201,""ProductName"":""Some Thing""}"
Dim serializer As New DataContractJsonSerializer(GetType(Product))
Dim stream As New MemoryStream(Encoding.UTF8.GetBytes(jsonSerializedProduct))
Dim product As Product = TryCast(serializer.ReadObject(stream), Product)
stream.Close()

Dim name = product.ProductName
```

The `DataContractJsonSerializer` class also serializes an object to JSON. This is beneficial when an entity has been modified in the Silverlight client application and it must be sent to a web service as JSON to be saved to a database. Example 9-16 shows a `Product` instance being serialized as JSON using the `DataContractJsonSerializer`.

Example 9-16. Serializing as JSON

```
Product product = new Product { ProductId = 301, ProductName = "Another Thing" };
DataContractJsonSerializer serializer = new
    DataContractJsonSerializer(typeof(Product));
MemoryStream stream = new MemoryStream();
serializer.WriteObject(stream, product);
string jsonSerializedProduct =
    Encoding.UTF8.GetString(stream.ToArray(), 0, (int)stream.Length);
```

```
Dim product As Product = New Product With _
    {.ProductId = 301, .ProductName = "Another Thing"}
Dim serializer As New DataContractJsonSerializer(GetType(Product))
Dim stream As New MemoryStream()
serializer.WriteObject(stream, product)
```

```
Dim jsonSerializedProduct As String = _
    Encoding.UTF8.GetString(stream.ToArray(), 0, CInt(Fix(stream.Length)))
```

In the sample Silverlight 2 client application `RESTfulClient`, one of the options is to
retrieve a list of products from the `RESTful` web service in JSON format and consume
it with the `DataContractJsonSerializer` class. When this option is executed the code
in Example 9-17 runs. First the JSON is pulled into a `MemoryStream`, then it is converted
to a `List<Product>`, and finally it is bound to the results `ListBox`'s `DataContext`. It is
important to make sure the appropriate encoding is used, which in this case is UTF8.
Figure 9-5 shows the results of running this operation.

Example 9-17. Deserializing JSON

C#
```
private void ParseProducts_AsJson_UsingDataContractJsonSerializer(
    object sender, DownloadStringCompletedEventArgs e)
{
    string json = e.Result;
    DataContractJsonSerializer serializer =
        new DataContractJsonSerializer(typeof(List<Product>));
    MemoryStream stream =
        new MemoryStream(Encoding.UTF8.GetBytes(json));
    List<Product> products = serializer.ReadObject(stream) as List<Product>;
    stream.Close();
    lstProducts.DataContext = products;
}
```

VB
```
Private Sub ParseProducts_AsJson_UsingDataContractJsonSerializer( _
        ByVal sender As Object, ByVal e As DownloadStringCompletedEventArgs)
    Dim json As String = e.Result
    Dim serializer As New DataContractJsonSerializer(GetType(List(Of Product)))
    Dim stream As New MemoryStream(Encoding.UTF8.GetBytes(json))
    Dim products As List(Of Product) = _
        TryCast(serializer.ReadObject(stream), List(Of Product))
    stream.Close()
    lstProducts.DataContext = products
End Sub
```

Posting Data to a RESTful Service

The previous sections demonstrated several different variations of building and invoking REST-friendly web services to retrieve data. All of the RESTful operations are decorated with the `WebGet` attribute, which indicates that they will be invoked with an
HTTP `GET`. RESTful operations also support other HTTP methods, such as `POST`, `PUT`,
and `DELETE`. However, Silverlight 2 is capable of directly issuing an HTTP `GET` or HTTP
`POST` method only through managed code. You can invoke `GET` requests from Silverlight
2 using the `WebClient` class's `DownloadStringAsync` method, and you can invoke `POST`
requests using the `UploadStringAsync` method.

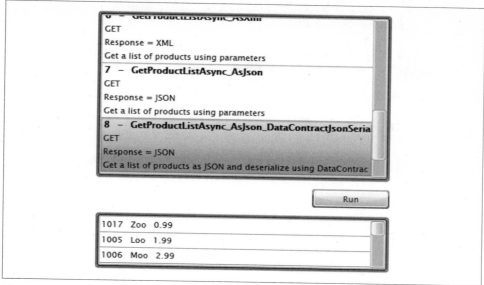

GET
Response = XML
Get a list of products using parameters

7 – GetProductListAsync_AsJson
GET
Response = JSON
Get a list of products using parameters

8 – GetProductListAsync_AsJson_DataContractJsonSeria
GET
Response = JSON
Get a list of products as JSON and deserialize using DataContrac

Run

1017	Zoo	0.99
1005	Loo	1.99
1006	Moo	2.99

Figure 9-5. Deserializing JSON

There are creative ways to pass a `PUT` or `DELETE` from Silverlight 2, such as passing the HTTP `PUT` or `DELETE` method as a parameter in the `X-HTTP-Method-Override` header. This technique, which is referred to as *POST Tunneling*, allows a `PUT` or `DELETE` method to be sent in the `X-HTTP-Method-Override` header of an HTTP `POST` method. Many firewalls allow only `GET` or `POST`, so this technique is commonly used to issue `GET`, `PUT`, `POST`, and `DELETE` methods when the web service expects them.

Defining POST Methods

Creating a `RESTful` web service that accepts an HTTP `POST` request using WCF requires that the operation be decorated with the `WebInvoke` attribute instead of the `WebGet` attribute. The code in Example 9-18 demonstrates how to decorate a web service operation with the `WebInvoke` attribute to indicate that the HTTP method is a `POST`. The `UriTemplate` indicates the unique URI that represents the `Product` resource.

The `UriTemplate` contains `?json` and the `RequestFormat` property is set to `WebMessageFormat.Json`, which indicates that the request body will contain a JSON object. Simply toggling the `RequestFormat` to `WebMessageFormat.Xml` would tell this method to expect the request to contain XML instead. You also can set the method to a `POST` by using a query string convention of `?Method=POST`, as shown in Example 9-18.

Example 9-18. Using WebInvoke

```
[OperationContract]
[WebInvoke(UriTemplate = "Product?json", Method = "POST",
```

```
        RequestFormat = WebMessageFormat.Json, BodyStyle = WebMessageBodyStyle.Bare)]
    void AddProductAsJson(Product product);
```

```
    <OperationContract, _
        WebInvoke(UriTemplate := "Product?json", _
        Method := "POST", RequestFormat := WebMessageFormat.Json, _
        BodyStyle := WebMessageBodyStyle.Bare)> _
    void AddProductAsJson(Product product)
```

Adding the ?json to the UriTemplate allows a similar web method to be created that performs the same operation but expects the request body to contain XML data instead of JSON. For example, the operation in Example 9-18 has a similar UriTemplate to the operation in Example 9-19. The two differences (shown in bold in the examples) in the WebInvoke attribute settings are in the UriTemplate and in the RequestFormat.

The slight difference in the UriTemplate creates two unique URIs that support a POST operation of a product resource. The first example expects XML and the second expects JSON. Both operations map to different public methods, which have identical implementations, as shown in Example 9-19.

Example 9-19. Mapping to different public methods

```
    [OperationContract]
    [WebInvoke(UriTemplate = "Product", Method = "POST",
        RequestFormat = WebMessageFormat.Xml,
        BodyStyle = WebMessageBodyStyle.Bare)]
    void AddProductAsXml(Product product);
```

```
    <OperationContract, _
        WebInvoke(UriTemplate := "Product", Method := "POST", _
        RequestFormat := WebMessageFormat.Xml, _
        BodyStyle := WebMessageBodyStyle.Bare)> _
    void AddProductAsXml(Product product)
```

As shown in Example 9-20, the AddProductAsJson method and the AddProductAsXml method receive a deserialized Product instance. The former is mapped to a RESTful URI that is invoked when JSON is sent and the latter is mapped to a RESTful URI that is invoked when XML is sent. Both call the private AddProduct method, which in turn inserts the new product into a database.

Example 9-20. Implementing the POST web service operations

```
    public void AddProductAsJson(Product product)
    {
        AddProduct(product);
    }

    public void AddProductAsXml(Product product)
    {
        AddProduct(product);
    }

    private void AddProduct(Product product)
```

```
{
    var query = @"INSERT INTO Products (ProductId, ProductName, UnitPrice) "
        + " VALUES (@productId, @productName, @unitPrice) ";

    const string connString = @"Data Source=(local)\SQLEXPRESS;Initial"
        + " Catalog=NorthwindEF;Integrated Security=True;";

    using (var conn = new SqlConnection(connString))
    {
        using (var cmd = new SqlCommand(query, conn))
        {
            cmd.Parameters.AddWithValue("@productId", product.ProductId);
            cmd.Parameters.AddWithValue("@productName", product.ProductName);
            cmd.Parameters.AddWithValue("@unitPrice", product.UnitPrice);
            conn.Open();
            cmd.ExecuteNonQuery();
        }
    }
}
```

VB
```
Public Sub AddProductAsJson(ByVal product As Product)
    AddProduct(product)
End Sub

Public Sub AddProductAsXml(ByVal product As Product)
    AddProduct(product)
End Sub

Private Sub AddProduct(ByVal product As Product)
    Dim query = "INSERT INTO Products (ProductId, ProductName, UnitPrice) " & _
        " VALUES (@productId, @productName, @unitPrice) "

    Const connString As String = "Data Source=(local)\SQLEXPRESS;Initial" & _
        " Catalog=NorthwindEF;Integrated Security=True;"

    Using conn = New SqlConnection(connString)
        Using cmd = New SqlCommand(query, conn)
            cmd.Parameters.AddWithValue("@productId", product.ProductId)
            cmd.Parameters.AddWithValue("@productName", product.ProductName)
            cmd.Parameters.AddWithValue("@unitPrice", product.UnitPrice)
            conn.Open();
            cmd.ExecuteNonQuery();
        End Using
    End Using
End Sub
```

Posting JSON and XML

You can use the `WebClient` class or the `HttpWebRequest` class to invoke an HTTP POST web service from a Silverlight 2 client, passing either JSON or XML as the `Request` body. Example 9-21 demonstrates this technique by first creating a sample `Product` instance and using the `DataContractJsonSerializer` to serialize the `Product` to JSON. Notice that the serialization encoding uses UTF8. This encoding must match the encoding set in the header of the POST request.

Example 9-21. POSTing JSON

C#
```csharp
private void PostProductAsync_AsJson_DataContractJsonSerializer()
{
    // Serialize a Product to JSON
    Product product = new Product
        {
            ProductId = 301,
            ProductName = "Another Thing",
            UnitPrice = (decimal)19.99
        };

    DataContractJsonSerializer serializer =
        new DataContractJsonSerializer(typeof(Product));
    MemoryStream stream = new MemoryStream();
    serializer.WriteObject(stream, product);
    string jsonSerializedProduct =
        Encoding.UTF8.GetString(stream.ToArray(), 0, (int)stream.Length);


    // POST the JSON to the Async Operation
    WebClient wc = new WebClient();
    wc.UploadStringCompleted += wc_UploadStringCompleted;
    wc.Headers["Content-type"] = "application/json";
    wc.Encoding = Encoding.UTF8;
    string urlString = string.Format("{0}/Product?json", BaseUri);
    wc.UploadStringAsync(new Uri(urlString), "POST", jsonSerializedProduct);
}
```

VB
```vbnet
Private Sub PostProductAsync_AsJson_DataContractJsonSerializer()
    ' Serialize a Product to JSON
    Dim product As Product = New Product With _
        { _
            .ProductId = 301, _
            .ProductName = "Another Thing", _
            .UnitPrice = CDec(19.99) _
        }
    Dim serializer As New DataContractJsonSerializer(GetType(Product))
    Dim stream As New MemoryStream()
    serializer.WriteObject(stream, product)
    Dim jsonSerializedProduct As String = _
        Encoding.UTF8.GetString(stream.ToArray(), 0, CInt(Fix(stream.Length)))


    ' POST the JSON to the Async Operation
    Dim wc As New WebClient()
    wc.UploadStringCompleted += wc_UploadStringCompleted
    wc.Headers("Content-type") = "application/json"
    wc.Encoding = Encoding.UTF8
    Dim urlString As String = String.Format("{0}/Product?json", BaseUri)
    wc.UploadStringAsync(New Uri(urlString), "POST", jsonSerializedProduct)
End Sub
```

Once the `Product` is serialized, the `WebClient` instance is created and a header is added to indicate that the content of the request body will contain JSON. A header is set to indicate that the encoding is UTF8, matching the encoding of the serialized `Product` instance. The URI is then created and passed to the `UploadStringAsync` method along with the `POST` action indicator and the JSON serialized `Product`. This asynchronous invocation is mapped to the `AddProductAsJson` method shown in Example 9-20.

It is important to make sure the content type matches what is being sent in the request's body. If JSON is being sent, the `content-type` header should be set to `application/json`. If XML is being sent, the `content-type` header should be set to `application/xml`.

> It is also important that the objects that are being serialized and deserialized on the Silverlight client and in the remote web service match each other. If the property names or even the namespaces are different, when the code tries to deserialize the object and it finds a difference in the object's structure, it will fail.

Posting XML data is a very similar process to posting JSON, with the obvious exceptions of serializing to XML. Example 9-22 shows how the `Product` instance is serialized to XML using the `DataContractSerializer` and the `content-type` header is set to `application/xml`.

Example 9-22. POSTing XML

```csharp
private void PostProductAsync_AsXml_DataContractSerializer()
{
    // Serialize a Product to XML
    Product product = new Product
    {
        ProductId = 301,
        ProductName = "Another Thing",
        UnitPrice = (decimal)19.99
    };
    DataContractSerializer serializer =
        new DataContractSerializer(typeof(Product));
    MemoryStream stream = new MemoryStream();
    serializer.WriteObject(stream, product);
    string xmlSerializedProduct =
        Encoding.UTF8.GetString(stream.ToArray(), 0, (int)stream.Length);


    // POST the XML to the Async Operation
    WebClient wc = new WebClient();
    wc.UploadStringCompleted += wc_UploadStringCompleted;
    wc.Headers["Content-type"] = "application/xml";
    wc.Encoding = Encoding.UTF8;
    string urlString = string.Format("{0}/Product", BaseUri);
```

```
        wc.UploadStringAsync(new Uri(urlString), "POST", xmlSerializedProduct);
    }

VB  Private Sub PostProductAsync_AsXml_DataContractSerializer()
        ' Serialize a Product to XML
        Dim product As Product = New Product With _
            { _
                .ProductId = 301, _
                .ProductName = "Another Thing", _
                .UnitPrice = CDec(19.99) _
            }
        Dim serializer As New DataContractSerializer(GetType(Product))
        Dim stream As New MemoryStream()
        serializer.WriteObject(stream, product)
        Dim xmlSerializedProduct As String = _
            Encoding.UTF8.GetString(stream.ToArray(), 0, CInt(Fix(stream.Length)))


        ' POST the XML to the Async Operation
        Dim wc As New WebClient()
        wc.UploadStringCompleted += wc_UploadStringCompleted
        wc.Headers("Content-type") = "application/xml"
        wc.Encoding = Encoding.UTF8
        Dim urlString As String = String.Format("{0}/Product", BaseUri)
        wc.UploadStringAsync(New Uri(urlString), "POST", xmlSerializedProduct)
    End Sub
```

So far this chapter has demonstrated how to issue HTTP GET and HTTP POST requests from Silverlight 2 client applications to RESTful web services. It also demonstrated how to design cross-domain, REST-friendly WCF web services that support various configuration and parameter options. The following section demonstrates a case study that combines many of these features and builds a Silverlight client application that interacts with the Twitter REST API.

Case Study: SilverTwit

The following example is an application called SilverTwit that exposes some of the most-used features of the Twitter API in a Silverlight 2 client application. SilverTwit pools many of the topics we've discussed in this book to build a Silverlight 2 client interface that uses data-binding techniques, builds a RESTful service, invokes remote web service calls asynchronously, uses type converters, handles cross-domain invocation, and sends GET and POST requests, among many other features. This section will go over the architecture of the application and jump into the details of its highlights. The full source code for the SilverTwit solution is located in the code for this chapter. SilverTwit exposes only some of the most commonly used features of the Twitter RESTful API. You can easily expand it to encompass many of the Twitter API features by extending the source code.

The SilverTwit solution is included in this chapter's code samples. To run this code, you must first change the constants' values at the top of the *Page.xaml.cs* file to use your Twitter credentials.

SilverTwit Architecture

The SilverTwit application has two major components, shown in Figure 9-6. The user interface is represented with a Silverlight 2 client application. It handles all interaction with the user and presents the data from the web services. It also communicates directly with the SilverTwit REST-friendly web services component. The Twitter API requires that credentials be passed to Twitter to perform some operations, such as obtaining a list of the latest direct messages for a user or posting a message to Twitter. The Silver-Twit RESTful web services component handles all calls to the Twitter API.

Figure 9-6. SilverTwit components

The `WebClient` class available in Silverlight is a subset of the `WebClient` class available in the full .NET 3.5 Framework's CLR. For example, in Silverlight the `WebClient` class does not have the `Credentials` property that is found in the `WebClient` class in the full .NET library. The `Credentials` property allows username and password credentials to be passed to a remote web service. If a web service requires credentials to be passed, a Silverlight application could call a custom web service that relays the calls to the remote web service. This way, the Silverlight application can pass the required credentials information to the relay web service as standard parameters (ideally through HTTPS), and the relay web service can package them in the `WebClient` library, because it has the full-blown `WebClient` class.

The SilverTwit web services do not necessarily need to be implemented as RESTful services. The services could easily be implemented as SOAP services using ASMX or WCF. However, as the calls to the Twitter API are RESTful, it made sense to make the relay web service also use the REST style.

SilverTwit UI

SilverTwit uses a `ListBox` to display all of the messages (also known as *tweets*) to the user. Figure 9-7 shows the application's user interface. When the user clicks the buttons on the top of the control, the types of tweets displayed are queried and bound to the `ListBox`. When the user clicks the Home button, all tweets for the logged-in user will

Figure 9-7. SilverTwit UI

be retrieved and bound. When the user clicks the Replies button, all replies to the logged-in user will be retrieved and bound. If the user clicks the Direct button, all direct messages sent to the logged-in user will be retrieved and bound.

The user can send a new tweet to Twitter using the `TextBox` and the Post button. When a user selects a tweet in the `ListBox` and clicks one of the small buttons above the `TextBox`, the author's username for the selected tweet will appear in the `TextBox`. This allows posts to be replied to a user or a direct message to be sent to a specific user.

The requests for the different types of tweets are sent from the Silverlight 2 client to the RESTful web service asynchronously via the `WebClient` class. When the SilverTwitWS web service returns the tweets via XML, they are parsed using LINQ to XML by the `LoadTweets` method shown in Example 9-23. `LoadTweets` parses the XML containing the tweets into the `TweetStatus` and `User` classes, which are then bound to the `ListBox`. Values are converted to the appropriate type inside the LINQ to XML query definition using the custom extension methods `ToDateTime`, `ToInt`, and `ToBool`. These extension methods, contained in the `MyExtensions` static class, simplify the conversions.

Example 9-23. LoadTweets method

C#

```csharp
private void LoadTweets(XElement xmlElement)
{
    XNamespace ns = "";
    var twitterQuery = from status in xmlElement.Descendants(ns + "status")
        let user = status.Element(ns + "user")
        select new TweetStatus
        {
            TwitterId = (status.Element(ns + "id").Value).ToInt(),
            CreatedAt = (status.Element(ns + "created_at").Value).ToDateTime(),
            Text = status.Element(ns + "text").Value,
            Source = status.Element(ns + "source").Value,
            Truncated = Convert.ToBoolean(status.Element(ns + "truncated").Value),
            InReplyToStatusId = status.Element(ns + "in_reply_to_status_id").Value,
            InReplyToUserId = status.Element(ns + "in_reply_to_user_id").Value,
            Favorited = (status.Element(ns + "favorited").Value).ToBool(),
            User = new User
            {
                UserId = (user.Element(ns + "id").Value).ToInt(),
                Name = user.Element(ns + "name").Value,
                ScreenName = user.Element(ns + "screen_name").Value,
                Description = user.Element(ns + "description").Value,
                Location = user.Element(ns + "location").Value,
                ProfileImageUrl = user.Element(ns + "profile_image_url").Value,
                Url = user.Element(ns + "url").Value,
                Protected = (user.Element(ns + "protected").Value).ToBool(),
                FollowersCount =
                    (user.Element(ns + "followers_count").Value).ToInt()
            }
        };
    List<TweetStatus> statusList = twitterQuery.ToList<TweetStatus>();
    lstTweets.DataContext = statusList;
}
```

VB

```vb
Private Sub LoadTweets(ByVal xmlElement As XElement)
    Dim ns As XNamespace = ""
    Dim twitterQuery = _
        From status In xmlElement.Descendants(ns + "status") _
        Let user = status.Element(ns + "user") _
        Select New TweetStatus With _
        { _
        .TwitterId = (status.Element(ns + "id").Value).ToInt(), _
        .CreatedAt = (status.Element(ns + "created_at").Value).ToDateTime(), _
        .Text = status.Element(ns + "text").Value, _
        .Source = status.Element(ns + "source").Value, _
        .Truncated = Convert.ToBoolean(status.Element(ns + "truncated").Value), _
        .InReplyToStatusId = status.Element(ns + "in_reply_to_status_id").Value, _
        .InReplyToUserId = status.Element(ns + "in_reply_to_user_id").Value, _
        .Favorited = (status.Element(ns + "favorited").Value).ToBool(), _
        .User = New User With _
            { _
            .UserId = (user.Element(ns + "id").Value).ToInt(), _
            .Name = user.Element(ns + "name").Value, _
            .ScreenName = user.Element(ns + "screen_name").Value, _
            .Description = user.Element(ns + "description").Value, _
```

```
                .Location = user.Element(ns + "location").Value, _
                .ProfileImageUrl = user.Element(ns + "profile_image_url").Value, _
                .Url = user.Element(ns + "url").Value, _
                .Protected = (user.Element(ns + "protected").Value).ToBool(), _
                .FollowersCount = _
                    (user.Element(ns + "followers_count").Value).ToInt() _
            } _
        }
        Dim statusList As List(Of TweetStatus) = twitterQuery.ToList(Of TweetStatus)()
        lstTweets.DataContext = statusList
End Sub
```

When a user enters a new tweet and clicks the Post button, the new tweet is sent to the SilverTwitWS web service, which in turn submits the tweet to the Twitter RESTful API. The tweet is wrapped in some simple XML, as shown in Example 9-24, and is sent to the SilverTwitWS RESTful web service. The tweet could have been sent as text or as JSON, or the entire TweetStatus object could have been serialized to XML and passed to the SilverTwitWS services. However, there is no need to pass the entire TweetStatus object for a new tweet when all that is required are the credentials of the user creating the tweet and the tweet text itself. This keeps the message that will be passed in the HTTP POST Request body small. The message and the URI are formatted and then passed through the UploadStringAsync method of the WebClient instance and on to the RESTful web service.

Example 9-24. Posting a tweet from Silverlight

C#
```
private void PostTweet()
{
    string uriString =
        string.Format("{0}/Tweet/{1}/?pw={2}", BaseUri, _userName, _password);
    Uri uri = new Uri(uriString);

    WebClient svc = new WebClient();
    svc.Headers["Content-type"] = "application/xml";
    svc.Encoding = Encoding.UTF8;
    svc.UploadStringCompleted += svc_UploadStringCompleted;

    string xml =
        string.Format("<TweetStatus><Text>{0}</Text></TweetStatus>", tbPost.Text);
    svc.UploadStringAsync(uri, "POST", xml);
}
```

VB
```
Private Sub PostTweet()
    Dim uriString As String = _
        String.Format("{0}/Tweet/{1}/?pw={2}", BaseUri, _userName, _password)
    Dim uri As New Uri(uriString)

    Dim svc As New WebClient()
    svc.Headers("Content-type") = "application/xml"
    svc.Encoding = Encoding.UTF8
    svc.UploadStringCompleted += svc_UploadStringCompleted

    Dim xml As String = _
```

```
        String.Format("<TweetStatus><Text>{0}</Text></TweetStatus>", tbPost.Text)
    svc.UploadStringAsync(uri, "POST", xml)
End Sub
```

SilverTwitWS RESTful Web Service

Example 9-25 defines the two RESTful operations and their matching UriTemplates. The
FindTweets method accepts all requests from the Silverlight client to retrieve tweets,
replies, and direct messages from the Twitter RESTful services. The tweetType parameter is passed in the URI's query string to indicate which of these types of retrieval is
being requested. The AddTweet method accepts the text that will be used to create a new
tweet. Both methods require the credentials of the user to be passed so that they in turn
can be passed on to Twitter via the Twitter RESTful API calls.

Example 9-25. ITwitterRESTService interface

C#
```
[ServiceContract(Namespace = "http://www.silverlight-data.com")]
public interface ITwitterRESTService
{
    [OperationContract]
    [WebGet(UriTemplate = "Tweet/{username}/{tweetType}/?pw={password}",
        ResponseFormat = WebMessageFormat.Xml)]
    XElement FindTweets(string username, string tweetType, string password);

    [OperationContract]
    [WebInvoke(UriTemplate = "Tweet/{username}/?pw={password}",
        RequestFormat = WebMessageFormat.Xml, Method = "POST")]
    void AddTweet(string username, string password, TweetStatus newTweetStatus);
}
```

VB
```
<ServiceContract(Namespace := "http://www.silverlight-data.com")> _
Public Interface ITwitterRESTService
    <OperationContract, _
        WebGet(UriTemplate := "Tweet/{username}/{tweetType}/?pw={password}", _
        ResponseFormat := WebMessageFormat.Xml)> _
    Function FindTweets(ByVal username As String, ByVal tweetType As String, _
        ByVal password As String) As XElement

    <OperationContract, _
        WebInvoke(UriTemplate := "Tweet/{username}/?pw={password}", _
        RequestFormat := WebMessageFormat.Xml, Method := "POST")> _
    Sub AddTweet(ByVal username As String, ByVal password As String, _
        ByVal newTweetStatus As TweetStatus)
End Interface
```

The FindTweets method, shown shortly in Example 9-27, uses the available
WebOperationContext.Current.OutgoingResponse object to set the HTTP status code for
the request. If the request receives an empty username, password, or tweetType
parameter, the HTTP status code is set to the HttpStatusCode.BadRequest enumerator
value. BadRequest implies that the server could not understand the request and it translates to a status code of 400. You can examine the status codes using a tool such as

Fiddler2 while testing the services. If the operation completes successfully, the HTTP status code is set to `HttpStatusCode.OK`, the most common HTTP status code for success. `OK` translates to a status code of 200. Table 9-2 lists some of the most commonly used status codes when creating RESTful services.

Table 9-2. Common HTTP status codes

HttpStatusCode enumerator	Code	Description
OK	200	The operation for the request was successful.
Created	201	The operation for the request successfully created a new resource.
BadRequest	400	Some aspect of the request was invalid. This is a fallback status code when no other status code fits.
Unauthorized	401	The request could not be made due to the lack of proper authorization.
NotFound	404	The resource requested is not found.
InternalServerError	500	A generic error occurred while processing the request.

 The Twitter API documentation lists all of the RESTful URIs and how to make requests to them. Some requests require authorization through credentials and others do not. You can return most requests using multiple formats, including XML, JSON, Atom, and RSS. You can view the documentation at *http://apiwiki.twitter.com*.

Depending on the value of the `tweetType` parameter, a different URI is used to communicate with the Twitter API. The URI to retrieve the default page for SilverTwit is *http://twitter.com/statuses/friends_timeline/{0}.xml?count=50*. The parameter is replaced with the name of the user, which allows the request to retrieve the 50 most recent tweets for the provided user and the user's Twitter friends.

Because this requires looking up a user's information, the username and password parameters are required, which are sent to the Twitter API request via the `WebClient.Credentials` object. The code in Example 9-26 packages the username and password parameters into a `NetworkCredential` class instance, and sets this new object to the `WebClient` instance's `Credentials` property.

Example 9-26. Checking and setting the credentials

C#
```
WebClient wc = new WebClient();
if (username.Length > 0 && password.Length > 0)
    wc.Credentials = new NetworkCredential(username, password);
```

VB
```
Dim wc As New WebClient()
If username.Length > 0 AndAlso password.Length > 0 Then
    wc.Credentials = New NetworkCredential(username, password)
End If
```

The other tweetType values indicate to use the URI to retrieve either the direct messages for the user or the replies sent to the user. Both of these requests require the credentials because they look for information that is directly sensitive to the user. Some requests do not require credentials, such as requesting the public timeline for Twitter. However, all requests that relate to a Twitter user's information require valid credentials to be passed. Example 9-27 shows the service's implementation of the FindTweets method defined in the interface in Example 9-25.

 The sample code for SilverTwit requires a valid Twitter username and password. You must set the values in the sample code in the Page class private fields in the SilverTwit client application. The fields are marked with TODO comments so that you can find them easily.

Example 9-27. Finding tweets from Twitter

```csharp
public XElement FindTweets(string username, string tweetType, string password)
{
    OutgoingWebResponseContext outResponse =
        WebOperationContext.Current.OutgoingResponse;

    if (string.IsNullOrEmpty(username)
        || string.IsNullOrEmpty(password)
        || string.IsNullOrEmpty(tweetType))
    {
        WebOperationContext ctx = WebOperationContext.Current;
        ctx.OutgoingResponse.StatusCode = HttpStatusCode.BadRequest;
        return null;
    }

    string uriString = string.Empty;
    switch (tweetType)
    {
        case "all":
            uriString =
              string.Format(
                @"http://twitter.com/statuses/friends_timeline/{0}.xml", username);
            break;
        case "dm":
            uriString = string.Format(@"http://twitter.com/direct_messages.xml");
            break;
        case "replies":
            uriString = string.Format(@"http://twitter.com/statuses/replies.xml");
            break;
        default:
            outResponse.StatusCode = HttpStatusCode.BadRequest;
            return null;
            break;
    }
    outResponse.StatusCode = HttpStatusCode.OK;
```

```
        return GetRequest(uriString, username, password, outResponse);
}
```

VB
```
Public Function FindTweets(ByVal username As String, _
        ByVal tweetType As String, ByVal password As String) As XElement
    Dim outResponse As OutgoingWebResponseContext = _
        WebOperationContext.Current.OutgoingResponse

    If String.IsNullOrEmpty(username) _
        OrElse String.IsNullOrEmpty(password) _
        OrElse String.IsNullOrEmpty(tweetType) Then
        Dim ctx As WebOperationContext = WebOperationContext.Current
        ctx.OutgoingResponse.StatusCode = HttpStatusCode.BadRequest
        Return Nothing
    End If

    Dim uriString As String = String.Empty
    Select Case tweetType
        Case "all"
            uriString = _
              String.Format( _
              "http://twitter.com/statuses/friends_timeline/{0}.xml", username)
        Case "dm"
            uriString = String.Format("http://twitter.com/direct_messages.xml")
        Case "replies"
            uriString = String.Format("http://twitter.com/statuses/replies.xml")
        Case Else
            outResponse.StatusCode = HttpStatusCode.BadRequest
            Return Nothing
    End Select
    outResponse.StatusCode = HttpStatusCode.OK
    Return GetRequest(uriString, username, password, outResponse)
End Function
```

Caching

Caching of web requests is important in terms of an application's performance and the user's experience. When designing a RESTful service, it is often beneficial to implement some sort of caching rules on requests to eliminate server overload. For example, if the same client makes the same request 10 times within a minute, it may be unlikely that the data returned from the request would change within that time frame. Therefore, all 10 requests may result in the same response message. RESTful services can easily set their own caching rules to dictate how a request should be cached on the client making the request. If after the first request the response is sent back to the client and it is marked to be cached for five minutes, all identical requests over the next five minutes from that same client will use the cached response instead of making a new request. This allows the client to load the data locally and not to overload the server with unnecessary calls.

It is a good practice to set the caching of RESTful services. The best caching policy depends on the requirements for the application. If the data is changed frequently—perhaps every few seconds—caching once per minute might be a good idea. If the data changes much less often, you can set the caching for a longer interval.

The Twitter AI caches some requests for 60 seconds, so as not to overload their servers. This policy can change, of course, as it is dictated by Twitter and defined in the Twitter API. The SilverTwitWS web service is also RESTful and can implement its own caching policy. The code in Example 9-28 shows that the SilverTwit service tells the client not to cache the response for the requests. This means that all requests made to SilverTwit will not be cached. Because Twitter caches for one minute, it could make more sense to set the cache for SilverTwitWS to one minute, as well. To do this, you can change the Expires setting from 0 to a time span of 60 seconds.

Example 9-28. Stop caching

```
private void SetNoCache(OutgoingWebResponseContext outResponse)
{
    //Tell client not to cache
    outResponse.Headers.Add("Pragma", "no-cache");
    outResponse.Headers.Add("Cache-Control", "must-revalidate");
    outResponse.Headers.Add("Cache-Control", "no-cache");
    outResponse.Headers.Add("Cache-Control", "no-store");
    outResponse.Headers.Add("Expires", "0");
}
```

```
Private Sub SetNoCache(ByVal outResponse As OutgoingWebResponseContext)
    'Tell client not to cache
    outResponse.Headers.Add("Pragma", "no-cache")
    outResponse.Headers.Add("Cache-Control", "must-revalidate")
    outResponse.Headers.Add("Cache-Control", "no-cache")
    outResponse.Headers.Add("Cache-Control", "no-store")
    outResponse.Headers.Add("Expires", "0")
End Sub
```

Tweeting

Tweeting refers to the action of an authorized Twitter user creating a new message in the Twitter database. The AddTweet method, shown in Example 9-29, invokes the URI (shown in bold) for the Twitter RESTful API that sends a new tweet. The contents of the tweet message are sent as part of the request message body and not as a parameter in the query string. All requests made in SilverTwit use XML; however, it's easy to have them use JSON by changing the extension for all of the URIs from .xml to .json.

The request is made using the HttpWebRequest class, as it allows more customization than the WebClient class. A WebRequest object instance is created from the URI using the HttpWebRequest.Create method. If the message for the new tweet is empty or has more than 140 characters (the limit for a tweet, according to the Twitter API), the HTTP status code is set to BadRequest. If the request contains a valid tweet, the credentials are set, the HTTP method is set to POST, the content-type is set appropriately, and the content length is set (see the code in bold in Example 9-29). Once the configuration of the WebRequest instance is complete, the request is made. This sends the new tweet along with the credentials and the configuration for the message as an HTTP POST to the Twitter RESTful services. If the request completes successfully, the HTTP status code is set to Created.

Example 9-29. Adding a tweet to Twitter

```C#
public void AddTweet(string username, string password, TweetStatus newTweetStatus)
{
    string uri = @"http://twitter.com/statuses/update.xml";
    IncomingWebRequestContext inRequest =
        WebOperationContext.Current.IncomingRequest;
    OutgoingWebResponseContext outResponse =
        WebOperationContext.Current.OutgoingResponse;
    WebRequest webRequest = HttpWebRequest.Create(uri);

    if (newTweetStatus.Text == null)
    {
        outResponse.StatusCode = HttpStatusCode.BadRequest;
        return;
    }

    string message = newTweetStatus.Text;
    message = message.Trim();
    if (message.Length > 140)
    {
        outResponse.StatusCode = HttpStatusCode.BadRequest;
        return;
    }

    // The TWEET_SOURCE constant below is a class level constant,
    // set to "SilverTwit".
    // It defines the name of the source program talking to Twitter.
    string parameters = string.Format("status={0}&source={1}",
        HttpUtility.HtmlEncode(message), TWEET_SOURCE);

    if (string.IsNullOrEmpty(username) || string.IsNullOrEmpty(password))
    {
        outResponse.StatusCode = HttpStatusCode.BadRequest;
        return;
    }

    // The username and password variables below are set as fields of this class.
    webRequest.Credentials = new NetworkCredential(username, password);
    webRequest.ContentType = "application/x-www-form-urlencoded";
    webRequest.Method = "POST";
    ASCIIEncoding encoding = new ASCIIEncoding();
    byte[] bytes = encoding.GetBytes(parameters);

    Stream os = null;
    try
    {
        webRequest.ContentLength = bytes.Length;
        os = webRequest.GetRequestStream();
        os.Write(bytes, 0, bytes.Length);
    }
```

```
        finally
        {
            if (os != null)
                os.Close();
        }

        // Set the outgoing status and response headers
        UriTemplate template = new UriTemplate("Tweet/{username}/?pw={password}");
        Uri newUri = template.BindByPosition(
            inRequest.UriTemplateMatch.BaseUri, username, password);
        outResponse.SetStatusAsCreated(newUri);
        return;
    }
```

```
Public Sub AddTweet(ByVal username As String, _
        ByVal password As String, ByVal newTweetStatus As TweetStatus)
    Dim uri As String = "http://twitter.com/statuses/update.xml"
    Dim inRequest As IncomingWebRequestContext = _
        WebOperationContext.Current.IncomingRequest
    Dim outResponse As OutgoingWebResponseContext = _
        WebOperationContext.Current.OutgoingResponse
    Dim webRequest As WebRequest = HttpWebRequest.Create(uri)

    If newTweetStatus.Text Is Nothing Then
        outResponse.StatusCode = HttpStatusCode.BadRequest
        Return
    End If

    Dim message As String = newTweetStatus.Text
    message = message.Trim()
    If message.Length > 140 Then
        outResponse.StatusCode = HttpStatusCode.BadRequest
        Return
    End If

    ' The TWEET_SOURCE constant below is a class level constant,
    ' set to "SilverTwit".
    ' It defines the name of the source program talking to Twitter.
    Dim parameters As String = String.Format("status={0}&source={1}", _
        HttpUtility.HtmlEncode(message), TWEET_SOURCE)

    If String.IsNullOrEmpty(username) OrElse String.IsNullOrEmpty(password) Then
        outResponse.StatusCode = HttpStatusCode.BadRequest
        Return
    End If

    ' The username and password variables below are set as fields of this class.
    webRequest.Credentials = New NetworkCredential(username, password)
    webRequest.ContentType = "application/x-www-form-urlencoded"
    webRequest.Method = "POST"
    Dim encoding As New ASCIIEncoding()
    Dim bytes() As Byte = encoding.GetBytes(parameters)

    Dim os As Stream = Nothing
    Try
        webRequest.ContentLength = bytes.Length
```

```
      os = webRequest.GetRequestStream()
      os.Write(bytes, 0, bytes.Length)
   Finally
      If os IsNot Nothing Then
         os.Close()
      End If
   End Try

   ' Set the outgoing status and response headers
   Dim template As New UriTemplate("Tweet/{username}/?pw={password}")
   Dim newUri As Uri = template.BindByPosition( _
      inRequest.UriTemplateMatch.BaseUri, username, password)
   outResponse.SetStatusAsCreated(newUri)
   Return
End Sub
```

As a result, the SilverTwit client application allows the user to create new tweets, view direct messages, view replies, and view his friend's timeline of tweets through a Silverlight 2 client application.

Summary

WCF provides for the means to design RESTful web services that include `UriTemplate` customization, HTTP status codes, caching policies, authorization through credentials, parameter and URI segment manipulation, and much more. The data can be formatted as JSON, XML, RSS, or Atom in many cases, and can be consumed with a variety of tools, including LINQ to XML, LINQ to JSON, `DataContractSerializer`, and `DataContractJsonSerializer`, among others.

This chapter showed you how to build custom RESTful services using WCF that send and receive requests that utilize many of these tools and features. It wrapped up with a case study showing how to build a Silverlight client application named SilverTwit that takes advantage of many of the concepts discussed in this book that are essential to building Silverlight client applications that communicate with cloud services. The next chapter will continue the discussion of accessing syndication data in the cloud and processing it with Silverlight 2.

CHAPTER 10

Syndication Feeds and Silverlight 2

Feed syndication has grown in availability as a web service. Many websites are now publishing their content as RSS or Atom feeds to provide news, press releases, sports updates, and other timely information. Syndicated information is just another form of data in the cloud that is available to be consumed. Instead of being provided through REST or SOAP, each feed gets a unique URI that returns a stream of XML containing the feed items using the popular RSS or Atom format.

Silverlight 2 includes several features that allow it to consume, manipulate, and display syndicated feeds. Feeds can be requested using `WebClient` or `HttpWebRequest`, the feed contents can be read and manipulated using `XmlReader`, LINQ to XML, or the `SyndicationFeed` class, and the results can be bound to Silverlight 2 target controls. There are several ways to work with feeds from Silverlight 2, each with its pros and cons. Because feeds are simply a web service, you must take cross-domain policy issues into consideration, as well. If a cross-domain policy is not available, services such as FeedBurner, Popfly, and Yahoo! Pipes offer valid alternatives. This chapter discusses the options, demonstrates the techniques for working with syndicated feeds, and provides solutions for working around some of the common pitfalls.

Syndicated Feeds

Silverlight 2 has syndication support for retrieving and processing feeds using the Atom and RSS protocols. Processing syndicated feeds with Silverlight 2 involves a handful of components that work in concert, as shown in Figure 10-1. Reading a feed from Silverlight 2 first requires using a communication library such as `WebClient` or `HttpWebRequest`. These classes issue the asynchronous request for the feed from the remote web service and help to assign the event handler to receive the feed from the web service.

RSS and Atom feed requests fall under the same set of rules as other HTTP requests when it comes to cross-domain policies. If a request has been made to a different domain than that of the web server that hosts the Silverlight 2 client application, a cross-domain policy is requested from the web service's server. If the file exists and it allows access

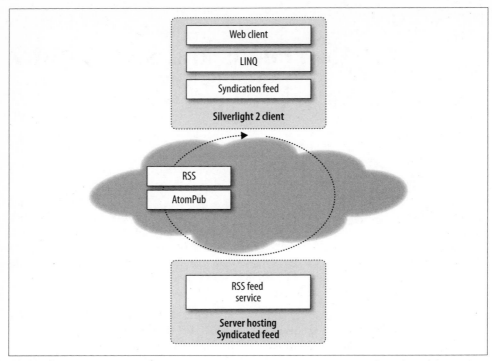

Figure 10-1. Reading syndication feeds from Silverlight 2

to the web service, the feed request is processed and a feed is returned in the `Response` message. The message is usually returned using the commonly accepted Atom or RSS protocol.

When the feed returns to the Silverlight 2 client application, the event handler for the asynchronous operation is executed. If it is returned as XML, you can examine the feed using LINQ to XML or you can load it into an instance of the `System.ServiceModel.Syndication.SyndicationFeed` class. This class, found in the `System.ServiceModel.Syndication.dll` assembly, has a structure that closely matches that of the RSS and Atom structures. `SyndicationFeed` allows a feed to be loaded into it from a string or a stream. Once it is loaded into the `SyndicationFeed` class instance, it can be bound to target user controls, examined by LINQ to XML, or its items can be iterated through using a `foreach` statement.

Once a request has returned containing the feed data, you can load it into an instance of the `SyndicationFeed` class. The `SyndicationFeed` class is an easy way to represent RSS and Atom feeds, because you can load it from either RSS or Atom. This flexibility is a nice advantage over reading the XML from the feed using an `XmlReader` and iterating through its contents. The `SyndicationFeed` class contains properties that represent the accepted standards for the RSS and Atom feed formats. It contains properties such as `Authors`, `Categories`, `Description`, and `Title`, for example. It also contains an `Items` property that represents a list of items in the feed. Each item contains properties that represent information such as the Title and Summary of the feed item.

Requesting a Feed

Both WebClient and HttpWebRequest can make asynchronous calls to web services, including requests for syndication feeds. WebClient is the simpler of the two class libraries as it uses HttpWebRequest under the covers. Using one of these classes to make a web request for a syndicated feed, you can retrieve the data as a string or as a stream, depending on what you desire. The examples in this chapter demonstrate techniques with both classes and both return formats.

The first step in requesting a feed is to find the feed's URI. Many websites publish their syndication feed address in a conspicuous spot on their web page. The format of the feed may be either RSS or Atom. Because both of these protocols are commonly used, any code that requests a feed should be prepared to work with either RSS or Atom. For the following examples, the *http://feeds.feedburner.com/johnpapa* feed will be requested.

 The code solution for the following example is named Syndication Reader and you can find it in the code folder for this chapter.

The example application (shown in Figure 10-2) will request a feed from an address that the user enters. When the feed is returned, it is loaded into a SyndicationFeed object and is bound to the control, where it displays information about the feed and its individual items.

The SyndicationReader application allows the user to choose between using WebClient and HttpWebRequest. Although a real-world application targeted at nondevelopers would likely not provide this choice, the example application does this to demonstrate both ways of making the request. When the user clicks the Go button, the GetFeeds event handler executes and calls a private method that makes the web request call using either the WebClient or the HttpWebRequest object based on the radio button the user selects, as shown in Example 10-1.

Example 10-1. Executing via HttpWebRequest or WebClient

C#
```
if (UseWebClient.IsChecked.Value)
    GetFeed_ViaWebClient();
else if (UseHttpWebRequest.IsChecked.Value)
    GetFeed_ViaHttpWebRequest();
```

VB
```
If UseWebClient.IsChecked.Value Then
    GetFeed_ViaWebClient()
ElseIf UseHttpWebRequest.IsChecked.Value Then
```

```
        GetFeed_ViaHttpWebRequest()
End If
```

Figure 10-2. Syndication reader in action

When the user selects the `WebClient` option, the `GetFeed_UseWebClient` method executes (shown in Example 10-2). The feed address that the user entered is extracted and parsed using the `Uri.TryCreate` method to make sure it is a valid URI. If it is a valid URI, an instance of `WebClient` is created, an event handler is assigned to the `DownloadStringCompleted` event, and `DownloadStringAsync` is executed. This fires off the web request asynchronously to retrieve the feed and tells the request what event handler to execute when the response is returned.

Example 10-2. Requesting the feed via WebClient

C#
```csharp
private void GetFeed_ViaWebClient()
{
    Uri feedUri;
    Uri.TryCreate(txtAddress.Text, UriKind.Absolute, out feedUri);
    if (feedUri == null)
        return;

    WebClient request = new WebClient();
    request.DownloadStringCompleted += ReadFeed_FromWebClient;
    request.DownloadStringAsync(feedUri);
}
```

VB
```vb
Private Sub GetFeed_ViaWebClient()
    Dim feedUri As Uri
    Uri.TryCreate(txtAddress.Text, UriKind.Absolute, feedUri)
    If feedUri Is Nothing Then
        Return
    End If

    Dim request As New WebClient()
    request.DownloadStringCompleted += ReadFeed_FromWebClient
    request.DownloadStringAsync(feedUri)
End Sub
```

Because the feed travels across domains, watching the request in a tool such as Web Development Helper (for Internet Explorer) or Firebug (for Firefox) makes it clear how Silverlight looks for the cross-domain policy file(s). Figure 10-3 shows Firebug watching the requests being made when the SyndicationReader application makes the web service request for the *http://feeds.feedburner.com/johnpapa* feed. Notice that the *clientaccess policy.xml* file is not found, but the *crossdomain.xml* file is found on the *feeds.feedburner .com* web server. Once the cross-domain policy validates the web request, the service returns the feed in the Response (Figure 10-3 shows a fragment of the Response).

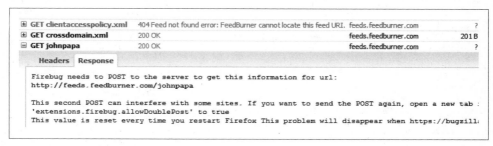

Figure 10-3. Watching requests in Firebug

  Appendix B demonstrates how to use Firebug and other tools to identify and resolve communication problems.

Reading a Feed

Once the feed returns in the `Response` message from the web service call, the `ReadFeed_FromWebClient` event handler processes the data (shown in Example 10-3). When a web request is made through `DownloadStringAsync`, the event handler catches the `Response` message body in an `e.Result` string parameter. If a stream is required, the string can be converted to a stream; alternatively, instead of using `Download StringAsync`, you can use the `OpenReadAsync` method to invoke the web service request. `OpenReadAsync` requests that a stream be created, which will have access to the response message body.

In `ReadFeed_FromWebClient`, the string is read into a `StringReader` object instance, which in turn is used to create an instance of an `XmlReader` object. The `XmlReader` is required to read the feed data (either RSS or Atom), because it is formatted as XML. The `XmlReader` instance is then passed to the `SyndicationFeed.Load` static method where it is parsed into a `SyndicationFeed` object and a collection of `SyndicationItem` child objects. The `SyndicationFeed` object has properties that are mapped to the standard RSS and Atom XML elements, thus making it easy to take the XML from a feed and use it in an object structure instead of reading it as XML.

Example 10-3. Reading the feed response

[C#]
```csharp
private void ReadFeed_FromWebClient(object sender,
    DownloadStringCompletedEventArgs e)
{
    string xml = e.Result;
    if (xml.Length == 0)
        return;
    StringReader stringReader = new StringReader(xml);
    XmlReader reader = XmlReader.Create(stringReader);
    SyndicationFeed feed = SyndicationFeed.Load(reader);
    LayoutRoot.DataContext = feed;
}
```

[VB]
```vb
Private Sub ReadFeed_FromWebClient(ByVal sender As Object, _
        ByVal e As DownloadStringCompletedEventArgs)
    Dim xml As String = e.Result
    If xml.Length = 0 Then
        Return
    End If
    Dim stringReader As New StringReader(xml)
    Dim reader As XmlReader = XmlReader.Create(stringReader)
    Dim feed As SyndicationFeed = SyndicationFeed.Load(reader)
    LayoutRoot.DataContext = feed
End Sub
```

Binding a Feed

Once the XML is parsed into the `SyndicationFeed` class instance named `feed`, the object is set to the `DataContext` of the `LayoutRoot` grid panel in the user interface. The feed

---

object is bound at this level instead of at the child `ListBox`, because properties of the feed object will be bound to the `Listbox` as well as to target controls outside the `ListBox`. Example 10-4 shows the data-bound sections of the XAML in bold.

`WebClient`'s completed event handler is placed back in the UI thread. This means that the feed can be bound to a control or panel in the XAML right in the event handler. In Example 10-4, the feed object is set to the `DataContext` of the `LayoutRoot` `Grid` panel. Because the event handler comes back from the asynchronous request and is placed in the UI thread, it is able to update the UI.

The `SyndicationFeed` class has `Title.Text` and `Description.Text` properties that are bound to `TextBlock` controls within the main `Grid` panel named `LayoutRoot`. `SyndicationFeed` also has an `Items` property that contains a collection of `SyndicationItem` instances. The `Items` property is bound to the `lstFeedItems` `ListBox`'s `ItemsSource` property.

By setting the `DataContext` of the `LayoutRoot` container panel to the `SyndicationFeed` instance, you ensure that all dependency properties can access the object. One alternative is to set the `ItemsSource` directly to the `feed.Items` property and bind the `TextBlock` controls for the feed title and description to the feed instance's properties directly. This works just as well, but using the `DataContext` at the lowest level that contains everything that needs to be bound helps to reduce the amount of code while getting the desired result.

Example 10-4. Syndication page XAML

```
<Grid x:Name="LayoutRoot" Background="#FF333333">
    <Grid.RowDefinitions>
        <RowDefinition Height="70"/>
        <RowDefinition Height="90"/>
        <RowDefinition Height="*"/>
    </Grid.RowDefinitions>
    <StackPanel HorizontalAlignment="Left" Margin="20,20,20,10"
            VerticalAlignment="Stretch" Width="560" Orientation="Horizontal"
            x:Name="FindPanel" Grid.Row="0">
        <TextBlock Text="Feed Address:" Margin="0,0,5,0" FontFamily="Trebuchet MS"
            FontSize="14" VerticalAlignment="Center" HorizontalAlignment="Left"
            FontWeight="Bold" Foreground="#FFC9C6C6"/>
        <TextBox Text="" Margin="5,0,5,0" FontFamily="Trebuchet MS" FontSize="14"
            HorizontalAlignment="Stretch" VerticalAlignment="Center" Width="457"
            x:Name="txtAddress" Style="{StaticResource TextBoxStyle}"/>
    </StackPanel>
    <Grid Grid.Row="1" Margin="20,5,20,5">
        <Grid.RowDefinitions>
            <RowDefinition Height="28"/>
            <RowDefinition Height="*"/>
        </Grid.RowDefinitions>
        <Grid.ColumnDefinitions>
            <ColumnDefinition Width="0.493*"/>
            <ColumnDefinition Width="0.507*"/>
        </Grid.ColumnDefinitions>
        <StackPanel Grid.Row="0" Grid.Column="1" Orientation="Horizontal">
```

```
        <RadioButton HorizontalAlignment="Left" Margin="0,0,7,0"
            VerticalAlignment="Center" Width="Auto" Content="WebClient"
            GroupName="RequestTypeGroup" x:Name="UseWebClient"
            Style="{StaticResource RadioButtonStyle}" Height="Auto"
            IsChecked="True" />
        <RadioButton HorizontalAlignment="Left" Margin="0,0,7,0"
            VerticalAlignment="Center" Width="Auto" Content="HttpWebRequest"
            GroupName="RequestTypeGroup" x:Name="UseHttpWebRequest"
            Style="{StaticResource RadioButtonStyle}" />
        <Button Width="80" Content="Go" Margin="0,0,0,0" x:Name="btnGo"
            Style="{StaticResource ButtonStyle}"
            HorizontalAlignment="Right" />
    </StackPanel>
    <StackPanel Grid.Row="1" Grid.ColumnSpan="2" Orientation="Vertical">
        <TextBlock Text="{Binding Mode=OneWay, Path=Title.Text}"
            Margin="2,2,5,2" FontFamily="Trebuchet MS" FontSize="24"
            x:Name="FeedTitleBlock" Foreground="#FFFFFFFF" />
        <TextBlock Text="{Binding Mode=OneWay, Path=Description.Text}"
            FontFamily="Trebuchet MS" FontSize="14" Margin="2,2,5,2"
            x:Name="FeedSubTitleBlock" Foreground="#FFC9C9C6" />
    </StackPanel>
</Grid>
<ListBox Margin="20,10,20,20" Style="{StaticResource ListBoxStyle}"
            Grid.Row="3" ItemsSource="{Binding Mode=OneWay, Path=Items}"
            x:Name="lstFeedItems">
    <ListBox.ItemTemplate>
        <DataTemplate>
            <SyndicationReader:FeedItem/>
        </DataTemplate>
    </ListBox.ItemTemplate>
</ListBox>
</Grid>
```

The lstFeedItems ListBox uses a DataTemplate named FeedItem to represent the items
in the feed. FeedItem's XAML, shown partially in Example 10-5 in the following section,
with data-bound sections in bold, displays information about each SyndicationItem in
the bound SyndicationFeed object instance's Items collection. Each feed item will be
displayed in the ListBox using the FeedItem user control as a template. Separating out
the contents of the ListBox's ItemTemplate into the FeedItem control abstracts the items
and makes it easier to work with the contents. Figure 10-4 shows a FeedItem from the
template.

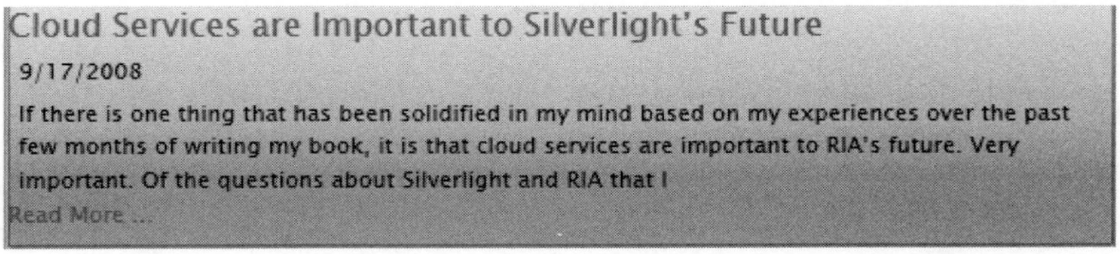

Figure 10-4. An individual FeedItem

Converters

The converters in the bindings help to format the date, strip HTML out of the feed item summaries, and create hyperlinks that point back to the post's origin site. You can find the full source code for all of the converters and the entire solution in the code folder for this chapter. For the `PublishDate` property binding, the `DateConverter` class simply grabs the `DateTimeOffset` value and converts it to a `DateTime` value that displays only the formatted date (no time). The binding goes in only one direction (to the target control), so there is a need to write code only for the `Convert` method, and no need to write code for the `ConvertBack` method. Example 10-5 shows some bindings that use converters.

Example 10-5. Assigning converters in XAML

```
<UserControl.Resources>
        <SyndicationReader:DateOnlyConverter x:Key="myDateOnlyConverter"/>
        <SyndicationReader:HtmlConverter x:Key="myHtmlConverter"/>
        <SyndicationReader:LinkConverter x:Key="myLinkConverter"/>
        <Style TargetType="TextBlock" x:Key="TextBlockSimpleStyle">
            <Setter Property="Margin" Value="3,0,3,0" />
            <Setter Property="FontFamily" Value="Trebuchet MS" />
            <Setter Property="FontSize" Value="11" />
            <Setter Property="HorizontalAlignment" Value="Left" />
            <Setter Property="VerticalAlignment" Value="Center" />
        </Style>
</UserControl.Resources>
<Grid x:Name="LayoutRoot" Width="535" Height="120">
    <StackPanel Orientation="Vertical" Grid.Row="0" Grid.Column="0">
        <HyperlinkButton Content="{Binding Title.Text,
            Converter={StaticResource myHtmlConverter}}"
            NavigateUri="{Binding Links,
            Converter={StaticResource myLinkConverter}}"
            TextWrapping="Wrap" FontSize="16" TargetName="_blank"
            x:Name="ItemTitleLink"/>
        <TextBlock Text="{Binding Mode=OneWay, Path=PublishDate,
            Converter={StaticResource myDateOnlyConverter}}"
            Style="{StaticResource TextBlockSimpleStyle}" Margin="5,2,5,2"
            x:Name="DatePublishedText"/>
        <TextBlock Text="{Binding ConverterParameter=250, Mode=OneWay,
            Path=Summary.Text, Converter={StaticResource myHtmlConverter}}"
            Style="{StaticResource TextBlockSimpleStyle}" Margin="5,2,2,2"
            TextWrapping="Wrap" x:Name="SummaryText"/>
        <HyperlinkButton Content="Read More ..."
            NavigateUri="{Binding Links,
            Converter={StaticResource myLinkConverter}}"
            TextWrapping="Wrap" FontSize="11" TargetName="_blank"
            x:Name="ReadMoreLink"/>
    </StackPanel>
</Grid>
```

The `LinkConverter` class accepts the value from the `SyndicationItem` instance's `Links` property. This is a great example of how a converter does not merely transform one scalar value to another scalar value. The `LinkConverter` accepts a `Links` collection property, and retrieves a single element from that collection and converts it to a URI. The `Links` property is a `Collection<SyndicationLink>` that defines the links from the feed item. Each feed item may have multiple links associated with it. The first link is generally accepted to be the link to the originating feed item. For example, the feed in this example is grabbing the posts from the blog at *http://feeds.feedburner.com/johnpapa*. The blog itself is read into a `SyndicationFeed` class and each blog post is read into a `SyndicationItem`. Each blog post's first link in the `SyndicationItem.Links` collection property points to the address of the blog post. So you convert the `Links` property to a URI through the following code in the `LinkConverter` class's `Convert` method.

[C#]
```
    return ((Collection<SyndicationLink>)value)[0].Uri;
```

[VB]
```
    Return (CType(value, Collection(Of SyndicationLink)))(0).Uri
```

The third converter used in this example, `HtmlConverter`, removes the HTML tags, newlines, and spaces, and then removes any leading spaces from a string. This converter is passed the `Summary` property from the current `FeedItem` instance in the `DataTemplate`. The converter also accepts a parameter value that indicates the maximum number of characters that the conversion process should return. Example 10-5 shows that the binding indicates that a value of 250 is passed into the converter, so at most 250 characters will be returned from the `Convert` method. Example 10-6 shows the full code for the `Convert` method of the `HtmlConverter` class.

Example 10-6. Stripping HTML from the feed summary

[C#]
```
public object Convert(object value, Type targetType,
    object parameter, System.Globalization.CultureInfo culture)
{
    int length = 0;
    int.TryParse((string)parameter, out length);

    // Remove HTML tags and empty newlines and spaces and leading spaces
    string formattedValue = Regex.Replace(value as string, "<.*?>", "");
    formattedValue = Regex.Replace(formattedValue, @"\n+\s+", "\n\n");
    formattedValue = formattedValue.TrimStart(' ');
    formattedValue = HttpUtility.HtmlDecode(formattedValue);

    if (length > 0 && formattedValue.Length >= length)
        formattedValue = formattedValue.Substring(0, length - 1);

    return formattedValue;
}
```

[VB]
```
Public Function Convert(ByVal value As Object, ByVal targetType As Type, _
    ByVal parameter As Object, ByVal culture As System.Globalization.CultureInfo) _
    As Object

    Dim length As Integer = 0
    Integer.TryParse(CStr(parameter), length)

    ' Remove HTML tags and empty newlines and spaces and leading spaces
```

```
    Dim formattedValue As String = _
        Regex.Replace(TryCast(value, String), "<.*?>", "")
    formattedValue = _
        Regex.Replace(formattedValue, "\n+\s+", Constants.vbLf + Constants.vbLf)
    formattedValue = formattedValue.TrimStart(" "c)
    formattedValue = HttpUtility.HtmlDecode(formattedValue)

    If length > 0 AndAlso formattedValue.Length >= length Then
        formattedValue = formattedValue.Substring(0, length - 1)
    End If

    Return formattedValue
End Function
```

You also can use WebClient to request that the response be returned via a stream. The WebClient.OpenReadAsync method invokes that HTTP web service request, and when it completes, a stream is presented to the event handler for the asynchronous operation. For example, you can modify the three lines of code from Example 10-2, shown here as Example 10-7, to request a stream.

Example 10-7. Asynchronous request via WebClient

C#
```
WebClient request = new WebClient();
request.DownloadStringCompleted += ReadFeed_FromWebClient;
request.DownloadStringAsync(feedUri);
```

VB
```
Dim request As New WebClient()
request.DownloadStringCompleted += ReadFeed_FromWebClient
request.DownloadStringAsync(feedUri)
```

You can also replace the three lines of code in Example 10-7 with the three lines of code in Example 10-8 to request a stream. Once the response has returned, the OpenRead_Completed method executes and has access to the stream containing the response. At this point, the stream can be read and loaded into a SyndicationFeed object instance.

Example 10-8. Requesting a stream

C#
```
WebClient request = new WebClient();
request.OpenReadCompleted += OpenRead_Completed;
request.OpenReadAsync(feedUri);
```

VB
```
Dim request As New WebClient()
request.OpenReadCompleted += OpenRead_Completed
request.OpenReadAsync(feedUri)Using HttpWebRequest
```

You also can call the request for the feed using the HttpWebRequest class instead of WebClient, if desired. For most cases, however, WebClient is sufficient to request syndicated feeds. But if you desire more control over the request, you can use HttpWebRequest, which returns a stream that provides access to the feed data. Example 10-9 shows the code that executes when the user chooses to retrieve the feed using HttpWebRequest.

Example 10-9. Feed request via HttpWebRequest

C#
```csharp
private void GetFeed_ViaHttpWebRequest()
{
    Uri feedUri;
    Uri.TryCreate(txtAddress.Text, UriKind.Absolute, out feedUri);
    if (feedUri == null)
        return;

    HttpWebRequest request = (HttpWebRequest)HttpWebRequest.Create(feedUri);
    request.BeginGetResponse(ReadFeed_FromHttpWebRequest, request);
}
```

VB
```vbnet
Private Sub GetFeed_ViaHttpWebRequest()
    Dim feedUri As Uri
    Uri.TryCreate(txtAddress.Text, UriKind.Absolute, feedUri)
    If feedUri Is Nothing Then
        Return
    End If

    Dim request As HttpWebRequest = CType(HttpWebRequest.Create(feedUri), _
     HttpWebRequest)
    request.BeginGetResponse(ReadFeed_FromHttpWebRequest, request)
End Sub
```

When the asynchronous request for the feed completes, the `ReadFeed_FromHttp WebRequest` event handler executes and processes the response (shown in Example 10-10). The handler receives a stream containing the feed data. The `IAsyncResult` parameter contains the reference to the `HttpWebRequest`, which in turn can yield the `HttpWebResponse`. The response is used to access the stream containing the feed through the `GetResponseStream` method. This stream can be accessed through an `XmlReader`, which can then be iterated through, or it can be loaded into a `SyndicationFeed` object instance, as shown in Example 10-10.

Once the feed is retrieved and loaded into the `SyndicationFeed` object instance, the desired effect is to bind the feed object to the UI target controls. However, the event handler for the `HttpWebRequest`'s event is executed on the background thread, which does not have direct access to the UI. Therefore, you cannot simply set the `SyndicationFeed` instance to the `LayoutRoot.DataContext`, as we did with the `WebClient` example.

The solution is to invoke a method that will set the `DataContext` using the feed data currently accessed in this background thread. The `Dispatacher` class handles this nicely. The `Dispatcher` object's `BeginInvoke` method accepts an action to perform, which can be an anonymous method, for example. The code shown in bold in Example 10-10 shows the `Dispatcher.BeginInvoke` method executing an anonymous method represented as a lambda expression. The lambda expression simply sets the `Grid` panel's `DataContext` to the feed. This line of code moves the feed and its contents from the background thread to the UI thread so that it can be bound. At this point, the feed object is bound to the user interface and the values are displayed to the user.

Example 10-10. Handling the response from HttpWebRequest

C#
```csharp
private void ReadFeed_FromHttpWebRequest(IAsyncResult asyncResult)
{
    HttpWebRequest request = (HttpWebRequest)asyncResult.AsyncState;
    HttpWebResponse response =
        (HttpWebResponse)request.EndGetResponse(asyncResult);
    if (response.ContentLength == 0)
        return;

    XmlReader reader = XmlReader.Create(response.GetResponseStream());
    SyndicationFeed feed = SyndicationFeed.Load(reader);
    Dispatcher.BeginInvoke(() => LayoutRoot.DataContext = feed);
}
```

VB
```vb
Private Sub ReadFeed_FromHttpWebRequest(ByVal asyncResult As IAsyncResult)
    Dim request As HttpWebRequest = CType(asyncResult.AsyncState, HttpWebRequest)
    Dim response As HttpWebResponse =
        CType(request.EndGetResponse(asyncResult), HttpWebResponse)
    If response.ContentLength = 0 Then
        Return
    End If

    Dim reader As XmlReader = XmlReader.Create(response.GetResponseStream())
    Dim feed As SyndicationFeed = SyndicationFeed.Load(reader)
    Dispatcher.BeginInvoke(Function() LayoutRoot.DataContext = feed)
End Sub
```

Cross-Domain Policies

One of the common issues with requesting feeds from a Silverlight 2 client application is that the web request is most often to a feed on another domain. The Silverlight client application must make a cross-domain web service request to obtain the feed data. Although this may seem obvious, many domains that host RSS and Atom feeds do not have a cross-domain policy file. Silverlight 2 cannot directly access and consume feeds hosted on another domain that does not have a cross-domain policy file that allows access to its web services.

The solution to obtaining a feed is to request the feed from a web service that does support a cross-domain call and that can request the feed directly. One such solution is to use a service such as FeedBurner. The examples in this chapter have requested the *http://feeds.feedburner.com/johnpapa* feed from the FeedBurner services. FeedBurner funnels syndicated feeds through its services and offers analysis of the feeds and other options.

One of the nice features of using a tool such as FeedBurner to publish syndication feeds is that the *feeds.feedburner.com* domain has a cross-domain policy file on its server root. The *clientaccesspolicy.xml* file exists at *http://feeds.feedburner.com/crossdomain.xml* and allows any client to make requests on its services. This makes requesting feeds from various sources much easier. If the feed was requested from *http://johnpapa.net/feed/*

default.aspx (which is the feed for that website) from another domain, the request would be denied if there were no cross-domain policy file on the *http://johnpapa.net* server. It is not realistic to place a cross-domain policy file on every web domain that hosts a feed, so services such as FeedBurner, Popfly, and Yahoo! Pipes are good alternatives. Example 10-11 shows the contents of the *crossdomain.xml* file hosted on the root of the FeedBurner domain.

Example 10-11. The crossdomain.xml file at FeedBurner

```
<?xml version="1.0"?>
<!DOCTYPE cross-domain-policy SYSTEM
    "http://www.macromedia.com/xml/dtds/cross-domain-policy.dtd">
<cross-domain-policy>
  <allow-access-from domain="*" />
</cross-domain-policy>
```

You could achieve the same effect by using a service such as Yahoo! Pipes to obtain the syndicated feed. One of the features of Yahoo! Pipes is that it can aggregate feeds and provide access to those feeds through a web service that it exposes. For example, the code from the previous examples cannot access the feed contained at *http://blogs.msdn .com/MainFeed.aspx?Type=AllBlogs*, because there is not a cross-domain policy file on the root of the *blogs.msdn.com* domain. Using Yahoo! Pipes the feed can be fetched (see Figure 10-5) and made accessible through a URI, hosted by Yahoo! Pipes. The pipe is accessible by requesting the feed data from the following URI:

> *http://pipes.yahooapis.com/pipes/pipe.run?_id=rLmJu9eE3RG5nJxzrLQIDg&_ren der=rss*

Yahoo! Pipes effectively fetches the feed data (as shown in Figure 10-6) from *http://blogs .msdn.com* and makes it accessible through this URI. Popfly is another service that supports the creation of services. Both of these services and FeedBurner are viable solutions to overcoming the issue of requesting feeds from Silverlight due to their support of cross-domain policy files on their web server roots.

Aggregating Feeds

Using the `SyndicationFeed` class, you can read and mash together both Atom and RSS feeds to create an aggregated list of feed items. The previous example showed how to consume a single feed and bind it to a `ListBox` control. The next example shows how to add and remove feeds from an aggregated list, and mash their feed items together into a list that you can bind to a list-based control.

Figure 10-7 shows the `Aggregator` Silverlight control from the sample code for this chapter. When the user enters a feed's URL in the `TextBox` and clicks the Add button, if the feed is valid and does not already exist in the `Aggregator` control, it is added to a private field, `_feeds`, of type `ObservableCollection<SyndicationFeed>`. When you use an `ObservableCollection<SyndicationFeed>`, every time a new feed is added or a feed is

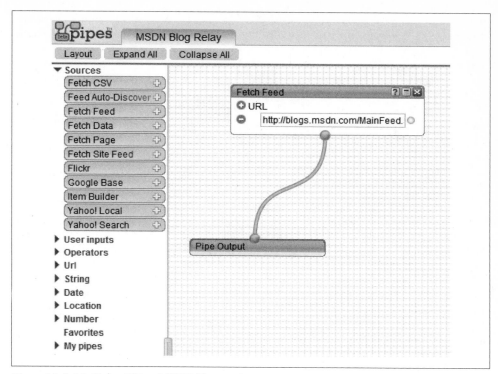

Figure 10-5. My Yahoo! Pipes MSDN blog service

removed from the _feeds class field, the ObservableCollection notifies the bound target controls that something in the list has changed. This makes it easy to add and remove items without having to rebind the list to the ListBox. The name of each feed is displayed in the upper ListBox, as shown in Figure 10-7.

When a feed address is entered the code uses the WebClient class to request the contents of the feed. When the asynchronous call to get the feed contents returns, the ReadFeed event handler processes the feed, as shown in Example 10-12. The feed is read into a SyndicationFeed object instance and then a check is made to see whether the feed already exists in the _feeds field. This check is made by passing a lambda expression to the _feeds.Where method, shown in bold in Example 10-12.

The lambda expression evaluates each instance of a SyndicationFeed in the _feeds field to see whether the feed title matches a feed's title already in the list. If the feed does not exist, the feed is added to the ObservableCollection<SyndicationFeed> _feeds, the lstFeeds ListBox is notified of the changes to its bound list, and the new feed is displayed in the ListBox.

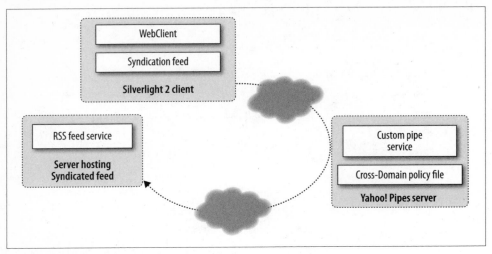

Figure 10-6. Using Yahoo! Pipes to fetch a feed

Example 10-12. Reading a new feed

```csharp
private void ReadFeed(object sender,
    DownloadStringCompletedEventArgs e)
{
    string xml = e.Result;
    if (xml.Length == 0)
        return;

    StringReader stringReader = new StringReader(xml);
    XmlReader reader = XmlReader.Create(stringReader);
    SyndicationFeed feed = SyndicationFeed.Load(reader);

    if (_feeds.Where(f => f.Title.Text == feed.Title.Text).ToList().Count > 0)
        return;

    _feeds.Add(feed);
    ReBindAggregatedItems();
    txtAddress.Text = string.Empty;
}
```

```vbnet
Private Sub ReadFeed_FromWebClient(ByVal sender As Object, _
        ByVal e As DownloadStringCompletedEventArgs)
    Dim xml As String = e.Result
    If xml.Length = 0 Then
        Return
    End If

    Dim stringReader As New StringReader(xml)
    Dim reader As XmlReader = XmlReader.Create(stringReader)
    Dim feed As SyndicationFeed = SyndicationFeed.Load(reader)

    If _feeds.Where(Function(f) f.Title.Text = feed.Title.Text).ToList().Count _
```

```
        > 0 Then
        Return
    End If

    _feeds.Add(feed)
    ReBindAggregatedItems()
    txtAddress.Text = String.Empty
End Sub
```

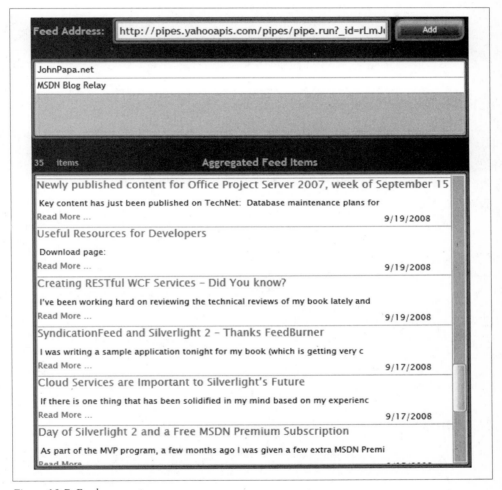

Figure 10-7. Feed aggregator

Once the feed has been validated and added to the list, the items from each feed must be mashed together and bound to the `ListBox` `lstFeedItems` on the lower part of the `Aggregator` control. The `ReBindAggregatedItems` method mashes the feed items from the `_feeds` together through a LINQ to Objects query. The query is defined to return an IEnumerable<SyndicationItem>. Once the query is executed, the results are converted to a List<SyndicationItem>, and the results are bound to the lstFeedItems ListBox.

Example 10-13 shows the code that mashes the feed items together using a LINQ to Objects query. The query retrieves all of the feed items from each Observable Collection<SyndicationFeed> and sorts them in descending order by their date published. Silverlight 2 does not support binding an anonymous type to XAML binding controls, so the LINQ query cannot return a projection in this case. The query is executed using the ToList method, which also converts the results to a List<SyndicationItem>. The result is a list of all feed items mixed together from various feed sources.

Example 10-13. Mashing the feed items using LINQ

C#
```
private void ReBindAggregatedItems()
{
    var query = from f in _feeds
                from i in f.Items
                orderby i.PublishDate descending
                select i;
    FeedItemsGrid.DataContext = query.ToList();
}
```

VB
```
Private Sub ReBindAggregatedItems()
    Dim query = _
        From f In _feeds , i In f.Items _
        Order By i.PublishDate Descending _
        Select i
    FeedItemsGrid.DataContext = query.ToList()
End Sub
```

When a feed is selected in the lstFeeds ListBox and the user presses the Delete key, the selected feed is removed from the ObservableCollection<SyndicationFeed> _feeds. Because this is an ObservableCollection<T>, the feed is instantly removed from the lstFeeds ListBox. The feed items are removed from the mashed feed item list in lstFeedItems by running the same LINQ to Objects query and rebinding the lstFeedItems ListBox.

Summary

Most feeds are going to be accessed across domains. This means that a feed's domain must contain a cross-domain policy file that permits the feed to be accessed by the Silverlight client's hosted server's domain. If the cross-domain policy file does not exist on the hosted domain's server, you can use services that support open cross-domain policies, such as FeedBurner, Yahoo! Pipes, and Popfly, to effectively relay the feed to the Silverlight client application.

Silverlight 2 applications can read RSS and Atom feeds using `WebClient` or `HttpWebRequest` and can consume them using the `SyndicationFeed` class, LINQ to XML, or the `XmlReader`. The `SyndicationFeed` class offers the most features for the least amount of work, as it encapsulates a lot of the functionality required to read and manage feed data, which is effectively a form of POX.

This chapter demonstrated how to consume feeds, mash them together, and work around the lack of cross-domain policy files. The next chapter discusses how to use ADO.NET Data Services and its RESTful style to communicate with Silverlight 2.

CHAPTER 11

Silverlight 2 and ADO.NET Data Services

The RESTful style of web services exposes representations of resources through unique URIs and query strings. Silverlight 2 can communicate with these resources using `WebClient` or `HttpWebRequest` as you have seen in the previous chapters. Alternatively, Silverlight 2 can communicate with services using the ADO.NET Data Services Silverlight client and to ADO.NET Data Services, as this chapter will demonstrate. Silverlight 2 can then consume the services using techniques such as LINQ to XML or LINQ to JSON, and translate the results into entities which you can bind to dependency properties in Silverlight 2 applications. ADO.NET Data Services provides an architecture that uses a RESTful-style web service that handles some of the heavy lifting and provides a rich set of functionality. ADO.NET Data Services is not a data access layer; rather, it helps client applications communicate with business layers and their entity models. It provides the architecture to consume resources and map them into entities, manage change tracking and save changes through a client API in Silverlight 2, expose an entire entity model via URIs with very little code, and customize the services by adding specialized service operations and the means to intercept service calls and perform business rules. There is a server and a client component with ADO.NET Data Services when working with Silverlight 2. On the server, ADO.NET Data Services provides the services and exposes them to clients. On the Silverlight 2 client, there is a client library that makes it easy to interact and communicate with the services.

The previous few chapters demonstrated several techniques that allow Silverlight 2 applications to communicate with web services using REST. This chapter explains how to create a Silverlight 2 application that interacts with ADO.NET Data Services to retrieve and modify data items via RESTful services. ADO.NET Data Services surfaces entity models (both custom entity models and models created through ORM tools such as the Entity Framework) as resources available through RESTful URIs. The `System.Data.Services.Client` client library provides a Silverlight 2 application with the ability to execute LINQ queries and save changes to the underlying data source exposed by ADO.NET Data Services.

This chapter demonstrates how to build a highly functional Silverlight 2 application using ADO.NET Data Services. This chapter first provides a brief overview of ADO.NET Data Services as it relates to Silverlight 2 client applications, including its goals, its RESTful style, and its client library. I discuss and demonstrate the features of ADO.NET Data Services to show how you can build them to benefit a Silverlight 2 application. The chapter wraps up by diving into the ADO.NET Data Services client library that you can use in a Silverlight 2 application to read data, change data, and manage change tracking.

ADO.NET Data Services Overview

The advantages of using ADO.NET Data Services can be considerable when developing Silverlight 2 applications. ADO.NET Data Services takes the best features of RESTful-style web services and makes them easier to implement over an entity model, and it provides features to account for authorization, business logic, and custom service operations. The ADO.NET Data Services Silverlight client offers proxy class generation for deserialization back into entities in the Silverlight 2 client application, and it provides LINQ queries to be defined and executed asynchronously, eliminating the need to put together an HTTP URI and execute it manually with `WebClient` or `HttpWebRequest`.

The ADO.NET Data Services framework provides an API that allows data to be created and consumed over HTTP using RESTful-style web services. ADO.NET Data Services exposes data items as resources that can be consumed via URIs. ADO.NET Data Services can expose an entity model via URIs, as long as the entity model supports an `IQueryable` implementation. Through the `IUpdatable` implementation, ADO.NET Data Services supports updates to data items via URIs. If a custom entity model exists in an architecture, it can be exposed for reading or writing if both implementations are executed on the entity model. These implementations make it possible for ADO.NET Data Services to provide a way to create, modify, delete, and read data items via RESTful web services.

Figure 11-1 shows how a Silverlight 2 client application can communicate through HTTP using the `System.DataServices.Client` library to ADO.NET Data Services. The services exposed can be either directly on top of the entity model or through custom operations, both through URIs.

HTTP Methods

ADO.NET Data Services supports HTTP calls to interact with data items using the standard HTTP methods. The `POST`, `GET`, `PUT`, and `DELETE` methods effectively map to Create, Read, Update, and Delete (CRUD), respectively. Calls can be made directly to services via HTTP calls through tools such as Fiddler2 or through a web browser's address box. Alternatively, calls can be made through the client library exposed by the

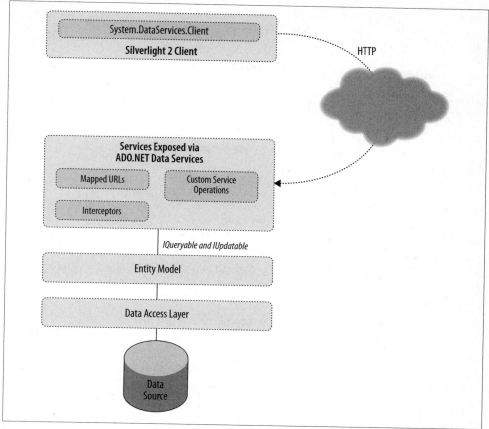

Figure 11-1. Silverlight 2 to ADO.NET Data Services

`System.Data.Services.Client` namespace. The client library for ADO.NET Data Services provides a thin layer on top of the plumbing that encapsulates the HTTP requests, eliminating the need for developers to manually craft HTTP requests.

 This section is a brief overview of ADO.NET Data Services. You can find more information in Appendix A, which lists all of the enumerators used with ADO.NET Data Services and Silverlight 2 along with their descriptions.

Message Formats

ADO.NET Data Services supports the data to be passed as XML or as JSON. The default message format is XML, specifically using the Atom Publishing Protocol (AtomPub) specification. JSON generally has a smaller footprint and is suited for consumption by Ajax clients due to the highest level of support for JSON in Ajax. The AtomPub message format is generated using a mapping of the entity model's structure to the AtomPub specification. Also, a few additional elements are included in the XML to represent entity-model-specific information.

AtomPub is the default message format and contains the most descriptive and readable version of the data. For example, executing the following URI against the `EFDataServices` data service included in the sample code for this chapter will return a response message containing the representation of the first two product entities. The response is formatted as XML using the AtomPub specification:

> *http://localhost:8890/NorthwindDataService.svc/Products?$orderby=Product Name&$top=2*

The URI maps to the *NorthwindDataServices.svc* file, which was created using ADO.NET Data Services. The URI indicates that the products should be accessed and sorted in sequential order by `ProductName`, and the first two should be returned. The AtomPub response, shown in Example 11-1, represents each entity inside a `feed` root XML element. Each data item is represented as an `entry` element, which is a child of the `feed` element. The `entry` elements each have an `id` element, whose value is a URI that represents the direct access path to the data item. Example 11-1 shows the URI for the first product item retrieved, in bold.

All of the properties for the resource are represented in the AtomPub response format. Whereas simple property values are embedded right in the XML response, navigation/association properties are represented as links by default. For example, the `Category` property of the first `Product` has a value that contains a URI that will return a representation of the category for the given product. (Example 11-1 shows this link in bold, too.)

Example 11-1. Sample AtomPub message response

```
<?xml version="1.0" encoding="iso-8859-1" standalone="yes"?>
<feed xml:base="http://localhost:8890/NorthwindDataService.svc/"
xmlns:d="http://schemas.microsoft.com/ado/2007/08/dataservices"
xmlns:m="http://schemas.microsoft.com/ado/2007/08/dataservices/metadata"
xmlns="http://www.w3.org/2005/Atom">
  <title type="text">Products</title>
  <id>http://localhost:8890/NorthwindDataService.svc/Products</id>
  <updated>2008-10-06T04:41:53Z</updated>
  <link rel="self" title="Products" href="Products" />
  <entry m:etag="W/&quot;X'0000000000000C6D'&quot;">
    <id>http://localhost:8890/NorthwindDataService.svc/Products(17)</id>
    <title type="text"></title>
    <updated>2008-10-06T04:41:53Z</updated>
    <author>
      <name />
    </author>
    <link rel="edit" title="Product" href="Products(17)" />
    <link
rel="http://schemas.microsoft.com/ado/2007/08/dataservices/related/Category"
type="application/atom+xml;type=entry" title="Category"
```

```
href="Products(17)/Category" />
    <link
rel="http://schemas.microsoft.com/ado/2007/08/dataservices/related/OrderDetails"
type="application/atom+xml;type=feed" title="OrderDetails"
href="Products(17)/OrderDetails" />
    <link
rel="http://schemas.microsoft.com/ado/2007/08/dataservices/related/Supplier"
type="application/atom+xml;type=entry" title="Supplier"
href="Products(17)/Supplier" />
    <category term="NorthwindModel.Product"
scheme="http://schemas.microsoft.com/ado/2007/08/dataservices/scheme" />
    <content type="application/xml">
      <m:properties>
        <d:Discontinued m:type="Edm.Boolean">true</d:Discontinued>
        <d:DiscontinuedDate m:type="Edm.DateTime">1996-07-
04T00:00:00</d:DiscontinuedDate>
        <d:ProductID m:type="Edm.Int32">17</d:ProductID>
        <d:ProductName>Alice Mutton</d:ProductName>
        <d:QuantityPerUnit>20 - 1 kg tins</d:QuantityPerUnit>
        <d:ReorderLevel m:type="Edm.Int16">0</d:ReorderLevel>
        <d:RowVersionStamp m:type="Edm.Binary">AAAAAAAADGo=</d:RowVersionStamp>
        <d:UnitPrice m:type="Edm.Decimal">39.0000</d:UnitPrice>
        <d:UnitsInStock m:type="Edm.Int16">0</d:UnitsInStock>
        <d:UnitsOnOrder m:type="Edm.Int16">0</d:UnitsOnOrder>
      </m:properties>
    </content>
  </entry>
    ...
    ...
    ...
</feed>
```

You can use the same URI to retrieve the data using the JSON format simply by changing the `Accept` header for the request to `application/json`. You can test this by opening Fiddler2 and issuing the same request (shown here) using the Request Builder tab of Fiddler2:

http://localhost:8890/NorthwindDataService.svc/Products?$orderby=Product Name&$top=2

You can add the `Accept` header to the request by entering the following text in the Request Builder's `Request Headers` section:

```
User-Agent: Fiddler
Host: localhost:8890
Accept: application/json
```

 The web application project in the `EFDataServices` sample for this chapter uses `localhost:8890` to host the services. This is configured in the project's properties.

The JSON response, shown in Example 11-2, is much terser than the AtomPub-formatted message response. The same data is embedded in both messages. Notice that the URI for the first product and the URI for the first product's category are in boldface in Example 11-2. The JSON message response format integrates more readily with Ajax applications, whereas the AtomPub format provides a more readable message. As discussed in the previous chapters, it is a good practice to provide both response formats from RESTful services. This allows the consumers of the service to concentrate on processing the responses in the format that suits them best. ADO.NET Data Services provides both message response formats by toggling the `Accept` header.

Example 11-2. Sample JSON message response

```
{ "d" : [
{
"__metadata":
    {
    "uri": "http://localhost:8890/NorthwindDataService.svc/Products(17)",
    "etag": "W/\"X\'0000000000000C6D\'\"",
    "type": "NorthwindModel.Product"
    },
    "Discontinued": true,
    "DiscontinuedDate": "\/Date(836438400000)\/",
    "ProductID": 17,
    "ProductName": "Alice Mutton",
    "QuantityPerUnit": "20 - 1 kg tins",
    "ReorderLevel": 0,
    "RowVersionStamp": "AAAAAAAADGo=",
    "UnitPrice": "39.0000",
    "UnitsInStock": 0,
    "UnitsOnOrder": 0,
    "Category": { "__deferred": {
    "uri":
    "http://localhost:8890/NorthwindDataService.svc/Products(17)/Category"
    }},
    "OrderDetails": { "__deferred": {
    "uri":
    "http://localhost:8890/NorthwindDataService.svc/Products(17)/OrderDetails"
    }},
    "Supplier": { "__deferred": {
    "uri":
    "http://localhost:8890/NorthwindDataService.svc/Products(17)/Supplier"
    }}
},
    ...
    ...
    ...
]}
```

Metadata

ADO.NET Data Services subscribes to the RESTful style of addressing, which uses URIs to refer to resources and perform operations. For example, the /Products(7) relative

---

URI could return the representation of the Product with a ProductID equal to 7. You can execute the URI directly over HTTP or through the ADO.NET Data Services client library (which also sends it over HTTP under the covers) and retrieve the response asynchronously. One of the features that ADO.NET Data Services provides is the option to retrieve metadata about the services and what they offer. This is helpful when determining the structure of a resource before requesting it.

ADO.NET Data Services makes metadata accessible that describes the resources it exposes and any custom service operations that can be executed. You can retrieve metadata for the service by using the URI for the service appended with the $metadata option. This returns information about the service, including the entity model that is available to be accessed, as well as any custom service operations. Here is an example:

http://localhost:8890/NorthwindDataService.svc/$metadata

Services over Custom Data Sources

You can create an ADO.NET Data Service that exposes query access to data where a provider with an IQueryable implementation exists over the data. If the provider also has an IUpdatable implementation, ADO.NET Data Services supports making modifications to the model, too. If you are looking to expose data from a relational database, the Entity Framework is tightly integrated with ADO.NET Data Services out of the box, allowing you to expose data from SQL Server and other third-party relational databases. As ADO.NET Data Services grows in popularity it is reasonable to think that other entity modeling tools will follow suit and will offer IQueryable and IUpdatable implementations. In the meantime, you can expose custom objects manually so that they can be consumed, in this case by Silverlight 2 applications through the ADO.NET Data Services Silverlight client library.

Using ADO.NET Data Services over a custom entity model requires that you have a custom entity model and that you then complete the following basic steps:

1. Create a custom data source.
2. Create a class that represents the model of the data for the services (a data context class).
3. Implement IQueryable and/or IUpdatable for the data model class.
4. Reference System.Data.Services.dll.
5. Create a service with ADO.NET Data Services.
6. Derive the service from DataService<CustomContextGoesHere>.

The *CustomDataService.Web* example project for this chapter contains a web application project with an ADO.NET Data Services service named CustomDataService that exposes the Product class entity. The Product class (shown in Example 11-3) is a simple representation for product information from the NorthwindEF sample database. This represents a simple entity model that will be exposed using ADO.NET Data Services.

Example 11-3. The Product class

C#
```csharp
public class Product : EntityBase
{
    public Product()
    {
    }

    private int _productId;
    public int ID
    {
        get { return _productId; }
        set
        {
            _productId = value;
            FirePropertyChanged("ID");
        }
    }

    private string _productName;
    public string ProductName
    {
        get { return _productName; }
        set
        {
            _productName = value;
            FirePropertyChanged("ProductName");
        }
    }
    ...
    ...
    ...
}
```

VB
```vb
Public Class Product
    Inherits EntityBase
    Public Sub New()
    End Sub

    Private _productId As Integer
    Public Property ID() As Integer
        Get
            Return _productId
        End Get
        Set(ByVal value As Integer)
            _productId = value
            FirePropertyChanged("ID")
        End Set
    End Property

    Private _productName As String
    Public Property ProductName() As String
        Get
            Return _productName
        End Get
        Set(ByVal value As String)
```

```
                    _productName = value
                    FirePropertyChanged("ProductName")
                End Set
        End Property
        ...
        ...
        ...
End Class
```

Before the ADO.NET Data Services service can expose the Product class (and any other custom entities), you must create a class that describes the entity model to ADO.NET Data Services in such a way that it can query it. This class will be used to generate the abstract entity data model that ADO.NET Data Services then uses. Creating a custom context class to describe the data requires that the class expose a field representing the collection of the Product entities, a way to fill the entity list, and a public property that exposes the entities and returns an IQueryable<T>, where T is the entity type. Example 11-4 shows the NorthwindData class that exposes the Products property, which returns the products as IQueryable<Product>. The Products property allows LINQ queries to be written against the Product entities.

Example 11-4. Class representing a custom data model

C#
```csharp
public class NorthwindData
{
    static List<Product> _products;

    static NorthwindData()
    {
        _products = new ProductMgr().FindProductList();
    }

    public IQueryable<Product> Products
    {
        get { return _products.AsQueryable<Product>(); }
    }
}
```

VB
```vb
Public Class NorthwindData
    Private Shared _products As List(Of Product)

    Shared Sub New()
        _products = New ProductMgr().FindProductList()
    End Sub

    Public ReadOnly Property Products() As IQueryable(Of Product)
        Get
            Return _products.AsQueryable(Of Product)()
        End Get
    End Property
End Class
```

Access Rules

Once the class representing the data model exists, you can create the service using the ADO.NET Data Services file template from Visual Studio. Figure 11-2 shows the *CustomDataService.svc* file being added to the web application project. This template creates the service with some basic placeholders where the service class must be modified. The service class must inherit from `DataService<T>`, where T is the class that represents the data model in this example.

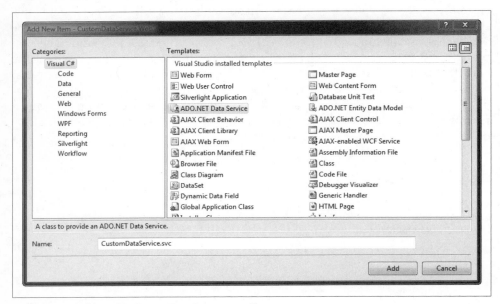

Figure 11-2. Adding the CustomDataService.svc file

Example 11-5 shows the `CustomDataService` service class inheriting from `DataService<NorthwindData>`. The template creates the `InitializeService` static method and provides a sample of how to enable access rules for the entities in the entity data model. By default, ADO.NET Data Services disables all access to the entity model. The entities require explicit action to allow access to them. The access rules define how the entities can be used. For instance, the sample wants to retrieve data items from the `Products` entity set. The access rules for the sample (shown in Example 11-5) set the entity access rules for the `Products` entity set to the `EntitySetRights.AllRead` enumerator value. This allows users of the service to execute queries against the `Products` entity set to return `Product` entities.

The `SetEntitySetAccessRules` method accepts two arguments. The first is the name of the entity set to which the rule will be applied. The second parameter is one or more `EntitySetRights` enumerator values that define the access rule for the given entity set. You can combine one or more `EntitySetRights` enumerator values to customize the rules for the entity set. Table 11-1 shows all of the valid enumerator values and their descriptions.

Table 11-1. System.Data.Services EntitySetRights enumerators

Enumerator	Description
All	All reads and writes are permitted on the specified entity.
AllRead	All reads are permitted.
AllWrite	All writes are permitted.
None	No access is permitted to the specified entity.
ReadMultiple	Reading multiple rows is permitted.
ReadSingle	Reading a single row is permitted.
WriteAppend	Creating new data is permitted.
WriteDelete	Deleting data is permitted.
WriteMerge	Merge updating is permitted.
WriteReplace	Replace updating is permitted.

Example 11-5. CustomDataService service class

C#

```csharp
using System.Data.Services;

namespace CustomDataService.Web
{
    public class CustomDataService : DataService<NorthwindData>
    {
        public static void InitializeService(IDataServiceConfiguration config)
        {
            config.SetEntitySetAccessRule("Products", EntitySetRights.AllRead);
        }
    }
}
```

VB

```vb
Imports System.Data.Services

Namespace CustomDataService.Web
    Public Class CustomDataService
        Inherits DataService(Of NorthwindData)
        Public Shared Sub InitializeService( _
            ByVal config As IDataServiceConfiguration)
            config.SetEntitySetAccessRule("Products", EntitySetRights.AllRead)
        End Sub
    End Class
End Namespace
```

Unlike the RESTful services that were created in Chapters 7 and 8 using Windows Communication Foundation (WCF) and that required `Uri Template` definitions, there is no need for explicit URI mapping with ADO.NET Data Services. ADO.NET Data Services automatically maps URIs to the entity model based on the entity set names. This can save you the effort and maintenance of explicitly mapping hundreds of URIs to entities in a large model. It also allows for a uniform URI format across services and the development of controls that are able to natively understand this format.

RESTful Addressing

You can call RESTful services through a web browser or through a tool such as Fiddler2. When requesting data items, a URI maps to one or more resources. The URI can contain resource names, parameters to retrieve a specific resource, and/or a query string with options to narrow the search for resources.

The `EFDataServices` sample for this chapter has an entity model generated from the Entity Framework tool over the sample NorthwindEF database (also available in the code samples). All of the tables in the database are mapped to entities in the entity domain model. ADO.NET Data Services provides services over all of these entities through the service named `NorthwindDataService`.

To view the AtomPub XML message response returned by an ADO.NET Data Service in Internet Explorer, select Tools→Internet Options, go to the Content tab, and make sure that Feed Reading View is turned off.

Once you have created the service, you can build and test it by executing a test request. The following URI requests the `Product` with a `ProductID` equal to 1 from the `CustomDataService`. When this is executed through a web browser or through Fiddler2, the response message contains the AtomPub content for the product.

> *http://localhost:3494/CustomDataService.svc/Products(1)*

You can execute a URI using `WebClient` or `HttpWebRequest` from a Silverlight 2 client against the ADO.NET Data Services public service asynchronously, just like you can execute any HTTP request. The Silverlight 2 client need not know that the service is using ADO.NET Data Services at all. You can pass the URI asynchronously via `WebClient` and receive and process the response using LINQ.

URI Options

You can write more complex queries as well by appending query string options, operators, and functions to the URI. These query string options, shown in Table 11-2, add sorting, filtering, and other customizations to the query. For example, you can use the orderby option in the URI to request all of the products sorted by product name:

http://localhost:3494/CustomDataService.svc/Products?$orderby=ProductName

 Appendix A lists all of the URI options, functions, and operators, along with descriptions for each of them.

Table 11-2. ADO.NET Data Services query string options

Option	Description	Example
expand	Requests set(s) of related entities to be retrieved	/Products(7)?$expand=Categories
orderby	Indicates the sequence entities to be retrieved	/Employees?$orderby=LastName asc,FirstName asc
skip	Skips a number of data items; useful for paging	/Products?$skip=10
top	At most, returns the top number of data items	/Products?$orderby=ProductName&$top=10
filter	Applies a filtering condition to narrow the data returned	/Products?$filter='ProductName eq Widget'

The URI options are prefixed with the $ symbol as part of the query string. You can combine them with other options, as well. For example, the following URI requests the first five products sorted by product name:

http://localhost:3494/CustomDataService.svc/Products?$orderby=ProductName& $top=5

The top option grabs the first *n* number of entities, and the skip option skips over *n* number of items, making it useful for paging. The filter option allows complex filters to be applied to queries through the URI, effectively limiting the rows of data items to those that match the filter conditions. The following example requests only those products that are not discontinued and cost more than $10, and returns them in sorted order:

http://localhost:3494/CustomDataService.svc/Products()?$filter=((Discontinued eq false)) and (UnitPrice gt 10M)&$orderby=ProductName

The expand option is helpful in requesting related graphs of entities. For example, the URIs shown in the previous examples return the Product items but do not return their associated categories or suppliers. Instead, the Category and Supplier properties of the Product are returned in the response's message as links which point to the Product's Category and Supplier, respectively. By default, queries return only those entities that are explicitly requested. The expand option allows a query to indicate which related entities to include in the response.

Creating the Proxy Class

Whereas you can communicate with these services using URIs through WebClient, the System.Data.Services.Client namespace allows Silverlight 2 client applications to execute LINQ queries against the service and receive the response as an entity (or collection of entities). This technique allows developers to skip formatting the HTTP URI and processing XML directly, and instead deal with a higher-level API and entities.

Silverlight 2 supports the Add Service Reference option which generates the proxy class for the entities that may be requested from the services. Figure 11-3 shows the reference being added to the *CustomDataService.svc* file and being named CustomDataServiceReference. This adds the *service.edmx* file to the Silverlight 2 client application, too. The *.edmx* file contains the XML that defines the structure of the entity data model, which in this case is the Products entity set and the Product entity type. Classes for NorthwindData and Product are also generated through this process. These supporting classes and files help to make the interaction between Silverlight 2 and ADO.NET Data Services much easier.

Async LINQ

Once you have generated the service, you can invoke it by executing a LINQ query through the API exposed by the System.Data.Services.Client namespace. First, you must create an instance of the service's context class. Example 11-6 shows the context class being created using the relative URI pointing to the name of the service file. Once you have created the context, you can define and execute queries asynchronously. The ADO.NET Data Service that is referred to in Example 11-6 is located in the same domain as the server that hosts the Silverlight client. This is why the URI uses a relative mapping.

 ADO.NET Data Services 1.0 does not support cross-domain service calls from Silverlight 2. Therefore, if a service exists on a different domain than the domain that hosts the Silverlight 2 client, the service calls will be denied.

Example 11-6. Creating the context

```
private NorthwindData _context;

public Page()
{
    InitializeComponent();
    _context = new NorthwindData(
        new Uri("CustomDataService.svc", UriKind.Relative));
```

```
        GetProductsAsync();
    }
```
VB
```
Private _context As NorthwindData

Public Sub New()
    InitializeComponent()
    _context = New NorthwindData( _
        New Uri("CustomDataService.svc", UriKind.Relative))
    GetProductsAsync()
End Sub
```

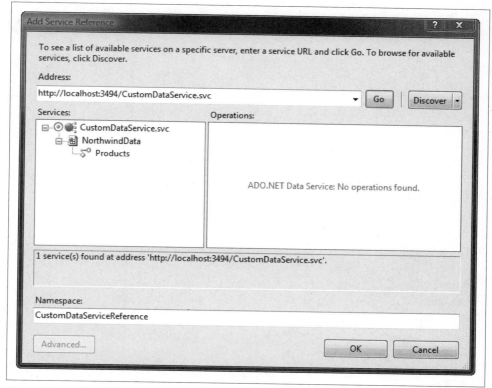

Figure 11-3. Adding the service reference

One of the advantages of using ADO.NET Data Services is that you can define and execute LINQ queries against the services instead of building a URI and executing it through the `WebClient` or `HttpWebRequest` class. You define the LINQ query using the context instance to access the entity sets from the generated classes. Because you must execute the query against the data on the remote server, you must pass the query to the server through the `CustomDataService` service. ADO.NET Data Services and Silverlight 2 handle this by translating the LINQ query to a URI and executing it asynchronously against the service.

Example 11-7 shows the LINQ query definition designed to request all products that have not been discontinued, cost more than $10, and are returned sorted by the ProductName property. This query is cast to a DataServiceQuery<T>, where T is the type of entity that will be returned (in this case, DataServiceQuery<Product>). The query is not executed on the client. Instead, the BeginExecute method of the DataServiceQuery class is executed asynchronously against the service. BeginExecute accepts a callback method, any user state information, and the query instance as arguments.

When this code executes, the LINQ query is translated into a URI that contains the query definition. As the query must be passed over HTTP, it is translated into the URI in terms the ADO.NET Data Service can understand. You can then examine the request using a tool such as Fiddler2, Firebug for Firefox, or Web Development Helper for Internet Explorer. This will show the query translated to the URI, as shown here:

> http://localhost:3494/CustomDataService.svc/Products()?$filter=((Discontinued eq false)) and (UnitPrice gt 10M)&$orderby=ProductName

Example 11-7. Executing a LINQ query with ADO.NET Data Services

C#
```csharp
private void GetProductsAsync()
{
    // Create a LINQ Query to be issued to the service
    var query = from p in _context.Products
                where p.Discontinued == false && p.UnitPrice > 10
                orderby p.ProductName
                select p;

    DataServiceQuery<Product> dsq = (DataServiceQuery<Product>)query;
    dsq.BeginExecute(new AsyncCallback(GetProductsComplete), dsq);
}
```

VB
```vb
Private Sub GetProductsAsync()
    ' Create a LINQ Query to be issued to the service
    Dim query = _
        From p In _context.Products _
        Where p.Discontinued = False AndAlso p.UnitPrice > 10 _
        Order By p.ProductName _
        Select p

    Dim dsq As DataServiceQuery(Of Product) = _
        CType(query, DataServiceQuery(Of Product))
    dsq.BeginExecute(New AsyncCallback(AddressOf GetProductsComplete), dsq)
End Sub
```

The URI is mapped through ADO.NET Data Services to create the response message containing the appropriate product information and is returned to the callback method. The callback method receives the response contained within the IAsyncResult parameter on the callback method (shown in Example 11-8). The IAsyncResult.AsyncState property is cast to a DataServiceQuery<T>, and its results are retrieved by executing the EndExecute method and converting the results to a List<Product>. ADO.NET Data Services provides this technique to retrieve results, which makes it easier to consume the response than invoking a URI through HTTP and consuming the XML directly with LINQ to XML.

Example 11-8. Receiving the results

C#
```
private void GetProductsComplete(IAsyncResult ar)
{
    DataServiceQuery<Product> qry = (DataServiceQuery<Product>)ar.AsyncState;
    var products = qry.EndExecute(ar).ToList();
    if (_syncContext != null)
    {
        _syncContext.Post(
            delegate(object state)
            {
                LoadProducts(products);
            }
            ,null);

    }
}
```

VB
```
Private Sub GetProductsComplete(ByVal ar As IAsyncResult)
    Dim qry As DataServiceQuery(Of Product) = _
        CType(ar.AsyncState, DataServiceQuery(Of Product))
    Dim products = qry.EndExecute(ar).ToList()
    If _syncContext IsNot Nothing Then
        _syncContext.Post( _
        Function(ByVal state As Object) _
        LoadProducts(products),Nothing) _

    End If
End Sub
```

In Example 11-8 there is an instance of the SynchronizationContext class named _syncContext. This SynchronizationContext class is used in this example to make sure that when the web service call completes, the code can access the UI thread. There is no guarantee that the event handler for the asynchronous operation will operate in the UI thread, so two common choices are to use the Deployment.Current.Dispatcher class or the SynchronizationContext class. This example creates an instance of the SynchronizationContext class in a place where the UI thread is available: the constructor.

 Code that accesses entities, accesses the DataServiceContext, or enumerates results of LINQ queries needs to happen on the UI thread.

You can execute a query through ADO.NET Data Services by passing a URI through WebClient or by using a LINQ query with the DataServiceQuery<T> class instance. Another technique crosses between both of these by creating a DataServiceQuery<T> through the context object's CreateQuery method. The CreateQuery method accepts a

URI referring to an entity set name (shown in bold in Example 11-9) and returns an instance of a `DataServiceQuery<T>`. This technique, shown in Example 11-9, is a good option for executing a query against ADO.NET Data Services when the URI is provided, perhaps as a parameter from an outside source.

Example 11-9. Executing a URI

```
DataServiceQuery<Product> dsq =
    _context.CreateQuery<Product>(
    "Products()?$filter=((Discontinued eq false)) and " & _
    "(UnitPrice gt 10M)&$orderby=ProductName");
dsq.BeginExecute(new AsyncCallback(GetProductsComplete), dsq);
```

```
Dim dsq As DataServiceQuery(Of Product) = _
    _context.CreateQuery(Of Product)( _
    "Products()?$filter=((Discontinued eq false)) and " & _
    "(UnitPrice gt 10M)&$orderby=ProductName")
dsq.BeginExecute(New AsyncCallback(AddressOf GetProductsComplete), dsq)
```

ADO.NET Data Services over the Entity Framework

When Silverlight 2 and ADO.NET Data Services communicate with each other, they form a symbiotic relationship. Silverlight 2 makes requests and passes information to ADO.NET Data Services, and ADO.NET Data Services provides a client library for Silverlight 2 to make the requests and serves up the information. The rest of this chapter demonstrates many of the features and possibilities that exist in this symbiosis through a sample application built on the Entity Framework, ADO.NET Data Services, REST, and Silverlight 2. The sample, found in `EFDataServices` in this chapter's sample code, also demonstrates authorization techniques and how to perform operations outside the standard URIs exposed by ADO.NET Data Services.

Out of the box, you can access the Entity Framework via the RESTful nature of ADO.NET Data Services. Once you have built an entity data model using the Entity Framework, you can access it through ADO.NET Data Services to perform CRUD operations, paging, and sorting, and to handle change tracking, implement transactions, and handle eager and delayed loading.

ADO.NET Data Services can be an integral component in a Silverlight 2 application's architecture. Although ADO.NET Data Services provides services to a variety of clients, its RESTful nature and its Silverlight 2 client library included in the `System.Data.Services.Client` library make it ideal for communicating with Silverlight 2. In the next section, we will build an entity data model using the Entity Framework, and we'll build services using ADO.NET Data Services on top of the entity data model.

Creating Services on an Entity Data Model

The `EFDataServices` example contains an entity data model created with the Entity Framework. The entity data model, shown partially in Figure 11-4, exposes all of

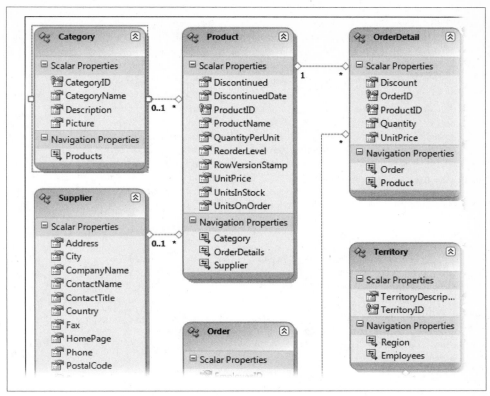

Figure 11-4. NorthwindModel.edmx

the tables in the NorthwindEF database. Hooking up the services to interact with the entity data model requires that the service class inherit from DataService<NorthwindEntities>, where NorthwindEntities is the object context for the Entity Framework-generated model. Then the access rules must be set for the entities that should be exposed through the service.

Read Access

For this sample application, the services should expose only the products, categories, and suppliers. Example 11-10 shows the NorthwindDataService class, which allows all types of reads to the Products, Categories, and Suppliers entity sets and disallows inserts, updates, and deletes. By default, all entity sets are inaccessible through ADO.NET Data Services unless an explicit access rule allows permissions to the entity set. The services allow all types of reads in this case by using the EntitySetRights.AllRead enumerator.

You can find the complete list of `EntitySetRights` enumerator values in Appendix A. The access rules are relatively self-explanatory, and you can combine them to create customized access rules or you can use the `All`, `AllRead`, or `AllWrite` rules to allow the most access. However, there are two types of update access rules: `WriteReplace` and `WriteMerge`. Both the `WriteReplace` and `WriteMerge` access rules are enforced, which allows both types of updates. A merge operation occurs when only the properties in the entity are included in the update to the entity. A property not included in the entity is ignored in the underlying data source. This is the most common type of update operation. A replace operation indicates that all fields on the underlying data source must be updated, even if they are not in the entity being used to update the data source. For every property that is not included in the entity, the replace operation uses the default value or null if allowed.

Example 11-10. NorthwindDataService

[C#]
```csharp
public class NorthwindDataService : DataService<NorthwindEntities>
{
    public static void InitializeService(IDataServiceConfiguration config)
    {
        config.SetEntitySetAccessRule("Products", EntitySetRights.AllRead);
        config.SetEntitySetAccessRule("Categories", EntitySetRights.AllRead);
        config.SetEntitySetAccessRule("Suppliers", EntitySetRights.AllRead);
    }
}
```

[VB]
```vb
Public Class NorthwindDataService
    Inherits DataService(Of NorthwindEntities)
    Public Shared Sub InitializeService(ByVal config As IDataServiceConfiguration)
        config.SetEntitySetAccessRule("Products", EntitySetRights.AllRead)
        config.SetEntitySetAccessRule("Categories", EntitySetRights.AllRead)
        config.SetEntitySetAccessRule("Suppliers", EntitySetRights.AllRead)
    End Sub
End Class
```

This is all that is required to allow the service to serve up the resources for these three types of entities, but not allow the client application to modify the entities. On the client side in the Silverlight 2 application, you can add a service reference to the `NorthwindDataService` that generates the proxy classes for the context and the entities. The `ProductView` user control invokes a LINQ query asynchronously to the service and receives a list of products. The list is then data-bound to a `DataGrid` control in the `ProductView` so that you can examine the products. Figure 11-5 shows the `Product View` user control with the list of products bound to the `DataGrid` control (Example 11-11 shows the XAML for the `DataGrid` control). On selection of each product row in the `DataGrid`, the current `Product` instance is bound to the `DataContext` of the `ProductDetailsLayout` grid panel.

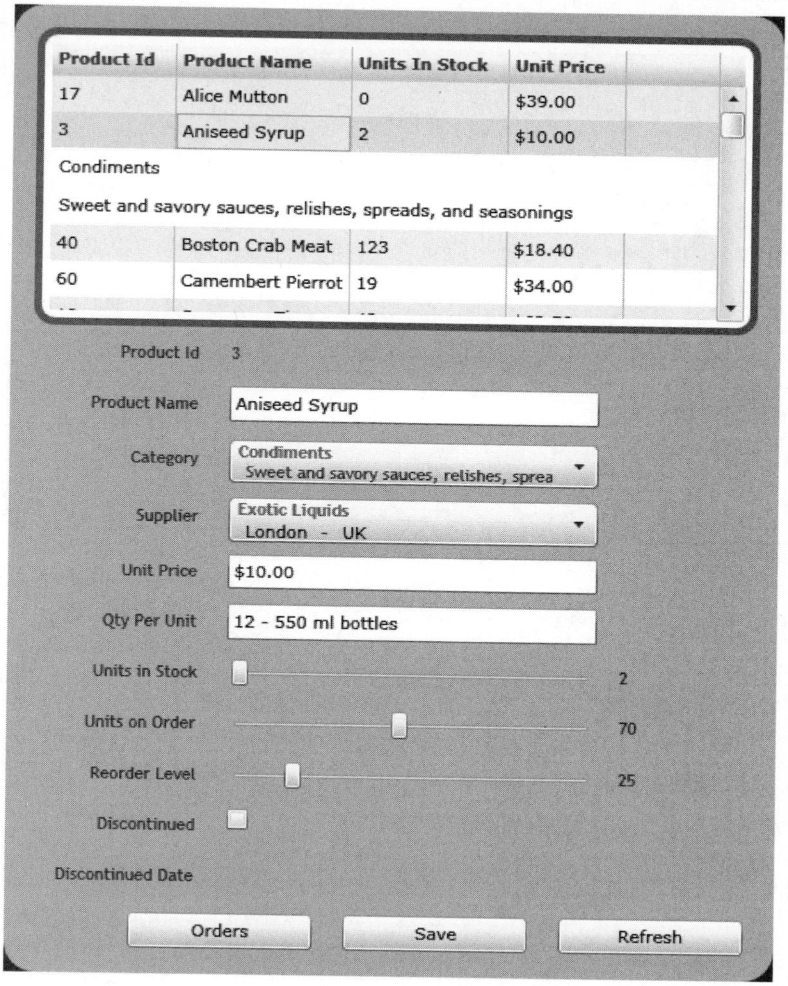

Figure 11-5. *ProductView user control*

Example 11-11. *DataGrid XAML with bindings*

```
<data:DataGrid Height="180" Width="Auto" BorderThickness="0,0,0,0"
    x:Name="productGrid"
    ItemsSource="{Binding Mode=OneWay}" AutoGenerateColumns="False"
    SelectionMode="Single" RowDetailsVisibilityMode="VisibleWhenSelected"
    RowDetailsTemplate="{StaticResource ProductDetailsTemplate}">
    <data:DataGrid.BorderBrush>
        <LinearGradientBrush EndPoint="0.5,1" StartPoint="0.5,0">
            <GradientStop Color="#FFA3AEB9"/>
            <GradientStop Color="#FF8399A9" Offset="0.375"/>
            <GradientStop Color="#FF718597" Offset="0.375"/>
```

```
                <GradientStop Color="#FFFFFFFF" Offset="1"/>
            </LinearGradientBrush>
        </data:DataGrid.BorderBrush>
        <data:DataGrid.Columns>
            <data:DataGridTextColumn Header="Product Id"
                Binding="{Binding ProductID}"/>
            <data:DataGridTextColumn Header="Product Name"
                Binding="{Binding ProductName}"/>
            <data:DataGridTextColumn Header="Units In Stock"
                Binding="{Binding UnitsInStock}"/>
            <data:DataGridTextColumn Header="Unit Price"
              Binding="{Binding UnitPrice,
              Converter={StaticResource myCurrencyConverter},
              ConverterParameter=C}" />
        </data:DataGrid.Columns>
</data:DataGrid>
```

Extending the Client Model

The Silverlight 2 client invokes a LINQ query to retrieve the products through an instance of the `DataServiceQuery<Product>` class. The process of invoking queries to request and save data can be very redundant. A LINQ query is defined, the instance of `DataServiceQuery` is created, the `BeginExecute` method is called, the query executes via the service, the response is returned to the callback method, and the results are deserialized into instances of the entities at the client. The varying factors in a basic read to get a list of entities are the query itself and the type of entity that is returned. For instance, in this example the query gets all products and returns a collection of `Product` instances. All of the remaining code is just plumbing that can be handled through inheritance and generics.

In this sample application, a `BaseList` class handles most of the plumbing for loading and saving data through communications with ADO.NET Data Services. This enables the individual customized list classes for each entity to contain a much smaller amount of code since they do not have to concentrate on the plumbing. For example, the `ProductList` class shown in Example 11-12 inherits from the `BaseList<Product>` and overrides the `LoadAsync` method so that it can define a specific LINQ query to retrieve all of the `Product` instances and their associated `Category` and `Supplier` instances. The method then calls the base class's `LoadAsync` method (inside `BaseList`), which passes the query to the service and sets the callback method. This technique keeps the derived classes for the lists short and very manageable while encapsulating all of the logic for executing the services and processing the results in the `BaseList` class.

Eager loading

The query uses eager loading to retrieve the related `Category` and `Supplier` entities for the `Product`. By default, the related entities would not be loaded. The `Expand` method shown in the `LoadAsync` method in Example 11-12 is an extension from the

System.Data.Services.Client namespace that is translated to the $expand option when the LINQ query is translated to a URI.

Example 11-12. The ProductList class

```csharp
public class ProductList : BaseList<Product>
{
    public ProductList(NorthwindEntities context)
        : base(context)
    {
    }

    public void LoadAsync()
    {
        //Eager loading
        var qry = from p in Context.Products.Expand("Category").Expand("Supplier")
                  orderby p.ProductName
                  select p;
        base.LoadAsync(qry);
    }
}
```

```vbnet
Public Class ProductList
    Inherits BaseList(Of Product)
    Public Sub New(ByVal context As NorthwindEntities)
        MyBase.New(context)
    End Sub

    Public Sub LoadAsync()
        'Eager loading
        Dim qry = _
            From p In Context.Products.Expand("Category").Expand("Supplier") _
            Order By p.ProductName _
            Select p
        MyBase.LoadAsync(qry)
    End Sub
End Class
```

Loading asynchronously

The BaseList class shown in Example 11-13 inherits from ObservableCollection. Before the LoadAsync method (shown in bold) passes the LINQ query to the service to be executed, the context's MergeOptions property is set to MergeOptions.Overwrite Changes. This enumerator indicates that when the data is retrieved it should replace any changes being tracked in the context. This effectively allows the Refresh button in ProductView to cancel all changes and retrieve a fresh set of data. The default value for MergeOptions is AppendOnly, which does not overwrite data elements it finds in the context. With AppendOnly, only data not found in the context is added to it. Appendix A provides the complete list of enumerator values for MergeOptions and their descriptions.

When the service returns the data, the OnLoadComplete event handler executes and processes the results. The Product instances are retrieved and are added to the BaseList collection. The collection inherits from ObservableCollection, so each item can implement the `PropertyChanged` event. This allows each item in the collection to raise a notification if the item changes. If the list is involved in a data-binding agreement with the `OneWay` or `TwoWay` binding mode, the target control will automatically be aware of the change. When properties change, the context's `UpdateObject` method is passed the entity instance. This notifies the context of any changes to the object.

Example 11-13. The BaseList class

```csharp
public abstract class BaseList<T> : ObservableCollection<T> where T : BaseEntity
{
    #region Event Declarations
    public event EventHandler LoadComplete;
    public event EventHandler<SaveDataEventArgs> SaveComplete;
    #endregion

    #region Constructors
    protected BaseList(){}

    public BaseList(NorthwindEntities context)
    {
        _context = context;
    }
    #endregion

    #region Fields
    private NorthwindEntities _context;
    #endregion

    #region Properties
    protected NorthwindEntities Context
    {
        get
        {
            if (_context == null)
                _context = new NorthwindEntities(
                new Uri("NorthwindDataService.svc", UriKind.Relative));
            return _context;
        }
    }
    #endregion

    #region Protected Methods
    protected void entity_PropertyChanged(
        object sender, PropertyChangedEventArgs e)
    {
        T entity = (T)sender;
        Context.UpdateObject(entity);
    }
    protected void LoadAsync(IQueryable<T> query)
    {
        this.Clear();
        Context.MergeOption = MergeOption.OverwriteChanges;
        DataServiceQuery<T> dataServiceQuery = (DataServiceQuery<T>)query;
        dataServiceQuery.BeginExecute(
```

```csharp
        new AsyncCallback(OnLoadComplete), dataServiceQuery);
    }

    protected void OnLoadComplete(IAsyncResult result)
    {
        DataServiceQuery<T> query = (DataServiceQuery<T>)result.AsyncState;
        try
        {
            List<T> entities = query.EndExecute(result).ToList();
            foreach (T item in entities)
            {
                item.PropertyChanged += entity_PropertyChanged;
                this.Add(item);
            }
        }
        catch (Exception ex)
        {
            Debug.WriteLine("Failed to retrieve data: " + ex.ToString());
        }

        if (LoadComplete != null) LoadComplete(this, new EventArgs());
    }

    protected void OnSaveComplete(IAsyncResult result)
    {
        bool succeeded = true;
        try
        {
            DataServiceResponse response =
            (DataServiceResponse)Context.EndSaveChanges(result);

            foreach (OperationResponse opResponse in response)
            {
                if (opResponse.Error != null)
                {
                    succeeded = false;
                }
            }
        }
        catch (Exception ex)
        {
            succeeded = false;
        }

        if (SaveComplete != null)
        SaveComplete(this, new SaveDataEventArgs { Succeeded = succeeded });
    }

#endregion

#region Public Methods

public virtual void SaveAsync()
{
    Context.MergeOption = MergeOption.AppendOnly;
```

```
        Context.BeginSaveChanges(SaveChangesOptions.Batch,
            new AsyncCallback(OnSaveComplete), null);
    }
    #endregion
}
```

```vb
Public MustInherit Class BaseList(Of T As BaseEntity)
    Inherits ObservableCollection(Of T)
    #Region "Event Declarations"
    Public Event LoadComplete As EventHandler
    Public Event SaveComplete As EventHandler(Of SaveDataEventArgs)
    #End Region

    #Region "Constructors"
    Protected Sub New()
    End Sub

    Public Sub New(ByVal context As NorthwindEntities)
        _context = context
    End Sub
    #End Region

    #Region "Fields"
    Private _context As NorthwindEntities
    #End Region

    #Region "Properties"
    Protected ReadOnly Property Context() As NorthwindEntities
        Get
            If _context Is Nothing Then
                _context = New NorthwindEntities( _
                New Uri("NorthwindDataService.svc", UriKind.Relative))
            End If
            Return _context
        End Get
    End Property
    #End Region

    #Region "Protected Methods"
    Protected Sub entity_PropertyChanged( _
        ByVal sender As Object, ByVal e As PropertyChangedEventArgs)
        Dim entity As T = CType(sender, T)
        Context.UpdateObject(entity)
    End Sub

    Protected Sub LoadAsync(ByVal query As IQueryable(Of T))
        Me.Clear()
        Context.MergeOption = MergeOption.OverwriteChanges
        Dim dataServiceQuery As DataServiceQuery(Of T) = _
            CType(query, DataServiceQuery(Of T))
        dataServiceQuery.BeginExecute( _
            New AsyncCallback(AddressOf OnLoadComplete), dataServiceQuery)
    End Sub

    Protected Sub OnLoadComplete(ByVal result As IAsyncResult)
        Dim query As DataServiceQuery(Of T) = _
```

```
                CType(result.AsyncState, DataServiceQuery(Of T))
        Try
            Dim entities As List(Of T) = query.EndExecute(result).ToList()
            For Each item As T In entities
                AddHandler item.PropertyChanged, AddressOf entity_PropertyChanged
                Me.Add(item)
            Next item
        Catch ex As Exception
            Debug.WriteLine("Failed to retrieve data: " & ex.ToString())
        End Try

        RaiseEvent LoadComplete(Me, New EventArgs())
    End Sub

    Protected Sub OnSaveComplete(ByVal result As IAsyncResult)
        Dim succeeded As Boolean = True
        Try
            Dim response As DataServiceResponse = _
            CType(Context.EndSaveChanges(result), DataServiceResponse)

            For Each opResponse As OperationResponse In response
                If opResponse.Error IsNot Nothing Then
                    succeeded = False
                End If
            Next opResponse
        Catch ex As Exception
            succeeded = False
        End Try

    RaiseEvent SaveComplete(Me, New SaveDataEventArgs With _
        {.Succeeded = succeeded})
    End Sub
    #End Region

    #Region "Public Methods"
    Public Overridable Sub SaveAsync()
        Context.MergeOption = MergeOption.AppendOnly
        Context.BeginSaveChanges(SaveChangesOptions.Batch, _
        New AsyncCallback(AddressOf OnSaveComplete), Nothing)
    End Sub
    #End Region
End Class
```

Enabling saves

The BaseList class also handles saving the changes made within the context. When a user changes product data in the ProductView, the BaseList.SaveAsync method invokes the context's BeginSaveChanges method and passes to it the SaveChangesOptions.Batch enumerator and the callback method that will be invoked when the save operation completes. The SaveChangesOptions.Batch enumerator indicates that all changes should complete as an atomic unit of work. If one save operation fails out of a set of entities that were modified, no changes will be saved.

You can find the complete list of SaveChangesOptions enumerator values in Appendix A.

When the ProductView user control runs and then makes and saves changes, ADO.NET Data Services executes the HTTP requests using the URIs and messages required to save the data. You can examine the URI and the message body for the save operation using a tool such as Fiddler2.

Appendix B contains tips on watching the RESTful operations and their URIs, requests, and responses to help debug the service calls. Fiddler2, Firebug, and the Web Development Helper are very useful for watching and debugging calls made through ADO.NET Data Services.

The Client Hookup

The ProductView user control creates an instance of the NorthwindEntities context and uses it to create each list of entities. Each list of entities is a class that inherits from BaseList<T>. When created, these classes are passed the context, so that all of the classes share the same context. The instance of the ProductList class will be loaded with the products that the user can examine and modify. The CategoryList and SupplierList class instances are loaded with all of their respective entities and are bound to their respective ComboBox controls. The code in Example 11-14 shows the setup of the ADO.NET Data Services context and the creation of the instances of the list classes for the Product, Category, and Supplier entities.

Example 11-14. Creating the context

```C#
private void Page_Loaded(object sender, RoutedEventArgs e)
{
    //Create the context for ADO.NET Data Services
    _context = new NorthwindEntities(
        new Uri("NorthwindDataService.svc", UriKind.Relative));

    // Create the lists of categories, suppliers
    // and products and set the ADO.NET Data Services context
    _categoryList = new CategoryList(_context);
    _supplierList = new SupplierList(_context);
    _productList = new ProductList(_context);
    ...
```

```VB
Private Sub Page_Loaded(ByVal sender As Object, ByVal e As RoutedEventArgs)
    'Create the context for ADO.NET Data Services
    _context = New NorthwindEntities( _
        New Uri("NorthwindDataService.svc", UriKind.Relative))

    ' Create the lists of categories, suppliers and
    ' products and set the ADO.NET Data Services context
```

```
_categoryList = New CategoryList(_context)
_supplierList = New SupplierList(_context)
_productList = New ProductList(_context)
...
```

Once the contexts have been set, the data bindings are established for each list. The product list is bound to the main `DataGrid` so that the user can examine the products and select a specific one. The category and supplier lists are then bound to the `ItemsSource` property of the `cboCategory` and `cboSupplier` controls. (See Example 11-15.)

Example 11-15. Binding the lists

C#
```
// Set the Bindings for all of the data binding operations
productGrid.DataContext = _productList;
cboCategory.ItemsSource = _categoryList;
cboSupplier.ItemsSource = _supplierList;
```

VB
```
' Set the Bindings for all of the data binding operations
productGrid.DataContext = _productList
cboCategory.ItemsSource = _categoryList
cboSupplier.ItemsSource = _supplierList
```

After the event handlers are set, the three asynchronous queries are executed to retrieve the entities for each respective list. Each list invokes its own `LoadAsync` method that defines LINQ queries that specifically retrieve each list of entities, as shown in Example 11-16.

Example 11-16. Loading the entities

C#
```
// Get the lists of categories, suppliers and products
_categoryList.LoadAsync();
_supplierList.LoadAsync();
_productList.LoadAsync();
```

VB
```
' Get the lists of categories, suppliers and products
_categoryList.LoadAsync()
_supplierList.LoadAsync()
_productList.LoadAsync()
```

When the user changes the selected product from the `productGrid DataGrid`, the event handler grabs the `Product` instance from the selected row. The selected `Product` instance is set to the `DataContext` of the `ProductDetailsLayout Grid` panel, which is the container control for all of the `TextBlock`, `TextBox`, `CheckBox`, and `Slider` controls that display the details of the selected product. (See Example 11-17.)

Example 11-17. Setting the DataContext for the product details

C#
```
void productGrid_SelectionChanged(object sender, SelectionChangedEventArgs e)
{
    Product product = productGrid.SelectedItem as Product;
```

```
        ProductDetailsLayout.DataContext = product;
    }
```

VB
```
    Private Sub productGrid_SelectionChanged(ByVal sender As Object, _
        ByVal e As SelectionChangedEventArgs)
        Dim product As Product = TryCast(productGrid.SelectedItem, Product)
        ProductDetailsLayout.DataContext = product
    End Sub
```

Loading and linking

When a user changes the value of a scalar property, the value is modified as per the binding mode. When a user changes the value of a navigation property, such as Product.Category, which contains an instance of a Category, some additional work must be done. To support these types of edits, the cboCategory ComboBox has a SelectionChanged event handler that does the dirty work.

When a user changes the category for a product, the selected Product is retrieved from the productGrid DataGrid and the selected Category is retrieved from the cboCategory ComboBox. Then the ADO.NET Data Services context instance is used to establish the new link between the Product instance and its Category instance. It does this through the context's SetLink method, as shown in Example 11-18. If the SetLink method is not called, the context will not capture the changes to the product's category.

Example 11-18. Linking the selected category to the product

C#
```
    private void cboCategory_SelectionChanged(
        object sender, SelectionChangedEventArgs e)
    {
        Product product = productGrid.SelectedItem as Product;
        if (product == null) return;
        Category category = cboCategory.SelectedItem as Category;
        if (category == null) return;
        _context.SetLink(product, "Category", category);
    }
```

VB
```
    Private Sub cboCategory_SelectionChanged( _
        ByVal sender As Object, ByVal e As SelectionChangedEventArgs)
        Dim product As Product = TryCast(productGrid.SelectedItem, Product)
        If product Is Nothing Then
            Return
        End If
        Dim category As Category = TryCast(cboCategory.SelectedItem, Category)
        If category Is Nothing Then
            Return
        End If
        _context.SetLink(product, "Category", category)
    End Sub
```

Notification Implications

After adding the service reference, the proxy class is generated on the client side. However, the INotifyPropertyChanged implementation on the entities (on the server) are not carried over to the Silverlight 2 client in the proxy class. This means that the generated classes will not support the change notifications even if the server's entity model class implements the INotifyPropertyChanged interface. Any Silverlight 2 XAML bindings that rely on OneWay or TwoWay binding modes to channel notifications to dependency properties will be affected by this. Without the notifications on the client, the bindings will not receive changes made to the class instances.

The generated classes that represent the entities in the Silverlight 2 client do not implement the INotifyPropertyChanged interface. The Product class in the service inherits from the EntityBase class (which implements the INotifyPropertyChanged interface). When any of its properties are set, the FirePropertyChanged event is executed.

This does not mean that notifications are unsupported, however. The generated class is created as a partial class, so it can be extended. The class also generates and raises two events inside each property setter. Example 11-19 shows the ProductName property from the generated Product class in the Silverlight 2 client application. This property raises the OnProductNameChanging and OnProductNameChanged events in the property setter code. You can handle the events by extending the Product class in the Silverlight 2 client application. The Product class is generated as a partial class when adding a service reference. Its change events are defined as partial methods, which makes extending these methods and firing the custom FirePropertyChanged method quite simple.

Example 11-19. Generated product class's ProductName property

C#
```csharp
public string ProductName
{
    get
    {
        return this._ProductName;
    }
    set
    {
        this.OnProductNameChanging(value);
        this._ProductName = value;
        this.OnProductNameChanged();
    }
}
```

VB
```vb
Public Property ProductName() As String
    Get
        Return Me._ProductName
    End Get
    Set(ByVal value As String)
        Me.OnProductNameChanging(value)
        Me._ProductName = value
        Me.OnProductNameChanged()
```

```
        End Set
    End Property
```

The code in Example 11-20 shows the partial Product class that is not generated. This extends the generated partial Product class by handling the change events. With this technique in place, the dependency properties involved in data binding with a Product class instance will be notified of any changes.

Example 11-20. Extending the Product class with PropertyChanged events

[C#]
```csharp
public partial class Product : BaseEntity
{
    partial void OnProductIDChanged() { FirePropertyChanged("ProductID"); }
    partial void OnProductNameChanged() { FirePropertyChanged("ProductName"); }
    partial void OnDiscontinuedChanged() { FirePropertyChanged("Discontinued"); }
    ...
}
```

[VB]
```vb
Partial Public Class Product
    Inherits BaseEntity
    Private Sub OnProductIDChanged()
        FirePropertyChanged("ProductID")
    End Sub
    Private Sub OnProductNameChanged()
        FirePropertyChanged("ProductName")
    End Sub
    Private Sub OnDiscontinuedChanged()
        FirePropertyChanged("Discontinued")
    End Sub
    ...
End Class
```

Delayed Loading

The default behavior is to retrieve only those entities that are explicitly requested in the DataServiceQuery. This means that when a list of Product instances is retrieved via ADO.NET Data Services, the Product instances' Category property values will not be available. This is where eager loading comes into play. Eager loading is beneficial when it is known in advance that an object graph should be loaded because the client will need it. For instance, the sample application requires the Product as well as each Product's Category and Supplier. In this case, eager loading is a good option, so the Expand method is used in the LINQ query to perform eager loading.

In some situations, you may not know whether the object graph containing the Product and its Category and Supplier are required. In such cases, you would not want the performance and memory hit for loading the extra data for the object graph if the data might not be used. For example, in the ProductView user control, when a product is selected the user may choose to click the Orders button which will display a pop-up control showing all orders for the selected product. Loading the orders for a product is necessary only if the button is clicked, so the data is not included in the eager loading directives in the LINQ query. But the data is needed if the user clicks the button. This is a scenario in which using delayed loading makes a lot of sense.

Delayed loading is a technique that ADO.NET Data Services supports to retrieve parts of an object graph on a "need to know" basis. In this example, the orders for the selected product data are not retrieved until the application "needs to know." You execute delayed loading using the context's `BeginLoadProperty` method. This method accepts the parent instance (in this case, the `Product` instance), a string value representing the name of the property to load (`OrderDetails`), and the handler that will execute when the results are returned.

The code in Example 11-21 handles the delayed loading for the `OrderDetails` to display the information for the selected `Product`. Notice that an embedded lambda expression is used to define the anonymous method that will process the results when the asynchronous operation completes. You could use a callback method instead, as in the previous examples in this chapter. However, the technique shown in Example 11-21 can be nice for embedding small bits of code that execute when an asynchronous operation completes. Also notice that the code in Example 11-21 uses the `Deployment.Current.Dispatcher` class's `BeginInvoke` method. As there is no guarantee that the asynchronous operation to the ADO.NET Data Services will come back on the UI thread, this ensures that the code can interact with the UI.

Example 11-21. Using an anonymous delegate on completion

C#
```csharp
Product product = productGrid.SelectedItem as Product;
if (product == null) return;
_context.BeginLoadProperty(product, "OrderDetails",
            (
                (IAsyncResult result) =>
                {
                Deployment.Current.Dispatcher.BeginInvoke(() =>
                {
                    _context.EndLoadProperty(result);
                    Product p = productGrid.SelectedItem as Product;
                    var query = (from od in p.OrderDetails
                                    orderby od.OrderID ascending
                                    select od);
                    ordersPopup.Show(query.ToList());
            });
                }
            ), null);
```

VB
```vb
Dim product As Product = TryCast(productGrid.SelectedItem, Product)
If product Is Nothing Then
    Return
End If
_context.BeginLoadProperty(product, "OrderDetails", _
            ( _
                Function(result As IAsyncResult)
                  _context.EndLoadProperty(result)
                  Dim p As Product = TryCast(productGrid.SelectedItem, Product)
                  Dim query = ( _
```

```
                    From od In p.OrderDetails _
                    Order By od.OrderID Ascending _
                    Select od)
              ordersPopup.Show(query.ToList())
         ), Nothing)
```

The results are loaded into the context through the context's `EndLoadProperty` method. At this point, the object graph (the product and its order detail information) is loaded in the context. This means that you can execute a LINQ to Objects query on the Silverlight 2 client to retrieve the `OrderDetails` instances. The LINQ query is not being sent through ADO.NET Data Services; instead, the LINQ query is hitting the local objects in the context. So, when the user clicks the Orders button, the `OrderDetails` for the selected product are retrieved and displayed in a pop-up control, as shown in Figure 11-6.

 The `NorthwindDataService` did not enable access to the `OrderDetails` entity set, so you must do this first in the ADO.NET Data Service. You do this by adding the following code to the `InitializeService` method in the `NorthwindDataService` class.

In C#:

```
config.SetEntitySetAccessRule("OrderDetails", EntitySetRights.AllRead);
```

In VB:

```
config.SetEntitySetAccessRule("OrderDetails", EntitySetRights.AllRead)
```

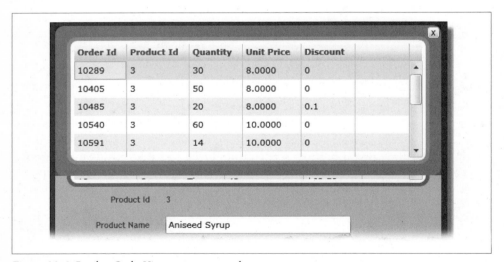

Figure 11-6. ProductOrderView pop-up control

Query Interceptors

You use the `EntitySetRights.AllRead` setting to indicate that a service will allow products to be retrieved. However, that does not help to narrow down which products can be retrieved based on business rules. For example, the application may allow the user to view only products that have not been discontinued. In this case, it is beneficial to intercept the query for the products and implement a business rule to filter out the discontinued products. The tool that handles this job is called an *interceptor*.

Interceptors come in two flavors. Query interceptors execute when retrieval queries are run on a specific entity set. Change interceptors execute when create, update, or delete operations are performed against a specific entity set. To intercept any queries on the `Products` entity set, you create a public method in the `NorthwindDataService` class. You then decorate the method with the `QueryInterceptor` attribute, which is passed the entity set name for which it should intercept queries. The public interceptor method returns an expression tree, not a list of the entities. The expression tree is defined in the method to filter out the discontinued products. The code in Example 11-22 shows the complete query interceptor for this task.

Example 11-22. Query interceptor

C#
```
[QueryInterceptor("Products")]
public Expression<Func<Product, bool>> OnQueryProducts()
{
    return p => p.Discontinued == false;
}
```

VB
```
<QueryInterceptor("Products")> _
Public Function OnQueryProducts() As Expression(Of Func(Of Product, Boolean))
    Return Function(p) p.Discontinued = False
End Function
```

Change Interceptors

Change interceptors execute when an update operation is performed on the indicated entity set. You can use change interceptors to implement business rules, such as preventing unauthorized users from making changes, preventing changes to discontinued products, or preventing a product's price from being less than $1. You represent a change interceptor via a public method in the data service class. You decorate the public method with the `ChangeInterceptor` attribute and pass to it the entity set name indicating which entity set saves it should intercept.

For example, the change interceptor in Example 11-23 enforces a business rule that states that only users in the administrator role can make changes to products. The public method has a parameter for the entity instance that is being saved (in this case, a `Product` instance). It also is passed a value for the `UpdateOperations` enumerator, which indicates whether the change is an add, change, or delete operation. In this example, the type of save is irrelevant, because only administrators can apply any type of save to a product. Instead, the interceptor checks to see whether the user is authorized to make the change using the `HttpContext.Current.User.IsInRole` method. The ASP.NET membership groups are available to the service, so this is used to handle the logic for the interceptor.

Example 11-23. Change interceptor

```csharp
[ChangeInterceptor("Products")]
public void OnChangeProduct_MustBeAdmin(
    Product product, UpdateOperations updateAction)
{
    if (HttpContext.Current.User.IsInRole("Administrators"))
        return; // Allow any updates.
    else
        throw new DataServiceException(400,
            "Update not allowed. Must be an administrator.");
}
```

```vb
<ChangeInterceptor("Products")> _
Public Sub OnChangeProduct_MustBeAdmin( _
        ByVal product As Product, ByVal updateAction As UpdateOperations)
    If HttpContext.Current.User.IsInRole("Administrators") Then
        Return ' Allow any updates.
    Else
        Throw New DataServiceException(400, _
            "Update not allowed. Must be an administrator.")
    End If
End Sub
```

 If a business rule exists that requires that a user be able to retrieve only his records, you can use `HttpContext.Current.User.Identity`. This returns the current user identity in the service, which can then be matched against a user record in a LINQ query to enforce the rule.

Change interceptors can use the `UpdateOperations` parameter value to implement business rules based on the type of save operation. For example, a business rule may state that a user cannot discontinue a product that is in stock or on order. The change interceptor can intercept product changes and evaluate the `UpdateOperations` parameter value, checking for Add or Change operations (as only additions or changes could render a product discontinued). If the operation is a delete, the rule is skipped and the save will continue as planned. Example 11-24 shows the code for this change interceptor.

Example 11-24. Change interceptor and UpdateOperations

```csharp
[ChangeInterceptor("Products")]
public void OnChangeProducts(Product product, UpdateOperations operation)
{
    switch (operation)
    {
        case UpdateOperations.None:
```

```
            break;
        case UpdateOperations.Add:
        case UpdateOperations.Change:
            if (product.UnitsInStock + product.UnitsOnOrder > 0
            && product.Discontinued)
                throw new DataServiceException(400,
                "Cannot discontinue a product that is in stock or on order.");
            break;
        case UpdateOperations.Delete:
            break;
        default:
            throw new ArgumentOutOfRangeException("operation");
    }
}
```

VB
```
<ChangeInterceptor("Products")> _
Public Sub OnChangeProducts( _
        ByVal product As Product, ByVal operation As UpdateOperations)
    Select Case operation
        Case UpdateOperations.None
        Case UpdateOperations.Add, UpdateOperations.Change
            If product.UnitsInStock + product.UnitsOnOrder > 0 _
            AndAlso product.Discontinued Then
                Throw New DataServiceException(400, _
                "Cannot discontinue a product that is in stock or on order.")
            End If
        Case UpdateOperations.Delete
        Case Else
            Throw New ArgumentOutOfRangeException("operation")
    End Select
End Sub
```

Extending the Service Operations

Although you can expose an entity data model using ADO.NET Data Services and allow access to the entity sets by issuing the SetEntityAccessRule method, sometimes you will need specialized operations that do not fit into this mold. If you require a custom service operation, you can add it by creating a public method in the data service class. You should decorate the service operation with the WebGet attribute and have it return an IQueryable<T>. This is different from creating a standard service operation, as shown in the earlier chapters, because this returns IQueryable<T>, which allows the results to be queried using LINQ.

For instance, the service operation in Example 11-25 exists in the NorthwindDataService class. It accepts a name of a city and creates a query that returns all of the customers for the given city. The query itself is returned, not the customers, as the query is not executed in this code segment.

Example 11-25. Custom service operation

C#
```
[WebGet]
public IQueryable<Customer> CustomersByCity(string city)
```

```
{
    var query = from c in CurrentDataSource.Customers
                where c.City == city
                select c;
    return query;
}
```

VB

```vb
<WebGet> _
Public Function CustomersByCity(ByVal city As String) As IQueryable(Of Customer)
    Dim query = _
        From c In CurrentDataSource.Customers _
        Where c.City = city _
        Select c
    Return query
End Function
```

You can run the service operation by executing an HTTP request using the following URI:

> *http://localhost:8890/NorthwindDataService.svc/CustomersByCity/?city='London'*
> *&$top=3&$orderby=CompanyName*

Service operations and interceptors are helpful when you are implementing custom behavior that may limit or run complex business rules. Service operations are also great when you require the flexibility to create a service that does not fit into the mold of simply intercepting queries through ADO.NET Data Services.

More Saving Options

If the provider implements IUpdatable, ADO.NET Data Services also supports adding and deleting single objects or object graphs. You add an object by creating an instance of the entity and using the context's AddTo[*EntitySetName*] method for the corresponding entity set. Then you can execute the context's BeginSaveChanges method to apply the changes and add the new entities to the underlying data source through ADO.NET Data Services. You can handle deletes by passing the object to delete to the context's DeleteObject method. Then you can execute the context's BeginSaveChanges method to apply the deletions through ADO.NET Data Services.

Inserts and Object Graphs

The DeepInsert user control in the sample code in the EFDataServices solution creates a series of related objects, links them together in an object graph, and adds them to the context. Then the object graph is saved via the data service. The DeepInsertTest method shown in Example 11-26 creates two Product instances and creates a new Category and Supplier instance for the new Product instances. The new Category and Supplier instances are linked to the new products using the context's SetLink method. Finally, the object graph is passed to the data service through the context's BeginSaveChanges method.

Example 11-26. Deep insert of an object graph

C#
```csharp
private void DeepInsertTest()
{
    Supplier sockSupplier = new Supplier
    {
        Address = "1 Lois Lane",
        City = "Somewhere",
        CompanyName = "Socks R Us",
        ContactName = "Ella",
        ContactTitle = "VP of Socks",
        Country = "US",
        PostalCode = "00000",
        Region = "SouthEast"
    };
    Category sockCategory = new Category
    {
        CategoryName = "Socks",
        Description = "Athletic socks"
    };
    Product soccerSocks = new Product
    {
        Discontinued = false,
        ProductName = "Soccer socks",
        QuantityPerUnit = "1 pair",
        ReorderLevel = 10,
        UnitPrice = (decimal)14.99,
        UnitsOnOrder = 0,
        UnitsInStock = 20
    };
    Product baseballSocks = new Product
    {
        Discontinued = false,
        ProductName = "Baseball socks",
        QuantityPerUnit = "3 pair",
        ReorderLevel = 7,
        UnitPrice = (decimal)11.99,
        UnitsOnOrder = 0,
        UnitsInStock = 10
    };
    _context.AddToCategories(sockCategory);
    _context.AddToSuppliers(sockSupplier);
    _context.AddToProducts(soccerSocks);
    _context.AddToProducts(baseballSocks);

    _context.SetLink(soccerSocks, "Category", sockCategory);
    _context.SetLink(soccerSocks, "Supplier", sockSupplier);
    _context.SetLink(baseballSocks, "Category", sockCategory);
    _context.SetLink(baseballSocks, "Supplier", sockSupplier);

    _context.BeginSaveChanges(SaveChangesOptions.Batch, (SaveComplete), null);
}
```

VB
```vb
Private Sub DeepInsertTest()
    Dim sockSupplier As Supplier = New Supplier With _
        { _
```

```
                .Address = "1 Lois Lane", _
                .City = "Somewhere", _
                .CompanyName = "Socks R Us", _
                .ContactName = "Ella", _
                .ContactTitle = "VP of Socks", _
                .Country = "US", _
                .PostalCode = "00000", _
                .Region = "SouthEast"_
                }
        Dim sockCategory As Category = New Category With _
                { _
                .CategoryName = "Socks", _
                .Description = "Athletic socks"_
                }
        Dim soccerSocks As Product = New Product With _
                { _
                .Discontinued = False, _
                .ProductName = "Soccer socks", _
                .QuantityPerUnit = "1 pair", _
                .ReorderLevel = 10, _
                .UnitPrice = CDec(14.99), _
                .UnitsOnOrder = 0, _
                .UnitsInStock = 20_
                }
        Dim baseballSocks As Product = New Product With _
                { _
                .Discontinued = False, _
                .ProductName = "Baseball socks", _
                .QuantityPerUnit = "3 pair", _
                .ReorderLevel = 7, _
                .UnitPrice = CDec(11.99), _
                .UnitsOnOrder = 0, _
                .UnitsInStock = 10_
                }
        _context.AddToCategories(sockCategory)
        _context.AddToSuppliers(sockSupplier)
        _context.AddToProducts(soccerSocks)
        _context.AddToProducts(baseballSocks)

        _context.SetLink(soccerSocks, "Category", sockCategory)
        _context.SetLink(soccerSocks, "Supplier", sockSupplier)
        _context.SetLink(baseballSocks, "Category", sockCategory)
        _context.SetLink(baseballSocks, "Supplier", sockSupplier)

        _context.BeginSaveChanges(SaveChangesOptions.Batch, (SaveComplete), Nothing)
End Sub
```

It is important to save object graph changes using the `SaveChangeOptions.Batch` enumerator so that all items in the object graph are saved as a single unit of work. Because the related entities were linked using the `SetLink` method, ADO.NET Data Services is smart enough to save the entities in the correct order based on the hierarchy of the object graph and the type of save operation (insert, update, or delete).

When the user clicks the Add Items button of the `DeepInsert` user control the following URI is executed as an HTTP `POST` operation:

http://localhost:8890/NorthwindDataService.svc/$batch

This URI indicates that a batch operation is being executed. You can examine the contents of the message using a tool such as Fiddler2. The request contains the entities of the object graph that will be saved and indicates that the HTTP method is a `POST`.

 Silverlight 2 applications should be designed to prevent the user from making multiple concurrent calls to `BeginSaveChanges`. The calls should finish completely before calling `BeginSaveChanges` again.

Optimistic Concurrency

ADO.NET Data Services supports the detection of conflicts when entities are saved. It uses the `ETag` value gathered from the request's response to check for concurrency conflicts. The `ETag` value contains the value of the concurrency token for the entity. The following URI might make a request, and Example 11-27 shows the response from this request to get the `Product` with a `ProductID` equal to 1.

http://localhost:8890/NorthwindDataService.svc/Products(1)

Inside the response is the `ETag` value for the entity, shown in bold. This value is used to check the state of the entity. In this case, the `ETag` represents the value for the `RowVersionStamp` property. The Entity Framework allows properties of an entity to be used for concurrency conflict checking by setting the property's `Concurrency Mode` attribute to `Fixed`. Figure 11-7 shows the `RowVersionStamp` property being selected, and Figure 11-8 shows the property's `Concurrency Mode` being set to `Fixed`.

Example 11-27. ETag for a product

```
<?xml version="1.0" encoding="iso-8859-1" standalone="yes"?>
<entry xml:base="http://localhost:8890/NorthwindDataService.svc/"
    xmlns:d="http://schemas.microsoft.com/ado/2007/08/dataservices"
    xmlns:m="http://schemas.microsoft.com/ado/2007/08/dataservices/metadata"
    m:etag="W/&quot;X'0000000000000C1D'&quot;"
    xmlns="http://www.w3.org/2005/Atom">
  <id>http://localhost:8890/NorthwindDataService.svc/Products(1)</id>
  <title type="text"></title>
  <updated>2008-10-08T06:27:45Z</updated>
  <author>
    <name />
  </author>
  <link rel="edit" title="Product" href="Products(1)" />
  <link
rel="http://schemas.microsoft.com/ado/2007/08/dataservices/related/Category"
    type="application/atom+xml;type=entry"
    title="Category"
    href="Products(1)/Category" />
```

```
  <link
rel="http://schemas.microsoft.com/ado/2007/08/dataservices/related/OrderDetails"
    type="application/atom+xml;type=feed"
    title="OrderDetails"
    href="Products(1)/OrderDetails" />
  <link rel="http://schemas.microsoft.com/ado/2007/08/dataservices/related/Supplier"
    type="application/atom+xml;type=entry"
    title="Supplier"
    href="Products(1)/Supplier" />
  <category term="NorthwindModel.Product"
        scheme="http://schemas.microsoft.com/ado/2007/08/dataservices/scheme" />
  <content type="application/xml">
    <m:properties>
      <d:Discontinued m:type="Edm.Boolean">false</d:Discontinued>
      <d:DiscontinuedDate m:type="Edm.DateTime" m:null="true" />
      <d:ProductID m:type="Edm.Int32">1</d:ProductID>
      <d:ProductName>Chai</d:ProductName>
      <d:QuantityPerUnit>10 boxes x 20 bags</d:QuantityPerUnit>
      <d:ReorderLevel m:type="Edm.Int16">10</d:ReorderLevel>
      <d:RowVersionStamp m:type="Edm.Binary">AAAAAAAADB0=</d:RowVersionStamp>
      <d:UnitPrice m:type="Edm.Decimal">18.0000</d:UnitPrice>
      <d:UnitsInStock m:type="Edm.Int16">39</d:UnitsInStock>
      <d:UnitsOnOrder m:type="Edm.Int16">0</d:UnitsOnOrder>
    </m:properties>
  </content>
</entry>
```

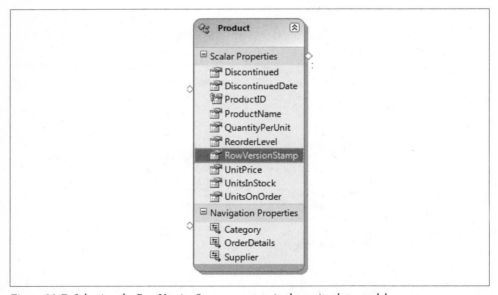

Figure 11-7. Selecting the RowVersionStamp property in the entity data model

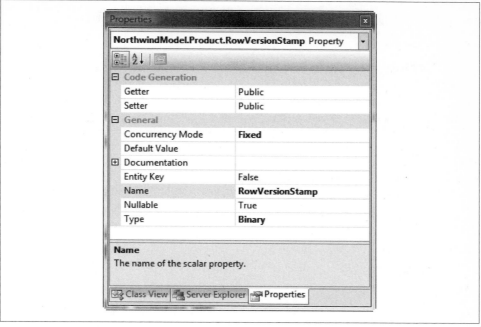

Figure 11-8. Setting the concurrency mode

If the data service is created using a custom data source, you can use the `System.Data.Services.ETagAttribute` to indicate which properties will represent the concurrency tokens for the entities. Setting this attribute or using the Entity Framework technique will cause all request queries for the entity to return an `ETag` with the concurrency token's data.

> If a response includes more than one entity, an `ETag` for each entity is returned within the payload. If the response includes a single entity, an `ETag` header is included in the response, as well.

The following steps will simulate a concurrency conflict where a product name is changed by two different users at the same time:

1. Execute the `EFDataServices` project and select the `ProductView` user control.
2. Select the product named Chef Anton's Cajun Seasoning.
3. Open SQL Server Management Studio (or any tool that can execute SQL).
4. Run the following SQL statement against the NorthwindEF database:

```
UPDATE Products
SET ProductName = 'Chef Anton''s Cajun Seasoning-hahaha!'
WHERE ProductID = 4
```

5. Back in the Silverlight 2 application, change the product name to Chef Anton's Popcorn.

6. Click the Save button.

When the changes are executed, the `ETag` values are compared to the values currently in the database. If they are different, a concurrency violation is thrown. If they are the same, the save operation is allowed. For this simulation, a concurrency violation occurs because the value of the `ProductName` column was changed in the database after the product was retrieved by the Silverlight 2 application but before it was saved again. This changed the `RowVersionStamp` value, causing the `ETag` values to be different and therefore a concurrency violation. Executing this code will cause a `DataServiceRequest` exception to be thrown. You can catch and examine this to see the following error message:

```
The etag value in the request header does not match with the current etag value
of the object.
```

Then the user can be notified of the problem and can take appropriate action.

Summary

The symbiosis between Silverlight 2 and ADO.NET Data Services can help you to create a rich application architecture that builds on the foundations of web services with Silverlight 2. This chapter demonstrated how to surface a data source with ADO.NET Data Services and manipulate it through RESTful services exposed by the service through URIs over HTTP directly, and through the Silverlight 2 client library in `System.Data.Services.Client`.

ADO.NET Data Services Quick Reference

ADO.NET Data Services has several enumerators and options that help define the way in which you can pass a URI and a query string over HTTP. Tables A-1–A-13 in this appendix list the most common enumerators, options, functions, and operators that ADO.NET Data Services relies on.

HTTP Methods

Table A-1. HTTP methods and their corresponding data actions

HTTP method	Data action
POST	Create
GET	Read
PUT	Update
DELETE	Delete

System.Data.Services.Client

Table A-2. System.Data.Services.Client SaveChangesOptions enumerators

Enum	Description
Batch	Changes will be sent in a single payload and will constitute an atomic unit of work
ContinueOnError	When multiple changes are sent, if an error occurs while saving one change, continue to attempt to save the other changes
None	No additional directions
ReplaceOnUpdate	Perform a Replace update instead of a Merge update; Merge updates only the values in the entity that is passed; Replace updates all properties, even if they are not in the passed entity

Table A-3. System.Data.Services.Client EntityStates enumerators

Enum	Description
Added	An entity was added since the last call to SaveChanges.
Deleted	An entity was deleted from the context. If SaveChanges is called, it will attempt to delete the data that the entity represents in the database.
Detached	An entity was detached from the context. This is not the same as Deleted. It simply flags the entity as removed from the context.
Modified	An entity was modified since the last call to SaveChanges.
Unchanged	No changes have occurred on the entity since the last call to SaveChanges.

Table A-4. System.Data.Services.Client MergeOption enumerators

Enumerator	Description
AppendOnly	Adds new entities, but existing entities and values will not be modified.
NoTracking	On retrieval, data is always refreshed from the server to the entity. No change tracking information is retained.
Overwrite Changes	On retrieval, current values are refreshed from the data service.
PerserveChanges	On retrieval, original values are refreshed from the data service. Client changes are retained.

System.Data.Services

Table A-5. System.Data.Services EntitySetRights enumerators

Enumerator	Description
All	All reads and writes are permitted on the specified entity.
AllRead	All reads are permitted.
AllWrite	All writes are permitted.
None	No access is permitted to the specified entity.
ReadMultiple	Reading multiple rows is permitted.
ReadSingle	Reading a single row is permitted.
WriteAppend	Creating new data is permitted.
WriteDelete	Deleting data is permitted.
WriteMerge	Merge updating is permitted.
WriteReplace	Replace updating is permitted.

Table A-6. System.Data.Services ServiceOperationsRights enumerators

Enumerator	Description
All	All rights are permitted to the service operation.
AllRead	The service operation is permitted to read one or more items.
None	The service operation is not permitted.
ReadMultiple	The service operation is permitted to read multiple items.
ReadSingle	The service operation is permitted to read one item.

Table A-7. System.Data.Services UpdateOperations enumerators

Enumerator	Description
Add	The item has been created.
Change	The item has been updated/changed.
Delete	The item has been marked for deletion.
None	No change occurred on the item.

ADO.NET Data Services URI Options

Table A-8. ADO.NET Data Services query string options

Option	Description	Example
expand	Requests set(s) of related entities to be retrieved.	/Products(7)?$expand=Categories
orderby	Indicates the sequence entities to be retrieved.	/Employees?$orderby=LastName asc,FirstName asc
skip	Skips a number of data items. Useful for paging.	/Products?$skip=10
top	At most, returns the top number of data items.	/Products?$orderby=ProductName&$top=10
filter	Applies a filtering condition to narrow the data returned.	/Products?$filter='ProductName eq Widget'

ADO.NET Data Services URI Operators

Table A-9. Logical operators

Operator	Description	Example
eq	Equal	/Products?$filter='UnitPrice eq 10'
ne	Not equal	/Products?$filter='UnitPrice ne 10'
gt	Greater than	/Products?$filter=UnitPrice gt 10
ge	Greater than or equal to	/Products?$filter=UnitPrice ge 10
lt	Less than	/Products?$filter=UnitPrice lt 10
le	Less than or equal to	/Products?$filter=UnitPrice le 10
and	Logical AND	/Products?$filter=UnitsInStock gt 0 and UnitsOnOrder eq 0
or	Logical OR	/Products?$filter=UnitsInStock eq 0 or UnitsOnOrder gt 0
not	Logical negation	/Products?$filter=not startswith(ProductName, 'Widget')

Table A-10. Math operators

Operator	Description	Example
add	Addition	/Product?$filter=(UnitPrice add 10) gt 100
sub	Subtraction	/Product?$filter=(UnitPrice sub 10) lt 100
mul	Multiplication	/Product?$filter=(UnitPrice mul 2) gt 100
div	Division	/Product?$filter=(UnitPrice div 2) lt 100
mod	Modulo	/Product?$filter=(UnitPrice mod 10) eq 0

ADO.NET Data Services URI Functions

Table A-11. String functions

Function	Description
bool substringof(string p0, string p1)	Evaluates whether a string exists within another string
bool endswith(string p0, string p1)	Evaluates whether a string ends with another string
bool startswith(string p0, string p1)	Evaluates whether a string begins with another string
int length (string p0)	Returns the length of a string
int indexof(string p0)	Returns the index of the occurrence in a string
string concat(string p0, string p1)	Returns the concatenation of two strings
string insert(string p0, int pos, string p1)	Inserts a string into another string, at a specific position

Function	Description
`string remove(string p0, int pos)`	Removes a string from a specific position
`string remove(string p0, int pos, int length)`	Removes a string from a specific position for a specific length
`string replace(string p0, string find, string replace)`	Replaces a string with another string starting at a specific position
`string substring(string p0, int pos)`	Returns the contents of a string starting at a specific position
`string substring(string p0, int pos, int length)`	Returns the contents of a string starting at a specific position for a specific length
`string tolower(string p0)`	Returns the string in all lowercase
`string toupper(string p0)`	Returns the string in all uppercase
`string trim(string p0)`	Returns the string with trailing spaces removed

Table A-12. Math functions

Function	Description
`double round(double p0)`	Rounds a double value
`decimal round(decimal p0)`	Rounds a decimal value
`double floor(double p0)`	Returns the floor of a double value
`decimal floor(decimal p0)`	Returns the floor of a decimal value
`double ceiling(double p0)`	Returns the ceiling of a double value
`decimal ceiling(decimal p0)`	Returns the ceiling of a decimal value

Table A-13. Type functions

Function	Description
`bool IsOf(type p0)`	Evaluates whether the value is of a given type
`bool IsOf(expression p0, type p1)`	Evaluates whether the expression is of a given type
`<p0> Cast(type p0)`	Casts to a type
`<p1> Cast(expression p0, type p1)`	Casts an expression to a type

Silverlight 2 Debugging with HTTP Sniffing Tools

SOAP, REST, ADO.NET Data Services, and other types of web services make a tremendous amount of information available to Silverlight 2 applications. When problems arise and the culprit is the communication between Silverlight 2 and web services, debugging the issues can be difficult. That is why it is good to have some solid tools and techniques to help with debugging problems between Silverlight 2 and web services.

Fiddler2, the Web Development Helper, and Firebug are three good, free tools that have many features, some of which overlap among the tools. This appendix discusses how to get started with the features of these tools that are most useful when debugging Silverlight 2 applications. It also provides tips on how to use the tools with Silverlight 2, and discusses key problems they can help you to solve. You can download the tools from the links shown in the following table.

Tool	Link
Fiddler2	http://www.fiddler2.com
Web Development Helper	http://projects.nikhilk.net/WebDevHelper/Default.aspx
Firebug	http://getfirebug.com

Fiddler2

Fiddler2 is a free, standalone tool that can log all HTTP network traffic. Developed by Eric Lawrence of Microsoft, Fiddler2 works independently of a web browser, as it can sniff network traffic from any source, web browser or otherwise.

Capturing Traffic

The F12 shortcut key toggles the setting for Fiddler2 to capture network traffic. Often, it is good to toggle traffic capture off after debugging so that all of the other traffic

Fiddler2 is watching is not being logged. This makes it easier to find the logged traffic for the debugging session. You can also find this setting on the menu under File→Capture Traffic, as shown in Figure B-1.

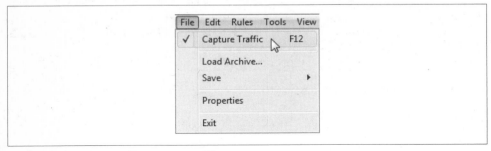

Figure B-1. Capture Traffic setting in Fiddler2

Executing Requests in Fiddler2

Fiddler2 can issue web requests over HTTP and can log the request, its response, headers, and status. Requests can include the POST, PUT, GET, and DELETE HTTP methods, any header, and request message content. This makes Fiddler2 a great tool for testing web requests for web services. For example, you can test the RESTful web service we created using ADO.NET Data Services in Chapter 11, using Fiddler2 and the following URI:

> *http://localhost:8890/NorthwindDataService.svc/Products/?$orderby=Product Name&$top=3*

The Request Builder window pane in Fiddler2, shown in Figure B-2, allows the user to enter and execute an address. You can select the HTTP method from the drop-down box, manually enter request headers in the space provided, and manually enter content in the large Request Body text box.

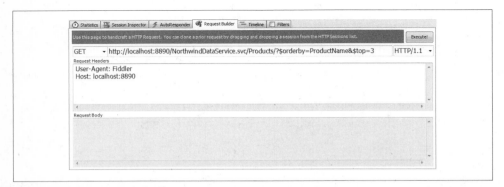

Figure B-2. Fiddler2 Request Builder

Inspecting Requests/Responses in Fiddler2

Once a request has been executed, Fiddler2 logs the traffic in the Web Sessions window pane. Figure B-3 shows the request being logged including the body size, caching settings, and content type.

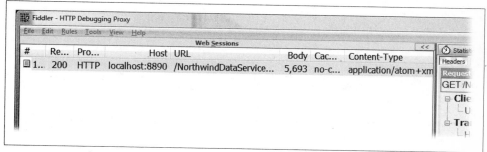

Figure B-3. Fiddler2 logging the request

When you double-click the web session shown in Figure B-3, the Session Inspector window provides detailed information about the request and its response. The Session Inspector window shows the original request, the header, caching, privacy, and other information. It also shows both the request and the response messages in raw text and in XML format (if appropriate). Figure B-4 shows the headers for both the request and the response. Figure B-5 shows the raw response and request messages for the HTTP request.

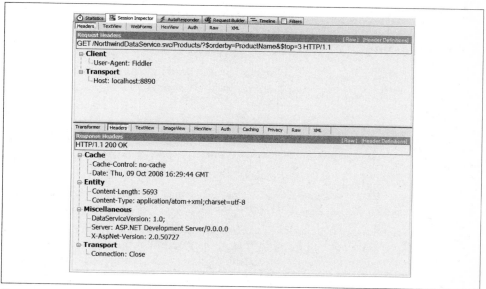

Figure B-4. Inspecting headers in Fiddler2

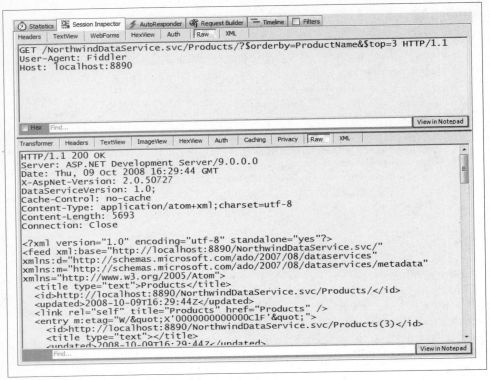

Figure B-5. Inspecting the request and response messages

Watching Localhost Requests

Many network communication tools do not support watching localhost out of the box. This section discusses a few common issues with watching localhost traffic and offers solutions to them.

IPv6

When you're making HTTP requests from Fiddler2's Request Builder, sometimes the following error may be returned with a status of 502:

```
[Fiddler] Connection to localhost failed.<BR>Exception Text: No connection could be
made because the target machine actively refused it ::1:8890
```

This message might occur because Fiddler2 tries to use IPv6 if it is detected, even though the IIS web server may not be bound to IPv6; therefore, the request is refused. Often, you can fix this by turning off the IPv6 setting in Fiddler2 by going to the Tools menu, selecting Options, and unchecking the "Enable IPv6 (if available)" checkbox on the General tab, as shown in Figure B-6.

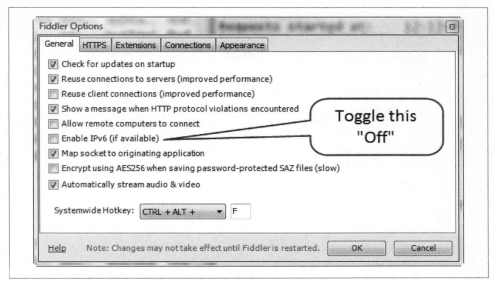

Figure B-6. Disabling IPv6

Using Fiddler2 to capture browser traffic in Firefox

Many web browsers do not send requests to *http://localhost* through proxies. Because Fiddler2 is a proxy, this means that without making changes to the settings in Fiddler2 or the web browsers, often Fiddler2 will not receive traffic sent to *http://localhost*. You can configure the Firefox web browser to pass its traffic through the Fiddler2 proxy by setting the proxy configuration through Firefox's Tools→Options→Advanced→Network→Settings menu (see Figure B-7). You can set the proxy server to 127.0.0.1 and the port to 8888, or you can use the autoconfiguration option. Setting these options will allow Fiddler2 to receive traffic from Firefox.

Select the autoconfiguration option and paste the following text in the URL text box for Windows Vista:

> *file:///c:%5Cusers%5CYOURNAMEHERE%5Cdocuments%5CFiddler2*
> *%5Cscripts%5Cbrowserpac.js*

Use the following URL for Windows XP:

> *file:///c:%5Cdocuments%20and%20settings%5CYOURNAMEHERE%5Cmy*
> *%20documents%5CFiddler2%5Cscripts%5Cbrowserpac.js*

Once you complete the proxy configuration and restart Firefox, Fiddler2 will receive the traffic from Firefox.

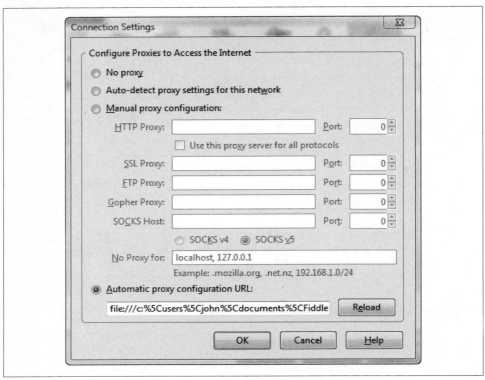

Figure B-7. Proxy configuration for Firefox

You also can configure Firefox and Internet Explorer by setting the manual proxy configuration through the same options dialogs. Figure B-8 shows the Firefox manual proxy configuration selected with the HTTP proxy set to 127.0.0.1 with port 8888, the standard address and port for Fiddler2. Internet Explorer also has the same proxy setting options in its Tools→Options→Connections→LAN Settings menu.

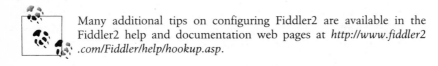

Many additional tips on configuring Fiddler2 are available in the Fiddler2 help and documentation web pages at *http://www.fiddler2 .com/Fiddler/help/hookup.asp*.

Web Development Helper

Web Development Helper is a plug-in for Internet Explorer that has many scripting and networking features. It is a great tool for watching traffic within Internet Explorer. You can display it by selecting the menu option View→Explorer Bar→Web Development Helper, as shown in Figure B-9.

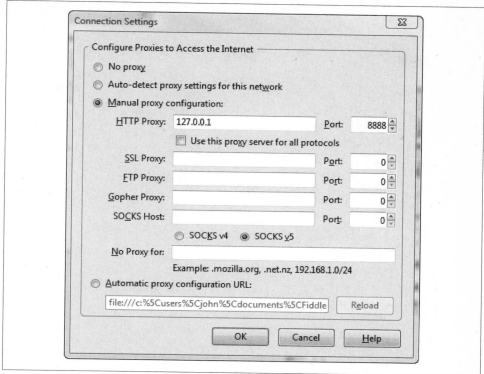

Figure B-8. Manual proxy configuration

Once enabled, Web Development Helper has a toggle switch that enables it to capture traffic in the Internet Explorer browser instance. Checking the Enable Logging checkbox turns logging on, which shows the traffic from the browser. When you enter the URI in the address bar (from the Chapter 11 ADO.NET Data Services service), the results are logged, as shown in Figure B-10.

You can view the request headers, request body, response headers, and response body by double-clicking the item from Figure B-10. This is a subset of the information that is viewable through Fiddler2 (shown in Figure B-11), but it is simpler in some senses, as it requires less setup work and has fewer options.

Cross-domain debugging

Like Fiddler2, Web Development Helper can also identify problems when web requests are made. For example, when a web request is made to a different domain, Silverlight 2 looks for one of the cross-domain policy files. If neither one is found, a status of 404 is returned and the web request is halted. Figure B-12 shows a web request in which

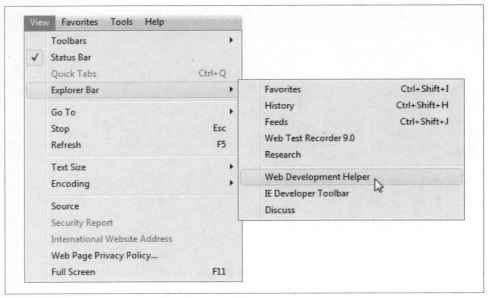

Figure B-9. Enabling the Web Development Helper plug-in

Figure B-10. Logging traffic in the Web Development Helper

neither cross-domain policy file is found. In this case, some possible causes for these results are that either the cross-domain files do not exist on the server, or the files are in the wrong location on the server (remember that cross-domain policy files must be located in the web root of the server, not in the application root).

Firebug

Firebug is an add-on for the Firefox web browser. It captures traffic in the Firefox browser, which is useful for debugging problems with web services. You enable Firebug

---

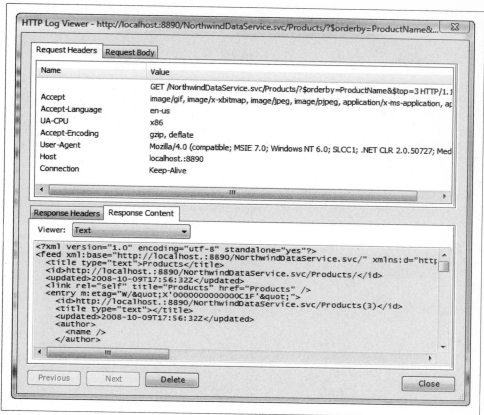

Figure B-11. Request and response information

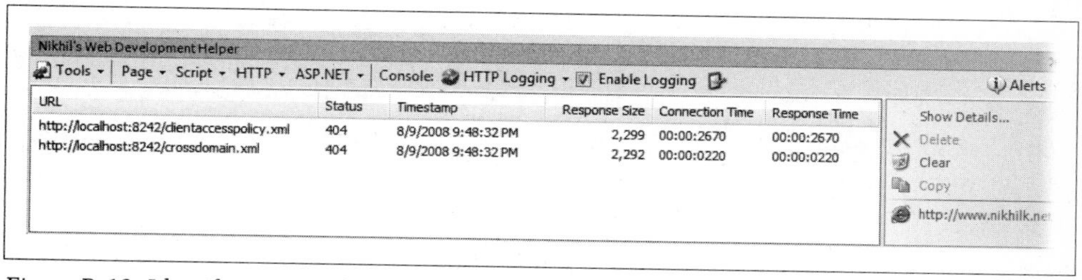

Figure B-12. Identifying cross-domain problems

by clicking the Firebug icon found in the lower-righthand corner of the Firefox web browser (shown in Figure B-13).

Figure B-13. Firebug icon

Firebug shows all web traffic from the web browser when the Net tab is selected. You can see the parameters, headers, and response from this view. Figure B-14 shows all of the requests that were made from the Firefox browser when running the **EFDataServices** sample from Chapter 11. Notice that the HTTP method, URI, status, domain, and size of the response are displayed. This can help you with debugging cross-domain issues, because you can watch the requests. It is also helpful when debugging, because you can examine the exact URI and request and compare them against the expected request.

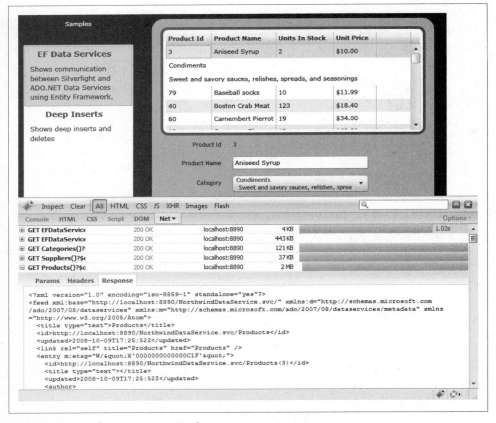

Figure B-14. Watching requests in Firebug

Index

We'd like to hear your suggestions for improving our indexes. Send email to *index@oreilly.com*.

331

AsyncCompletedEventArgs object, 107
AsyncState property, IAsyncResult interface, 180
Atom protocol, 251
AtomPub (Atom Publishing Protocol) message format, 274
    sample message response, 274
attributes, serialization, 132
automatic properties, 8
    use in Product class (example), 56

B

BaseList class, 292
    code example, 294–297
    saving changes made within context, 297
basicHttpBinding, 115
BeginGetResponse method, HttpWebRequest class, 182
binding (see data binding)
Binding attribute, 28
Binding class, 31
binding modes, 45–67
    adding notifications, 61–64
    considerations for ListBox controls, 72
    deciding whether to use notifications, 56
    different modes for list-based control with item selection, 81
    effect of binding modes and INotifyPropertyChanged, 46
    implementing INotifyPropertyChanged interface, 56–61
    indicated in Mode property, XAML bindings, 29
    OneTime, 46
    OneWay, 48
    oneWay value, XAML binding markup in Expression Blend, 42
    setting for conversions between source and target values, 89
    TwoWay, 49
    without notifications, 50–55
Binding objects
    creating for target and source pair, 32
    removing a binding, 35
    Source property, 36
    WPF versus Silverlight 2, 34
BindingValidatorError event, 29
Blend (see Expression Blend)

browsers (see web browsers; individual browser names)

C

C#, 16
    (see also language enhancements in .NET 3.5)
    automatic properties, 8
    language enhancements in version 3, 6
caching, web requests by RESTful services, 246
CancelAsync method, WebClient class, 179
CartCreate operation, 207
CartModify method, 191
Cassini web server, 101
change interceptors, 305
change notifications (see notifications)
classes
    creating and initializing, 11
    proxy classes, generation by Silverlight client, 5
client library for ADO.NET Data Services, 273
client model, extending, 292–298
    eager loading, 293
    enabling saves, 297
    loading asynchronously, 293–297
clientaccesspolicy.xml file, 109
    for ASMXEmailService website, 111
    more restrictive (example), 112
    Silverlight-enabled WCF web service, 121
clientaccesspolicy.xml file (for Live Search), 125
collection initializers, 11
Collection type, customizing for return values, 101
CollectionChanged event, 83
concurrency conflict, 313
concurrency mode, 311
content negotiation, 225
content-type header, JSON or XML data, 237
context, creating for ADO.NET Data Services, 298
contract name, modifying, 118
contracts (see service contracts)
Control class, controls deriving from, 24
controls
    data binding to, 17
    manual binding, 18–23

UI thread access for ADO.NET Data
Services query, 287
WebClient and HttpWebRequest
invocations of web services, 184
tweeting, 247
tweets, adding to Twitter, 248–250
Twitter API, 238
TwoWay binding mode, 46, 49

U

UI thread, 183
access for ADO.NET Services query, 287
UIs (user interfaces), rich, cross-browser web
UIs, xiii
UpdateOperations parameter, use by change
interceptors, 306
URI templates
modifying to allow default values, 222
RESTful WCF service, 161
URIs
executing in ADO.NET Data Services
queries, 288
options for ADO.NET Data Services query
string, 283
RESTful web service resources, 282
unique URIs for RESTful web service
resources, 160
web service, 165
URLs, base URL for BookSearch, 194
UserControl class, 36

V

ValidatesOnExceptions property, 29
var keyword
anonymous type declarations, 15
implicitly typed variable declarations, 14
variables, implicitly typed, 14
VB (Visual Basic), 16
(see also language enhancements in .NET
3.5)
declaring implicitly typed variables, 14
Visual Basic 9, 6
Visual Studio 2008, 3
data binding in XAML, 39
Silverlight 2 Tools for, 3

W

WCF (Windows Communication Foundation),
95
creating RESTful services (see RESTful web
services)
creating Silverlight-enabled service, 114–
121
bindings, 115
invoking WCF service, 119
service setup, 116
passing entities via, 127–156
example application, 134–143
passing between physical tiers, 127
RESTful web methods built with, 161
service consuming entities from Entity
Framework, 151
web applications
data-centric, communicating with web
services, xiv
rich user interfaces, xiv
web browsers
cross-browser web application UIs, xiii
supporting Silverlight 2, 2
Web Development Helper tool, 110, 326
cross-domain debugging, 328
web services
ASMX, 96–100
calling services written by other developers,
121
communications with, xv
creating Silverlight-enabled WCF service,
114–121
cross-domain access, 109–114
data access through, 2
discoverable, 101
discoverable, Silverlight and, 95
invoking, basic steps in process, 102
third party applications, open SOAP and
RESTful APIs, 187
Web Services Description Language (see
WSDL)
web.config file
changing service contract configuration,
138
WCF service, 115
WebClient class, 164–179
callbacks invoked on UI thread, 184
CancelAsync method, 179

About the Author

John Papa is a Microsoft C# MVP, MCSD.NET, and INETA speaker who has been working with Microsoft distributed architectures for more than 10 years. He has enterprise experience architecting and developing .NET technologies focusing on architecture, patterns and practices, data access, and mobile development. John has authored or coauthored several books on data access technologies, and he is the author of the "Data Points" column in *MSDN Magazine*. He has presented MSDN WebCasts and can often be found speaking at industry conferences, such as DevConnections and VSLive. You can contact John at *http://www.johnpapa.net*.

Colophon

The animal on the cover of *Data-Driven Services with Silverlight 2* is a white-cheeked turaco (*Tauraco leucotis*). The bird is prized for its beauty: its feathers contain rich blue, green, and copper hues that are not found in other birds, and, when flying, the bird's vibrant red secondary feathers become visible. A white stripe runs along one cheek (hence its common name), and its beak and a circular patch around its eye are bright orange.

White-cheeked turacos live in families of no larger than six birds. Researchers believe the birds show their distinctive red coloring while flying to let their family members know where they are and also to help set the boundaries of their territory.

Although the bird's natural habitat is in Africa, white-cheeked turacos can be found in zoos around the world. Visitors to zoos find the birds are popular not only for their colorful appearances, but also for their colorful personalities, as the birds have curious natures and often enjoy being approached by humans.

Throughout the mating season, male and female white-cheeked turacos will usually spend time apart when not breeding; if the birds are forced together during this time, they will fight and occasionally harm each other. However, after the female lays her eggs, the parents again become attentive toward each other and others of their kind, and it is not unusual for adult white-cheeked turacos to become foster parents to other chicks within their species.

The cover image is from *Cassell's Natural History*. The cover font is Adobe ITC Garamond. The text font is Linotype Birka; the heading font is Adobe Myriad Condensed; and the code font is LucasFont's TheSansMonoCondensed.